THE ZONDERVAN 2018
PASTOR'S
ANNUAL

For a *FREE* downloadable copy of the book, please visit:
http://downloads.zondervan.com/zpa2018.

THE ZONDERVAN 2018
PASTOR'S ANNUAL

AN IDEA AND RESOURCE BOOK

T. T. CRABTREE

ZONDERVAN

The Zondervan 2018 Pastor's Annual
Copyright © 1977, 1997, 2017 by Zondervan

This title is also available as a Zondervan ebook

Requests for information should be addressed to:
Zondervan, *3900 Sparks Dr. SE, Grand Rapids, Michigan 49546*

Much of the contents of this book was previously published in *Pastor's Annual 1998.*

ISBN 978-0-310-53663-5

Cover design: Angela Grit
Cover photo: Mark Veldheer
Interior design: Sue Vandenberg Koppenol

Printed in the United States of America

17 18 19 20 21 22 23 24 25 26 27 /DHV/ 15 14 13 12 11 10 9 8 7 6 5 4 3 2 1

CONTENTS

MISCELLANEOUS HELPS

Messages on the Lord's Supper

Messages for Children and Young People

Funeral Meditations

Weddings

Sentence Sermonettes. 433

Contributing Authors

Morris Ashcraft	AM	November 4, 11, 18, 25
Tom S. Brandon		Miscellaneous Section
Harold T. Bryson	PM	July 1, 8, 15, 22, 29
		August 5, 12, 19, 26
Hiram Campbell	WED	September 5, 12, 19, 26
		October 3, 10, 17, 24, 31
		November 7, 14, 21, 28
		December 5, 12, 19, 26
James E. Carter	AM	February 25
		March 4, 11, 18, 25
		April 1
	PM	December 2, 9, 16
T. T. Crabtree		All messages except those attributed to others
Charles O. Dinkins	PM	April 1, 8, 15, 22, 29
		May 6, 13, 20, 27
		June 3, 10, 17, 24
David R. Grant	WED	June 6, 13, 20, 27
		July 4, 11, 18, 25
		August 1, 8, 15, 22, 29
James F. Heaton	AM	June 24
		July 1, 8, 15, 22, 29
		August 5, 12, 19, 26
W. T. Holland	AM	December 2, 9, 16, 23, 30
	PM	December 30
David L. Jenkins	PM	January 7, 14, 21, 28
		February 4, 11, 18, 25
		March 4, 11, 18, 25
Jerold McBride	AM	April 8, 15, 29
		May 6
Lowell D. Milburn	PM	October 7, 14, 21, 28
Leonard Sanderson	AM	October 7, 14, 21, 28
Bob Wood	AM	January 14
Fred M. Wood	AM	January 21, 28February 4, 11, 18
		April 22
		September 2

PREFACE

Favorable comments from ministers who serve in many different types of churches suggest that the *Pastor's Annual* provides valuable assistance to many busy pastors as they seek to improve the quality, freshness, and variety of their pulpit ministry. To be of service to a fellow pastor in his or her continuing quest to obey our Lord's command to Peter, "Feed my sheep," is a calling to which I respond with gratitude.

I pray that this issue of the *Pastor's Annual* will be blessed by our Lord in helping each pastor to plan and produce a preaching program that will better meet the spiritual needs of his or her congregation.

This issue contains series of sermons by several contributing authors who have been effective contemporary preachers and successful pastors. Each author is listed with his sermons by date in the section titled "Contributing Authors." I accept responsibility for those sermons not listed there.

This issue of the *Pastor's Annual* is dedicated to the Lord with a prayer that he will bless these efforts to let the Holy Spirit lead us in preparing a planned preaching program for the year.

SUGGESTED PREACHING PROGRAM FOR THE MONTH OF

JANUARY

■ Sunday Mornings

We will start the new year with a Sunday morning sermon titled "A Controlling Motive for the New Year." Then, on the second Sunday morning, we will begin a series on "Jesus, the Word." After an initial sermon on Jesus as God's "last Word," on the following Sundays we will examine some of Jesus's first sayings.

■ Sunday Evenings

"God Continues to Speak" is the theme for messages based on some selected great chapters from the Old Testament. These relevant messages deal with the needs and problems that confront us in daily living.

■ Wednesday Evenings

"The Words of Jesus Christ" is the theme for the Wednesday evening meditations. Paul's exhortation to the Colossians, "Let the word of Christ dwell in you richly," is the scriptural theme for these meditations on some of Jesus's great statements. You may want to implement a memorization program using the passages from the Wednesday evening services.

WEDNESDAY EVENING, JANUARY 3

Title: The Words of Jesus Christ

Text: "Let the word of Christ dwell in you richly, as you teach and admonish one another in all wisdom, and as you sing psalms and hymns and spiritual songs with thankfulness in your hearts to God" **(Col. 3:16 RSV)**.

Scripture Reading: Matthew 6:21–29

Introduction

Our attitude toward Jesus's words will determine our success, happiness, and usefulness as his servants.

Jesus pronounced a beatitude upon his disciples because they were perceptive in that they used their eyes to see and their ears to hear (Matt. 13:16). He said imperatively, "He who has ears, let him hear" (v. 43 RSV). Our Lord brings the Sermon on the Mount to a climactic conclusion by illustrating the value of not only hearing his words but also doing them if we want to escape a life of waste and disappointment and find a life of security and happiness (Matt. 7:14–27).

Accepting Jesus's words into our innermost being as the great guidelines for our life will affect the vitality and the effectiveness of our prayer life (John 15:7). To be a mere hearer of the word and not a doer is to fall into self-deception (James 1:22–25). The apostle Paul was not wasting his breath when he urged believers at Colossae to "Let the word of Christ dwell in you richly."

What are you doing with the words of Jesus Christ? Do you study his words? Do you accept as authoritative the great truths, the warnings, the guidelines, the instructions that fell from his lips? As we begin this new year, let us determine that we are going to study and memorize some of the great truths that Jesus spoke.

The psalmist asserted that we can bring charity into our lives by letting the Word of God be our guide (Ps. 119:9). He also declared that we can avoid the way of sin by storing up the Word of God within our hearts (v. 11).

I. Let the words of Christ commend you.

It is interesting to note in the seven letters to the churches of Asia Minor that, following a salutation, our Lord spoke words of commendation to at least six of the churches. These words of commendation were spoken first, indicating that our Lord is positive and affirmative and that he looks for the best in us.

If we will let the words of Jesus Christ dwell in us richly, they will serve to commend and encourage us and will help us to properly evaluate ourselves as those for whom Jesus Christ died.

II. Let the words of Jesus Christ correct you.

All of us are mistake makers. We sin against ourselves, against others, and against God. We all stand in need of correction. And if we will let Christ's words abide in us richly, we will hear, along with his words of commendation, words of complaint concerning those characteristics of our lives that are self-destructive or are harmful to others. Christ is eager to correct us—not to condemn us and put us down, but so that we can achieve our highest possible destiny in life. Any criticism from our Lord will always be positive and helpful rather than vindictive.

III. Let the words of Christ commission you.

As we read the words of our Lord, we should look for words of command, for there are things God wants to accomplish through us. He comes in love to commission us to service in his name.

The Great Commission is all-inclusive in its claims upon our lives and resources. Each of us is to be a witness and a worker for our Lord in the personal world in which we live. If we will let his words live in us richly, he will commission us from day to day as we walk the road of life.

IV. Let the words of Christ cheer you.

It is easy to become weary in well-doing. All of us have experienced discouragement as we have faced the uphill struggles of life and as we have sought to carry the burdens that befall us. Discouragement is one of Satan's chief methods for bringing about our personal defeat.

All of us stand in need of having a cheerleader along at times to encourage us as we face the obstacles to living a victorious Christian life. Jesus Christ is the faithful witness who wants to give testimony to you in the deepest zone of your being as you face the problems in your life. If you will memorize his great teachings, he will have the Holy Spirit recall these to your remembrance when you need them most.

Conclusion

No one can do your sleeping for you, and no one can do your eating for you. Likewise, no one but you can let the words of Christ dwell in you richly. Begin today a personal program of memorizing some selected verses of Scripture, the words of Jesus Christ, and write them on the walls of your mind and heart. Let them become plaques with messages from God to your heart.

SUNDAY MORNING, JANUARY 7

Title: A Controlling Motive for the New Year

Text: "And many other signs truly did Jesus in the presence of his disciples, which are not written in this book: But these are written, that ye might believe that Jesus is the Christ, the Son of God; and that believing ye might have life through his name" (**John 20:30–31**).

Scripture Reading: John 1:35–50

Hymns: "God, Our Father, We Adore Thee," Frazer
"He Leadeth Me," Gilmore
"I Will Sing the Wondrous Story," Rowley

Offertory Prayer: Holy Father, we come to you on this first Lord's Day of the new year thankful that we are inclined to worship you and to seek your will in all of our ways. We come praying for your help that we might give ourselves completely to you as we walk through this year. Today we bring tithes and offerings as symbols of our desire to commit ourselves to you. Bless both the gifts and the dedication of our hearts to your honor and glory and to the proclamation of the good news of your love both in this community and to the ends of the earth. In Jesus's name we pray. Amen.

Introduction

The apostle John, writer of the fourth gospel, leaves his readers with no question about his motive for writing the gospel that bears his name: He is trying to convince them that Jesus Christ is the Son of God. Yet he encourages his readers to not only believe this with their minds but also to make Jesus Christ the Lord of their lives.

Some say that the law of self-preservation is the first law of nature. John

15

appeals to this motive in his presentation of the gospel. He affirms that God the Father is vitally interested in our eternal preservation (3:16) and that Christ the Son came and gave his life that we might experience abundant life in the here and now (10:10).

In John's statement of purpose, he affirms that he was selective in choosing the contents of his gospel. He did not tell everything that could have been told concerning the life, work, and teachings of the Lord. He left out many things so that he might emphasize his controlling motive. He was eager to share the Good News so that people could come to know Jesus Christ as Lord and Savior. John, the beloved apostle, was an evangelist. We should give serious consideration to letting John's controlling motive be the guiding principle for our lives as we walk through another year toward eternity.

John selected seven great signs, miracles, wonders, and illustrations under the guidance of the Holy Spirit to convince the minds and hearts of people that Jesus Christ was indeed the Son of God and worthy of all of the confidence they could place in him.

I. The turning of water into wine (John 2:1–11).

To understand the significance of this event, we need to look at the historical situation. We find Christ, the Lord of life, attending a wedding in a simple home in Cana of Galilee.

    A. *Jesus prevented embarrassment to those who were not able to provide an abundance of wine for the crowd who came to the wedding.*

    B. *Jesus made this festive social occasion even more joyful.*

    C. *Jesus demonstrated his unique power over nature.*

    D. *Jesus illustrated his availability, his ability, and his desire to make the last of life better than the first.*

Christ can make your life richer, fuller, and more joyful if you will trust him and obey him in love and gratitude.

II. The healing of the nobleman's son (John 4:46–54).

    A. *In this miracle Jesus revealed his power over disease.*

    B. *Jesus revealed his power over distance.* The nobleman's son was twenty miles away from where the nobleman and Jesus were having their conversation. Jesus said to the man, "Go thy way; thy son liveth."

    C. *This sign revealed Jesus's compassionate concern for people with heavy hearts.*

    D. *The nobleman and his household responded properly to Jesus by believing.* The nobleman now had a new Master.

III. The healing of the lame man (John 5:1–6).

    A. *Jesus healed a man who was helpless, lonely, and poor.*

    B. *The compassionate Savior genuinely cares for those who are totally helpless and seemingly worthless to others.*

C. *This miracle took place on the Sabbath.* By acting on the Sabbath, Jesus showed that the work of God is continuous and that it must not be limited by custom or tradition.

D. *Christ was also interested in the man's soul.* He was not content merely to render a medical ministry to the man. Jesus sought him out and encouraged him to forsake the way of sin (5:6–14).

IV. The feeding of the five thousand (John 6:1–14).

A. *The compassionate Christ was concerned and continues to be concerned about those who suffer from physical hunger.*

B. *Jesus was willing to use his power to meet the needs of those who suffered the pangs of hunger.*

C. *Christ demonstrated his capacity and desire to use small things to bless a great multitude.* He used this occasion of feeding people with bread to talk about the Bread of eternal life.

V. Walking on the sea (John 6:15–21).

A. *Christ the Creator demonstrated his power over nature.*

B. *Christ illustrated his power over the causes of human fear.* He said, "It is I; be not afraid" (v. 20).

C. *By coming to his disciples during the storm, Christ revealed his availability to aid the helpless and fearful in times of distress.*
   1. He sees us today and knows about our fears and our insecurity.
   2. He comes to us today walking across the sea of life to where we are.
   3. He comes to help us in our times of need.
   4. He saves us from the catastrophes we fear.

VI. The healing of the man born blind (John 9).

A. *Christ is the source of illumination concerning the mysteries of time and eternity.*

B. *Christ is the source of real life because he is the Son of God.* It is interesting to note the progression in the man's understanding of Jesus. He knows Jesus simply as "a man" (v. 11), and then he speaks of him as "a prophet" (v. 17). He finally comes to believe in him as "the Son of God" (vv. 35–38).

VII. The raising of Lazarus (John 11:1–54).

A. *By this miracle we perceive the sincere sympathy of the Son of God for those who suffer grief and sorrow (vv. 17–35).*

B. *By this miracle Jesus revealed his lordship over life, death, and the grave (vv. 39–45).* John the apostle was fully convinced that Jesus Christ had the power to resurrect. He can bring life to your individual heart and soul. He has the power to resurrect your family and to give you a new life and a new future.

Conclusion

We are not on the way to death. Instead, through Christ, we are on the way to abundant, eternal life. During this year we must serve as those who do believe and live so as to persuade others to believe that Jesus Christ is indeed the Son of God who should also be the Lord of their lives.

SUNDAY EVENING, JANUARY 7

Title: Two Character References

Text: "How blessed is the man who does not walk in the counsel of the wicked, nor stand in the path of sinners, nor sit in the seat of scoffers! . . . The wicked are not so, but they are like the chaff which the wind drives away" (**Ps. 1:1, 4 NASB**).

Scripture Reading: Psalm 1

Introduction

Tonight we begin a series of sermons exploring great chapters in the Old Testament. Where do you look among the outstanding biblical chapters to find a New Year's challenge? Perhaps we should take a spiritual inventory. Psalm 1 is a good point of departure.

In a sense, we might compare this first psalm to a "spiritual examination room." It is as though the psalmist is having us subject our total selves to the glaring light of God's testing. This literary artist paints two portraits that provide two character references. The first one—a portrait of a godly man—is finished and is framed beautifully. The second one—a portrait of an ungodly man—is merely sketched in with dark and foreboding colors, as though the artist became so depressed with the prospect of the finished picture that he could not complete it. He leaves the finished portrait to the imagination of the beholder.

I. The godly man.

This man is alert. He understands the importance of certain refusals in the process of building character. He sees the importance of driving down a few stakes to use as boundary lines for his life as he pursues the way of God.

The first red light of warning that flashes on his way is the danger of walking "in the counsel of the wicked." He refuses to expose himself to the attitudes and ideas of those who have no place for God in their thoughts and in their lives. A brilliant and promising young preacher became attracted to the study of philosophy. His fascination grew until he began to study all kinds of life philosophies. He listened to those who proclaimed these philosophies until his own faith became weak and insecure. Eventually he abandoned the Christian ministry with the sad explanation, "I no longer have anything to say." It is one thing to become knowledgeable concerning the philosophies of life that are in opposition to Christianity; it is something else when one's obsession with such a study produces confusion and fosters doubt.

The second flashing red light has written over it, "Don't stand in the path of sinners." Not only does this man refuse to walk in the direction of those who would poison his faith, but he also refuses to associate himself with them. This group is a bit more destructive than the first. These people do more than talk; they throw obstacles in the way of those who would follow God. What actually happens when a person listens to these enemies of Christian faith? The person becomes spiritually dull and morally weak, finding it increasingly difficult to make moral distinctions. One who "stands in the path of sinners" will ultimately begin to lose his or her sensitivity to sin.

The brightest warning light of all flashes on the third step: "sit in the seat of scoffers." Here are the cynics who sneer and scoff at truth and at sacred things. The cynic possesses a soured personality. He snaps and growls and snarls like a mongrel. His life is miserable, and he devotes himself to making the lives of others equally miserable. The psalmist infers, "If I pass by the first two warning lights, this is where I will be! I will have joined this disillusioned and hopeless crowd!"

So what have we here? We have the potential tragedy of a person walking by a questionable place without any intention of going into sin. He merely wants to see what it is like. The next step is to loiter long enough to let evil get its grip on him. He begins to savor what he sees and hears. Finally, he walks blatantly into the midst of these enemies of God and seeks membership in their society. But the godly man has taken certain steps to protect himself from such an end.

II. The ungodly man.

Before we examine the preventive measures taken by the godly man, we must see his counterpart as the psalmist describes him. Here is the penciled-in sketch of a ruined life. The psalmist leaves us the task of filling in the details.

"They are like the chaff which the wind drives away" (Ps. 2:4 NASB). "Chaff" is one of the most useless forms of refuse to be found in the vegetable world. The ancient threshing floors were on elevated ground, and the mixture of straw, stubble, chaff, and grain was taken off the heap left by the threshing and tossed into the breeze. The breeze did the winnowing, and the husbandman would either burn the chaff or let the wind dispose of it. The picture is that of the futility of a life without God, yielding nothing more substantial than chaff.

The end of the ungodly man is that he will not be able to stand his ground when the judgment comes. He must retire in the shame and confusion of the guilty. Thus, as if eager to be done with his description, the psalmist then turns back to the righteous man.

III. The prescription for godliness.

The "godly man" the psalmist describes in verse 1, in contrast with the ungodly man in verse 4, did not take his stand in life all by himself. What was his secret?

"His delight is in the law of the LORD" (v. 2 NASB). The Word of God was a necessity in his life. He not only read it, but he "delighted" in it. He found in it God's message to his soul. It revealed God to him.

"And in his law he meditates day and night" (v. 2 NASB). God's Word never grew stale to the psalmist. It was as fresh to him as the first rose of June and as inexhaustible as the sparkling spring in the hills. The Word of God was so vital in his life that wherever he was, whatever the circumstance might be, a choice portion of Scripture came to his mind and gave him strength to carry on.

The results in the psalmist's life were thrilling. "And he will be like a tree firmly planted by streams of water" (v. 3). The word "planted" here implies purpose. The tree is not where it is by mere chance. An intelligent God planted it there. And as it grows, it is fulfilling a purpose. So it is with this godly man. As he grows, he will be able to discern in his own life the outworking of God's plan. He will be able to say to God, "To this end was I born, and for this cause came I into the world, that I might do this bit of work for you."

Furthermore, as a planted tree, this man is steadfast. He is not the plaything of every capricious breeze. He is rich in usefulness, for he is as a tree "which yields its fruit in its season" (v. 3 NASB). Wherever he plants his seed, the fields produce, and the golden grain heads in rich profusion.

Conclusion

Which path are you walking today? Are you trifling with the ungodly? Are you playing with their dangerous fire? Or are you finding your delight in the eternal Word and plan of God for your life? On this threshold of a new year, take close inventory of the energies and the opportunities God has granted you.

WEDNESDAY EVENING, JANUARY 10

Title: The Invitation Continues to Come

Text: "And he said to them, 'Follow me, and I will make you fishers of men'" (**Matt. 4:19 RSV**).

Scripture Reading: Matthew 4:18–22

Introduction

Down through the centuries, even to this hour, the invitation our Lord issued to the fishermen on the shores of the Sea of Galilee has continued to be extended.

How do you respond to these words of Jesus? Do you see them as being merely a part of a conversation that comes from the ancient past? Do you limit this invitation to those who were to be Jesus's future apostles? To do so is to miss the spiritual impact of the living Lord as he spoke then and as he continues to speak to us in the present. In these words our Lord describes the nature and the fruits of discipleship.

Later, following his resurrection, Jesus was to again speak this word of command—in the form of an invitation—to the apostle Peter (John 21:19, 22). To be a true disciple of Jesus Christ is to be his follower. When we follow him, there will be results in our lives and also in the lives of others.

I. "Follow me" is an encouragement to have faith.

Jesus Christ, God's Son, sought to instill and to develop faith in the hearts and lives of his disciples in the God of love, grace, mercy, and power. The call "Follow me" is not only an invitation to begin a life of discipleship, but it is also an imperative that requires a response of trust and commitment each day.

II. "Follow me" is an invitation to friendship (John 15:12–15).

By God's grace we have the privilege of being the *children* of the heavenly Father. It is granted to each of us that we might be the *servants* of our Lord in his continuing ministry to others. Through faith and obedience it is possible for us to become the *friends* of Jesus Christ.

Jesus did not think of his disciples in terms of their being his personal servants. He saw them as friends in a common cause of making known the good news of God's love to a needy world. As his disciples followed him in love and obedience, he opened up to them the great truths of God's character and purpose. They became sharers with him.

Abraham had the distinction of being called "the friend of God" (James 2:23). To truly become a follower of Jesus Christ is to become his friend, and it is to enjoy the privilege of friendship with the friend who sticks closer than a brother (see Prov. 18:24).

III. "Follow me" is an invitation with a promise of fruitfulness attached: "I will make you fishers of men."

The men to whom our Lord spoke the words of our text were fishermen by trade. They not only fished for fish, but they also caught fish. There is a vast difference between being a *fisherman* and a *catcherman*. Jesus issued a promise that if these men would truly become his followers, he would enable them to labor on a much higher and more productive level. Instead of measuring their reason for being in terms of catching fish, he would lead them to measure their purpose for being in terms of a ministry to people.

Satisfaction comes to a fisherman when he lands a large fish and has it safely in the net. A much greater thrill comes to the person who is used by the Holy Spirit to help another human being come to know God through faith in

Jesus Christ. Jesus was extending an invitation to a life of high adventure for those who would follow him. He was extending an invitation that encouraged them to invest their lives in the richest possible venture of faith. To accept his invitation, and to follow faithfully, is to discover the highest possible human happiness. To follow Jesus and to abide in him in faith and love and obedience enables one to be fruitful and productive in spiritual ministries to others. This brings joy to the heart of the Father God and deep inward satisfaction to the follower of Christ (John 15:8).

Conclusion

If we would follow Jesus, we need to yield ourselves completely to the Holy Spirit and follow wherever he guides. If we truly follow Jesus, we will go alone into the place of prayer regularly for communion with God. To truly follow Jesus means that regular public worship will be a vital part of our spiritual ministry. To follow Jesus means that we will define our purpose for being in terms of ministry to others for the glory of God (Mark 10:45). To truly follow Jesus may lead us to a cross on which to suffer. To truly follow Jesus will enable us to enter heaven at the end of the way.

SUNDAY MORNING, JANUARY 14

Title: Jesus: God's Last Word

Text: "God, after He spoke long ago to the fathers in the prophets in many portions and in many ways, in these last days has spoken to us in His Son" **(Heb. 1:1–2 NASB)**.

Scripture Reading: Hebrews 1:1–12

Hymns: "All Hail the Power of Jesus' Name," Perronet
"How Great Thou Art," Boberg
"Wonderful Words of Life," Bliss

Offertory Prayer: Holy heavenly Father, we come to give you the adoration of our hearts, the praise of our lips, and the gifts of our hands. Accept our tithes and offerings as an expression of our gratitude and as an indication of our recognition of your ownership and our trusteeship of all that we are and of all that we possess. Bless the use of these gifts toward the coming of your kingdom on earth. We pray in Jesus's name. Amen.

Introduction

The Bible is God's Word. Millions have had their lives changed by its message. Many attempts have been made to destroy the Bible, but all have failed. In AD 303 Diocletian, emperor of the Roman Empire, set out to destroy all the Bibles in the land together with the people who possessed them. He believed that Christians could not exist apart from the Book they claimed as their rule of faith. Thousands of Christians were cruelly martyred in this bloody onslaught. Within a few years Diocletian felt his drive had been so successful that he erected a column over a burned Bible and wrote on the column these words: *extincto nomine Christianorum* ("The name of Christian is extinguished"). Yet by AD 313 the new Roman emperor, Constantine, had declared himself a Christian and had adopted the symbol of the cross for the standards of his Roman army.

The Bible remains, not because of some magical power, but because of the risen Christ who stands behind it. He is the ultimate Word of God.

I. God's last word in communication (Heb. 1:1).

Ever since the garden of Eden, God has sought to communicate to people the message of life. The Bible is not only a record of God's communication, but is itself a part of God's communication. People can discover many things about the created universe, but only God can reveal to people the spiritual truths so needed for life. In revealing himself to people, God had to lead them a step at a time, much like a father leads his child through the first faltering steps of walking. Sin had so blinded the minds of people that God could reveal only a small portion of truth at a time. God had to work slowly because people were slow to understand. The writer of Hebrews says it this way: "God, after He spoke long ago to the fathers in the prophets in many portions and in many ways, in these last days has spoken to us in His Son, whom He appointed heir of all things, through whom also He made the world" (Heb. 1:1–2 NASB).

The Old Testament prophets worked like people putting together a giant puzzle. Here and there God handed to them a piece of the picture. Each fragment was accurate but was only a part of the total picture. The puzzle took final shape with the coming of Jesus Christ. Everything else remained in fragmentary form until Christ came to give unity to the picture and fullness to the prophecies. To look upon the Old Testament prophets is to look upon God's messengers, but to look upon Jesus is to look upon God in terms we can understand—God pictured in human terms. God began a communication to people thousands of years before he was to present his final communication—his last Word—as Jesus Christ.

II. God's last word in salvation (Heb. 1:2–3).

Where salvation of the soul is concerned, Jesus Christ is God's last Word. Prior to Jesus's coming, people experienced salvation through faith in God's promised Savior. Since Jesus's coming, people have experienced salvation through faith in the revealed Savior. Christ was truly God in the flesh! In "being the radiance of His glory" (v. 3 NASB), the word translated "radiance" depicts a radiant beam of glorious light descending from the heavenly Father upon the earthly Christ in such a way that the same glory shines out from both. John too used the idea of light to speak of Christ: "And the light shines in darkness" (John 1:5 NASB).

Jesus Christ is divine, and for a brief moment during his earthly life, on the Mount of Transfiguration, the divine radiance shown through. The writer of Hebrews further describes Christ's divinity: "The exact representation of His [God's] nature" (v. 3 NASB). This scriptural image denotes the imprint of a king's seal left when applied to warm wax. The image left on the wax is an exact reproduction of the royal seal. The writer of Hebrews is trying to say that Jesus Christ is the exact reproduction of God's essence—God's being.

Finally Christ is pictured as the Redeemer: "When He had made purification of sins, He sat down at the right hand of the Majesty on high" (v. 3 NASB). Christ personally effected the removal of our guilt. He provided the cleansing of our sins. Here the idea of his high priesthood is introduced. People need no other high priest, for Christ has provided the cleansing for sins. No one else can remove the stain of guilt from people's souls. Thus, Christ is God's last Word on what people can do about sin. Simon Peter realized this truth as he answered Jesus's question as to whether the disciples would also leave him: "Lord, to whom shall we go? You have words of eternal life" (John 6:68 NASB).

III. God's last word in exaltation (Heb. 1:3).

When Jesus came in the flesh, the Jewish people were anticipating a conquering Messiah who would dispose of their Roman captors. Jesus tried to make clear to his disciples that his kingdom was not an earthly kingdom (John 18:36). Yet there would be a final triumph—a final exaltation—and again Jesus would be God's last Word in it. The final exaltation will come when "the Lord himself shall descend from heaven with a shout" (1 Thess. 4:16).

The apostle Paul reminded the Philippians: "Wherefore God also hath highly exalted him, and given him a name which is above every name: That at the name of Jesus every knee should bow, of things in heaven, and things in earth, and things under the earth; and that every tongue should confess that Jesus Christ is Lord, to the glory of God the Father" (Phil. 2:9–11). Of course Christ was exalted following his resurrection when he "sat down on the right hand of the Majesty on high" (Heb. 1:3 NASB), but this final exaltation will not be fully manifested until the return of Jesus Christ.

The writer of Hebrews puts it like this: "And, Thou, Lord, in the beginning hast laid the foundation of the earth; and the heavens are the works of thine hands: They shall perish; but thou remainest; and they all shall wax old as doth a garment; and as a vesture shalt thou fold them up, and they shall be changed: but thou art the same, and thy years shall not fail" (Heb. 1:10–12).

Heaven and earth, as we know them, will grow old. Christ will roll them up as one rolls up an old garment and lays it aside to be worn no more. Heaven and earth, as we know them, will be exchanged for new heavens and a new earth (Rev. 21:1). Scientists have set forth what is called the "second law of thermodynamics," the belief that the universe is gradually losing heat and is thus slowly running down. The Bible says it more poetically by describing the universe as an old garment that gradually is becoming worn out. In the face of such prospects, God promises a final exaltation: "The kingdoms of this world are become the kingdoms of our Lord, and of his Christ; and he shall reign for ever and ever" (Rev. 11:15).

Conclusion

The prophets were great men, but they were only spokesmen for God. The Bible speaks of angelic beings, but they are only messengers of God to do his bidding. Only Jesus Christ is the Son of God.

James I of Scotland often traveled about his kingdom in disguise in order to acquaint himself with the real needs of his people. He disguised himself as a farmer and went under the name of "The Good Man of Ballengiech." Over the years he developed close friendships with humble people who never dreamed that he was the king. During one of his disguised travels, the king was befriended by a poor countryman who risked his own life to do so. Later the same countryman was summoned to Stirling Castle where the king kept midwinter court. Naturally the poor fellow was horrified, because in those days to be summoned to the king's court usually was to be condemned for some crime. Little did the poor fellow know that the king before whom he was to appear was one and the same with "The Good Man of Ballengiech." Imagine the surprise on the face of the poor countryman when he looked up into the eyes of the one sitting on the throne, fearing that he would hear a condemnation of death and seeing for the first time that the king was in reality an old friend. The summons to the king's court was not for condemnation but for reward (James Hastings, ed., "The Epistle to the Hebrews," in *The Speaker's Bible* [Grand Rapids: Baker, 1961], 13).

Jesus comes to us in much the same manner. He came among us as one of us to become both our Friend and Lord. He came as God's last Word to us. The salvation that he offers is never obsolete or irrelevant. In these last times God seeks to speak to us through his Son. We will do well to listen and to follow.

SUNDAY EVENING, JANUARY 14

Title: Sinning Man and Seeking God

Text: "When the woman saw that the tree was good for food, and that it was a delight to the eyes, and that the tree was desirable to make one wise, she took from its fruit and ate; and she gave also to her husband with her, and he ate" **(Gen. 3:6 NASB)**.

Scripture Reading: Genesis 3

Introduction

From the earliest times of recorded history, Genesis 3 has been a battleground. Some have cast it aside as fiction or mythology, scorning any literal or historical significance whatsoever. Others have said that it is allegorical—that it has spiritual meaning and is not literal in any sense of the word.

Actually, we must classify the chapter as a combination of the literal and the historical and note that it does contain some allegory. We have in this chapter the story of the actual events that took place in a man's physical life. Spiritual evil, in the person of the devil, is represented as taking physical form in order to reach spiritual man through his physical being.

Why should we consider Genesis 3 as one of the great chapters of the Old Testament? Its significance lies in the fact that it is here we meet sin and the devil for the first time. Here also we have the first promise of redemption and the symbolic act God performed in providing a covering for the nakedness of Adam and Eve. We will examine the chapter from three perspectives.

I. The method of the devil.

"Now the serpent" are the opening words of chapter 3. We must blot out of our minds the picture suggested by a writhing reptile. The Hebrew word translated "serpent" is *nawchash,* which means "a shining one." The evil personality that approached Eve in the garden of Eden was not a snake as we think of it, which would have been inferior to her, but "a shining one," obviously superior. In 2 Corinthians 11 Paul refers to this event when he says that "the serpent deceived Eve by his craftiness" (v. 3 NASB). Later, in the same context, Paul says, "Even Satan disguises himself as an angel of light" (v. 14 NASB). There is every reason to believe that the creature inhabited by the devil in the garden of Eden was appealingly beautiful.

What was the devil's method in approaching Eve? He began with a question: "Indeed, has God said, 'You shall not eat from any tree of the garden'?" (Gen. 3:1 NASB). Then he followed with a negation: "You surely shall not die!" (v. 4 NASB). His last line of attack was an affirmation: "For God knows that in the day you eat from it your eyes will be opened, and you will be like God, knowing good and evil" (v. 5 NASB).

What did the question accomplish? It raised a doubt in Eve's mind as to the goodness of God. A simple question is sometimes one of the best tools that can be used to cause doubt or to suggest evil. The question can be asked, "Did you hear about John?" And immediately, human nature being what it is, the person asked thinks, "Aha! What has John done? What kind of scandal is he involved in? What evil has befallen him?" The question is often the forerunner of the doubt.

Satan's question was not merely an inquiry. He was making an evil suggestion that God was unkind in withholding something from Adam and Eve. The devil followed this suggestion with a denial: 'You surely shall not die!" Not only had he suggested that the restriction God placed on man was unkind, but also that it was unreal. God did not really mean what he said. Last, Satan moved in for the kill by implying that God was unjust because he knew that when the fruit was eaten, man would know good and evil as God knew it.

Sunday Evening, January 14

II. The experience of man.

Eve apparently had no difficulty following the devil's line of reasoning, for the record states that she "saw that the tree was good for food, and that it was a delight to the eyes, and that the tree was desirable to make one wise" (Gen. 3:6 NASB). What had Eve actually done? She saw (or thought she saw) and her will acted on what she saw. She put two and two together but left out God, the supreme quantity, and thus got the wrong answer!

When Eve took the forbidden fruit, her act was a direct rebellion against God and consequently an act of spiritual suicide. Immediately she became afraid. For the first time since she was created, she experienced fear. She had not been afraid before because where there is no sin, there is no fear.

After fear came on Adam and Eve, dejection followed. For the first time they experienced an overwhelming consciousness of the physical, which filled them with a sense of shame. Sin puts blinders on people so that they see only the physical. Only when their sins are forgiven are they able to perceive the spiritual and understand their intended relationship with God.

III. The reaction of God.

"And they heard the sound of the LORD God walking in the garden in the cool of the day, and the man and his wife hid themselves from the presence of the LORD God among the trees of the garden" (Gen. 3:8 NASB). Satan had challenged God's goodness, and the fact that God came looking for Adam and Eve, who had sinned and who had tried to hide themselves from God, is proof of his great goodness.

"Then the LORD God called to the man, and said to him, 'Where are you?'" (Gen. 3:9 NASB). The garden of Eden in the cool of the evening—what a high and holy time of fellowship Adam and Eve had enjoyed in their daily meetings with God! Again, as usual, God came seeking. Here is a lesson concerning the attitude of God toward sinners—he takes the initiative and seeks them! No move came from Adam and Eve. They were silent and hidden.

God's question, "Where are you?" was not the call of a policeman arresting a criminal, but the wail of a father who had lost his child! It was God's heart quivering with grief. This is the first question of God in the Old Testament. (In contrast, the first question of the New Testament is recorded in Matthew 2:2: "Where is he?" It is the question of a sinner, convicted of his sins, seeking the Savior.)

God's question was a convicting one, for it could be answered only by a confession of guilt. Adam's answer reveals the damage sin had done. "I heard the sound of Thee in the garden, and I was afraid because I was naked; so I hid myself" (Gen. 3:10 NASB). God countered, "Who told you that you were naked? Have you eaten from the tree of which I commanded you not to eat?" (v. 11 NASB).

The reaction of Adam and Eve was despicable as they tried to shift the blame. Adam blamed Eve and even indirectly blamed God ("The woman

27

whom Thou gavest to be with me," NASB). Eve blamed the serpent, and God did not argue with her, for he knew that what she said was so. God asked no question of the devil, probably because confession on the devil's part is impossible and irrelevant, and redemption and restoration for him are also impossible.

Verse 15 is the mountain peak of the chapter, for it contains the first promise of redemption. It came immediately upon the fall of man. This was the first movement of God in grace toward the sinner. The sequel to this drama is described in verse 21: "And the Lord God made garments of skin for Adam and his wife, and clothed them." Any adequate covering for man's sin that will make him acceptable to God must be provided by God himself. The skins required the death of an innocent animal, which was symbolic of the death of Christ, the sinless substitute, on the cross.

Conclusion

"God clothed them." He did not say, "Here, Adam and Eve, is the covering for your sins. Come and get it if you want it. Take off your old coverings and put my covering on!" No! "God clothed them" means that he personally removed the poor and inadequate coverings that they had made for themselves and put on them his own covering.

God still works this way. Because sinful man is "dead in trespasses and sin," he cannot help himself. All he can do is present himself, in response to the seeking call of God, and allow God to do the cleansing and the clothing.

WEDNESDAY EVENING, JANUARY 17

Title: Jesus's Assumption Concerning Prayer

Text: "But when you pray, go into your room and shut the door and pray to your Father who is in secret; and your Father who sees in secret will reward you" **(Matt. 6:6 RSV)**.

Scripture Reading: Matthew 6:5–14

Introduction

Jesus made a great assumption concerning the fact that his disciples would give themselves to the habit of prayer. He gave them instructions concerning errors to avoid and procedures to follow in the practice of prayer. He warned them against praying like the hypocrites who looked upon prayer as a speech to be made to impress God and others. He also warned them against praying like the pagans who repeated many empty phrases in an effort to impress their helpless and reluctant deities to hear their pious phrases. Jesus declared that such repetition is unnecessary because of the nature and character of the God they were worshiping.

Our text contains a great assumption about prayer—not a command-ment—an assumption. We should let these words on prayer dwell in our hearts and encourage us as we give ourselves to the practice of prayer.

Why did Jesus assume that we would pray?

I. Because God is our heavenly Father.

Jesus gave himself to prayer because, as the Son of God, he hungered for fellowship and for the strength that came through dialogue with the heavenly Father. He assumed that, as the children of God, we would hunger and thirst for fellowship and would dialogue with the heavenly Father.

Jesus taught his disciples to think of God not as the eternal almighty exalted God, but as "Our Father who art in heaven." Jesus did not teach his disciples to approach the throne of God as beggars looking for a castoff; he encouraged them to come into the presence of the eternal God as needy children approaching a wise and generous father.

Why did Jesus assume that we would pray?

II. Because each of us has a violent and evil enemy in the devil.

Jesus had a personal experience with Satan at the beginning of his min-istry (Matt. 4:1–11). Satan was his foe. Jesus describes the devil as his enemy and our enemy (Matt. 13:25, 28, 39).

Peter warned his readers about our enemy the devil (1 Peter 5:8). James gave advice on how we can overcome the devil (James 4:7–8). John assured his readers that victory could be found through him who dwells within us (1 John 4:4).

Why did Jesus assume that we would pray?

III. Because life brings many troubles and hardships.

Many of us never make any allowance for the possibility of the tragic and the catastrophic happening in life. Suffering is in the pathway of each of us sooner or later. Peter encourages us to bring our anxieties and burdens to the Lord because he cares for us (1 Peter 5:7). Paul declared to the Philippians that by faith he had learned to be master of the adverse circumstances that befell him (Phil. 4:11–13).

Why did Jesus assume that we would pray?

IV. Because the pathway of life is uncertain.

Tomorrow is a mystery for all of us. Because we do not know what tomor-row holds, many of us feel the need to go into the closet of prayer to receive the strength we need and the assurance of the guidance of him who is the Light of the World (John 8:12).

Why did Jesus assume that we would pray?

29

V. Because prayer brings the strength and the help of the Lord to those who wait on him in faith and faithfulness (Isa. 40:31).

Our Lord gave himself continuously to the practice of prayer. It restored the vital energies of God to his life as he faced life's burdens and responsibilities. It brought the freshness of God's grace into his life continually.

It is the testimony of saints of the past and the present that, when we neglect the private place of prayer, we do so to our own impoverishment.

Conclusion

We should give ourselves to the practice of prayer because of the commandment of God, because of the invitation of Jesus, because of the hunger of our own heart for God, and because we live in the midst of so many unsaved people who need to know Jesus Christ as Savior and Lord. Jesus assures us that prayer is productive and brings rich rewards to those who give themselves to dialogue with the heavenly Father.

SUNDAY MORNING, JANUARY 21

Title: Be About God's Business

Text: "How is it that ye sought me? wist ye not that I must be about my Father's business?" **(Luke 2:49).**

Scripture Reading: Luke 2:40–52

Hymns: "All the Way My Saviour Leads Me," Crosby
        "I'll Live for Him," Hudson
        "I Love to Tell the Story," Hankey

Offertory Prayer: Our Father, as we worship you today, may we resolve to use our gifts and talents effectively in your service throughout the world. Give us a sense of mission. Make us and keep us aware that we were born for tasks that will not be done unless we do them. May we give of our resources this morning cheerfully and enthusiastically that your Word may be preached here at home and unto the uttermost part of the earth. We pray in Jesus's name. Amen.

Introduction

Much has been said about Christ's last words from the cross, but during the next few weeks we will concentrate on some of the things Jesus said early in his ministry. Although the words we will use this morning are unquestionably the first recorded words of our Savior, subsequent Sundays will not be quite so easy. We will depend, however, on the best scholarship to guide us step by step in the unfolding life of Jesus. By comparing the Gospels, we will seek to trace chronologically the events in the early part of Jesus's life and his reaction, as well as his comments concerning both the happenings and the people associated with them.

This morning we see Jesus in the temple at the age of twelve. He had accompanied his mother and father to the Passover feast. When the feast was concluded, Mary and Joseph traveled along in the caravan back toward home thinking Jesus was with the group. Suddenly they discovered he was missing, and they retraced their steps to Jerusalem. They found him talking with the learned men of the day in the temple. When they expressed their concern for him at their discovery of his absence, he replied that they should have understood he must already be about his Father's business. These words have gone down in history as expressing the early awareness of the young boy that he was a special person on a special mission for God.

I. The divine-human Jesus.

No one has ever been able to answer satisfactorily the question of when the boy Jesus first realized his unique relationship to God. He was completely divine, but he was also completely human. As a boy he must have studied the Scriptures (our Old Testament). On the other hand, God must have revealed to him early in his life his role as Savior and Redeemer. Nevertheless, the Father's business was not preaching and working miracles, but remaining at home as an obedient child, happy that he could be of help to his parents and developing as an industrious growing man.

There are times in the life of a young person when he or she must get preparation. Part of that preparation is accepting discipline. There are two kinds of discipline—being subject to others and controlling oneself. Both are important. This divine-human Jesus was completely God and yet completely man. Years later, when Christian theologians tried to define his nature, they wrote in a famous church council that he was one man with two natures and that we should never seek to confuse the natures nor divide the person. It is difficult, if not impossible, to improve upon this group's decision.

II. The work of Jesus.

The time came, however, when Jesus had to launch out into God's work. His years of preparation were important even though we do not have a record of them. Some of the fanciful tales that are told in noncanonical literature concerning his childhood should not be taken seriously. Traditions and stories have come to us about how he astounded his playmates by performing miracles as a child, but these have never been historically proven. They are fanciful and contrary to the life and ministry of Jesus as we understand him. He did not begin his work of redemption as a small child except that he lived a sinless life that could be accepted later by God in sacrificial death for our sins.

The work of Jesus was redemptive. Even as the Old Testament is not a history of Israel, but a history of God's redemptive work, so the New Testament is not a record of Jesus's life nor the life of any other person, but rather a record of God's redemptive work. The gospel writers were not compiling a biography of Jesus. They were telling of God's redeeming grace through his Son. This was the work in which Jesus was constantly engaging.

31

III. The world does not understand.

Luke tells us that his parents "understood not the saying which he spake unto them" (2:50). This is the reaction of the world today. Those who do not know Jesus Christ in personal redemption do not understand the mission of Christian people. Those who are born again have a task. They are to witness concerning the grace of Jesus Christ and of the change that can come when the Holy Spirit transforms a life. The secular world simply does not understand. An outstanding preacher was once attacked by a secular newspaper reporter who wrote, "I simply do not understand how a red-blooded he-man could devote his life to preaching such a message." The minister replied the next day from the pulpit, "I agree with that newspaper reporter. He does not understand." Those of us who know Jesus Christ as personal Savior do understand and consider it a great privilege and joy to invest our lives in our Father's business.

IV. To do God's will brings fulfillment of life.

One of the greatest statements ever made about a young man was made concerning Jesus when the gospel writer says that he "increased in wisdom and stature, and in favour with God and man" (Luke 2:52). Often we hear people speak of the sacrifices they made to follow Jesus. Actually, no one ever left anything for Jesus without being fully and completely rewarded many times and in many ways. Once, during the ministry of Jesus, Simon Peter said, "Lo, we have left all, and followed thee" (Luke 18:28). Jesus replied, "Verily I say unto you, There is no man that hath left house, or parents, or brethren, or wife, or children, for the kingdom of God's sake, who shall not receive manifold more in this present time, and in the world to come life everlasting" (vv. 29–30). We become more in this world by following Jesus than we could ever become without him.

One of our great preachers of another generation, Dr. M. E. Dodd, used to speak laughingly of how people told him that he would have made a great businessman if he had not gone into the ministry. He once said, "At one time I began to feel sorry for myself when I thought of how much I had left to follow Jesus. Then I remembered who I was and what I was before I surrendered to him. I was a little country boy hid away on a farm in West Tennessee. I realized that all that I had become was because I had followed Jesus." Dodd used to love to say, "The only thing I left to follow Jesus was a flop-eared mule, a bull-tongued plow, and a patch of new ground in Gibson County." Jesus was constantly busy with his Father's work, and this made him an even greater person. .

Conclusion

Where do you fit into God's work? This is closely related to the question of God's will for your life. Not only preachers, but laypeople as well, are to be busy in the Father's business. William Carey, founder of the modern missions movement, used to say, "My business is preaching the gospel of Christ. I mend shoes to pay expenses." So the layman ought to consider his secular employment as only the means for earning a living so that he may give himself completely to the Christian life. It is important to have full-time religious workers such as pastors, evangelists, teachers, and missionaries, but if the world is ever won to Christ, it will be because nonordained people, the rank-and-file Christians, take seriously God's work and give their best to it.

As Jesus grew from innocence into holiness by being obedient to God and being about his work, so we will grow in the grace and knowledge of our Lord as we commit ourselves to his work. We shall never, of course, be like Jesus in the ultimate sense of the word, since he was the eternal Word of God become flesh. On the other hand, we can grow into his likeness as we are busy for him in constructive service and personal witnessing. Let's always, wherever we are, be about our Father's business!

SUNDAY EVENING, JANUARY 21

Title: Down Life's Dead-End Streets

Text: "And he said, 'Take now your son, your only son, whom you love, Isaac, and go to the land of Moriah; and offer him there as a burnt offering on one of the mountains of which I will tell you"' **(Gen. 22:2 NASB)**.

Scripture Reading: Genesis 22:1–24

Introduction

When we are born into the family of God, we become the object of God's loving care. And the attention of God toward his people is not the doting care of a parent who seeks to give his children everything they want. Rather, immediately upon our entrance into the heavenly family, God begins to work with us. We are like shapeless lumps of clay in his hands. With the precision of a master potter, God begins to mold and fashion us.

Occasionally, because of our belligerence and stubbornness, the process is slowed. Yet in his own sovereign way, God keeps on working with us until one day we shall stand before him "having no spot or wrinkle or any such thing" (Eph. 5:17 NASB), having been formed into the image of God's dear Son. Sometimes these testing experiences that God either permits or initiates in our lives appear to us as dead-end streets. Such was the case with a particularly difficult testing time in Abraham's life.

As far as we know, this was the last great test that came to Abraham, for when this experience was finished, the life of that venerable old patriarch came to a close. In effect, this was Abraham's "final exam."

I. Difficult instructions.

"Now it came about after these things, that God tested Abraham" (Gen. 22:1 NASB). The words "after these things" are significant. This test that was about to come to Abraham came after God had proved his power in fulfilling his promise to Abraham and Sarah in the birth of Isaac. After a long process of molding and fashioning, Abraham's faith was ready for the supreme test. It is reassuring to know that God will never allow to come into the life of one of his children a test or temptation that is beyond the strength of that believer's faith to bear (see 1 Cor. 10:13).

There was no softening of the blow when God said plainly to Abraham, "Take now your son, your only son, whom you love, Isaac, and go to the land of Moriah; and offer him there as a burnt offering on one of the mountains of which I will tell you" (Gen. 22:2 NASB). The analogy between Abraham and God himself in this incident begins at once. Human fatherhood and sonship are but shadows of the perfect relationship that existed between God the Father and Jesus Christ the Son. Just as Isaac was Abraham's "only son," so Jesus was the "only begotten Son of God." The land of Moriah is generally considered to be the area around Jerusalem, which further compares with the sacrifice of Christ, which took place just outside the city of Jerusalem.

God instructed Abraham to offer Isaac as "a burnt offering." According to Leviticus 1, there are two essential requirements concerning a burnt offering. First, it must be offered freely and voluntarily. Christ came to do his Father's will knowing full well that it demanded the sacrifice of his life. Second, a burnt offering was to be offered whole. Nothing must be kept back. Christ withheld nothing, and in Romans 12:1 believers are called on to offer to God all that they are and have. Abraham was called on to offer to God all that he had.

Abraham was to offer Isaac "on one of the mountains" in Moriah. He was not to do this in the valley or out of sight in a secluded place. It was to be done in a high and exposed place. Likewise, Jesus was openly crucified on a hilltop, and his crucifixion was the most open of all events in human history.

II. Deliberate obedience.

"So Abraham rose early in the morning" (Gen. 22:3 NASB). There is no evidence in the narrative that Abraham had wrestled through the night with this command from God. However, we can be almost certain that this was the longest night in his life! But when dawn came, Abraham's faith in God enabled him to see that the road down which God was leading him was not a dead-end street after all! A thrilling commentary on Abraham's experience is given by the writer of Hebrews: "By faith Abraham, when he was tested, offered up Isaac; and he who had received the promises was offering up his only begotten son; it was he to whom it was said, 'In Isaac your seed shall be called.' He considered that God is able to raise men even from the dead; from which he also received him back as a type" (Heb. 11:17–19 NASB). Some say Abraham did not struggle with this at all. Yet it would have been no test had Abraham not agonized through the experience, allowing his faith to be perfected so that he could see God's wisdom.

The writer is careful to note that Abraham "went to the place of which

God had told him" (Gen. 22:3 NASB). It was a specified place. God is concerned about the details in our lives and in the development of our faith. Nothing that concerns his children is unimportant to God. When Abraham and Isaac reached the mountain God had pointed out, Abraham carried out God's orders explicitly. He built the altar, laid the wood for the fire in order, bound Isaac, and placed him on the altar. Even though Abraham's faith had won the initial battle, doubtlessly he still found great difficulty in carrying out God's orders. Peter commented on the fact that trials and tests often are extremely difficult in a Christian's life (see 1 Peter 1:6–7).

Furthermore, Abraham was prepared to carry out everything God had commanded. "And Abraham stretched out his hand, and took the knife to slay his son" (Gen. 22:10 NASB). And it was at that moment, when Abraham had done everything God had told him to do up to the point of taking Isaac's life, that God intervened.

III. Divine compensation.

God allowed the test to go to its full length, just short of Isaac's death. Then, for the second time, God called out in the voice of the angel of the Lord, "Abraham, Abraham!" God was pleased with his servant Abraham and said, "Do not stretch out your hand against the lad, and do nothing to him; for now I know that you fear God, since you have not withheld your son, your only son, from Me" (Gen. 22:12 NASB).

"Now I know . . . ." God knew from the beginning what kind of faith Abraham had; he simply meant by that statement that the testing of Abraham's faith was exhaustive and conclusive. James says that Abraham's "works" perfected or completed his faith—brought it to maturity (see James 2:21–26). This is the intended result of tests and trials in Christians' lives.

At this point, God revealed the "detour" on this seemingly dead-end street. "Then Abraham raised his eyes and looked, and behold, behind him a ram caught in the thicket by his horns; and Abraham went and took the ram, and offered him up for a burnt offering in the place of his son" (Gen. 22:13 NASB). The "detour" was there all along, but Abraham could not see it until the trial of his faith was completed.

Conclusion

It is not uncommon for Christians to find that they are trudging along what appears to be a dead-end street—a dreary road of trial and heartache. It was so for Abraham. But the Scripture says that "Abraham raised his eyes and looked." When he did, he saw God's provision for the happy ending of his trial. He didn't waste time trying to figure out where the ram came from or how the ram came to be caught by its horns in the thicket. That was of no consequence. God had provided! And Abraham called that place "Jehovah-Jireh," which means "the Lord will provide" (Gen. 22:14).

WEDNESDAY EVENING, JANUARY 24

Title: The Savior's Encouragement Regarding Prayer

Text: "Ask, and it will be given you; seek, and you will find; knock, and it will be opened to you" **(Matt. 7:7 RSV).**

Scripture Reading: Matthew 7:7–11

Introduction

These words from the lips of the Savior contain an imperative for all of us. If we would obey our Lord, we must pray and keep on praying with persistence. Jesus dealt with the subject of prayer earlier in the Sermon on the Mount, giving us a pattern to follow (Matt. 6:9–13). Prayer is the only subject dealt with twice in the Sermon on the Mount. In the words of our text, our Lord is declaring that God answers prayer in his own divine way.

In these words Jesus speaks to those who have entered the family of God through the gateway of the new birth. He encourages us to ask, to seek, and to knock at the door of the heavenly Father, who is the great giver. Jesus is speaking of three degrees of intensity in our prayer efforts. We are to ask as children, as dependents. We are to ask with persistence. And we are to pray for specific gifts, for our Father is "too wise to err, too good to be unkind." Our heavenly Father is too wise and good to give us some things we ask for. Instead he sometimes finds it better to substitute something else or to withhold giving altogether. All of the precious promises of God are subject to certain great spiritual conditions. He will not be inconsistent with his own character, and he will not give us that which is contradictory to his own redemptive purpose. The Father God always gives in conformity to his character, his wisdom, and his goodness.

I. The Father God gives the good gift of himself to those who pray (Matt. 6:6; James 4:8).

The greatest gift that comes to us in the experience of prayer is the gift of himself that God grants to those who come to his throne of grace.

II. The Father God gives us forgiveness of sin and cleansing from the pollution of sin (I John 1:9).

With the gift of new life comes the gift of cleansing associated with forgiveness. No one enjoys being dirty. Everyone feels better after a good bath. To truly pray a prayer of repentance and confession is to experience a cleansing of the soul that brings joy to the heart.

III. The Father God gives us wisdom for living in difficult times (James 1:5–6).

The Father God was pleased when Solomon requested above all things "wisdom and knowledge" that would enable him to be a good king for his nation (2 Chron. 1:10). God granted to him the wisdom and knowledge he needed (2 Chron. 1:12).

Every one of us stands in need of divine wisdom—the capacity to see through to the end of a way of thinking or a way of acting. We need this divine insight to enable us to steer away from that which is destructive and to choose that which is good and excellent. Divine wisdom will come to those who pray for it.

IV. The Father God gives us the Holy Spirit to help us (Luke 11:13).

The gift of the Spirit is the gift of God when we receive Jesus Christ as Lord and Savior. The fullness of the Spirit comes to those who invite him to fill every portion of their being. He can guide the minds of those who are willing to let God's thoughts come into their intellect. He can aid us in controlling emotions that often would lead us to wrong actions. The more we pray with faith, the more we let the Holy Spirit have his way in our lives.

V. When we pray, the Father God gives us the grace, mercy, and help we need (Heb. 4:14–16).

If we would live triumphant lives, then we should give ourselves to prayer every day. We are encouraged to come boldly before the throne of grace that we may obtain the mercy, grace, and help that we need. Many of us live impoverished lives because we have neglected to follow the guidelines given to us in the words of our text.

Conclusion

Why not open every day with a prayer for divine guidance. The very moment you awake, thank God for the privilege of being able to see the light of day. Thank him for what he is going to do for you during the day. Ask him for grace and guidance and help that you might make wise choices and that you might give yourself to good causes.

Keep on asking. Keep on seeking. Keep on knocking. And God will keep on giving.

SUNDAY MORNING, JANUARY 28

Title: Do the Things That Are Right

Text: "Suffer it to be so now: for thus it becometh us to fulfil all righteousness" (Matt. 3:15).

Scripture Reading: Matthew 3:13–17

Hymns: "O Happy Day," Doddridge
"My Faith Looks Up to Thee," Palmer
"Trust and Obey," Sammis

Offertory Prayer: Our Father, we know that you are infinite and we are only human. In you alone can we conquer our selfishness and hatred of others. In you alone can we find the joy unspeakable that makes life worth living and gives us peace when we must face death. May we find joy this morning in sharing our material possessions with those who stand in spiritual need. Reveal to us that only what we give away do we really have, and only what we invest in the work of your kingdom will remain with us always. May the Savior who, though rich, became poor that we through his poverty may be rich, bless us as we give. We pray in the Redeemer's name. Amen.

Introduction

The second recorded time that Jesus speaks is at his baptism. John was six months older than his cousin and was on the scene first preaching about the kingdom of God. His was a "repentance baptism," and some have raised the question as to why Jesus was baptized when he certainly had no sin in his life. In fact, this was no doubt part of John's problem as he insisted that Jesus should baptize him rather than vice versa. Whether John realized at that moment that Jesus was the promised Messiah and without sin or whether he realized that shortly thereafter, we cannot be certain. We do know, however, that as John faced Jesus he recognized a man who was spiritually his superior. Thus, he said, "I have need to be baptized of thee" (Matt. 3:14). Jesus, however, insisted that in order that they "fulfil all righteousness" (v. 15), John should baptize him. John accepted this reasoning and fulfilled the request.

What does it mean to "fulfil all righteousness" in one's life? *Fulfill* means literally "to fill full." Jesus was thus saying concerning his life and John's that which we need to say concerning our own. Whatever the cost, we should do the things that are right. For Jesus at that particular time, it meant being baptized by John. Later it meant resisting temptation. Still later it meant preaching fearlessly about sin and teaching simplistically about righteousness. Much later it meant going to the cross and dying for the sins of the world. Always, in every place, Jesus was committed to doing the thing that was right.

I. To confess Jesus publicly is a right thing to do.

Regardless of the many denominational views on baptism, one thing is so evident we should all agree immediately concerning it. Baptism is a public confession and commitment to Christ. Christendom is in full agreement that followers of Jesus should confess openly and publicly their faith in the Savior and their desire to follow him. Orthodox Christianity has rejected the views of those who have suggested that Jesus in some way "became the Son of God in the fullest sense" at his baptism. Jesus was the Son of God because of his entrance into the world through the supernatural virgin birth. He did not become the Son of God nor become even more the Son of God at his baptism.

This act was a declaration to the world that he was committed to the spread of God's righteousness. As the life, death, and resurrection of Jesus unfolded in his ministry, deeper truths could be seen. At this stage, however, Jesus was declaring to the world the importance of public commitment.

II. To identify with good people is a right thing to do.

John the Baptist was a man of God. He proclaimed righteousness as a necessity for pleasing God. He defined righteousness in terms of fairness in dealing with others, unselfishness in meeting human needs, and sincerity in every aspect of life. When one group asked him what to do, he replied, "He that hath two coats, let him impart to him that hath none; and he that hath meat, let him do likewise" (Luke 3:11). When soldiers asked him the same question, he replied, "Do violence to no man, neither accuse any falsely; and be content with your wages" (v. 14).

When Jesus was baptized, he was identifying himself with the things for which John the Baptist stood. In this world of lowered moral and ethical standards, we need to identify ourselves in loyalty and allegiance to those who are preaching righteous living. Years ago, in the British Parliament, one man arose and said, "I propose that England base her foreign policy on the Sermon on the Mount." A skeptical member of the body said, "If we do that, God help England." The first man arose and said quietly, "I am persuaded that if England will base her foreign policy on the Sermon on the Mount, God will help England." Likewise, when we identify ourselves with those who are seeking, in Christ's name, to bring justice, righteousness, and peace to this world, we are doing that which is right.

III. When we do the right thing, God will honor us.

A strange thing occurred when Jesus came up out of the water. The heavens opened and the Spirit of God descended upon him. A voice from heaven said, "This is my beloved Son, in whom I am well pleased" (Matt. 3:17). This was God's approval of Jesus's action. A great lesson comes to us from this incident. God will bless the person who seeks to do his will. This does not mean he will always make him rich, although we can note many times that God has blessed Christian businesspeople with wealth. Neither does it mean that we shall never suffer. Some of the greatest Christians have suffered most but have learned lessons in suffering that have blessed their lives. God nowhere promises those who please him that they will be popular with the world or successful as the world counts success. He does promise, however, to honor those who honor him. Righteousness will win the struggle even if it does not win every individual battle. The team that wins the ball game is the one that is ahead at the end of the game, not at the end of a particular inning. Whatever else the book of Revelation teaches, one great lesson is clearly evident: God's people will never be stamped out by the satanic forces of wickedness. When we align ourselves with the cause of righteousness, we will not only be preserved but also be blessed and greatly rewarded. Washington Gladden wrote:

> I know that right is right;
> That it is not good to lie;
> That love is better than spite,
> And a neighbor than a spy;
>
> I know that passion needs
> The leash of a sober mind;
> I know that generous deeds
> Some sure reward will find;
>
> In the darkest night of the year,
> When the stars have all gone out,
> That courage is better than fear,
> That faith is truer than doubt;
>
> And fierce though the fiends may fight,
> And long though the angels hide,
> I know that Truth and Right
> Have the universe on their side.

Conclusion

A sermon such as this one must not be misunderstood. Salvation does not come by doing things. We are justified from the guilt of sin by faith in Christ. The deeper meaning of baptism, even that of John's baptism, was that it pointed to the time when Christ would be crucified for our sins, be buried, and rise from the dead. The first "work of righteousness" that we can do is to believe on Christ, whom God sent to be our Savior. Growth in grace and knowledge of our Lord can come only after a new-birth experience. To do the things that are right thus involves repentance of sin and receiving the Savior as entrance into the new life. After that, we develop as a Christian by doing good things. Priorities must always be kept in proper perspective. Redeemed people should obey the Lord. They do this, however, because they have been saved, not in order to be saved.

SUNDAY EVENING, JANUARY 28

Title: A Token Forever

Text: "Now this day will be a memorial to you, and you shall celebrate it as a feast to the LORD; throughout your generations you are to celebrate it as a permanent ordinance" **(Ex. 12:14 NASB)**.

Scripture Reading: Exodus 12:1–51

Introduction

The intervention of God in human history—in nations and in the lives of individuals—always comes at the right hour. After nearly four hundred years in Egypt, much of which was spent in prosperity and favor, the Hebrew people had become the helpless victims of a pharaoh who "knew not Joseph." Unlike the friendly pharaoh who held Joseph in high esteem and consequently honored Joseph's people, this new pharaoh's concern was for his own countrymen. He felt that these descendants of Joseph were becoming a growing threat to the security of Egypt.

As a result, he began to put burdensome tasks on the Hebrews. They were required to build treasure cities in Egypt. Finally, as the rigors of this bondage became harder and harder, we are told that "a great cry went up in Egypt." The Hebrews were nearing the breaking point. They had lost their self-respect, their spirit, and their dignity. This sense of insufficiency opened the way for God to work on their behalf. We often work ourselves down to the point of spiritual exhaustion before we turn to God and he comes to our rescue. It is only then that we recognize our need.

Thus, the time had come for the Hebrews to be brought out into a new and thrilling liberty. Exodus 12 describes the rite that was established in connection with this victorious emancipation and which has remained a memorial throughout history to God's miraculous deliverance.

I. The preparation.

In Exodus 11:7 we are told that the Lord will "make a distinction between Egypt and Israel." What was this distinction? It was not a racial or ethnic one—not even a moral one. The difference existed only because the blood of the Passover lamb, the innocent sacrifice, had been prescribed and applied. It was in the "blood of the lamb" that mercy and truth met together and that righteousness and peace kissed each other (Ps. 85:10).

When the divine pronouncement came to Moses in regard to the death angel's passing through Egypt, the sentence was passed on Egyptians and Hebrews alike. Any Hebrew family could have refused to make these preparations. If they had, their firstborn sons and the firstborn males of all their flocks and herds would have died just as the pharaoh's firstborn died.

Specific instructions were given regarding the sacrificial lamb. It had to be just a year old and without blemish. It had to be chosen from the flock on the tenth day of the month and kept until the fourteenth day. On the fourteenth day the lamb was to be killed, its blood caught and then sprinkled on the doorposts and lintel of the houses wherein the Hebrew people lived. Then, on the fateful night when the death angel passed through the land and saw the blood on the houses of the Israelites, he would not enter (v. 23). Why? Because death had already done its work in those houses! The innocent had died in the place of the guilty. Thus, God's justice was satisfied.

II. The application.

The first direct reference to the "lamb" in the Bible is in Genesis 22:8. Abraham said to Isaac that the Lord would "provide himself a lamb." The lamb was provided to glorify God's character, to vindicate his holiness, to satisfy his justice, and to magnify his being. This is what Paul had in mind when he wrote: ". . . being justified freely by his grace through the redemption that is in Christ Jesus: Whom God hath set forth to be a propitiation through faith in his blood, to declare his righteousness . . . that he might be just, and the justifier of him which believeth in Jesus" (Rom. 3:24–26).

In the instructions to the Hebrews concerning the lamb, we can see an amazing parallel with the life of Jesus. The year-old lamb was neither newborn nor old. Jesus was crucified when he was yet a young man in his prime. The lamb was "kept up" for four days with the family. The animal identified with the family, and a relationship was established. Jesus likewise came and identified with humanity in a special way. He lived among people, ate with them, rejoiced and wept with them. Jesus was thus a "personal" Savior.

On the fourteenth day of the month the lamb was killed. Why? Because death had to be inflicted either upon the guilty transgressor or upon an innocent substitute. Then its blood was to be applied to the doorposts and lintel of the house in which each Hebrew family lived. Without the shedding of blood and the sprinkling of this blood, there is no remission of sins (Heb. 9:22). These two acts are not synonymous. The first, the shedding of the blood, was to satisfy God's righteous demands; it is the propitiation for our sin. The second act is to save people—the appropriation, or application, of the sacrificial blood to our sin.

A person can accept intellectually the facts of the life and death of Jesus and still not apply that sacrificial death to his or her own personal need. Intellectual acceptance of the life and death of Jesus will not bring about the new birth. A Savior "provided" is not sufficient. He must be received. There must be "faith in his blood" (Rom. 3:25), and faith is a personal expression.

Note Exodus 12:23 (NASB): "For the LORD will pass through to smite the Egyptians; and when he sees the blood on the lintel and on the two doorposts, the LORD will pass over the door and will not allow the destroyer to come in to your houses to smite you." Note that the eye of the Lord was upon the blood, not on the house. It might have been a strong house or a miserable hovel. That was no matter. God looked for the blood on the doorposts and lintel.

Nor was his eye on those within the house. It mattered not that they were blood descendants of Abraham. It was not their genealogy, their ceremonial observances, or their works that secured deliverance from God's judgment. It was their personal application of the shed blood. It is likewise true that when God looks toward us, he looks to see the cleansing, redeeming blood of his Son. He is not impressed with anything we might have done to "prepare" ourselves for salvation.

III. The proclamation.

"And it will come about when your children will say to you, 'What does this rite mean to you?' that you shall say, 'It is a Passover sacrifice to the LORD who passed over the houses of the sons of Israel in Egypt when he smote the Egyptians, but spared our homes.' And the people bowed low and worshiped" (Ex. 12:26–27 NASB).

When God established this ritual of the Passover feast, he did so in the interest of the children. He was making provision for the generations that were to come. What God did was based on the philosophy that we are slow to grasp—the hope of the future lies in the child! If children are properly trained and informed, a highway is opened in every generation for the Holy Spirit to prepare hearts to receive the gospel.

God is constantly putting in front of children things that make them ask questions, and there is no work more important than that of answering their questions. Their impressionable minds need to be carefully programmed with the incomparable truths of God's Word. Then, at the proper time, the Holy Spirit will trigger their memories, and those holy truths will spring to life within them.

Conclusion

In succeeding Scripture references, the Passover is described as an ordinance, a feast, and a sacrifice. It is an ordinance in that it is an authoritative arrangement. God set it forth and ordered it. He conceived it. Likewise, "salvation is of the Lord." Man could never have devised such a holy and righteous plan.

The Passover is a feast, an occasion of rejoicing because of deliverance. One's eternal salvation is ever an occasion for joy unspeakable, for it is a mighty stroke of divine grace in which believing people are delivered from eternal death.

The Passover is a sacrifice—it speaks of a substitutionary death that spelled "life" for those on whose houses the blood was sprinkled. So Jesus became the substitution on the cross of death for all people. Yet until that blood is applied by faith to one's personal sin, it is of no avail.

WEDNESDAY EVENING, JANUARY 31

Title: The Nature of Prayer

Text: "Then he said to his disciples, 'The harvest is plentiful, but the laborers are few; pray therefore the Lord of the harvest to send out laborers into his harvest'" **(Matt. 9:37–38 RSV)**.

Scripture Reading: Matthew 9:35–38

Introduction

Of all the words that fell from the lips of our Savior that we should let dwell within us, we should rejoice in and respond to the gracious invitation contained in our text: "The harvest is plentiful, but the laborers are few; pray therefore the Lord of the harvest to send out laborers into his harvest."

Many have lived with only a partial understanding of what our Lord was seeking to communicate in these words. Consequently, our response to his command, his gracious invitation, has been only fractional rather than full. Many have seen in this verse an encouragement to pray for Christian workers when there are vacancies within the church. Congregations have lifted their hearts to God when they were without a shepherd. Pastors have used this verse as a basis for praying that God would send workers to lead singing, to teach Bible classes, or to work with children. Certainly this type of a petition is encouraged by the text, but to see this as the full meaning is to miss the best part of the verse.

Many of us have failed to enter into the meaning of this passage because of our limited concept of prayer. We have thought of prayer in terms of bringing our requests to God and asking him to do certain things for us or to do certain things in the hearts and lives of others. We have seen prayer as a monologue in which the needy child approaches the throne of the Father God and presents his or her needs. We have failed to see that prayer is in reality a dialogue in which the needy child comes to the Father God and the Father God also comes to the needy child. We offer our petitions to God and should also give God the opportunity to offer his petitions, suggestions, commandments, and directions to us.

I. Prayer is listening to God and listening for God.

Those who would pray effectively should pray often in private and should spend a considerable portion of that time in silence waiting for God to speak. God may use the Scriptures to speak to us or a phrase from a great hymn or perhaps an observation concerning the events of life. He may speak to us by laying on us such a burden of concern that we feel compelled to do his will.

II. Prayer is hearing what God has to say.

Many of us make the sad mistake of rushing into the presence of God with our "grocery list" of requests, and we speak to him as if we were the chief executive officer of a corporation and he was nothing more than a divine office boy. We need to reverse this concept and see God as the executive who has the right to give us guidelines, suggestions, and even orders and commissions.

As we read through the great prophetic books of the Old Testament, we find over and over the indictment brought against the people that they would not heed what God was saying to them. Are we guilty of the same sin? Is this the reason why much of our prayer efforts fail to accomplish anything either in our lives or in the lives of others?

III. Prayer is consenting to what God does say.

The call for repentance basically is a call to agree with God concerning all the issues and values we face in life. To repent is to change the mind, to alter the attitude, to accept a new philosophy and a new scale of values in the innermost being. When this basic change in our attitude toward God, self, sin, others, and things takes place, a radical transformation in our conduct and activities is the inevitable result. Are we like stubborn and unthinking children who turn a deaf ear to the wise counsel of the Father God who is eager to communicate to us his good and perfect will?

IV. Prayer is asking God for both the disposition and the energy to obey his good will.

The fields are white unto harvest. We do not have to persuade the Lord of the harvest to send forth laborers. Rather, we should ask the Lord of the harvest concerning what portion of the field he would have us to engage ourselves in for the harvest of souls. He is eager to give each of us directions concerning our participation in harvesting the fields that are white unto harvest.

Conclusion

What is prayer? Prayer is listening to God, hearing what God has to say. Prayer is also agreeing with what God says and asking God for the power to obey him in every area of life.

FEBRUARY

- ### Sunday Mornings
  Complete the series on the first sayings of Jesus.

- ### Sunday Evenings
  Continue the series "God Continues to Speak."

- ### Wednesday Evenings
  Continue the series "The Words of Jesus Christ."

SUNDAY MORNING, FEBRUARY 4

Title: No, Satan, I Will Not Serve You

Text: "Get thee hence, Satan: for it is written, Thou shalt worship the Lord thy God, and him only shalt thou serve" **(Matt. 4:10)**.

Scripture Reading: Matthew 4:1–11

Hymns: "Yield Not to Temptation," Palmer
"I Would Be True," Walter
"What a Friend We Have in Jesus," Scriven

Offertory Prayer: Almighty God, in our minds there are many recesses, and we need constantly to purge them from all falsehood and selfishness. Shine on us with the light of your Holy Spirit and help us to both recognize and confess our sins and put them far from us. As we bring our offerings this morning, may we count it a joy to worship by giving and to remember always the words of our Savior, who said that it is better to give than to receive. We pray in Christ's name. Amen.

Introduction

Each time our Savior refused one of Satan's temptations in today's Scripture text, he was saying in essence the same thing: "No, I will not serve you." Satan made his strongest attack on Jesus shortly after his most exciting moment, his baptism by John in the Jordan. Satan was doing more than tempting to get Jesus to sin by doing specific acts. He was trying to get him to make wrong decisions that would affect his entire earthly ministry.

What kind of messiah would Jesus be? Would he conform to the popular opinion of the people, or would he do things God's way? Would his ministry be mere showmanship or deep spiritual commitment? Each of the three temptations had overtones of the decisions that Jesus would have to make throughout his ministry.

Also, these temptations represent frontal attacks on the three vulnerable points of human nature. Satan's temptations appeal to the appetite, to avarice, and to ambition. These represent the three categories into which sin falls. John calls them "the lust of the flesh," "the lust of the eyes," and "the pride of life" (1 John 2:16). In the garden of Eden the woman saw that the tree was "good for food, and that it was pleasant to the eyes, and a tree to be desired to make one wise" (Gen. 3:6). Both of these passages are in harmony with the categories of sin as outlined in the account of our Lord's temptations.

I. I will not compromise my body.

One thing should be emphasized at the outset. Jesus did not ignore the necessity of bread. He rather refused to give it priority in his life. He would not be imprisoned within the narrow limits of fleshly desires.

The needs of the body are real. God has made us with certain drives that call constantly for fulfillment. He has also, however, set limits to our liberty. When a life is given over completely to an "eat, drink, and be merry" philosophy, pessimism is the logical outcome. Personal pleasure and spectacular amusement actually represent nothing but the worship of the body. When it is placed first in life, there can be no real conviction of immortality and perhaps hardly even the wish for it. One of communism's early leaders once said, "Religion is the opiate of the people." He was wrong! In America the opiate of the people is commercialized entertainment that seeks to immediately satisfy every drive of the physical body and the lower nature that is so often associated with such drives.

A depressed patient was once told by his doctor, "You need an uplift. You need to forget the cares of the world. I advise that you go and become acquainted with Grimaldi, a great entertainer who lives the free and easy life. If you will associate with him and gain his philosophy, you will find that your depression will give way to delights and joys in life. He knows how to enjoy life to the fullest in an unbridled and uninhibited way." The patient replied, "I'm sorry, doctor; you did not get my name when I came in. I am Grimaldi."

Jesus refused to compromise. He had come into the world to be a spiritual leader and would not adopt methods that compromised his basic philosophy of what the Messiah should be. He would take the long, hard, rugged road to provide for humankind's redemption and not use the power that was his to gain a shortcut to the fulfillment of his messiahship. Likewise, although in a different way, we too must remain true to our convictions. God has given us a body to be used to his glory. There is no shortcut in service. We must keep our body under subjection, disciplining it to the utmost that we might be useful in his kingdom. To fail to do so means forfeiting our opportunities for effective service. Paul had this in mind when he wrote, "I pommel my body and subdue it, lest after preaching to others I myself should be disqualified" (1 Cor. 9:27 RSV). Paul did not mean that he would lose his salvation if he yielded to temptation. He meant rather that if he did not discipline his body

47

continuously, he would fail to be the servant of Christ that God intended him to be.

II. I will not have unholy ambitions.

Matthew and Luke reverse the order of Jesus's second and third temptations. We cannot be certain which of the two came first, but we are dealing with Matthew's account in this message. Jesus had answered Satan with Scripture in refusing the first temptation. Now Satan quotes Scripture to reinforce his second attempt to sidetrack Jesus and get him to sin.

What was involved in Satan's suggestion that Jesus cast himself down? The devil wanted him to gain popularity with the crowds in a cheap and theatrical way. In short, he wanted Jesus to be a "worldly" messiah rather than a spiritual one. This temptation came often to Jesus, for the crowds constantly wanted to place a crown on his head and make him an earthly king.

Jesus affirmed to the end, however, that he had not come to be an earthly king. He said plainly to Pilate, "My kingdom is not of this world" (John 18:36). Far too many of us today, however, have never seen the spiritual nature of Christ's kingdom. Perhaps I am not going too far when I say that the basic reason Jesus was crucified was that he would not conform to the wishes of the crowd that he become a political ruler. Multitudes were willing to follow him in a crusade against the Roman government, but he would not allow himself to be led into that kind of situation.

The devil quoted Scripture. At first his use of Scripture seemed logical. Had not God promised to protect his own? But there was another side to it. We are not to put ourselves in a dangerous position by our own foolishness and then expect that God is obligated to deliver us. While we are in God's will, we can expect him to be with us, but when we stray from his will in order to feed our own ego or satisfy some vain ambition, we must not expect him to feel any obligation to rush to our rescue.

Pride is one of the greatest sins. Early Christians listed it as first of the "seven deadly sins," indicating how strongly they felt about it. James Russell Lowell said that "pride and weakness are Siamese twins." Benjamin Franklin gave a graphic picture as "Pride breakfasted with Plenty, dined with Poverty, and supped with Infamy." William Knox inquired searchingly of his generation:

> Oh, why should the spirit of mortal be proud?
> Like a swift-flitting meteor, a fast-flying cloud,
> A flash of the lightning, a break of the wave,
> He passeth from life to his rest in the grave.

III. I will not worship the material.

The third temptation was probably the most direct and frontal attack! There were no subtle innuendoes or nuances in the devil's speech. Nor was there any effort to reinforce his temptation with a scriptural quotation. The proposition was clear: Put material things first in your life. Sell out your soul, and I will give you the treasures of this world.

Can the devil do it? In a sense, he can. When one ignores all spiritual values and concentrates solely on the material, he or she, for a limited time, can succeed in this realm. But eternity will come! If, however, a Christian tries to serve the devil for material gain, God will chastise the born-again believer. There is a great difference in the way God deals with his own redeemed family and his attitude toward those who are of Satan's household. If you can continue to sin without chastisement, you should examine your experience and see if you are truly a born-again Christian. In the old play, Faust, or Faustus, sold himself to do the devil's bidding and was promised all this life had to offer. His day of doom came, however, and he met a terrible end. Although this is only fiction, it is certainly a true picture of one who falls down and worships the devil, hoping to receive the treasures of this world.

Conclusion

What is the best course of action when we are tempted? For the lost person, it is to repent of sin and trust Jesus as personal Savior. No other course is open. Until one has become a Christian, he or she has no basis for dealing with temptation.

For the Christian, however, it is different. We have Jesus, our High Priest, who has been tempted in all points like as we are and is yet without sin. We are to claim his presence, study his Word, and seek his will in every choice. If we live in fellowship with the Savior, we will find it much easier to resist the devil and see him flee from us.

> Temptations around me are heavy to bear
> But when I am tempted my Saviour is there,
> My grace is sufficient I read in his word,
> No promise so precious has man ever heard.

SUNDAY EVENING, FEBRUARY 4

Title: Following the Shepherd

Text: "The LORD is my shepherd; I shall not want. . . . Surely goodness and mercy shall follow me all the days of my life: and I will dwell in the house of the LORD for ever" **(Ps. 23:1, 6)**.

Scripture Reading: Psalm 23

Introduction

Probably the most familiar New Testament passage is the model prayer our Lord gave to his disciples when they asked him, "Lord, teach us to pray" (Luke 11:1–4). The most familiar Old Testament passage is the beloved Twenty-Third

Psalm. These words have lingered on the lips of more of God's people than any others in all of Holy Scripture.

Who is the author of this psalm? David, the great shepherd-king of Israel. He probably wrote it in the winter years of his life out of long experience with the providential care of a loving God. He remembered the tender care of a loving Shepherd who watched over his wandering and disobedient sheep.

The psalm is exceedingly simple. There are no hidden mysteries here; it is within the reach of every child of God, at whatever stage of spiritual growth and development he or she may be. In verse 1 we find David's proclamation, which is majestic, marvelous, and all-inclusive. The provision the great Shepherd makes for his sheep is delineated in verses 2–5, and the thrilling promise concludes the psalm in verse 6.

I. The proclamation.

"The LORD is my shepherd; I shall not want" (v. 1). In the King James Version the verb "is" appears in italics, which indicates that it was not found in the original manuscripts. The translators supplied the verb for smoothness in reading. Leaving out the verb makes this opening statement an exclamation: "The LORD my shepherd!"

Notice also that David has the unmitigated presumption to say, "The LORD is *my* shepherd!" suggesting not only that he knows who his shepherd is but that his shepherd knows him!

Astronomers tell us that at least 250 million times 250 million stars, each larger than our sun (which is one of the smallest of the stars), have been scattered across the vast universe by the Creator. Earth, our temporary home for the few short years of our existence, is so minute a speck of matter in space that if it were possible to transport our most powerful telescope to our nearest neighbor star, Alpha Centauri, and look back this way, the earth could not be seen, even with the aid of that powerful instrument.

All of this is considerably humbling to proud and pompous humans. Yet the staggering fact remains that the Creator of such a universe descends to call himself *my* shepherd, and invites *me* to consider myself *his* sheep. Jesus said in John 10:14, "I am the good shepherd, and know my sheep, and am known of mine." Thus, because of his great love, God made provision through the death of his Son for us to become his very own.

"I shall not want." Note the equation: The Lord of heaven as my Shepherd equals the fact that I shall not suffer want. But this does not mean that, because of my privileged relationship as a sheep of the great Shepherd, every whim and fancy I have shall be provided. It simply means that only my heavenly Father truly understands my needs, and he will meet them accordingly.

II. The provision.

Because the Lord is my Shepherd, he has made certain basic provisions for my care. First, "He maketh me to lie down in green pastures: he leadeth me beside the still waters." Phillip Keller, in his book *A Shepherd Looks at Psalm 23*, says that a strange thing about sheep is that because of their makeup, it is almost impossible for them to be made to lie down unless certain requirements are met. First, owing to their timidity, they refuse to lie down unless they are free from all fear. Second, because of the social behavior within a flock of sheep, they will not lie down unless they are free from friction with others of their own kind. Third, if tormented by flies or parasites, sheep will not lie down. Only when free of these pests can they relax. Fourth, sheep will not lie down as long as they feel in need of finding food. They must be free from hunger. The unique thing about all of these needs is that only the Shepherd himself can provide them (Grand Rapids: Zondervan, 1970, 35)!

An undefined fear dogs the steps of many in our world today. They are searching—like sheep without a shepherd—for something new, something different, something exciting. All the while, our Great Shepherd has provided "green pastures and still waters" for those who will let him be their Shepherd.

"He restoreth my soul: he leadeth me in the paths of righteousness for his name's sake." Is it possible that one who enjoys the bountiful care of the great Shepherd of the sheep could ever become so distressed in spirit that he would need restoration? The author of this psalm knew the arid wastelands of spiritual distress. He had tasted the bitter gall of yielding to temptation; he had experienced the cold emptiness of estrangement from God. In another psalm he cries out, "Why art thou cast down, O my soul? and why art thou disquieted within me?" (42:11).

Keller says that a "cast down sheep" is an old English shepherd's term for a sheep that has turned over on its back and cannot get up again by itself. He describes the pathetic sight of such a sheep lying on its back with its feet in the air trying frantically to get up but not being able to do so. Sometimes it will bleat a little for help, but usually it just lies there lashing about in frightened frustration. It is necessary that the shepherd find the "cast down" sheep right away, for predatory animals and birds know that a cast down sheep is an easy meal (p. 60).

After coming to our rescue, the Shepherd leads us in "paths of righteousness." He retrieves us from the dangerous detours we often take in life. These detours are comparable to those times when we presume that God is going to take care of us even though we have acted irresponsibly as his independent sheep. However, because ours is a Shepherd who is ever alert and attentive to his cast down sheep, he is instantly responsive to their cries for help. Through the prophet Isaiah, God expressed his concern for the needs of his people: "And it shall come to pass, that before they call, I will answer; and while they are yet speaking, I will hear" (Isa. 65:24).

When David speaks of "the valley of the shadow of death," he is portraying life's bitterest experiences. One can almost feel the chill and the loneliness suggested by the valley. The Hebrew word translated "shadow of death" means "deepest darkness." But even in these agonizing experiences, one can know the warmth of the Shepherd's presence. For, after leading his sheep through these dark stretches on the way, the Shepherd "prepareth a table" for them in the midst of those who would destroy them and applies healing oil to their bruised bodies and the oil of gladness to their wounded spirits. The "cup running over" suggests the abundant life our Lord promises to all who drink from his fountain.

III. The promise.

"Surely goodness and mercy shall follow me all the days of my life: and I will dwell in the house of the LORD for ever." Here is a picture of the complete confidence of the sheep in his Shepherd, who has, through the long journey of life, proved again and again his concern for his sheep. Every moment of the way, even on the detours he has foolishly chosen, the sheep has been followed by the "goodness and mercy" of his Shepherd.

Jesus said to his distraught disciples on the night before his crucifixion: "In my Father's house are many mansions: if it were not so, I would have told you. I go to prepare a place for you" (John 14:2). Psalm 23 covers the full spectrum of life—from the helpless state of the young lamb through the wilds and storms of his adult life. Then the end of this life is but the beginning of a grander life that has no termination!

Conclusion

"Following the shepherd" each step through life is the only way to maintain one's equilibrium even in the midst of the most ferocious storm. When the sun is shining and the Shepherd's care for us is obvious or when we are in the subterranean passageways of the valley of deepest shadows and cannot feel his presence, we can have "peace . . . which passeth all understanding" (Phil. 4:7), because we know that the Shepherd's "goodness and mercy" follow us all the days of our lives.

WEDNESDAY EVENING, FEBRUARY 7

Title: The Necessity for Privacy

Text: "And he said to them, 'Come away by yourselves to a lonely place, and rest awhile'" **(Mark 6:31 RSV).**

Scripture Reading: Psalm 46:8–11

Introduction

Jesus's words from this evening's text describe an action and an activity of our Lord. Jesus speaks not only by his words but also by his actions. We should let his actions speak to us even as we let his words dwell within our minds.

It is significant that the Savior who said, "We must work the works of him who sent me, while it is day" (John 9:4), also said, "Come away by yourselves to a lonely place, and rest a while." Our Lord was an activist who worked to meet the great needs of humanity, but he also recognized the limitations of the human frame and its need for constant restoration. Although the work is still great, we should follow Jesus's example and "rest a while." Each of us should find a place of solitude for rest and relaxation and for communion with our loving Father.

I. Jesus went into the place of solitude to determine his priorities (Mark 1:12).

Our Lord was led, under a sense of divine compulsion, to go into a solitary place that he might make some decisions about accomplishing his redemptive mission. It is possible that during the entire forty days of his fast he was tempted by Satan, and yet when you read the three synoptic accounts (Matt. 4:1–3; Mark 1:12–13; Luke 4:1–4), either the real temptation began or it reached a new intensity following Jesus's forty days of fasting. The Holy Spirit led our Lord into the desert that victory over Satan might be accomplished. For practical purposes today, we need to recognize the significance of this period of solitude in the life of our Savior.

II. Jesus sought the place of privacy when he needed communion with the Father God (Mark 1:35).

It might not be possible for all of us to find a private place in the great outdoors for communion with God. Nevertheless, we all have the same need. In some manner, even in the midst of a crowd, we must draw aside to listen to what our Lord would say to us (Isa. 26:3).

III. Our Lord needed privacy when opposition arose (Mark 3:6–7).

The successful general knows when not to fight as well as when and how to fight a battle. There comes a time when retreat is in reality a forward march. When life becomes difficult and perplexing, we need to search for a private place so that we might make sure that our thoughts and values are in balance.

IV. Our Lord suggested privacy for purposes of rest and relaxation (Mark 6:30–31).

Many people look upon themselves as machines of perpetual motion. They do not recognize that the Sabbath was made for man and not man for the Sabbath. People need to be workers, but they must also rest if they are going to be efficient workers. This was true for our Lord and his disciples, and it is just as true for us today, perhaps more so for those who live in an urban and technological context.

V. Jesus withdrew to the place of solitude when he was misunderstood by his disciples (Mark 6:46).

The parallel passages of Matthew 14:22–32 and John 6:15–21 give us the impression that the crowd that had eaten the miraculous loaves was being led by Jesus's apostles in an effort to make Jesus king. After compelling his disciples to get into the boat, Jesus went up into the hills to pray. Evidently our Lord was disappointed that even his most intimate followers still did not understand the nature of his kingdom. He needed divine reinforcement for this time of discouragement and thus sought out a quiet place to meet with his Father.

Conclusion

Are you in a rush at all times, coming and going, doing and being? Do you feel at times that you are at the end of your rope and that there is a possibility you are going to have some kind of an emotional breakdown? Perhaps you need a regular dose of solitude. Try to find a time during the day when you can turn off the world and get alone with God. Find a quiet place in your home or yard where you can be alone with God and meditate on his Word, evaluate your circumstances, and rededicate your life to him. Our Lord did. You and I must.

SUNDAY MORNING, FEBRUARY 11

Title: What Are You Looking For?

Text: "Then Jesus turned, and saw them following, and saith unto them, What seek ye?" **(John 1:38)**.

Scripture Reading: John 1:35–39

Hymns: "Beneath the Cross of Jesus," Clephane
             "Blessed Assurance, Jesus Is Mine," Crosby
             "Jesus Is All the World to Me," Thompson

Offertory Prayer: Our Father, we pray this morning for our Christian brothers and sisters no matter who they are or where they are. We pray for those who are not Christians, and we ask that the offering we bring today will be used both here at home and unto the uttermost part of the earth to preach the gospel to those who need the message of Christ and him crucified. Reveal unto us how we can be used to take the gospel to those near us even as we bring our gifts to take the gospel to those who are far from us. Help us to remember that at our best, we are still only sinners redeemed by the blood of Christ and forgiven because you have come to earth to pay the price for our salvation. We thank you for yourself and for your faithfulness to us. Help us to show our faithfulness not merely in words but also in the lives that we live and by committing ourselves completely to your service. We pray for Jesus's sake. Amen.

Introduction

When Jesus left Satan and the temptations, where would he go? One answer emerged. He would go back to John and the people who were like-minded. When he returned, John took one look at him and then knew that, beyond the shadow of a doubt, this man whom he had baptized was indeed the coming Messiah. John said, "I saw, and bare record that this is the Son of God" (John 1:34).

As Jesus was walking by one day, John looked upon him and said to those nearby, "Behold the Lamb of God!" Two of the disciples heard John and followed Jesus. He turned to them and said, "What are you looking for?" Their reply was, "Where do you live?" Jesus answered, "Come, and you will see."

Jesus's question to the two disciples of John is a timeless one. It applies to all people in all generations. We never see more than we are looking for. In fact, whatever we are looking for, we probably will find. If we are looking for the good in people, we can find it; and if we are looking for the evil, we can find that. Furthermore, whatever we start out to do in life, we probably will do it. We should therefore be careful what we make our aim.

I. Do you have a goal?

A former prime minister of Canada once said, concerning our country, "What America needs is the tonic of a great task." Likewise, one of the superlative needs for individuals is a great purpose in life that will give meaning and motivation to everyday existence. Far too many people have no specific, and some not even a general, idea of what they really want to do and be in the years to come. When Jesus saw the two disciples of John following him, the question he asked was more than a casual one. He was inquiring concerning their basic attitude toward God and the things of the Spirit. There was, of course, a curiosity concerning Jesus of Nazareth, since John had pointed him out as "the Lamb of God, which taketh away the sin of the world" (John 1:29). This would indeed excite the people and cause them to inquire further. People are incurably religious, and when anyone comes on the scene who professes to meet spiritual needs, most people have at least a passing interest.

Religious goals are the most important ones! Assuming that you have a relationship to God through Jesus Christ, do you have a day-by-day fellowship with him that enriches life? Everyone should have some spiritual goals toward which he or she is working. A friend of mine told a group of us that he made a list of personal goals in Christian growth. He typed them on a card and kept them at a certain place in his desk. Every morning he would take them out in the solitude of his own office and study them reflectively. He sought day by day to reach the goals he had set for himself.

II. How do we obtain our goals?

First and foremost, we must keep our fellowship with Jesus active if we are to do the things we feel God has planned for us. This truth underlies any other practical suggestions that might be given.

Perhaps the first matter in realizing our goals is to be certain they are definite and concrete. Short-range goals can be reached because they are definite. Long-range goals sometimes are modified as time moves along. We should try to set out some definite ends toward which we will work and never forget that they are a part of our life's plan.

Never minimize hard work! Too often we somehow get the idea that someday the moment of inspiration will come to do that difficult task, and then it will be easy to accomplish. Nothing could be further from the truth! Genius has been defined as 10 percent inspiration and 90 percent perspiration. The same is true of reaching our goals. There is absolutely no substitute for hard work. If a goal can be reached easily, it is, in all probability, not a worthy goal. A young person once said rather flippantly to an outstanding pianist, "I'd give anything if I could play the piano like you can." The older man replied with a smile, "Would you give eight hours of practice a day for twenty years?"

In reaching our goals, we must realize that there will be days of disappointment as well as days of optimism. At certain periods in our life we will decide that we have chosen the wrong goals and will never be able to reach them. When such times come, we must simply say to ourselves, "This is one of my bad days. Tomorrow will be better. I must not give up on my goals."

Above all, we must be certain that we are seeking to accomplish a goal that has God's approval. This means that the goal will be in harmony with New Testament teaching. God can certainly reveal his will in the privacy of a person's own prayer life, but he will never reveal a goal that is inconsistent with biblical teaching. Test every ambition by the Spirit of Christ and the clear-cut teachings of God's Word!

Know that God will help you in realizing your goal. William Shakespeare wrote, "There's a divinity that shapes our ends, rough hew them how we will." Paul was a little more specific when he said, "All things work together for good to them that love God, to them who are the called according to his purpose" (Rom. 8:28). The Revised Standard Version says, "We know that in everything God works for good with those who love him, who are called according to his purpose." The difference in the two translations is that in the former "things" work while in the latter "God" works. We know of course that things work because God works them. If we keep our fellowship with God vital, he will work things so that we can realize our goal. A great Christian of another generation prayed, "Lord, let your will be my will that my will may be your will." It is difficult, if not impossible, to improve on such an attitude!

III. Don't forget to have patience.

Perhaps the greatest reason goals are not met is that we are not willing to wait. There is a time to labor, but there is also a time when we can do nothing but wait for the proper time of fulfillment to come. Many years ago, as a young man, I came across a plaque that impressed me so much I placed it in my room above my desk. It reads, "All things come to those who hustle while they wait." That motto has lived with me through the years. Timing is of superlative importance! To reach our goals, we must be willing to accept the fact that God works on a time schedule and never becomes frantic. Jesus never hurried, never worried, and never doubted the outcome.

Conclusion

So much depends on what one can see. Someone once observed that for every thousand people who can talk, there is only one who can think; and for every thousand people who can think, there is only one who can see. A good prayer to pray is this: "God grant us the wisdom to see the angel in the marble, the oak in the acorn, the blossom in the bud, the dawn in the darkness, the gold in the boulder, the future in the present, and God in everything."

SUNDAY EVENING, FEBRUARY 11

Title: The King of Glory

Text: "Lift up your heads, O ye gates; and be ye lift up, ye everlasting doors; and the King of glory shall come in. Who is this King of glory? The LORD strong and mighty, the LORD mighty in battle" **(Ps. 24:7–8)**.

Scripture Reading: Psalm 24

Introduction

Psalm 23 presents Jesus as the Great Shepherd, resurrected and ascended, who shall not only provide for our needs in this life but also shall receive us in "the house of the Lord" where we shall dwell forever. Psalm 24 presents Jesus as the Chief Shepherd who is coming again in power and glory to bring everlasting blessing to his people. The apostle Peter described that event in his first epistle: "And when the chief Shepherd shall appear, ye shall receive a crown of glory that fadeth not away" (1 Peter 5:4). Therefore, Psalm 24 is a joyous victory shout rising out of the Psalter. It is the affirmation and confirmation of the returning King of Kings and Lord of Lords to rule forever and ever.

I. The King's sovereignty.

The first two verses of this psalm state plainly that the Lord's rulership of the world is established by right of creation. In the first verse, we have a broad and unchallengeable claim concerning God's dominion over the world. To the Hebrews he was a "confined God," concerned chiefly with their religious acts. They did not believe he was concerned with the rest of the world.

The psalmist's majestic statement in verse 1 portrays the concern of God for all people and his desire to become involved in their lives. Because he is a God of love, he is in every corner of the earth, bombarding humanity with grace, with undeserved blessings, and with undeniable evidences of his presence.

When the psalmist says that "the earth is the LORD's, and the fulness thereof; the world, and they that dwell therein," he is speaking only in terms of creation. When God reasoned within himself and said, "Let us make man

57

in our image, after our likeness" (Gen. 1:26), he imparted to man an attribute which, up to that point, had been exclusively divine. He gave man freedom of choice. God desires to have fellowship with people on the basis of their choice. Thus, in the profound mystery of God's sovereignty, he made man, surrounding him with evidences of divine love and concern, and then backed away to let him make his own choices.

In verse 2 the psalmist describes the incomparable manner in which God made the earth. He "founded it on the seas" (NIV) and then restrained the waters lest, in their greediness, they attempted to swallow up the land! Jeremiah expressed it this way: "'Should you not fear me?' declares the LORD. 'Should you not tremble in my presence? I made the sand a boundary for the sea, an everlasting barrier it cannot cross. The waves may roll, but they cannot prevail; they may roar, but they cannot cross it'" (Jer. 5:22 NIV). God has "founded" the earth, and it shall not be moved until God is finished with it. The reason is simply that there dwells on this earth a creature into which God has breathed the breath of life. God loves people in spite of their sinfulness and rejection, and to the last moment of his mercy, he will exert every effort short of violating their free will to secure his repentance and make of them "new creatures in Christ Jesus" (see 2 Cor. 5:17).

II. The King's subjects.

In verses 3–6 the psalmist has set forth the conditions whereby people can come before the Lord and recognize him as Lord of Lords and King of Kings. The question is asked and then answered in plain terms: the person who is qualified to "ascend into the hill of the LORD" and "stand in his holy place" is the one who has "clean hands, and a pure heart" and who has "not lifted up his soul unto vanity, nor sworn deceitfully" (v. 4).

But where can we find such a person? Not one of us would present ourselves as a candidate for this honor! Yet there is hope, for Jesus Christ has filled all of God's requirements. When we cast ourselves upon him and put our trust totally in him, we are "accepted in the beloved" (Eph. 1:6)—that is, God accepts us in Christ. "As we walk in the light, as he is in the light, we have fellowship one with another, and the blood of Jesus Christ his Son cleanseth us from all sin" (1 John 1:7). As we live daily and consciously in the light of God's holy Word and its declarations and promises, the blood of Jesus, which has already established our position as children of God, keeps on cleansing us daily from sins that would bar us from the Father's presence and from "the hill of the LORD."

All of this makes possible the truth included in verse 5: "He shall receive the blessing from the LORD, and righteousness from the God of his salvation." The last phrase could be interpreted, "the God who is saving him." For salvation is in three tenses: we *have been saved* from the presence of sin, and we *shall be saved* from the power of sin. Because of what Jesus has done, the past is taken care of! The future is out of our hands and is committed to God for safekeeping. It is the *present* with which we wrestle and grapple! Yet God will take our "present" also and "keep on saving us" from the presence of sin that surrounds us and bombards us on every hand.

III. The King's reception.

Verses 7–10 comprise the grand finale of this majestic psalm. Here is portrayed the King of Kings poised and ready to come to receive his subjects and to take his throne.

George Whitefield was one of the great preachers of England during the Great Awakening. A story is told of Whitefield preaching on Psalm 24 one day at Keswick, in the region of the famed English Lakes. Apparently it was an outdoor service, for from where Whitefield stood, he could see the highest peaks in England, which encircled the far end of the lake. It was a scene of unparalleled natural beauty and dignity. Whitefield began preaching quietly and with a gentle appeal to his listeners. Then, all of a sudden, he pointed to those mountain peaks, and with a full, thunderous voice, he shouted, "The trumpeters have crossed the hills! The trumpeters have crossed the hills! The King is coming! Open the doors of your hearts and let him in!" And there was a tremendous stirring among the people as, in the imagery of that fearless preacher, this psalm came alive.

The promise rings through the pages of the Bible: "The King is coming!" His outriders are on the hills, and they are shouting, "Lift up your heads! Be prepared! Trim your lamps! See to your oil supply!"

Conclusion

Only the Father in heaven knows the time of Jesus's glorious second coming. The program is God's; the timing and the details are in his hands. We are commissioned to assist in the preparation for this great event. We are to point the world to Jesus, "the Lamb of God, which taketh away the sin of the world" (John 1:29).

WEDNESDAY EVENING, FEBRUARY 14

Title: Have Faith in God
Text: "And Jesus answered them, 'Have faith in God'" (**Mark 11:22 RSV**).
Scripture Reading: Mark 11:20–25

Introduction

Repeatedly and continuously our Lord sought to instill within the hearts of his disciples a great faith in God. He was grieved because of the little faith his followers had (Luke 12:28). Jesus responded graciously to the faith of his disciples in such a manner as to encourage them to have even greater faith.

Unbelief was the undoing of ancient Israel. It was because of their lack of faith that they missed many of the blessings God wanted to bestow on them (Ps. 78:22).

Our Lord spoke pointedly to his disciples and said, "Have faith in God." This great statement of our Lord contains a message that we should let dwell in our hearts richly at all times so that it might speak to our spirit, challenge our mind, and motivate our emotions.

Having faith in God is more than just having a firm belief in his existence. To really have faith in God means to unite with him in a union similar to that which exists between a man and a woman who are ideally related to each other in marriage. To have faith in God means to let Jesus Christ come and live within your life. To have faith in God is to make a constant response to the indwelling Holy Spirit.

If we would let this great statement of Jesus dwell in us richly, there are a number of different responses that we should and can make.

I. Have faith in God's person.

What kind of a God do you worship? What is his nature and character?

A. *The God of whom Jesus speaks is a good God.* Everything about him is good. There is no flaw in his character, and there is no blemish on his life. He relates to us in terms of grace and love at all times (John 3:16). Even while we were yet sinners, he revealed his love for us in that Christ died for our sins (Rom. 5:8).

B. *God is our heavenly Father.* Jesus taught his disciples to think of the eternal God as our loving heavenly Father who has a perfect love and who is perfectly wise and who is generous in all dealings with us (Matt. 7:11).

The God in whom Jesus encourages us to have faith is a dependable, consistent God whose character is described as love.

II. Have faith in God's presence.

The eternal God who came in the person of Jesus Christ has chosen to live within the heart of each of us in the person of the Holy Spirit (1 Cor. 3:16). The God whom we are to trust is not a god who dwells at a great distance away from us. He is as close as the air we breathe, and we can be absolutely certain that whatever happens to us, he will be on the scene working to bring out every possible good for those who love him (Rom. 8:28).

III. Have faith in God's purpose.

Some people do not trust in God because they have false ideas about his purpose in the world. They question his motives. Some people see God as a bully. Others see him as a robber or a thief. Others see him as a dictator who would take away their freedom.

The purpose or will of God is not that which a harsh fate imposes on us. God's purpose is God's wonderful plan for our lives. It is something for us to reach up to and to search for rather than to avoid and run from. Paul reveals what we need to do in our own mind and heart if we would personally discover how good and perfect God's will is.

IV. Have faith in God's power.

There can be no question that our God is all-powerful. He is the creator and sustainer of the universe. Paul writes in his epistle to the Philippians of the availability of this power for those who trust and obey Jesus Christ. Paul had experienced God's power many times when God enabled him to triumph in the most adverse of circumstances—imprisonment, loneliness, stonings, beatings, shipwreck. Through the power and goodness of God, Paul was able to adjust to these things in a triumphant manner through the strength that came to him through faith in Jesus Christ (Phil. 4:10–13).

V. Have faith in God's promises (Rom. 4:18–19).

The great men and women of faith have been those who discovered God's promises written on the pages of the Bible. They have claimed these promises and moved forward depending on the trustworthiness of the God who made the promise. The richness of your faith and the vitality of your spiritual life will be determined largely by the degree to which you discover, apply, and cling to God's promises.

VI. Have faith in God's provisions.

A. *God has provided for you full salvation from the penalty of sin through the death of his Son on the cross.* Trust in Christ's substitutionary death for your sins if you want peace when guilt tries to disturb you.

B. *Have faith in the provisions of the living Lord who has promised his personal presence to you as you give yourself in service to him (Matt. 28:20).*

C. *Have faith in God's provisions for you in the future (John 14:1–3).* Our Lord, the carpenter of Galilee, has moved on ahead in order that he might prepare for his followers a home that will meet every need of the redeemed for eternity.

Conclusion

Use the faith that you do have to grow a greater faith in God. Ask the heavenly Father to grant to you the gift of greater faith. Cling to the precious promises of God and let God give proof to you of his dependability.

SUNDAY MORNING, FEBRUARY 18

Title: God's Time Is Always Best

Text: "Woman, what have I to do with thee? mine hour is not yet come" **(John 2:4).**

Scripture Reading: John 2:1–11

Hymns: "Lead, Kindly Light," Newman
            "God Will Take Care of You," Martin
            "Great Is Thy Faithfulness," Chisholm

Offertory Prayer: Our Father, you know that we live continually in the midst of many and great dangers. Because of our frailty, we need the strength and protection that can come to us only through you. Support us in our dangers and carry us through our temptations. Live and reign in our hearts. Help us to purify ourselves even as you are pure. As we bring our offerings this morning, receive them and use them to spread the message of Christ to those who do not know him. We pray in Jesus's name. Amen.

Introduction

According to most scholars, Jesus left Judea shortly after the incidents recorded in the first chapter of John and returned to Galilee for a brief visit. Perhaps he wanted to go back home for a short time before beginning his public ministry. While there he accompanied his mother to a wedding. We see in this account that Jesus loved to be with people and to share in their joys. He never isolated himself from the everyday routines of life but stayed in touch with the happinesses as well as the sorrows of those to whom he ministered.

A crisis arose. The reception host was about to be embarrassed because the drinks had run out. Perhaps more guests had come than he had anticipated. We cannot be sure of all that was involved in Mary's request to Jesus, but obviously she felt that he could meet the need. At first, however, Jesus was reluctant to perform such a miracle. After all, he had refused to turn stones into bread. We should remember, however, that his first refusal was his unwillingness to satisfy his own personal need. The situation was different here in that someone else had a need, and his miracle saved that person from embarrassment.

One of the most significant statements in the entire story is when Jesus answered his mother by pointing out to her that his time had "not yet come." Again, we cannot know exactly how much Mary understood about Jesus's answer, although she must have been aware of his unusual abilities since she was his mother and knew the facts concerning his birth. We can lift this statement of Jesus out from the rest of the story and find some great spiritual truths in these early words of our Savior.

I. Don't run ahead of God.

Timing is of the utmost importance! God has a purpose for every life, but he also has a timetable. Sometimes in our zeal we want to do God's will quicker than he wants it done. Years ago a seminary president told the students how, when he was a pastor, a young man moved into the city to serve as pastor of one of the churches. He visited the older pastor and outlined with great enthusiasm all that he was going to do in his new church. The older pastor said with tenderness, "Those plans are fine. But let me give you a word of caution. Don't try to do all of this the first year or two you are at the church." Unfortunately, the young man failed to heed the advice. In a little more than a year he was asking this man to recommend him to another church.

> Impatient hearts want action . . . now!
> They fear God's time will be too late;
> How prone we are to rush ahead—
> When God says, "Wait!"

God had a great plan for Moses. Unfortunately, however, Moses tried to do the job too quickly and too early. His mother must have whispered many times during the years at the palace, "God will send a leader to free his people from slavery and oppression." Moses decided God was calling him to do it—and now! Why wait? One day Moses saw an Egyptian oppressing a Hebrew, so he killed him and hid his body in the sand. He thought no one knew it, but he was wrong. Our secret sins are seldom as secret as we think. The next day a fellow Hebrew shattered his illusions: "Who made thee a prince and a judge over us?" (Ex. 2:14). This pushed Moses's panic button! He thought, *Everyone knows I killed the Egyptian; I'd better get out of town.* His trying to run ahead of God cost him forty years in the wilderness. Moses should have waited for God's time.

II. Don't drag behind God.

The Greeks were impressed with the value of time. They had two words for it. One signified "time viewed in its extension or succession of moments" while the other suggested "time charged with opportunity." The latter belongs to us as our personal possession. We have the privilege of seizing and vitalizing it by human energy and transforming it into purposeful activity. In Greek art this word is represented as a wrestler or charioteer, swift but pure in decision. Sometimes it is pictured as a youth pushing forward with wings on his back and with long hair in front but bald behind. The explanation is that opportunity must be seized by the forelock or it cannot be captured at all.

There are opportunities in life of which we must take advantage or lose. God has certain plans for us. If we fail to act when he is ready for us, we may never have the opportunity again. Certainly we shall never have the opportunity quite as full and open. Young people need to be reminded often that when they miss one year of preparation through carelessness or because of sin, it might take them four or five years to "catch up" what they have lost. When you know God wants you to do something, don't delay. Do it immediately!

> But hearts debate and question God,
> Our hesitating feet are slow;
> We yield to cautious reasoning
> When God says, "Go!"

God has a time for you as well as a plan for you. One day he will be ready to put us in the place of service he has chosen for us. A mature, godly professor used to pray, "Lord, prepare us for the place of labor you are preparing for us." Not all of God's calls are dramatic, but they are all important.

III. Stay in touch with God.

One factor that permeated the life of Jesus was his constant, unbroken fellowship with the Father. If he had allowed anything to come between him and his Father, he would have yielded to temptation and ruined any chance to be the world's Redeemer. Although you and I do not have the same unique relationship to God and fellowship with him as Jesus does, the basic principle is the same. We enter into a relationship with the Father through the new birth. Nothing can destroy this filial relationship. We are members of God's redeemed family because we have been born into that family. Jesus is our elder brother. We are heirs of God and joint heirs with Christ. Our fellowship, however, is another thing. For time to time we sin and break fellowship. We constantly must be asking for forgiveness in order that this fellowship be restored. When we speak of "staying in touch with God," we mean keeping fellowship with him intact. When we do this, we are able to pace ourselves, neither running ahead nor dragging behind his purpose for us.

Although Jesus possessed perfect knowledge of God's plan for him, he also realized that he had a ministry to perform before going to the cross to die for humankind's sin. At the close of this ministry, Jesus, while praying in the garden of Gethsemane, said, "Father, the hour is come; glorify thy Son, that thy Son also may glorify thee" (John 17:1).

Conclusion

Victor Hugo has received credit for the profound statement "Nothing is so powerful as an idea whose time has arrived." Likewise, the most powerful and effective life is the one that has sought God's will earnestly, prepared itself completely, and waited with patience for the right time to stand forth boldly and do God's will whatever the cost. There are two dangers we must avoid. First, rushing in quickly before we are ready and before God is ready for us to do the job. Second, holding back when God is ready for us to act. The poet says it well:

> So fast, so fast, time's current flows,
> Yet cannot rush the budding rose.
> While life goes by at breakneck speed,
> All in its time will burst the seed.
> Though planes increase their miles per hour
> Only the sun can speed the flower.
> And though man set ahead his clocks

He cannot speed the equinox.
Let him accept the truth with grace:
God alone can set the pace!
Mae Winkler Goodman

SUNDAY EVENING, FEBRUARY 18

Title: When Guilt Is Gone

Text: "Blessed is he whose transgression is forgiven, whose sin is covered. Blessed is the man unto whom the LORD imputeth not iniquity, and in whose spirit there is no guile" **(Ps. 32:1–2)**.

Scripture Reading: Psalm 32

Introduction

There is a vast difference between being declared guilty of some crime and actually experiencing guilt. One of the most devastating enemies of mental health and happiness is that of guilt feelings, whether real or imaginary.

When God created man in the beginning, it was his intention that man be a whole person, fulfilling the highest divine plan for his being. But man sinned. He deliberately transgressed the law God had set down for him. The result of this violation was that the net of guilt fell down around man, encompassing him and imprisoning him. Immediately a yawning chasm of separation existed between man and God.

However, in spite of man's seemingly hopeless and desperate plight, God did not vacate his creation. When Adam and Eve sinned, they ran and hid themselves from God. The beauty of that primeval tragedy lies in the fact that God came searching for them and calling for them! Thus, as it has been from the beginning, the initiative for reestablishing communion between God and man lies with God. Man, blinded by his sin and imprisoned in his guilt, could never have restored the communication lines between himself and God.

Psalm 32 is the first of thirteen psalms bearing the superscription "Maschil." This simply means that it is a psalm of instruction containing divine insights into the condition and plight of humanity. Psalm 32 also takes its place beside the inimitable Psalm 51, in which David, a heartbroken king, bares his soul before God in confession of his humiliating sin and receives forgiveness and restoration. There are echoes of Psalm 51 in Psalm 32. David is talking about the time when he made an "about face" in his relationship with God.

I. A declaration.

David lays the groundwork for his psalm in the first two verses. He makes a declaration based on a firsthand experience. He tells how God removes the burden of guilt and brings joy and gladness to the repentant sinner. He describes his present condition before God in the form of two beatitudes. Note that each verse begins with the word "blessed."

In the first verse, there are three great words: *transgression, forgiven*, and *covered. Transgression* implies a willful disobedience of a divine command. It is the despicable label plastered on that person who knows better but who, at the moment, doesn't care and steps across the line God has drawn that says, "Off limits!"

Forgiven is the second word, and its original meaning in the Hebrew language is "to lift off a weight." It suggests the picture of a slave bent over with a heavy burden on his back. There steps up beside him a strong man who tenderly and with no rebuke takes the burden and throws it on his own shoulders. With the other hand, the strong man reaches down and lifts up the exhausted slave. In essence, this is what God does in regard to the repentant sinner.

The word *covered* is used in several ways in the Old Testament. It describes God's covering the deep with the waters of the sea. Scripture says that God will cast the sins of his repentant people "into the depths of the sea" (Mic. 7:19). There, covered by the waters, our sins cannot be seen again. The word *covered* also was used in Old Testament times in connection with sacrifices. Man's sins were symbolically covered by the blood of innocent animals and birds. The symbolism became reality, of course, when Jesus was crucified, making it possible for man's sins to be covered once and for all by his atoning sacrifice.

In the second verse, the word *imputeth* appears, which means "to lay the responsibility or blame for something upon a person." In ancient days, sundials used to be inscribed with the motto *"Pereunt et imputantur,"* which indicated that, though the hours may pass away, they come back and are "cast up into our teeth." It is a grim reminder that time will not let man escape what he does not do. In Kipling's poem *If* he speaks of the "unforgiving minute." Thus David used the word *impute* to say that, in God's mercy, this shadow of man's past that normally would come back and haunt him, is removed forever. People say, "I forgive you, but I can never forget." Only God is capable of a total and complete forgiveness.

II. A contemplation.

In verses 3 and 4 David describes with vivid metaphors the inner torment he experienced preceding his forgiveness. First, he says that his body ached with anguish, and he groaned like a suffering animal. His suffering was made all the more acute because God's hand of judgment seemed to rest heavily on him. As a result, he felt as though he had been out in the scorching summer sun for many hours. He had dehydrated, and his strength and vitality were gone.

This is David's way of expressing his experience with guilt. There is a great difference between guilt as a result of humankind's awareness of God's law and the nebulous, undefined guilt feelings that fester in people's subconscious and cause them to become mentally ill. The guilt allowed by God focuses on and locates sin in people, bringing about an awareness of their transgression.

David also discovered that, although God is longsuffering, patient, and loving, he is also righteous. Conviction of sin acts to the soul as fever acts to the body. It is an indicator that there is an infection that needs attention. Thus conviction of sin, like fever, is a blessing in disguise.

III. A confession.

"I finally admitted all my sins to you and stopped trying to hide them. I said to myself, 'I will confess them to the Lord.' And you forgave me! All my guilt is gone" (v. 5 TLB).

Finally, David had come to himself, just as the prodigal son did in the far country. In a flash, he saw clearly the pathway to God's forgiveness. He did not try to hide anything from God. He made a full confession of his sins. David felt the burden of his soul fall off immediately, for God had heard his cry for forgiveness, and without a moment's delay he lifted the heavy weight and granted full pardon.

But there is more: not only is David's heavy weight gone, but he was cleansed and purified even from sin's foul touch! He was restored to full life again with a clean body and mind and a newly created heart. He was ready to live the abundant life, for there was no accusing record left in heaven to stand against him. The pardoning grace of God had provided a means whereby his sins were borne far away and covered from God's sight. The ugly record had been washed away completely.

IV. An exhortation.

The remainder of the psalm, beginning at verse 6, provides David an opportunity to "preach." Verses 6, 7, 10, and 11 are David's words, and verses 8 and 9 are God's words to him. We learn here that conversion does not bring perfection in people. Redeemed people know that God has forgiven them, and the festering guilt feelings that had immobilized them are gone. They find that they can forgive themselves because God has forgiven them. At the same time, they must be realistic. They are not saved *out* of the world but *in* it. At times the waters will swell at their feet. They will be tempted, and in moments of weakness, they may yield. But even then the stumbling children can return to their Father who will pardon and restore them.

God reminds David—and us—that he is the teacher, the guide, the leader of his people. He warns us against being like the beast who must be compelled by force to submit to human will. When people refuse to be led by God, they lower themselves to the level of brute beasts!

Conclusion

David brings his joyful psalm to a close by declaring that God's "steadfast love surrounds him who trusts in the LORD." But only people who have confessed, admitted their guilt, and experienced this "weight lifted off" can be aware of this surrounding love of God.

> *O safe to the Rock that is higher than I*
> *My soul in its conflicts and sorrow would fly;*
> *So sinful, so weary—Thine, Thine would I be:*
> *Thou blest "Rock of Ages," I'm hiding in Thee.*

WEDNESDAY EVENING, FEBRUARY 21

Title: The Golden Rule for Human Relationships

Text: "So whatever you wish that men would do to you, do so to them; for this is the law and the prophets" **(Matt. 7:12 RSV)**.

Scripture Reading: Matthew 7:1–12

Introduction

We should let the words of Jesus Christ dwell in us as the guiding principles for the abundant life in the here and now. Only as we take seriously his teachings can we hope to experience the changes he sought to bring about in the lives of his followers. The words of our text have been called the Golden Rule. It calls for action on the second of the greatest commandments, "Thou shalt love thy neighbor as thyself." It is not only a summary statement of all that Jesus said about our treatment of our fellow humans, but it expressly says that it covers all that the law and the prophets taught about the matter. In this one verse our Lord gives us a great guiding principle that would settle a hundred different points of difference that constantly arise to upset human relationships.

The critics of Jesus have collected the great sayings of other religious leaders and have come to the conclusion that Jesus made no distinctive contribution in this Golden Rule. The great Hebrew master Hillel said, "Do not do to thy neighbor what is hateful to thyself." The great Greek philosopher Socrates said, "What stirs your anger when done to you by others, that do not to others." Aristotle said, "We should bear ourselves toward others as we would desire they should bear themselves toward us." The great Chinese teacher Confucius gave what someone has called the Silver Rule. He said, "What you do not want done to yourself, do not do to others." There is one radical difference between the Golden Rule enunciated by Jesus and the above guidelines articulated by some of the world's great teachers. The Golden Rule of Jesus is positive and active while their statements are negative and passive. While they would say, "Stand still; do not do to others what you would not want them to do to you," Jesus approaches the matter from a positive and creative standpoint. He says that we should "go and do what we would have others do to us."

I. A very significant "therefore."

The challenge of Matthew 7:12 is based on the great truth of God's goodness expressed in verse 11: "If you then, who are evil, know how to give good gifts to your children, how much more will your Father who is in heaven give good things to those who ask him!"

    A. *As your heavenly Father is good and as he showers upon you the best of heaven, even so, you are to give good things to your neighbor.*

    B. *We cannot expect to continue to receive the good gifts of God if we do not serve as a channel through which his mercy and grace flow out to bless the hearts and lives of others.*

    C. *We are to treat our fellow human beings as we desire to be treated by our heavenly Father.*

    D. *Pious talk and righteous looks will accomplish nothing if we do not treat our fellow humans in terms of what is right and generous.*

    E. *We must be absolutely sure that we do not let the conduct of others determine our treatment of them, but rather we must let God's treatment of us determine the manner in which we relate ourselves to others.*

II. The Golden Rule contains a divine commendation.

"For this is the law and the prophets."

    A. *To faithfully and fully observe the spirit of the Golden Rule is to rise up to the highest teachings of both the law of Moses and the precepts of the prophets.*

    B. *To faithfully follow the spirit of the Golden Rule is to fulfill the essence of our Christian duty toward our fellow humans.*

Conclusion

    Only Christians can truly live by the Golden Rule. While people may say, "The Golden Rule is my religion," they cannot be telling the full truth unless they have the Christ who gave the Golden Rule as the Lord of their heart and mind. Only those who have experienced the love of God as it is revealed in Jesus Christ can truly love their neighbor as themself. May God give to each follower of Jesus Christ the grace, guidance, and support we need to live by the Golden Rule.

SUNDAY MORNING, FEBRUARY 25

Title: Resisting Reality

Text: "And they that had laid hold on Jesus led him away to Caiaphas the high priest, where the scribes and the elders were assembled" **(Matt. 26:57)**.

Scripture Reading: Matthew 26:57–66

Hymns: "All Hail the Power of Jesus' Name," Perronet
             "Jesus, Lover of My Soul," Wesley
             "Blessed Redeemer," Christiansen

Offertory Prayer: Our Father, accept our gratitude for your many blessings, not the least of which is the life that you have given us and the new life that we have through faith in Jesus Christ as our Savior. Forgive us our sins, failures, and weaknesses. Empower us with your Holy Spirit for the tasks, trials, and temptations of the week we face. And Lord, as we give to you this money which represents our labor, our interest, and our very lives, we pray that you would accept it, bless it, and cause it to be used for your glory throughout the world. We pray in Jesus's name and for his sake. Amen.

Introduction

In the play *Harvey*, Elwood P. Dowd lives in a dream world. He has a faithful friend and companion, Harvey, a six-foot rabbit. The play revolves around the attempts of Dowd's family to get him to come down to earth and face reality. This he resists. He finds life much more enjoyable and exciting when he lives in his dream world with his rabbit friend, Harvey.

Elwood P. Dowd is not the only person throughout history who has resisted reality. Many of us have spent much time hoping for a condition that will never exist, yearning for a time that can never return, or glamorizing days that were never quite as glamorous or glorious as we imagine them to have been. This is not quite facing the realities of life. But there are times when it is more comfortable and convenient to resist reality.

It happens in spiritual life too. There are times when we resist spiritual reality. That is what the priests in the crowd that surrounded the cross of Jesus were doing.

As we draw near to Easter, we remember a familiar spiritual that asks, "Were you there when they crucified my Lord?" Let us join the crowd at the cross during the next few weeks. By looking at some of the faces around the cross, we can understand better our place, our reaction, and our faith. We begin with the priests. Religiously we would say that the priests resisted reality. They could neither understand nor accept that God had a new way of dealing with people.

I. In resisting reality there is a distinction.

The distinction that must be made is between being religious and being Christian. The priests were religious all right. They made sure that religion kept going. In Jesus's time it is estimated that there were a hundred thousand priests. There were so many of them that they were divided into twenty-four courses that served in the temple two weeks during the year. The only time they all served was during the three major feasts of Passover, Pentecost, and Tabernacles.

The only qualification for priesthood was unbroken physical descent from Aaron. There were no spiritual or moral qualifications. If a man did not descend from Aaron, nothing could make him a priest; if he did descend from Aaron, nothing could keep him from being a priest. A few physical defects could keep him from serving, but nothing could disqualify him from being counted as a priest. The priesthood was a position of privilege and power, for priests stood between God and man. Then came Jesus.

Jesus was not a priest or a recognized, trained teacher. The things that Jesus taught ran counter to the religious leaders' teaching. He taught the kingdom of God rather than the temple, the sacrifice of self rather than the sacrifice of animals, a relationship by faith to God rather than dependence on the sacrificial system, love rather than law. It became clear: *If Jesus was right, the priests were wrong.*

We still struggle with this distinction between merely being religious and being Christian. It was the German martyr Dietrich Bonhoeffer who introduced the phrase "religionless Christianity." There is always the danger of a lapse into legalism. Many people are trying a "do-your-own-thing," "follow-your-own-conscience" kind of religion. And always some will take refuge in sincerity. The forms of religion may be structured or unstructured, but the issue is the same: the distinction must be made between being religious and being Christian.

The challenge is to follow Christ. Three college students who were selling Bibles went to an evangelical church in Oklahoma. They had been to church quite a lot, they said, but they also said they had never been challenged with the decision to accept Christ personally. This they did and were baptized into the fellowship of that church.

II. In resisting reality there is a determination.

When our position is called into question, we usually increase our determination.

This the priests did. The plot thickened. The priests had always opposed Jesus. They then decided that he must die. But they were confronted with the problem of his popularity with the people. After his arrest he was brought before the council and the high priest, who questioned him and sought a means of condemning him. False witnesses were brought forth, but they could not agree on their stories. Then Caiaphas confronted him directly with the question of whether he was the Christ. Jesus then indicated that Pilate had expressed it himself. Upon this charge of blasphemy they began to build their case. They were determined to find some reason why Jesus could be condemned.

Why can't we be as determined for good? There are many times when good could be done, witness could be given, mission could be accepted and fulfilled if people showed just a little more determination. If the priests could be that determined to condemn Jesus, couldn't we be as determined to confess him?

This kind of determination has saved opportunities for Christian witness. In June 1862 at the close of the third session of the young Southern Baptist Seminary, school was suspended due to the Civil War. Early in the summer of 1865, the faculty met to consider the possibility of beginning the work again in October. The picture was dark. The South was prostrate and the churches weak. The school had no financial resources, and many of the finest youth of the land had died in the dreadful conflict.

There was some talk among Southern Baptists that the seminary should remain closed. Four faculty members, who constituted the entire faculty, met and prayed. Then John A. Broadus said, "Gentlemen, suppose we quietly agree that the seminary may die, but we'll die first." With that kind of determination it lived.

III. In resisting reality there is a decision.

The priests had come to a decision: Jesus must die. The charges were twofold—religious and political. The religious charge had to do with his destruction of the temple. While faith in Christ would ultimately mean that the temple would be unnecessary, that is not what he meant when he said that the temple would be destroyed and raised up again in three days. He was talking about himself. The political charge had to do with his claims to kingship, but it was a spiritual kingdom he proclaimed, not a political kingdom.

The political and religious areas of life are two of the most emotionally charged areas. The situation is now reversed. Jesus is not on trial. You are on trial. You have to make a decision, and that decision will determine your life. At an outstanding art gallery a student observed that she did not like a certain picture. The attendant answered by saying, 'Young lady, the picture is not on trial. You are on trial before the picture."

What will your decision about Jesus be? It is established that he is the Christ, the Savior. What is your decision?

Conclusion

Resisting reality cannot continue for long. Jesus was right. Now what will you do?

SUNDAY EVENING, FEBRUARY 25

Title: Let's Just Praise the Lord!

Text: "Bless the LORD, O my soul: and all that is within me, bless his holy name" **(Ps. 103:1).**

Scripture Reading: Psalm 103

Introduction

Many Christians find it difficult to think about the privilege of prayer without doing so in terms of asking for something or complaining to God about some life situation. Of course, petitionary praying is a part of our communication with God. We are exhorted in numerous places in Scripture to bring our needs to God in prayer. In fact, James says that "ye have not, because ye ask not" (James 4:2). At the same time, however, the Word of God also enjoins us to praise the Lord, to express gratitude, more often than it tells us to ask God for things.

Why, indeed, should we express praise and thanksgiving to God? When we cultivate the habit of praising God, we enlarge our capacity to appreciate the greatness and the glory of God, and we diminish our own self-centeredness. In short, we "grow up" spiritually.

Psalm 103 is a pure song of praise with not one single petition in it. There is a progression in the design of the psalm. First, David addresses himself, driving home the need for "blessing the Lord," or praising God. Then he turns to his people, Israel. He expresses amazement that God would even consider these creatures of clay, and finally he builds to a crescendo of praise as he addresses the entire universe, calling on everyone and everything to give praise to God.

I. An exhortation to oneself (vv. 1–5).

David begins his psalm by talking to himself. In examining his own life, he has discovered a need for genuine introspection. To his chagrin, he finds that the winsome blossom of praise and thanksgiving is missing from the garden of his heart. So he addresses himself: "Bless the Lord, O my soul: and all that is within me, bless his holy name" (v. 1). The soul is the total personality, that unique entity that makes us what we are. It is the whole person.

But David doesn't stop there. He adds, "all that is within me." He is saying, "Everything inside me that makes up my soul needs to praise the Lord!" He lifts up his whole being in gratitude to God.

In verse 2 David reminds himself to "forget not all his benefits." While he was praising God from the innermost recesses of his being, he was not to overlook the specifics of God's unmerited grace and mercy. David knew that he could not *remember* all of God's blessings; on the other hand, he must not *forget* them all. In other words, he was not to take for granted God's expressions of goodness and blessing to him.

Beginning with verse 3, the psalmist starts to list some of God's blessings. The first reason for praise is *forgiveness*, or moral cleansing. That is where God's activity on behalf of sinful people always begins. Without this basis, there can be no relationship at all. Second, David thinks of the blessing of *health*. The words *holy* and *healthy* come from the same root. It would be just as correct to speak of a "holy body" and a "healthy spirit." Disease is failure, whether it be spiritual, mental, or physical. God is the healer, says the psalmist.

David continues his recital of blessings for which he must praise God with the declaration, "who redeemeth thy life from destruction" (v. 4). *Redeemeth* as it is used here means "preserves." David praises God for the sustaining and preserving life that is his. Then he adds, "who crowneth thee with loving-kindness and tender mercies." *Mercies* are God's acts of benevolence toward us, whereas *grace* is his general attitude of love toward us.

The psalmist brings his opening solo to a close with an all-inclusive statement: "Who satisfieth thy mouth with good things; so that thy youth is renewed like the eagle's" (v. 5). Man is indeed a needy creature, and in God's wisdom and lovingkindness he supplies man's need with *good* things. As a result, we continually have fresh strength. The human spirit is renewed from day to day.

II. An encouragement to others (vv. 6–12).

In these seven verses, David gives two reasons for uniting our hearts and voices in a choir of praise to God. First, we should be grateful for the government of the Lord (vv. 6–7). Two facts are emphasized: God's way of governing his people is righteous, not selfish or capricious. Second, God's way of governing his people is practical. There is a reason behind every law and commandment he has set down in his holy Word. These commandments must not be taken lightly.

The second reason for praise is the patience and longsuffering of the Lord. He is full of compassion, slow to anger, with mercy as great as the heaven is high above the earth. He removes our transgressions from us as far as the east is from the west. This is not permissiveness on God's part; he is not a weak and indulgent heavenly Father. Yet upon our repentance, he sends away the haunting specter of our sins forever.

III. An expression of amazement (vv. 13–18).

It is hardly possible for David to believe the truth that is revealed: God will indeed have mercy on and bless imperfect and vacillating humans, the products of the dust of the earth! G. Campbell Morgan calls this "the pity of the Lord." God never forgets our frailty. When he administers chastening because of our disobedience, he does so in love and for corrective purposes.

In verses 15 and 16 David compares man's earthly existence with "the grass of the field" that withers and is carried off by the wind. The point he is making is that, in spite of our human expendability, God's love is steadfast. He has locked our souls securely to his bosom. He will be our God and we shall be his children throughout eternity.

The point of this third movement is to show the beautiful lovingkindness of God that is bestowed upon this weak creature, man, who in no way deserves the mercy and grace of God.

IV. An exclamation to the universe (vv. 19–22).

In this last movement, David invites the whole universe to lift its voice along with the choir. He praises God for the sovereignty of his rule, which is marvelously tempered with grace. He calls on the angels in heaven to join in the song. Then he includes the "ministers" of God. Here he likely means other heavenly creatures who minister to God in their various acts of service in heaven. We may not even have any biblical record of these particular beings to whom David refers. God may not have seen fit to tell us everything that goes on in heaven; it is doubtful that we could comprehend it if he had told us!

David's purpose, in this majestic climax, is to include every being in the universe who in any way exists to fulfill the purposes of God to join in this celebration of praise. Finally, feeling there might yet be music not expressed by intelligent beings, the psalmist calls on all nature, inanimate as well as animate, to join in the praise fest. "Bless the LORD, all his works in all places of his dominion" (v. 22).

Conclusion

Suddenly the chorus is over. The choir, the angels, the ministers of God, and all nature are quiet. Once again the soloist, who began the psalm of praise, steps forward. Intense with emotion, pure with praise, his voice reverberates throughout the entire universe: "Bless the LORD, O my soul" (v. 22).

When we lift our heart and soul, our total personality, in a pure offering of praise to God, we are linked with the universe and we are in tune with the Infinite! This teaches us a valuable lesson about worship: It must never be haphazard and careless. Our coming together for worship should never be "just church." The worship assembly of God's people must be a place where his children are ever searching their hearts and preparing themselves to lift up an offering of pure praise to their heavenly Father because of the work and the continuing ministry of his Son and our Savior, Jesus Christ.

WEDNESDAY EVENING, FEBRUARY 28

Title: Are You Living the Abundant Life?

Text: "The thief comes only to steal and kill and destroy; I came that they may have life, and have it abundantly" **(John 10:10 RSV)**.

Scripture Reading: John 10:7–10

Introduction

Many professing Christians find themselves living far short of what could be classified as the abundant life. Many who confess Jesus Christ as Lord find life to be a barren desert with one disappointment after another. Some have become cynical over whether or not Jesus Christ is able to produce what he said he came to accomplish.

The abundant life is not to be equated with the affluent life. Some people think of happiness only in terms of the possession of things. Our Lord had little of this world's valuable things. He did not find happiness and joy in the mere possession or control of things.

This text from Jesus's lips should be planted deep within our mind and heart that we might be reminded over and over of God's generous purpose. Jesus is affirming his concern for us and his desire that we experience more

75

than just mere existence. The Christian life is meant to be a feast rather than a fast. God means for our life to have a surplus rather than a deficit.

Why is it that so many who profess to know Jesus Christ as Lord fall far short of the abundant life? Is it because they have a false concept of what the abundant life is? Is it because they expect God to hand them something on a silver platter merely because they have received Jesus Christ as Lord? The abundant life is promised to those who totally commit their lives to the lordship of the Good Shepherd.

I. Abundant living comes to those who live a life of genuine faith.

To really trust God—to have faith in God—means to unite with him and let him be the controlling partner in your life. To trust in him is to believe that he is and that he is a rewarder of those who diligently seek him. It means to depend on him and to accept his suggestions and corrections.

II. Abundant living comes to those who live a life of prayer.

Prayer is much more than bringing a grocery list to God. It is a precious experience of dialogue between a loving, trusting child and a generous and wise heavenly Father. The needy child brings his or her needs and aspirations to the attention of the heavenly Father. The Father is too wise to be in error and too good to do his child harm. He will always grant our request in a manner consistent with his nature and character.

III. Abundant living comes to those who live a life of obedience.

The true sheep of our Lord hear his voice and follow him in a life of loving obedience (cf. John 10:27). There is no substitute for obedience, and there is no joy in the life of a person who is disobedient to the known will of our great God. If you would find the abundant life in the here and now, it will be along the pathway of obedience to God as he seeks to keep us from evil and lead us in growth and ministry.

IV. Abundant living comes to those who live a life of giving.

Those who are selfish may possess many things, but this will not mean that they are enjoying the abundant life our Lord came to provide. The more selfish people are, the less they will truly enjoy God's blessings. Only those who learn the joy of giving will experience the joy of living. This is true in the business world, in marriage relationships, and in spiritual things.

Conclusion

Make a total response to the Lord of life and love. He wants to help you experience an abundant, fulfilled life. Do not be satisfied with a fractional response. "The measure you give will be the measure you get."

Suggested preaching program for the month of

MARCH

■ **Sunday Mornings**

On the first Sunday of the month, begin a series titled "The Crowds at the Cross," which will take you through Easter. These messages make a contemporary application of the various responses of those who were on the scene at the time of Jesus's crucifixion.

■ **Sunday Evenings**

Complete the series of messages based on great chapters from the Old Testament using the theme "God Continues to Speak."

■ **Wednesday Evenings**

Continue the series "The Words of Jesus Christ," which is based on Colossians 3:16: "Let the word of Christ dwell in you richly."

Sunday Morning, March 4

Title: Trafficking in Treachery

Text: "Then one of the twelve, called Judas Iscariot, went unto the chief priests, and said unto them, What will ye give me, and I will deliver him unto you? And they covenanted with him for thirty pieces of silver. And from that time he sought opportunity to betray him" **(Matt. 26:14–16)**.

Scripture Reading: Matthew 27:3–8

Hymns: "O Thou to Whose All-Searching Sight," Zinzendorf
"Jesus Is All the World to Me," Thompson
"Satisfied with Jesus," McKinney

Offertory Prayer: Our Father, we thank you for this day. Whenever we see its beauty and know its opportunities, we are grateful that you have given it to us. And we thank you for other blessings that have come to us by your hand: salvation, worship, the time and place to serve in your name. We realize, our Father, that we are not and never will be worthy of all that you have given us. But we pray that you would indeed make us grateful and make us adequate to the task before us. At this time we return to you a portion of what you have provided for us. Bless it, we pray, and use it for your glory. And always make us aware of your presence and your power. We pray these things in Jesus's name and for his sake. Amen.

Introduction

Traitor. The very word sends chills down the spine and awakens images of treachery, trickery, and tragedy. There is an aura of horror and unwholesomeness about it.

The most infamous American traitor during the Revolutionary War was Benedict Arnold. Arnold began well. In fact, he received recognition, honors, and promotions, and in 1777 after the second battle of Saratoga, Congress voted him a resolution of the nation's thanks and promoted him to major general.

But Arnold also received some disappointments along the way. Then in 1780 while in command of West Point, he worked out a plan to surrender the fort to the British. His plan was discovered when Major John Andre was captured, for Arnold had been sending messages in Andre's boot. Arnold then deserted to the British and finished his life with them. But he had betrayed his country.

While Benedict Arnold is the most notorious American traitor, Judas Iscariot has to be the most infamous traitor of all time, for he betrayed Jesus Christ into the hands of his enemies. The priests had already decided that Jesus must die. Judas made it possible.

He, too, began well. Something in Judas must have appealed to Jesus, for he gave Judas a position of trust.

Why, then, did Judas betray Jesus? At least three basic answers are given to this question: (1) it was because of greed and avarice; (2) it was because of bitter hatred based on disillusionment; and (3) it was an attempt to force Jesus to bring in the kingdom of God.

Although Judas committed suicide before Jesus's crucifixion, we certainly see Judas in the crowd at the cross. And whenever we think of him, we think of one who trafficked in treachery. Let's for a few moments give Judas the benefit of the doubt. Suppose he was well intentioned and simply meant to force Jesus's hand. Suppose he was trafficking in treachery and it went differently than he had planned.

I. We traffic in treachery when we misinterpret the kingdom of God.

Apparently Judas tragically misinterpreted the meaning of the kingdom of God. He looked for a national kingdom that would run off the Romans, restore grandeur, and give him personal power.

Evidence shows that Judas may have been a Zealot. Some find the meaning of the name Iscariot in the *sicarri*, a group of dedicated, fanatic loyalists. But that was not the meaning of the kingdom of God. The power of the kingdom of God is love.

Love cannot be understood; it must be experienced. The scene just before Judas's deal with the priests was the one of the woman who anointed Jesus's feet. Judas had only one question then: How much did it cost? He never understood love.

Jesus cannot be changed; he must be trusted. Judas wanted to change Jesus. That, however, is the wrong order. Jesus must change us, and he does that when we trust him in faith.

II. We traffic in treachery when we try to manipulate God's will.

Judas tried to manipulate God's will. He wanted things done, and he wanted Jesus to do them. But he wanted Jesus to do things his way, not God's way. Judas thought he knew more than God about running God's business. For instance, the cross was God's will. Hebrews 9:22 says, "Without shedding of blood is no remission" (Heb. 9:22). But Judas wanted another way.

How often we try to chart our own way. Whether witnessing, praying, or serving God, we try to do it our own way rather than God's way. A popular television commercial several years ago had a woman proclaiming in anger to her mother, "Please, mother, I would rather do it myself!" How often have we expressed that to God!

It is interesting that the first thing Jesus told the disciples to do between the Resurrection and Pentecost was nothing. He told them to wait. That must have seemed strange to them, but it was God's way. They waited. And they received the power of the Holy Spirit for their ministry.

This often comes about when we have lost our glory, our vision of what God is about and what we are to do. Archibald Rutledge once asked an engineer on a southern riverboat how he kept everything in such perfect working order and so immaculately clean. As he laid down a Bible he had been quietly reading, the engineer explained, "I've got a glory!"

When you lose your willingness to follow God, when you lose your glory, then you try to manipulate the will of God by pushing the promises of God. You want to bring about the desired results rather than letting God work them out in your life. One of the primary examples of this is Abraham taking Sarah's maid Hagar to produce a son when God's promise of a family had apparently not been fulfilled. Rather than waiting on God's promise, Abraham pushed the promise, and Ishmael was born. But trouble followed.

III. We traffic in treachery when we misapply repentance.

The final scene in Judas's life is horrible. He repented of his sin all right, but he waited too long. He tried to make right his wrong by returning the money, but he waited until it was too late. He had betrayed the only one who could forgive him, so in remorse he hanged himself.

Charles Griffin described a seventeenth-century fresco portraying Judas, which he saw in a church in Bucharest, Hungary: "There we see the ugly, giant figure of Satan sitting on some hot stones in Hades, holding the doll-like person of Judas, along with the infamous bag of bribe money; and Judas is weeping in remorse" (R. Earl Allen, *Persons of the Passion* [Nashville: Broadman, 1972], 31). This tells us at least two terrible things about sin.

A. *It is impossible to turn back the clock.* We cannot undo what has been done no matter how sorry we are about having done it. The harm has already been done. The character has been set; the trust has been broken; the act has been committed; the heart has been hardened to that extent.

This truth has been expressed poetically:

> The Moving Finger writes; and, having writ,
> Moves on: nor all your Piety nor Wit
> Shall lure it back to cancel half a Line,
> Nor all your Tears wash out a Word of it!

B. *You can come to hate the very thing that was gained by sin.* Judas hated the money that was gained by his betrayal. He got his way and was even paid for his trouble, but he hated it—and hated himself as well.

This is not an isolated case in life or in literature. In Shakespeare's play *Macbeth*, Macbeth murdered Duncan, the king. Macbeth got his heart's desire, but it did not make him a peaceful person. In accomplishing what he had set out to do, all that made life beautiful departed from him. He soon could not sleep and life became unbearable. It was said that "Macbeth hath murdered sleep."

Conclusion

You can apply repentance properly. You can come to this same Christ in faith. Even when you have trafficked in treachery, you can live in faith and trust. Christ forgives.

SUNDAY EVENING, MARCH 4

Title: The Travail and the Triumph

Text: "But he was wounded for our transgressions, he was bruised for our iniquities; the chastisement of our peace was upon him; and with his stripes we are healed" **(Isa. 53:5)**.

Scripture Reading: Isaiah 52:13–15; 53:1–12

Introduction

The book of Acts gives an unforgettable account of a divinely arranged encounter between Philip and the Ethiopian eunuch. The Ethiopian, apparently a God-fearer (a Gentile who worshiped Jehovah), was returning to his country from Jerusalem, where he must have attended one of the great feast weeks. He was sitting in his chariot, poring over the Scriptures. He had a yearning in his soul to understand what he was reading. Upon instructions from the Holy Spirit, Philip stopped the chariot and got inside and sat down beside the Ethiopian.

Imagine the thrill Philip experienced when he saw that the portion of the scroll the Ethiopian was reading was that which we know as Isaiah 53.

When he asked the Ethiopian, "Understandeth thou what thou readest?" (Acts 8:30), the pathetic reply of the Ethiopian was, "How can I, except some man should guide me?" (v. 31). And Luke records that Philip "began at the same scripture, and preached unto him Jesus" (v. 35).

I. The prologue (52:13–15).

Isaiah's favorite attention-getter is the word *Behold*. He uses this word nearly seventy times as a means of pointing out a new object or referring to a new thought. It means "Come to attention! Concentrate with all of your mental powers on what I am about to say!" The words of this prologue actually constitute the words of God himself speaking through Isaiah.

"Behold, my servant shall deal prudently" (v. 13). God's servant, the Messiah, will be successful; he will prosper. He will be the embodiment of wisdom, and because of that, nothing shall halt his mission. All the powers of evil cannot deter him from the completion of his mission on earth. The remainder of the verse, "he shall be exalted and extolled, and be very high," is a prediction of complete victory. The key phrase is "lifted up." It is a prophetic foregleam of the cross.

In verse 14 there is a scene change. We are plunged into the darkness and terror of a depraved humanity. Here is a picture of suffering and agony. A face is marred so that it does not look like a human face; a form, a body, is torn and mutilated so that it does not even resemble a human being. Thus, the exaltation, the victory of the Servant of God, will come on the heels of this inconceivably horrible scene.

Jesus was indeed "lifted up" in sorrow, anguish, and humiliation. But this very terror that struck the sinless Son of God catapulted him even higher, to the place of sovereignty and victory, so that the kings of the earth shut their mouths because of him (v. 15).

II. The travail of suffering (53:1–9).

These nine verses can be divided into three movements: the rejected Person (vv. 1–3), the vicarious Sufferer (vv. 4–6), and the atoning Lamb (vv. 7–9).

A. *Verses 1–3 give us one of the most tender and beautiful references to the relationship between Jesus and his heavenly Father in all of Scripture.* But before Isaiah unveils this exquisite gem, like a herald before the appearance of a king, he says, "Who hath believed our report? and to whom is the arm of the LORD revealed?" (v. 1). Indeed, Jesus was the "arm of the LORD" for humankind. The arm is that part of the body by which work requiring strength is accomplished. It carries out the will of the mind. It is a fitting description of Jesus.

"For he shall grow up before him as a tender plant" (v. 2). Here is the Father watching his Son as he "grows up" and becomes the joy and fulfillment of his Father's dreams. The "tender plant" is a poetic description of Jesus in all the beauty and strength suggested by youth. But that is not how people saw him. People said of him, "As a root out of dry ground: he hath no form nor comeliness; and when we see him, there is no beauty that we should desire him" (v. 2). There is no contrast more stark than that between a tender plant in its growth and a root pulled up out of the earth lying on the pathway exposed and ugly. The pulled root is something people count as useless and kick out of the way as they walk by. People were blind to the beauty, the worthiness of the Son of God.

B. *In verses 4–6 Isaiah shows that the Messiah's sorrows were vicarious sorrows.* In fact, the prophet states boldly that the sorrows of the Messiah were not his own; he was suffering for others. People were saying, "Those who suffer are always afflicted of God because of their wrongdoing. Look at this so-called Messiah! Look at his suffering! God did it to him because of his sins!" But Isaiah says, "Not so! It was our transgressions, our sins, that caused his suffering. He was totally innocent, completely righteous before God."

C. *In verses 7–9 we have the consummation and the climax of the suffering and travail of Jesus as presented by Isaiah.* We see Jesus silent in the presence of all the wrong done to him. What kind of silence was this? It was the silence of one who was in perfect agreement with God and with God's determination to provide redemption for sinful people.

III. The triumph of victory (53:10–12).

The prophet opens this new scene with the statement: "Yet it pleased the Lord to bruise him" (v. 10). The conjunction "yet" is important; it is Isaiah's way of drawing the contrast between two opposite scenes. In verses 1–9 we have the picture of our Lord being wronged by people yet silently bearing their sins. Now, beginning with verse 10, we are told that all of this was within the will of God. Isaiah's statement harmonizes beautifully with Peter's words on the Day of Pentecost: "Him, being delivered by the determinate counsel and foreknowledge of God, ye have taken, and by wicked hands have crucified and slain" (Acts 2:23).

In short, Isaiah begins with the prediction of the wrong done by people and ends with the affirmation that God overruled that wrong. Peter begins with the declaration that God determined the death of Jesus from the beginning and ends with the affirmation that the sin of people caused the suffering of the Lord Jesus! Indeed, it was "the pleasure, the permission" of the Lord for Jesus to suffer for humankind's sin. The plan of God, delineated from eternity past, was carried out in history, in time. It was completed, finished, sealed to become forever irrefutable and irreversible.

When Jesus was made an offering for sin, his "soul," as Isaiah says, entered into that sacrificial death. Jesus's total self suffered, and the purposes of God were assured of accomplishment. Through travail, our Lord came to triumph.

"He shall see the travail of his soul, and shall be satisfied" (v. 11). And what is the satisfaction of the Lord God in seeing the travail of the soul of his Son? It is the birth of many into the kingdom!

Conclusion

Isaiah 53 is undoubtedly the Mount Everest of the Old Testament prophecies concerning the Messiah. And the marvel of it all is that this clear and graphic description of the Lord Jesus and his atoning death was given through a prophet hundreds of years before its historic fulfillment. The great theologian Delitzsch, reflecting on this, wrote, "This whole passage looks as if it might have been written beneath the Cross on Golgotha!"

Perhaps we can find the focal point of Isaiah 53 in the thrilling words of Paul: "God was in Christ, reconciling the world unto himself" (2 Cor. 5:19).

WEDNESDAY EVENING, MARCH 7

Title: As I Have Loved You

Text: "A new commandment I give to you, that you love one another; even as I have loved you, that you also love one another. By this all men will know that you are my disciples, if you have love one for another" **(John 13:34–35 RSV)**.

Scripture Reading: John 13:31–38

Introduction

In a world filled with hate and torn by strife, modern followers of Jesus are urged to love each other by the same measure with which Christ loved his disciples. The love Jesus commands is not a shallow, emotional kind of love. Instead, it could be defined as a "persistent, unbreakable spirit of goodwill that is always devoted to the highest good of others."

Note that in this commandment Jesus moves beyond the measure of love listed in the second great commandment, "You shall love your neighbor as yourself" (Matt. 22:39 RSV). In this condensation of the commandments that are concerned with our relationship to others, Jesus declares that the measure of love we have for ourselves is the measure by which we are to love our neighbors. In the new commandment, Jesus declares that his disciples are to love each other, "even as I have loved you." How did Jesus love these disciples?

I. Jesus's love for his disciples was unmerited.

We live in a performance oriented society in which people come to a feeling of personal worth because of their performance. This makes it difficult for us to understand unmerited love. Jesus loved his disciples not because they were lovely, but because he was loving. The source of his love was in his own heart and in his relationship to the Father God. His love was not pulled out of him toward them because they are exceedingly lovely. Jesus's love was unmerited in that he took the initiative in manifesting goodwill toward others. This is the kind of love we are to demonstrate toward others.

II. Jesus's love was always appropriate.

Jesus manifested divine love in different ways to different people. There was no stereotyped manner by which he expressed God's love. He could talk to a public figure like the Pharisee Nicodemus under the curtain of darkness. He could approach a hated publican like Zacchaeus on a city street filled with community citizens. He could stoop down and write in the sand, refusing to look upon the shame of a woman who had been accused of adultery. Our Lord in tenderness could bless and pray for children. His love was always expressed in an appropriate manner. As his followers, we must seek to appropriately manifest our concern for others.

III. Jesus's love for his disciples was a working love.

Jesus thought of success and greatness not in terms of mere noble sentiments, but in terms of deeds of kindness and helpfulness to the unfortunate. He was a worker, a servant who ministered to the needs of people.

At a time when Peter wanted to stay on the mountaintop, our Lord insisted that they depart from the place of spiritual ecstasy and move down into the valley of human need because there was suffering at the foot of the mountain.

Our Lord calls us not into the sheltered cloister to spend our total time in prayer, but rather he calls us out into the fields that are white unto harvest to be his laborers.

IV. Jesus's love for his disciples was forgiving.

On the cross Jesus demonstrated in practice what he had taught by precept. He had insisted on his disciples practicing forgiveness toward those who mistreated them even to the point of forgiving seventy times seven (Matt. 18:21–22). Jesus believed in forgiveness that was free, full, and forever. Genuine Christian love does not harbor hate and carry a grudge. Genuine Christian love will manifest itself in forgiveness.

V. Jesus's love for his disciples was persistent.

Jesus continued to love even when his disciples were unlovable in their responses to him and in their treatment of others.

Paul was able to rejoice greatly and join in singing a doxology of praise to the permanence of God's great love revealed in Jesus Christ (Rom. 8:38–39).

VI. Jesus's love for his disciples was sacrificial (Mark 10:45).

Jesus saw life as an opportunity to serve, to help, and to minister. He saw it as a goblet to be emptied rather than a vessel to be filled. His sacrificial life and his substitutionary death on the cross illustrate the great truth he expressed when he said, "Truly, truly, I say to you, unless a grain of wheat falls into the earth and dies, it remains alone; but if it dies, it bears much fruit" (John 12:24 RSV).

Conclusion

The command to love is Jesus's foremost command to his disciples. Love is the supreme gift of the Spirit. Only as we let the Holy Spirit do his work within our innermost being can we fully respond to this commandment of our Lord (Rom. 5:5). Paul declares love to be the greatest of all the gifts of the Spirit (1 Cor. 13:13). Because of Jesus's command and with the help of the Holy Spirit, each of us needs to relate to each other in terms of love even as Jesus has loved us.

SUNDAY MORNING, MARCH 11

Title: Dallying with Denial

Text: "But Peter said unto him, Although all shall be offended, yet will not I. And Jesus saith unto him, Verily I say unto thee, That this day, even in this night, before the cock crow twice, thou shalt deny me thrice. But he spake the more vehemently, If I should die with thee, I will not deny thee in any wise. Likewise also said they all" **(Mark 14:29–31)**.

Scripture Reading: Mark 14:27–31, 50, 66–72

Hymns: "Stand Up, Stand Up for Jesus," Duffield
"O for a Faith That Will Not Shrink," Bathurst
"My Faith Looks Up to Thee," Palmer

Offertory Prayer: Our Father, accept our gratitude for your blessings. Accept our lives as we give them to you in faith and commitment. And please accept these gifts as we give them into your hands in response to your graciousness in giving us life, love, and new life. Help us, Lord, to so dedicate ourselves to you and to your will that we will not deviate from your direction. Please give to us the strength to carry out the resolves that we so quickly and glibly make. Forgive us now of our sins and guide us with your Spirit. We pray in Jesus's name and for his sake. Amen.

Introduction

Andrew Jackson's mother once gave him this advice: "In this world, you will have to make your own way. To do that, you must have friends. You can make friends by being honest, and you can keep them by being steadfast.... To forget an obligation, or be ungrateful for a kindness, is a base crime."

This is the thing that has always bothered us so much about Peter's denial of Jesus: It seems like a betrayal of friendship.

Look at the crowd at the cross. Among those there you must see Simon Peter, the boisterous, impetuous, impulsive disciple of Christ. Peter had followed afar off when Jesus was carried before the council for his trial. Peter probably stood afar off when Jesus was being crucified. But you can be sure that he must have been in the crowd somewhere.

Peter's denial of Jesus stands in stark contrast with his boast that he would never forsake Jesus. Yet when the time came, he definitely denied his Lord.

Is it not possible that we all dally with denial? Are we not like Simon Peter, always standing at the borderline of confession and cowardice, of affirmation and denial? No one who has ever noticed in his or her own life the grim possibility of denial can throw stones at Peter. In the face of Peter's affirmed strength, the Lord saw the possibility of failure. We stand in much the same position.

I. You dally with denial when you deny the principles of peace.

At the Last Supper, Peter had asserted that he would never leave Jesus. He even argued with Jesus that he never would leave him. But he did.

Peter first denied Jesus by his actions. He denied him at the arrest when he tried to kill the high priest's servant. He succeeded in cutting off the servant's ear, but you can be sure that was not his original intention. This was a denial of the principles of peace. Jesus's kingdom was a kingdom of peace. By his violent action Peter denied that Jesus's kingdom was one of peace. He tried to make it violent.

   A. *We never carry out Christ's principles by violence.* Violence does not bring in the kingdom of God. When Clovis the Frank first heard the story of Jesus's crucifixion, he jumped from his seat, grabbed his sword, and said, "If I and my Franks had been there, they never would have done that to Jesus!" Peter displayed much the same attitude. But the principles of Christ's kingdom are never carried out by violence.

   B. *We never carry out Christ's principles by pressure.* The form of force we often use to coerce people is pressure rather than violence. While we may never threaten people with death if they do not receive Christ, we may use means to try to force them to make a decision. A well-known preacher and teacher of preachers indicates that he delayed making a public profession of faith in Christ for many years because of this. In the small community in which he lived, and in the small church he attended, often he was the only prospect for membership during the annual revival meeting. The people found such ways of putting pressure on him to join the church that he resisted it. And thus he resisted Christ for several years.

   C. *We never carry out Christ's principles by isolating and rejecting people.* Jesus accepted people and brought them to himself. We often reject and isolate the very people who need Christ. Jimmy Karam had been a leader in the Little Rock race riots before his conversion. He was the successful owner of a clothing store in that city, a former football coach, a typical secular and unchurched man. He told the moving story of how his daughter had become a Christian. She and her husband had asked the pastor of their church to call on him in his store. When the minister, a well-known Baptist pastor, came to see him, Jimmy Karam said it was the first time anyone had ever come to talk with him about attending church or giving his heart to Christ. He said in his testimony, 'You know, all my life I wanted to be like you. I wanted to be nice, fine, respectable Christian people like you. But no one ever asked me. Everyone knew that I was a sinner, and I didn't think they wanted Jimmy Karam in their churches" (Leighton Ford, *The Christian Persuader* [New York: Harper and Row, 1966], 70–71).

Often we want to hurry things up, so we take them in our own hands. This was exactly what Peter did. He would save Jesus himself. In doing this we forget the parables of the mustard seed and leaven and the principles of peace by which the kingdom of peace grows.

II. You dally with denial when you deny the Prince of Peace.

Peter's second denial of Jesus was in the courtyard. The denial of Jesus often comes after just such a boast of courage and loyalty. Those who boast are the ones to watch. In our boasting we may simply be covering up for a weakness of which we are much aware. The person who boasts that he is strong and does not need the rules by which other people live is the one headed for moral trouble. The drinker who says that she can take it or leave it alone is the one often destined to become an alcoholic. The gambler who says that he can quit at any time is likely already a compulsive gambler. The only real defense is to live in humility and dependence on Christ's strength. Paul warned, "Wherefore let him that thinketh he standeth take heed lest he fall" (1 Cor. 10:12).

A. *The denial of Jesus comes when you think of evil and sin only abstractly.* As long as we think of sin only abstractly, we know we can be strong enough to stand against it. When Peter boasted in the Upper Room about his strength, he had not actually been tempted to forsake Christ. However, when the girl questioned him in the courtyard, that which he had considered only abstractly became very concrete.

B. *The denial of Jesus is sometimes silent as well as verbal.* There are times when we deny the Savior by the things we do not say as well as by those things we do say. By a refusal to speak up for the right, to stand for convictions, and to witness for Christ, we deny Christ.

In Robert Bolt's play about Sir Thomas More entitled *A Man for All Seasons*, Thomas Cromwell addressed the jury at the trial of Sir Thomas More. In his address he indicated that there were several kinds of silence, including the silence of death. In some circumstances silence could speak. In the case of

Sir Thomas More's silence in refusing to accept the king's act of succession to make him the rightful king, everyone knew what that silence meant. It meant that More did not consider the king's title valid. In that case it was not silence at all, but eloquent denial. And so is our silence at times.

Conclusion

Even in denial God still loves us and claims us. It is never too late to repent. Denial can be turned into acceptance.

SUNDAY EVENING, MARCH 11

Title: God's Social Register

Text: "Ho, every one that thirsteth, come ye to the waters, and he that hath no money; come ye, buy, and eat; yea, come, buy wine and milk without money and without price" (**Isa. 55:1**).

Scripture Reading: Isaiah 55

Introduction

An examination of Isaiah 55 reveals that God has a "social register" that is prominently displayed and referred to throughout the Scriptures. God's social register includes the world! No one is snubbed, overlooked, or discriminated against. In spite of the exclusivism of the Hebrew people, God's universal invitation is found even among the proclamations of the Hebrew prophets. Isaiah stood tallest of all when he proclaimed, "Ho, everyone that thirsteth, come ye" (55:1). The perfect climax came when Jesus said, "Come unto me, all ye that labor and are heavy laden, and I will give you rest" (Matt. 11:28); and again, "Him that cometh to me I will in no wise cast out" (John 6:37).

There are three divisions in Isaiah 55: verses 1–5 proclaim a worldwide invitation, verses 6–9 issue a call to repentance, and verses 10–13 constitute a declaration of victory.

I. A worldwide invitation.

Ho! is another of Isaiah's favorite words. It is even more arresting than the word *behold.* The expression *Ho!* is akin to a verbal trumpet call. One can almost picture Isaiah taking up a megaphone and, with ear-splitting volume, catching everyone's attention. The reason? What he is about to say is for everyone! He is about to set forth the one requirement everyone can meet. Some may not choose to meet it, but no one is excluded due to not being able to meet it.

What is the requirement? Thirst! Are you utterly dissatisfied with your life as you are living it now? If so, then you thirst for something better. Are you turned off by what the world has offered you? Then you thirst for that which will satisfy. Three times within the scope of this first verse, the imperative "Come" appears. This is the insistency of God's invitation.

Three things are mentioned for which one is to "come" when he or she senses thirst. First, there is *water*. "Come ye to the waters." The plural form indicates that there is an abundant supply. Water, in the Scriptures, is a symbol of life. So water comes first, since a human's first need is to be infused with divine life.

Next the prophet mentions *wine*. Wine is ever a symbol of joy in the Scriptures. The wine is for the soul, the total personality of a person. After one drinks of the Water of Life, there comes the joy, the radiating and overflowing joy that must be shared.

Third, Isaiah speaks of *milk*. This is an excellent progression. The new Christian needs the milk of God's Word to grow spiritually. The water *gives* life, the wine *expresses* life in joy, and the milk *sustains* life and causes growth.

The prophet then offers a delightful alternative for those inclined to spend their substance on that which does not satisfy. "Eat ye that which is good, and let your soul delight itself in fatness!" With this, the intensity of emotion reaches its peak. It is almost as if the audience is holding its breath. "Incline your ear, and come unto me." That means, "Bend down a little closer; don't miss a word of this!" Then Isaiah begins to deliver his message. He describes the purpose and the mission of the coming Messiah.

II. A call to repentance.

When does a person seek God? When that person sees God coming in grace—not to judge, condemn, strike, or curse, but to bless, to save at awful cost, to love everlastingly. God seeks people first, as he surrounds their lives with blessings too numerous to count.

What is there about people that is presupposed in God's offer of forgiveness? It is *guilt*. Guilt is one of the bedrock problems of human life. Some try to get rid of their guilt by persuading themselves that there is no God. Others attempt to drown out the voice of an accusing conscience by drink, work, entertainment, gambling, drugs, or whatever other means of escape they can find. Still, the problem of guilt does not go away.

Paul Tournier, the eminent Swiss psychiatrist and author, says in his book *Guilt and Grace*, that a vast number of illnesses and difficulties that lead people needlessly to physicians have their origin in unresolved guilt. Assurance of forgiveness is a universal need of people. However, pardon and forgiveness, in the final analysis, can be obtained only from the one who has been offended. The only true relief people can receive from the torture of guilt must come from God.

A solemn note is added: the day of opportunity and pardon will pass. One can wait too long. God's grace and mercy are not to be equated with an indulgent weakness. When Isaiah says, "Seek ye the LORD while he may be found," he means that there is a limit to the longsuffering and patience of God.

Verse 7 tells us the way to seek the Lord. The wicked man is to forsake his evil way, the unrighteous man his evil thoughts, and he is to "return unto the Lord." Seeking the Lord begins with an awakened conscience and requires that one turn in the Lord's direction. When this "turning" takes place, there is a cleansing. Both a radical transformation of thought and change of conduct are required. When this is done, God will abundantly pardon.

III. A declaration of victory.

Verses 10 and 11 contain a parable from nature. First, the rain is called to witness. It descends from heaven, its source. So it is that the word God speaks comes from him. The rain falls on the thirsty earth, and so the Word of God falls on a person's dry and thirsty spirit. The rain falls on mountain and valley, but the hard, lofty mountain sheds it, and the valleys receive it and profit by it. Thus, the Word of God is for all; but some, like the lofty craggy mountains in their pride, cast it off. Others, like the lowly valley, receive it in penitence. Because of the rain, the valleys are fertile and are covered with every form of vegetation. The redeemed person who receives the Word grows and in turn shares the Word with others.

So what happens? Finally the rain is drawn back to the heavens. Likewise the Word returns to God, accompanied, as it were, by the multitudes of those who have received it and have been transformed by its power.

It seems as though Isaiah can hardly contain himself as he writes the words recorded in verses 12 and 13. He is telling us that God's Word, like the mysterious powers of germination in nature, will be effective in the world. Its impact on human life will be miraculous. Peace and joy will be produced by it. Mountains and hills will ring with song because of it. Even the trees will "clap their hands" as a result of it.

Conclusion

Through these metaphors, the prophet is telling us that there is a transforming power in the good news of salvation and that it is for all people everywhere. The change that it brings in the lives of people would be as if fir trees came up instead of thorns, and myrtle trees instead of briers! In this beautiful and thrilling fashion, Isaiah is giving expression to the glorious and universal power of the Word of God. It is for everyone who will receive it.

WEDNESDAY EVENING, MARCH 14

Title: The Untroubled Heart

Text: "Let not your hearts be troubled; believe in God, believe also in me" **(John 14:1 RSV)**.

Scripture Reading: John 14:1–6

Introduction

The text on which we concentrate at this time is one of the most precious that ever fell from the lips of our Lord. It contains for us the secret of the tranquil heart and provides us with the clue that will enable us to live a life of inward poise in the midst of storm.

Jesus was assuring his dear friends that as they had believed in God in the past, they could continue to believe in him as he had revealed himself in the Son. Out of this great faith in Jesus Christ come many bases for our being able to live a tranquil life with inward peace even in the midst of turmoil. Let us consider a few of them.

I. We have the guidance of the inspired Word (Josh. 1:8).

Joshua, the new leader of the people of Israel, was promised divine guidance and success if he would meditate on the Word of God day by day and use it as the source for guidance and help. This promise comes down to us today, and we need to have a greater confidence in the imperatives and the suggestions that come to us through the pages of the Holy Word.

II. We have the presence of the Holy Spirit.

Jesus calmed the fears and encouraged the hearts of his disciples by promising them "another comforter." The word translated "another" means "another of like kind." He was referring to the gift of the Holy Spirit that would be poured out in fullness on the Day of Pentecost. The Holy Spirit indwells each believer. We need to remind ourselves of this thrilling truth so that we won't fear, but will have courage in our hearts.

III. We have the unclosed gate of prayer that is always open (Matt. 6:6).

The needy child of God is invited into the throne room for a conversation with the heavenly Father, the giver of good gifts. His greatest gift is an awareness of his own loving and abiding presence. If we come confessing our sin and seeking God's will for our lives, we can be certain that the door to the throne room of answered prayer will always remain open.

IV. We can rejoice in the fellowship of God's people (John 13:35).

We love because God first loved us. This new love that comes from God in the conversion experience causes us to love God's people. In the fellowship of the church, in worship, in Bible study, in prayer, in hymn singing, we receive the strength that comes from God through his people. An hour spent with God's people can do much to settle the troubled waters that threaten to destroy us.

V. We have the sure promise of the coming of our Lord (Rev. 22:12).

Over and over our Lord promised to return to the earth to claim his own. At that time the battle with sin will be over and death will be a defeated foe. We shall rejoice in God's grace and with God's people for ages without end.

Conclusion

Our Lord does not want us living our lives trembling with fear. He wants us to be calm and courageous in the midst of whatever circumstances may befall us. If we would live confidently in a troubled world, we must trust in God and believe in Jesus Christ with all our heart. God is trustworthy, and we can depend on our Lord to be with us at all times.

SUNDAY MORNING, MARCH 18

Title: Cavorting with Cowardice

Text: "And so Pilate, willing to content the people, released Barabbas unto them, and delivered Jesus, when he had scourged him, to be crucified" **(Mark 15:15).**

Scripture Reading: Mark 15:1–15

Hymns: "O Love That Wilt Not Let Me Go," Matheson
"Have Faith in God," McKinney
"I'll Live for Him," Hudson

Offertory Prayer: Our Father, thank you for your blessings to us. Help us, our Father, to live life with courage and strength. There are so many times and so many situations in which it would be easier to take the coward's way out. But strengthen our resolve, touch our lives, and give understanding to our minds that we might stand for you. This day we will offer to you some of our earnings. Help us to realize that you are interested in how we earn our money and how we spend our money as well as how we give our money. May we then give with clean hands and a ready heart. Use our gifts for your glory. And we also ask for the forgiveness of our sins. In Jesus's name we pray. Amen.

Introduction

At one time the ever-popular "Humor in Uniform" section of the *Reader's Digest* had the story of two paratroopers who collided in midair. As they collided, one of the chutes collapsed. One of the chutists then grabbed the other in a bear hug, and they rode the good chute to safety. Commended for his quick thinking, the paratrooper modestly admitted that he deserved no praise. "We had only one chute," he said, "and I wasn't about to let go to see if it was mine."

Most of our acts of courage are about that courageous. Actually, we may be more cowardly than courageous. There are times, however, when we are able to summon enough strength, enough nerve, and enough faith to act with courage. Most of us play around with cowardice with about as much frequency as we act with courage.

Whenever we think of cowardice, we think of Pontius Pilate. He was the governor of Judea at the time of Christ's crucifixion. The Jews had a good bit of freedom in running their own affairs, but they could not pronounce the death sentence. For this, they depended on Pilate. Pilate had risen through the military ranks. His governorship was given to him as a political plum, and he knew little about law and justice—and public relations. It seemed as though he went out of his way to antagonize the Jews. They hated him bitterly, but they were willing to use him. According to Luke's account, three political charges were leveled against Jesus: (1) being a revolutionary, (2) inciting people not to pay taxes, and (3) claiming to be king (Luke 23:2).

Pilate knew Jesus was innocent. His wife sent him word about a dream she had had and pleaded with him to have nothing to do with Jesus. Pilate attempted a trade-off with the people in offering to release either Jesus or a known criminal. Then he bowed to the pressure. Protesting his innocence of the affair, he washed his hands. But still he acted cowardly. So we see him in the crowd at the cross: Pilate the coward.

I. You cavort with cowardice by a failure to resist the pressures.

Pilate knew what he should do legally. This was a religious problem, not a political problem. And he knew, too, that Jesus was innocent. But Pilate could not resist the pressure. The religious leaders threatened to report him to Rome, and he could not stand an adverse report to Rome. He had already antagonized the Jews enough and had already proved himself to be an inept governor. So they continued to apply pressure to him to do what he knew was wrong.

Pressure is what gets to us most. It may be pressure to excel. Reared on the success image, we may feel that we have to excel in order to be accepted and appreciated. It may be on the athletic field, in the classroom, in the business office, or out on the field selling something—wherever it is, the pressure to excel often builds to the bursting point. Or it may be the pressure to produce. You may feel that you have to produce results no matter what the cost. It may also be the pressure to be accepted by others. Young people, and not so young people, often are willing to go to almost any means to be accepted and liked by their peers. This produces a pressure on them to do things they might not do otherwise.

How can you resist this kind of pressure? Someone has spoken about the "inner braces." These inner braces are what allow us to resist the pressures of life. Albert Einstein has been quoted as saying that only the church opposed Hitlerism when it came to Germany. He had expected the universities to oppose it, but they accepted it. He had expected the newspapers to oppose it, but they propagated it. The leaders in institutions that should have opposed it bowed to its authority. Only the Christian church met Hitlerism with opposition. A *Time* magazine cover in May 1940 had a picture of Martin Niemoeller with this caption: "In Germany only the cross has not bowed to the Swastika." Niemoeller had preached a famous sermon in which he said, "God is my Führer." The inner braces of faith and dependence on God held.

II. You cavort with cowardice by a failure to act on what you know is right.

Pilate knew what was right, but he would not act on it. He knew that Jesus was not guilty of a criminal offense, but he would not free him. It is sin not to do what we know is right. We sin by the bad things we do but also by the good things that we do not do. For nice, respectable people, this is the way sin most often finds its way.

The result of this is that many people actually die before their funeral. Robert Hastings told the story of the funeral of Anderson McCrew, a one-legged hobo who was buried sixty years after his death. In 1913 McCrew fell from a freight train when it passed through Marlin, Texas. He lost both his leg and his life. A Marlin funeral home mummified McCrew's body to preserve it until a relative might show up. But none did. Somehow McCrew's remains became part of a carnival. Dressed in a tuxedo, his body was carried across the United States as the "Petrified Man." But the carnival went broke, and a Dallas mortuary buried McCrew sixty years after he had died.

Sixty years is a long time to wait for a funeral. But many people die years before their funerals. They may turn bitter, cynical, and dead inside. This can result from failing to do what they know is right.

III. You cavort with cowardice by a failure to accept responsibility.

Pilate did not want to accept the responsibility for his actions. He even ordered a wash basin so that he could publicly wash his hands as a sign of the position he had taken.

There are some things that we cannot blame on others. We have tried to shift the blame for what we are, but in the end we cannot do it. We have to accept the responsibility for our actions. President Truman had a sign on his desk at the White House that read, "The buck stops here." He was in the position where the responsibility finally lay. And so are we with our own life and our own choices.

Conclusion

In many ways we cavort with cowardice. Now take a step of courage. Step toward Christ in faith.

SUNDAY EVENING, MARCH 18

Title: The Night of the Lions

Text: "Then was the king exceeding glad for him, and commanded that they should take Daniel up out of the den. So Daniel was taken up out of the den, and no manner of hurt was found upon him, because he believed in his God" (**Dan. 6:23**).

Scripture Reading: Daniel 6

Introduction

Someone has called Daniel the first lion tamer recorded in history! What is more amazing is that he accomplished his feat without the aid of a whip or a chair or a weapon at his side. Of course, the truth of the matter is that Daniel had nothing directly to do with the lions not eating him. He was God's man, and he had implicit faith that his God would take care of him. God did the rest.

It is a bit unusual to find this account of Daniel's experience in the lion's den in the midst of his prophecy of the great events that are to come at the end of time. Thus, there is one conclusion we must draw: It was important enough in God's sight to be included in Holy Scripture; therefore, its message is important for all generations.

I. The exaltation.

The first three verses of the chapter provide us with the account of Daniel's exaltation in the kingdom of Babylon. A number of years before, Nebuchadnezzar and his armies had carried many of the Jews captive into Babylon. Among them were four splendid young Hebrew men, one of whom was Daniel. They were the pick of the young men of Judah, and they were to be educated at Nebuchadnezzar's court.

Daniel distinguished himself from the beginning by taking a stand for God and for his faith. The king changed Daniel's name from Daniel to Belteshazzar, just as he had changed the names of the other three young men. But the king could not change the faith of Daniel or make him forget the name of his God.

One of the first issues that Daniel and his companions had to deal with was the menu at the king's table. Set before them was wine that had been offered to heathen gods and meat that the law of Moses forbade them to eat. Daniel purposed in his heart that he would not defile himself with the king's meat nor drink the king's wine. The result was that Daniel prospered and grew strong with the simple diet of water and vegetables, and he won the respect of the king's officials and of the king himself.

Under several kings and through successive reigns, Daniel rose from honor to honor in the kingdom. In the day of the great King Darius, Daniel was exalted to the office of prime minister of the empire. Inevitably, Daniel's contemporary Babylonian peers became jealous of him, but he maintained "an excellent spirit" (6:3). Daniel knew how to handle his success! This was true because he kept in touch with God through daily prayer.

II. The plot.

The purity of Daniel's life was constantly chafing to the Babylonian officials who worked beside him. The record states, "Then the presidents [the other two men who served with Daniel] and princes sought to find occasion against Daniel . . . but they could find none . . . forasmuch as he was faithful, neither was there any error or fault found in him" (6:4).

These enemies of Daniel were like the snowbird who asked the snowflake why it hated him so. And the snowflake answered, "Because you are going up, and I am going down!" When one man is going up, and others are slipping down, you can count on it that some of them will try to vent their envy upon the person who is going up. Thus, Daniel's enemies began to plot his downfall.

The diabolical scheme they devised was to place him in a position where his loyalty to the God of Israel would be in conflict with the laws of the kingdom of Babylon. Through flattery, they persuaded King Darius to sign a royal decree stating that for a period of thirty days no one would ask a petition of any god or any man, save of the king. If anyone prayed to any but the king, he would be cast into the den of lions. The decree appealed to the vanity of the king.

What did Daniel do when he heard about the decree? He opened his window toward Jerusalem "and prayed, and gave thanks before his God, as he did aforetime" (6:10). And when the king realized that he had been trapped into signing the decree (for he loved and respected Daniel deeply), he was grieved and very frightened. But he could not lose face; he had to order Daniel cast into the den of lions.

"Then the king commanded, and they brought Daniel, and cast him into the den of lions. Now the king spake and said unto Daniel, Thy God whom thou servest continually, he will deliver thee" (6:16). In verse 14 we discover that the king had "laboured until the going down of the sun to deliver him." But he had not succeeded, for there was a law among the Medes and Persians that said that no decree or statute which the king had established could be changed. What Darius was saying to Daniel was this: "Daniel, I have done everything that I can to save you from the lions, but I have failed. Now it is up to your God. If you are saved at all, he must do it!"

III. The victory.

As the day was dawning, the king rushed to the lions' den. The lions were quiet, and Darius must have thought, as he trembled with fear: "That can mean only one thing: they have full stomachs! Daniel is not just inside the den; he is inside the lions!" Verse 20 says that the king "cried with a lamentable voice unto Daniel." There was grief in the king's voice, for he loved and respected Daniel. There was self-reproach, for he was aware of his own weakness and gullibility in being trapped by his own princes. Then there was fear, for though he was a pagan, he respected Daniel's God.

Hear the king's quivering question as he bent down over the den's opening: "O Daniel, servant of the living God, is thy God, whom thou servest continually, able to deliver thee from the lions?" (6:20). Then, up from the depths of that dark and foreboding den came the sound of Daniel's voice: "O king, live for ever. My God hath sent his angel, and hath shut the lions' mouths, that they have not hurt me" (vv. 21–22).

"Then was the king exceeding glad for him, and commanded that they should take Daniel up out of the den. So Daniel was taken up out of the den, and no manner of hurt was found upon him, because he believed in his God" (v. 23). There is no way that we can measure the influence of a godly person. Daniel's experience doubtless shook the entire empire, for we can be sure that the news traveled the length and breadth of the land.

God rewarded Daniel for his faithfulness, for in visions of overwhelming glory God revealed the future to him. His prophecy is a delightful handbook for those who would study "the things which are to be hereafter."

Conclusion

What is the great sermon, the inspiration, of Daniel's life? He tells us how to dare, how to stand, and how to overcome. And what was the far-reaching effect of Daniel's victory? We are told, in the latter part of this chapter, that Darius issued a decree to be sent throughout the entire empire calling on men everywhere to fear the God of Daniel. The inscription on which the decree was addressed read, "Unto all people, nations, and languages, that dwell in all the earth" (6:25).

WEDNESDAY EVENING, MARCH 21

Title: Jesus Sets Us Free

Text: "So if the Son makes you free, you will be free indeed" (**John 8:36 RSV**).

Scripture Reading: John 8:31–38

Introduction

Jesus came into the world to set people free. As Moses had been used by God to set the Israelite slaves free from the bondage of Egypt, so Jesus came to set people free from the slavery of sin.

People have always loved freedom. The Revolutionary War was a war for freedom. World War I was fought to make the world free and safe for democracy. World War II was fought because the freedom of people was being threatened. People love and hunger for religious freedom, political, freedom, and economic freedom.

Dr. Elton Trueblood has stated six positive freedoms: freedom to (1) learn, (2) debate, (3) worship, (4) work, (5) live, and (6) serve. The four great freedoms as defined by President Franklin D. Roosevelt in 1941 are precious to us all: (1) freedom of speech, (2) freedom of worship, (3) freedom from want, and (4) freedom from fear.

I. Many have confused license for freedom.

This false definition of freedom thinks primarily in terms of anarchy rather than in terms of harmony and happiness for all. Freedom is no invitation to anarchy and selfish indulgence.

II. Jesus came to deliver people from slavery to freedom.

A. *Jesus saw people in bondage to ignorance, superstition, and tradition.*
B. *Jesus saw people enslaved by their own passions growing out of their own fallen nature.*
C. *Jesus saw people enslaved by sin and Satan.*
D. *Christ came to set people free from that which enslaves the soul and destroys the heart and life.*

Paul speaks concerning Christ, "who gave himself for our sins to deliver us from the present evil age, according to the will of our God and Father" (Gal. 1:4 RSV). Paul wrote to the Colossians about the great redemption that we have in Jesus Christ, and he declared that Christ "has delivered us from the dominion of darkness and transferred us to the kingdom of his beloved Son, in whom we have redemption, the forgiveness of sins" (Col. 1:13 RSV).

1. Christ is able to deliver us from the guilt of sin.
2. Christ is able to deliver us and to set us free from the power of sin over our lives.
3. Christ is able to set us free from the fear of death.
4. Christ is able to set us free from the power that Satan would exercise over us.

III. True freedom comes only through the Son.

"For freedom Christ has set us free; stand fast therefore, and do not submit again to a yoke of slavery" (Gal. 5:1 RSV).

A. *Christ grants to us a freedom from the condemnation that sin brings because he has purchased us with his own precious blood (1 Peter 1:18–19).*
B. *Christ sets us free with a liberty that is instantaneously received.*
C. *Christ grants us a freedom that lasts forever.*
D. *The freedom that comes from Christ is received as a free gift to those who come to him in the faith that surrenders (Rom. 6:23).*

Conclusion

Are you free? If not, then make peace with God through faith in Jesus Christ. If you have received Jesus Christ, then enter fully into the freedom that God offers to you.

1. You are free to call God your Father.
2. You are free to claim the protection of your heavenly Father's house.
3. You are free to bring your needs to the throne of grace in prayer.
4. You are free to be genuine workers in his church.
5. You are free to journey toward Christlike character.
6. You are free to live a victorious Christian life.

"For freedom Christ has set us free."

SUNDAY MORNING, MARCH 25

Title: Choosing with Carelessness

Text: "But the chief priests and elders persuaded the multitude that they should ask Barabbas, and destroy Jesus. The governor answered and said unto them, Whether of the twain will ye that I release unto you? They said, Barabbas. Pilate saith unto them, What shall I do then with Jesus which is called Christ? They all say unto him, Let him be crucified. And the governor said, Why, what evil hath he done? But they cried out the more, saying, Let him be crucified" **(Matt. 27:20–23)**.

Scripture Reading: Matthew 27:15–26

Hymns: "God of Grace and God of Glory," Fosdick
         "O Master, Let Me Walk with Thee," Gladden
         "Take My Life and Let It Be," Havergal

Offertory Prayer: Our Father, it is not that we have a lack of choices. The choices of life confront us and confuse us day after day. It almost seems as though we have more choices to make than we have the strength and wisdom to make them. And the choices, our Father, are not always between the good and the bad. Sometimes the choices are between the good and the best. Give to us the wisdom to make the right choices. Give to us the perspective to see things in the light of eternity. Give us the courage to stand for you even when it may not seem the popular thing to do. And, Father, help us to make the right choices concerning our Christian stewardship. We acknowledge that you have given us the ability and opportunity to earn money. We are aware that all the things that we have are gifts from you. Help us, then, to give to you in proportion to your blessings to us. We give this gift and we give our lives into your hands. Accept us we pray. Forgive us our sins we ask. And bless us with your presence both now and forevermore. In Jesus's name we pray. Amen.

Introduction

Having worked as a salesman from time to time in my life, I have always been intrigued by the way people make decisions. Some people make decisions carefully. They compare, contrast, examine, price, and weigh their decisions. Other people make decisions quickly with little thought or determination. It would seem that they were choosing with carelessness.

In John Patrick's play *The Teahouse of the August Moon*, there is an interesting exchange between the interpreter Sakini and Captain Fisby. The scene takes place during the occupation of Okinawa. Sakini says, "Explain what is democracy." And Fisby replies, "Well, it's a system of determination. It's . . . the right to make the wrong choice" (in Charles L. Wallis, ed. *Speaker's Resources from Contemporary Literature* [New York: Harper and Row, 1965], 62).

And that is exactly what the people did on that fateful day when they were offered the choice between Jesus and Barabbas. They made the wrong choice. They chose Barabbas for freedom and Jesus for death. They were choosing with carelessness.

Pilate was on the spot. He knew that there were no valid legal grounds for the execution of Jesus. He was aware that this was basically a religious question that had taken on political overtones for the purpose of accomplishing the religious leaders' will. So Pilate thought of a way to get off the hook. As an act of mercy in keeping with the Passover season, they always released a prisoner. Pilate had two possibilities at hand: Jesus, whom he insisted on calling the king of the Jews, and Barabbas, who was a notorious robber and insurrectionist. Probably thinking that they would choose Jesus, he offered the people their choice.

Pilate misjudged on two counts: (1) the mob may have been Barabbas's supporters, and (2) the religious authorities were deeply dedicated to the destruction of Jesus. And so the people chose Barabbas to be released.

The people chose with carelessness. And many times we also choose with carelessness.

I. We choose with carelessness when we choose without making a comparison.

Pilate felt that he was giving the people a clear contrast. Look at the comparison: Barabbas was known to be a robber, an insurrectionist, a notorious criminal. Jesus was known to be a man of compassionate kindness and noble character.

William Barclay has pointed out that when the people chose Barabbas, they chose lawlessness instead of law, war instead of peace, and hatred and violence instead of love.

Notice another comparison. Barabbas is a surname. The name usually given to him is Jesus Barabbas. Jesus (the Hebrew form was Joshua) was a common name. Barabbas means "son of the father." Who were they to choose? Jesus Barabbas, the son of the father, or Jesus Christ, the Son of *the* Father?

II. We choose with carelessness when we choose without consulting our conscience.

There is a tragic, yet revealing, statement in Mark's account: "So Pilate, wishing to satisfy the crowd, released for them Barabbas" (Mark 15:15 RSV). Pilate's choice was because of expediency and pressure, not because his conscience told him this was the right thing to do.

And the same thing was true with the crowd. This was a conscienceless choice they made. They allowed themselves to be manipulated by the religious authorities and pressured by mob violence until they reacted without conscience.

How often do you make a decision on the same basis?

You choose between two courses of actions, and you choose the expedient. You choose between two persons, and you choose the one who pressures most. You choose between two places of service, and you choose the easiest.

The knights of an ancient order were rewarded for valor by a mystical glow on their shields at the close of a victorious battle. Independent and compassionate, they never became puppets of religious or political systems. Before gathering at evening around the table or banquet hall, the knights looked with unrestrained curiosity from one shield to another until they found one that glowed. According to legend, the owner of this shield had fought more valiantly than others.

Once at early dawn the leader assigned the boldest warrior to sentry duty at the outside entrance of the moat. The knight chafed at this assignment while his comrades dashed forth to heroic battle. During the day an impostor disguised as a sickly hermit approached him with a plea to come help a wayfarer who had fallen into a marsh. His noble instincts tempted sorely, the knight almost abandoned sentry duty to go help the unfortunate. In spite of the taunting of the hermit, he would not neglect his duty and abandon his post, leaving the gate unguarded. That evening at the banquet table they dressed their wounds and looked at the stacked shields. They were amazed when they saw that the shield of the sentry had the brightest glow. Amazement turned to understanding, however, when they heard of the inner battle he fought.

III. We choose with carelessness when we choose without considering the consequences.

The crowd glibly stated that they would take the consequences of their act in choosing with carelessness. One of the consequences was the guilt of having chosen wrong. They took that consequence even as they glibly said they would.

But there is more to the blood of Jesus than their off-the-cuff statement that Jesus's blood should be upon them. It is indeed by the blood of Jesus that we have forgiveness of sin. When the blood of Jesus is on us, we are forgiven of our sin and have a new life.

It has been stated that of all the people in Jerusalem, Barabbas could most definitely say that Jesus died for him. And of all the theories of the atonement, the best explanation is still the simple statement that Jesus died for my sins. He died for Barabbas's sins. And he died for your sins.

Conclusion

Indeed, we have the freedom of making the wrong choice. Those people did that day in Jerusalem when they carelessly chose Barabbas instead of Jesus. Don't you do the same thing today.

SUNDAY EVENING, MARCH 25

Title: God's Irresistible Love

Text: "For the children of Israel shall abide many days without a king, and without a prince, and without sacrifice, and without an image, and without an ephod, and without teraphim: Afterward shall the children of Israel return, and seek the LORD their God, and David their king; and shall fear the LORD and his goodness in the latter days" **(Hos. 3:4–5)**.

Scripture Reading: Hosea 3

Introduction

In the first two chapters of Hosea's prophecy, we see the accounts of a broken home (a broken relationship between a man and his wife) and of a broken nation (a broken relationship between a people and their God). Yet there is something unique about this broken home. First, the tragedy is heightened in that the one sinned against is a prophet of God charged with the responsibility of preaching to a nation. Second, the Lord God knew what was going to happen in Hosea's home even before he commanded his prophet to marry this woman, Gomer. In his sovereign purpose, God used this heartbreaking tragedy to add a dimension of compassion and love to Hosea's life and ministry that he could never have had otherwise. It enabled Hosea to catch a fleeting glimpse of the unfathomable suffering God experiences when his people sin against him.

In the five verses comprising Hosea 3, the love of God is described and demonstrated in four ways. We might compare God's love here with a finely cut diamond having four distinct facets, each of which flashes its fire in a different color or hue.

I. God's seeking love.

Verse 1 reflects the heart of Hosea's entire message: God's love toward those who are not worthy of it. God was showing Hosea and commanding him to demonstrate a revolutionary concept of the love of God. Throughout the Old Testament era, God's people had placed a confining limitation on God's love. They believed that God's mercy and love were limited to those who feared him and remembered his commandments; or, in other words, God's mercy was for those who merited it.

When Jesus came, he redefined love. Paul expressed it like this: "For scarcely for a righteous man will one die: yet peradventure for a good man some would even dare to die. But God commendeth his love toward us, in that, while we were yet sinners, Christ died for us" (Rom. 5:7–8). Thus, through Hosea's experience with his unfaithful wife, Gomer, God was revealing the love of his "new covenant," a love that seeks all people, regardless of their moral, social, or spiritual condition.

There is no way Hosea could have obeyed God's command to "go again, love the same woman, Gomer . . . [now] an adulteress" with human love. By every human standard, Gomer had forfeited her right to any degree of acceptance by her fellow humans. Yet in this command God was giving Hosea the first and basic lesson of New Testament evangelism: God's love goes out to humanity not because humanity is lovely but because God is love. Thus, when we say that God loves humanity, we are not saying anything about humanity and their moral qualifications, but we are saying volumes about God and his seeking love. This, then, is the kind of love with which Hosea went out seeking Gomer, and it is the kind of love with which God seeks sinful people.

II. God's redeeming love.

As we gently turn the diamond of God's love, another facet catches fire: "So I bought her to me for fifteen pieces of silver, and for an homer of barley, and an half homer of barley" (3:2). Here is the redeeming love of God.

Gomer had become a slave, a concubine. She had voluntarily sold herself. So Hosea bought her back at the price of a slave. This is the love that seeks not its own, that takes no account of evil, that "bears all things, believes all things, hopes all things"—it is redeeming love. When Hosea bought Gomer back from the slave market—a woman who had defiled herself in prostitution—he saw her in a way he had never seen her before, through the eyes of God, and he loved her with the heart of God. That, again, is New Testament evangelism!

What kind of man was Hosea? He was gentle, sensitive, a man of unquestioned integrity, whose personal life was above reproach. This makes his redemptive act, his willingness to take Gomer to himself again, all the more meaningful. Had Hosea been of questionable character himself—had he compromised with sin in his own life—he might have lightly brushed aside Gomer's sin. Instead, Hosea suffered agony because of her sin.

This is a part of our redemption that we often do not see. This is why Jesus, in the garden of Gethsemane, sweat "as it were great drops of blood" (Luke 22:44). He was experiencing the agony, the suffering involved in taking to himself our sins. Hosea was not Jesus; he was not perfect and sinless, nor did he take on himself the sins of Gomer, as Jesus took on our sins. Yet there was within his situation the human counterpart of the relationship between Jesus Christ and sinful humanity.

III. God's disciplining love.

The third facet is found in verse 3, which describes a love that disciplines: "And I said to her, You shall be [betrothed] to Me for many days; you shall not play the harlot and you shall not belong to another man. So will I also be to you [until you have proved your loyalty to Me and our marital relations may be resumed]" (AMP).

Gomer was the prodigal wife who had been bought out of the slave market. The beautiful and pure flower of chastity and godly womanhood had been torn from its stem and trodden in the dirt. Now she is told that she must remain for a time in seclusion. It will be a period of discipline; she is not to enter her new relationship with Hosea in a flippant way. She needs time for reflection, for a realization of where she had been, where she was at the moment, and where she must go henceforth.

Jesus told of a man who, in the heat of enthusiasm and excitement, began to build a tower. But he had to abandon the project before it was finished because he had not counted the cost (Luke 14:30). There are doubtless many Christians whose spiritual growth and development have been aborted because there was no discipline following conversion. They needed to have been taught, nurtured, and instructed. Hosea instituted this program of discipline for Gomer, just as the church should consider itself the spiritual custodian of new believers who come into its midst. This is the discipline of love, which is more than mere sentimentality and emotion.

IV. God's triumphant love.

The fourth facet of our diamond flashes its fire: "Afterward shall the children of Israel return, and seek the Lord their God, inquiring of and requiring Him, and [from the line of] David, their King [of Kings]; and they shall come in [anxious] fear to the Lord and to His goodness and His good things in the latter days" (3:5 AMP).

Here is that which is always typical of our God: the last word is love, not wrath; grace, not judgment; return, not exile. To fear God is not to be afraid of him as one would fear a tyrant. That kind of fear "hath torment." Rather it is to stand in awe of him, to bow reverently before his majesty and holiness. For God's goodness places a person under much heavier obligation than evil. If the father of the prodigal son had been hard or cruel, then the far country would not have been nearly as tormenting to the wayward son. But to sin against love, to return evil for good, is a heavy burden for people to bear.

Conclusion

What should be our response to this irresistible love of God? We must remember that a good God is far more to be feared—reverenced, held in awe—than an evil God. For a "good" God requires goodness of his people, a goodness that is found in his righteousness, which is imputed to them "by grace, through faith . . . not of works, lest any man should boast" (Eph. 2:8–9).

WEDNESDAY EVENING, MARCH 28

Title: What Reward Will You Receive?

Text: "And, behold, I come quickly; and my reward is with me, to give every man according as his work shall be" **(Rev. 22:12)**.

Scripture Reading: Matthew 25:32–40

Introduction

From beginning to end, the Bible teaches that we will one day give an account of ourselves to our creator God (Rom. 14:12). In the words of our text, which come from the lips of our risen, ascended, and reigning Lord, there comes the promise of a sure reward to those who faithfully serve him. The reward of which he speaks is not the gift of eternal life. Eternal life is the gift of God through faith in Jesus Christ. There is no way by which we can earn or merit the privilege of spending eternity in the Father's heavenly home. This comes as a gift of his grace to those who receive Jesus Christ as Lord and Savior. The reward of which our Lord speaks is a reward for faithful service to those who have chosen to trust him and follow him in a life of helpfulness to others. This verse, which should dwell in our hearts always, has several great truths for our consideration.

I. These words affirm the fact of rewards.

Jesus is speaking dogmatically concerning the fact that at the end of the ages when history is consummated and when he returns, rewards will be bestowed on people. This great truth is taught in the Old Testament (Dan. 7:9–10) and is reemphasized by the apostle Paul (2 Cor. 5:10). Repeatedly the final book of Holy Scripture affirms that there is going to be a final day of reckoning for unbelievers and of rewarding for the saved (see, e.g., Rev. 20:11–15).

II. These words identify the giver of rewards.

"My reward is with me, to give every man according as his work shall be." Jesus identifies himself as the giver of the rewards on that final day when we stand before him. The purpose of the judgment is not to determine whether or not we are saved or lost. That is determined before we leave this life by the response we make to Jesus Christ whom God has appointed to be our Lord. The Scriptures tell us that God has commanded "all men everywhere to repent: because he hath appointed a day, in which he will judge the world in righteousness by that man whom he hath ordained; whereof he hath given assurance unto all men, in that he hath raised him from the dead" (Acts 17:30–31).

The Lord who gave his all for us on the cross will distribute the rewards at the end of the age with a nail-scarred hand. Since Jesus is to be the bestower of these rewards, it seems that we should seek at all times and under all circumstances to do those things that would be pleasing to him. Instead of seeking the applause of people, we should concentrate on receiving the applause of our Lord in the here and now as well as in the hereafter.

III. These words clarify the measure of the rewards.

"To give every man according as his work shall be." The gift of eternal life is a free and equal gift given to all who come to Jesus Christ in faith. The rewards at the end of the age will be individualized in that they will be given to each one on the basis of loyalty, faithfulness, and service. Not everyone will receive the same reward. Everyone who is in heaven will have received the gift of eternal life on an equal basis—that is, on the basis of his or her faith in Jesus Christ.

What kind of rewards do you hope to have when you stand before your Savior? Let us consider some possibilities.

A. *Each of us can have the record of being a giver (Matt. 10:41).* Jesus affirmed that even the giving of a cup of cold water would bring its reward from his loving hand. Nothing that we do is hidden from his eyes. The cup of cold water is something that everyone needs. It is symbolic of something that everyone can do on behalf of others, something to meet a deep basic need in the life of another and to bring refreshment and joy and strength to them. There are many cups of cold water that we can distribute. If we do so, we will be rewarded.

B. *We can strive to have a record of many good and profitable words (Matt. 12:36).* Our Lord warns us concerning the misuse of our tongue. He affirms that the use of our tongue will have something to do with the rewards that we receive on the final day. Proper use of the tongue will bring favorable rewards, while destructive use of the tongue could cause us to miss and even to lose some of the rewards that we might have had. In James's epistle we find the classic statement concerning use of the tongue (1:27; 3:1–13).

An unknown author has described the power of words:

> A careless word may kindle strife,
> A cruel word may wreck a life;
> A bitter word may hate instill,
> A brutal word may smite and kill;
> A gracious word may smooth the way,
> A joyous word may light the day;
> A timely word may lessen stress,
> A loving word may heal and bless.

Let us always recognize that the use of our tongue points either to profit or to our loss on the Judgment Day.

C. *We can strive to have a record of ministry to the unfortunate (Matt. 25:32–46).* Let it be understood that the judgment of which our Lord speaks here is not one determining whether one is saved or lost. Notice in verse 34 that the children of the king are to inherit the kingdom rather than receive it as a reward. Their conduct reveals their relationship to the king because the king is concerned about the suffering and the unfortunate. They have given themselves in ministries of mercy to these. They have ministered to the king without even being aware of it as they ministered to the unfortunate.

D. *We can strive for a record of faithfulness in service (Matt. 25:21–23).*
Not all of us can be brilliant. Not all of us can be prominent. Not all of us can achieve greatness in the eyes of the world. But each of us can be faithful, loyal, dependable, and trustworthy. Our rewards will be determined by the degree of faithfulness we have demonstrated to the opportunities that were given to us.

Conclusion

What will the heavenly record say? It will be determined by the manner in which we live and serve day by day. While we have time and opportunity, let us strive to serve our Lord in such a manner that he will be able to bestow rewards on us on the final day.

Suggested Preaching Program for the Month of

APRIL

■ **Sunday Mornings**

Celebrate Easter with a sermon on Christ's resurrection on the first Sunday of the month. Then, until the Sunday before Mother's Day, use the theme "More Than Conquerors."

■ **Sunday Evenings**

The theme for this month's messages is "The Way of Faith." It is based on the lives and experiences of the great patriarchs in the book of Genesis.

■ **Wednesday Evenings**

Continue with the theme "The Words of Jesus Christ."

Sunday Morning, April 1

Title: Witnessing the Resurrection

Text: "And as they went to tell his disciples, behold, Jesus met them, saying, All hail. And they came and held him by the feet, and worshipped him. Then said Jesus unto them, Be not afraid: go tell my brethren that they go into Galilee, and there shall they see me" **(Matt. 28:9–10)**.

Scripture Reading: Matthew 28:1–10

Hymns: "Christ the Lord Is Risen Today," Wesley
"Low in the Grave He Lay," Lowry
"One Day," Chapman

Offertory Prayer: Our Father, on this resurrection day we are so grateful to you for the risen Lord. We recognize that this means that your power has triumphed over the power of sin and the grave. We realize that this means we serve a living Lord. Help us, Father, to live our lives in the power of Christ's resurrection. As you have defeated even the final foe of death, make us ever aware that you can defeat the common foes that we face day by day. And on this day we gratefully return to you a portion of ourselves, for on this day, as perhaps on no other, we have a renewed awareness of our debt to you. We know that we can never repay that debt simply by the giving of our money. But we know also that the giving of our money is an indication of the strength of our commitment to you. As you have given yourself for us in the death of Christ and as you have shown your commitment to us and our salvation through his resurrection from the dead, help us to give of ourselves and to commit our lives to you in this gift. Please forgive us our sins and accept our gifts as you accept us. In Jesus's name we pray. Amen.

Introduction

William Faulkner's novel *The Sound and the Fury* tells the story of how the Compson family suffered heavily and how each family member reacted to the suffering. Mr. Compson put himself beyond the reach of suffering by means of a cynical philosophy and a decanter of whiskey. Mrs. Compson evaded her responsibilities through a nauseating self-pity and a convenient hypochondria. Quenton Compson committed suicide; his brother Jason put on the armor of callousness; sister Candace reacted irresponsibly; and Benjy, being an idiot, did not react at all.

Only one character in the novel—Dilsy, the black "mammy"—could stand up to the sound and the fury of life with tenderness and courage. She was to the Compson family everything their mother should have been, and her presence alone prevented them from sinking into an even more complete state of collapse. There could be no more apt description of the Dilsys of the world than that which Faulkner gives them: "They endured."

And Faulkner gives us a glimpse into the secret of their endurance. Dilsy's strength came from a powerful sermon of a black preacher from St. Louis on Easter Day 1928. Here was the promise that gave her hope and sustained the spirit in her fatigued and debilitated body: "I sees de resurrection en de light; sees de meek Jesus sayin, Dey kilt me dat ye shall live again; I died dat dem what sees en believes shall never die. Breddren, O breddren! I sees de doom crack en hears de golden horns shoutin down de glory, en de arisen dead what got de blood en de ricklickshun of de Lamb." Beyond the darkness of Good Friday, Dilsy was able to see the light of Easter.

The secret of Christian stability is the Resurrection. Actually, the symbol of Christianity is more an empty tomb than a cross. The empty tomb gives meaning to the cross. Were it not for the empty tomb, the cross would have been a tragedy.

It was only right that the witnesses of Jesus's crucifixion and burial were also witnesses of his resurrection. Mary Magdalene and the other Mary were the first to receive news of the risen Lord and to encounter him. They had been at the cross; they had been there when he was laid in the tomb; and now they received love's reward—they were the first to know the joy of the resurrection.

We have been looking at the crowd at the cross these last few weeks. Part of the crowd at the cross was also at the empty tomb. They were witnesses of the Resurrection. And so do we witness resurrection, the return to life, the defeat of death.

I. Witnessing the Resurrection affirms the reality of resurrection.

Our Christian faith is built on the reality of the Resurrection. It does not, alone, prove the deity of Christ, but it is consistent with it. Because Jesus is Lord, we can believe that he is the resurrected Lord.

Was the Resurrection real? Many scholars say that it is the best-attested fact in history. Yet skeptics try to explain away the Resurrection by saying that the women went to the wrong tomb; or that Jesus fainted and later revived; or that thieves stole his body, the disciples removed his body, or the Roman or Jewish authorities took his body into their own custody.

But the tomb is empty! Jesus was resurrected and set loose in the world. In John Masefield's drama The *Trial of Jesus*, there is a passage in which Longinus, the Roman centurion in command of the soldiers at the cross, comes back to Pilate to hand in his report on the day's work. The report is given. Then Procula, Pilate's wife, beckons to the centurion and begs him to tell her how the prisoner died. When the story has been told, she suddenly asks, "Do you think he is dead?" "No, lady," Longinus answers, "I don't. "Then where is he?" she asks. "Let loose in the world, lady, where neither Roman nor Jew can stop his truth," is his answer.

II. Witnessing the Resurrection gives witness to the Resurrection.

Knowing that the Resurrection is real, what are we to do? Tell others. Notice that the angels told the women to "go quickly, and tell" (28:7). The first declaration of the Resurrection was a call to action. "Go, quickly, tell." This is the kind of news that you do not keep to yourself. Sit with a family in the waiting room of a hospital with a desperately sick child. When the physician comes to say that the crisis has passed and the child will live, you do not just quietly continue to sit there. You run down the hall to find the mother; you go to the coffee shop to find the uncles and aunts; you rush to the telephone to call the grandparents. There is some news that you do not keep to yourself. The Resurrection is that kind of news—news that gives courage: "Fear not"; news that gives assurance: "He is not here"; news that gives joy: "with great joy." This is news that gives life!

III. Witnessing the Resurrection reminds us of the greatest witness: changed lives.

Carefully note the change in the men who followed Jesus at the close of the Gospels and the opening of the book of Acts. Notice particularly Peter and James.

Peter had denied the Lord three times. He had cursed and sworn as though he had never known the restraining influence of Jesus. He had gone out and wept bitterly. And he had joined the other disciples behind closed doors after Jesus died. But then turn over about two pages in your Bible, and you will see that he is standing outside that same upper room of the Last Supper preaching Christ boldly. He defied the same Sanhedrin that had condemned Jesus to death. And he slept in his jail cell the night before he was to be executed. What changed Peter? The power of the resurrected Christ.

James later assumed a position of leadership in the Jerusalem church. But in Jesus's lifetime he did not believe in him. After the Resurrection this earthly brother of the Lord was transformed from a doubter into a believer just as Simon Peter was turned from fear to courage. Lives are changed by the resurrected Lord. This is the greatest assurance of the Resurrection in our lives. We have met the resurrected Christ, and he has changed us.

Then he charges us. He gives us a job to do and the power to do it.

Conclusion

We are witnesses of the resurrection as we experience his power and presence in our lives.

SUNDAY EVENING, APRIL 1

Title: The Way of Faith

Text: "By faith Abraham, when he was called to go out into a place which he should after receive for an inheritance, obeyed; and he went out, not knowing whither he went. By faith he sojourned in the land of promise" **(Heb. 11:8–9).**

Scripture Reading: Genesis 12:1–10

Introduction

"Without faith it is impossible to please God" is a declaration asserting the importance of faith. Genuine salvation is a result of personal faith (Eph. 2:8–9). Certainly that which Jesus commands is worthy and essential. One of his finest commendations is to the woman of Phoenicia, "O woman, great is thy faith" (Matt. 15:28).

From Abel (Heb. 11:4) to the prophets (Heb. 11:32), the triumph of victory resulting in heroic achievement was the principle of a dynamic faith. "This is the victory that overcometh the world, even our faith" (1 John 5:4). Since faith is so essential, let us discover the way of faith in the life and experience of Abraham.

I. Faith begins with the divine initiative (Gen. 12:1–3).

Human nature is not such that people desire or seek a personal and holy God. In contrast, it is the nature of a loving God to seek sinful people. In the verses before us it is noteworthy that God takes the initiative with Abraham and issues a *call*, a *command*, and a *promise.*

A. *The call: "Now the LORD had said" (Gen. 12:1).* The first question of the Bible, "Where art thou?" is more of a call than a question. Adam is hiding, evading, guilty, but God is on a quest of love. The call of God is notable because it is personal, as is seen in Hebrews 11:8: "Abraham, when he was called." The call of God is worthy because it is holy (2 Tim. 1:9; 1 Peter 1:15). The call of God is high because it is heavenly (Heb. 3:1). The call of God is apart from human merit (1 Peter 5:10). The call of God is to a plan and purpose: "Whom he called, them he also justified: and whom he justified, them he also glorified" (Rom. 8:30).

B. *The command: "Get thee out . . ." (Gen. 12:1)*. Following the *call* is the *command* to get out from. The command is *from* country, kindred, and the father's house, but it is *to* a land to be shown to Abraham. The command is to separate from the undesirable in order to embrace that which is far better.

   1. There is a command to forsake the familiar: "thy country." The familiar can become commonplace. Faith grows better in the midst of uncertainty rather than in the certain. We are challenged more by that which we lack than by that which we possess.

   2. There is a command to forsake that which is dearest: "thy kindred" (cf. Luke 14:33). Just as that which is nearest (familiar) may be a fetter, so may that which is dearest be a hindrance to faith. Our loved ones cannot impart faith by proxy. Faith is and must be personal. Thus, Abraham must discover God for himself. One's country cannot provide faith; neither can family bestow faith.

   3. There is a command to embrace that which God will show to Abraham: "a land that I will shew thee." There is no provision here to give the land to Abraham, only to show him the land. But at a subsequent experience (Gen. 15:7), God did promise to give the land to him.

      The way of faith is one step at a time. God will first reveal (show the land) and afterward bestow. The fundamental foundation for all religious experience is an accurate revelation of God. The way of faith will show us something and afterward give us something.

C. *There is a promise to bless: "I will bless thee" (Gen. 12:2)*. The blessing is both inclusive and universal. The promise is to include Abraham plus those who bless him and even all the families of the earth.

   1. The promise concerning Abraham. The way of faith begins with a call and command but issues in a blessing of God. The dual blessing of Abraham is that of his descendants becoming a great nation and of his name becoming great.

      One of the finest ways to perpetuate influence is through descendants. The true heirs of Abraham are those of faith. "For ye are all the children of God by faith in Christ Jesus. . . . And if ye be Christ's, then are ye Abraham's seed, and heirs according to the promise" (Gal. 3:26, 29; cf. Rom. 4:17–18).

   2. The promise concerning those who bless him: "I will bless them that bless thee" (Gen. 12:3). Those who bless Abraham are those of faith, both Jew and Gentile (Gal. 3:14, 16, 28).

3. The promise concerning the world: "In thee shall all families of the earth be blessed" (Gen. 12:3).

II. The way of faith requires a personal response (Gen. 12:4–10).

Three responses of Abraham are indicted in verses 4 and 5. The first response was personal and a display of obedience. The second was communal and involved others. The third was a climactic realization, "into the land of Canaan they came."

A. *The response of personal obedience: "So Abram departed, as the LORD had spoken."* A true evidence and an initial response to faith is personal obedience. It is better to obey than to sacrifice.

B. *The response of personal involvement with others.* Faith is personal, but the way of faith requires that we are to become involved with persons and possessions. We may identify faith by obedience, but we demonstrate it by relationships to persons and possessions (see James 2:14–17). Abram took Sarai, his wife, and Lot, his nephew, with him. Likewise, he took his servants and his possessions.

C. *The response of the joy of realization.* And into the land of Canaan they came. This realization of being in the place where God had called Abraham to must have brought a sense of real joy and satisfaction. A personal faith in the Lord plus personal involvement with others leads to a personal realization that is incomparable.

III. The way of faith leads in paths of difficulties (cf. James 1:12 and 1 Peter 1:7).

There is a tendency to think that the way of faith is all sweet and not bitter, but such is not true. On the flush of joy and realization of having obeyed God, there are three trying experiences. Canaanites were in the land, there was a famine in the land, and there was family strife in the land.

A. *The way of faith leads us into conflict with the ways of the world.* The Canaanite is hostile to the Israelite.

B. *The way of faith may lead us to the area of extreme want.* "There was a famine in the land." Faith is never fully satisfied.

C. *The way of faith may lead to family strife (Gen. 13:6–7).*

IV. The way of faith may mature in peculiar ways and places (Gen. 12:7–9).

Two things occupy our thoughts—"the altar" and "the tent."

A. *Abraham built an altar (v. 7).* Faith needs to grow to maturation (see 2 Thess. 1:3). One of the fine places for faith to grow is at the altar. The altar is a peculiar place:
   1. It is the place of sacrifice (cf. Rom. 12:1).
   2. It is the place of worship.

3. It is the place of fellowship. God meets with us in the moment of sacrifice (self-giving) and in the moment of worship. Note in verse 7 that the Lord appeared to Abraham.

B. *Abraham pitched his tent (Gen. 12:7).* The tent (tabernacle) is temporary. Its value is in what it anticipates more than what it accomplishes. The incarnation of Jesus was a "tenting" among men (John 1:14). Abraham is ever on the move. In verse 6 he is passing "through the land"; in verse 8 he is moving from there; in verse 9 he is journeying, going on toward the south. Why? He is in anticipation of that which is eternal (see Heb. 11:10). Faith grows as we anticipate, desire, and look to the eternal.

Conclusion

The way of faith is the way to begin, continue, and finish the Christian life. The examples of Hebrews 11 are proof of the victory of faith. Those who need Christ need to begin the life of faith today. Others of us need to grow in faith. May it be so.

WEDNESDAY EVENING, APRIL 4

Title: The Great Commission
Text: "Go therefore and make disciples of all nations" **(Matt. 28:19 RSV).**
Scripture Reading: Matthew 28:16–20

Introduction

Our text is Jesus's command to his disciples and to his church to make disciples of all people of all nations. The emphasis in this command is not on going; the emphasis is on making disciples. The only imperative in these words is "make disciples." The word translated "go" is actually a participle with the force of an imperative. It means that in our going about from place to place, we are to concern ourselves with making disciples.

I. Our Lord asserts his authority (Matt. 28:18).

The word translated "authority" means "the power to command, the power to issue orders or requisitions, the authority to take charge." On the basis of his unique person, and because of his sacrificial death, victorious resurrection, and ascension to the right hand of God, our Lord asserts his authority.

Today's disciples need to recognize and respond to the lordship of Jesus Christ. He is not only our Savior; he is also our owner. To him has been given the right to lay claims on all we are and have. He should be the great authoritarian figure in our lives. As we emphasize Christ's authority, we need to remember his love and devotion, which he demonstrated by dying on the cross for us sinners.

II. Our Lord reveals his continuing redemptive program (Matt. 28:19).

Our God has been a missionary God from the beginning of human history. He called Abraham to go out on a missionary trip. He called the people of Israel out of Egypt that they might be the instrument for his redemptive purpose.

A close study of the Psalms and the prophetic books of the Old Testament will indicate that God was always seeking to communicate with his people the broadness, the depth, and the range of his love for all people.

The book of Jonah is a missionary book in which God seeks to reveal to the prophet and the people the extent of his concern for an unbelieving world. The book of Jonah is a stinging rebuke to the narrow nationalism and spiritual isolationism of those who considered themselves to be the people of God during that day.

In many instances our Lord revealed his concern for those outside the nation of Israel. He gave the Water of Life to a despised Samaritan woman, and in the parable of the Good Samaritan, he highly commended the Samaritan who ministered to the man left for dead by robbers. He called attention to the fact that it was a Samaritan who expressed gratitude for his healing power. He heard the prayer of the Phoenician woman as she prayed for deliverance for her daughter. Our Lord was to pour out the Holy Spirit on the Day of Pentecost to prepare his disciples for a ministry to the whole world.

Many followers of the Lord have professionalized the words of this Great Commission and have applied it only to the clergy. To do this is to do violence to the Scripture and to rob Christ's followers of their heritage and their opportunity as servants of the Lord. Many others have internationalized the words of this Great Commission, applying it only to foreign missions. A closer reading will indicate that it is all-inclusive and that each of us is to evangelize our own area of the world.

III. Our Lord promises his personal presence (Matt. 28:20).

If we would obey the words of this Great Commission, we would enjoy the fulfillment of the promise of the Lord to bless with his presence those who give themselves to the task of witnessing. The abiding presence of Jesus Christ can bring great joy and comfort to the fearful, can motivate us to do our best, and can make us bold when we would be fearful. He is with us always as we serve him and minister to others.

Conclusion

Let each of us individualize this Great Commission and respond to this mandate from our Master. Let us not miss the opportunity to be a coworker with him.

SUNDAY MORNING, APRIL 8

Title: You Can Conquer Disappointment

Text: "But he said unto her, Thou speakest as one of the foolish women speakest. What! shall we receive good at the hand God, and shall we not receive evil? In all this did not Job sin with his lips" **(Job 2:10)**.

Scripture Reading: Job 2:9–10

Hymns: "Tell It to Jesus," Rankin
"I Must Tell Jesus," Hoffman
"Precious Lord, Take My Hand," Dorsey

Offertory Prayer: Heavenly Father, when we give our tithes and offerings to you this day, we acknowledge that we are merely stewards of your possessions. We pray that you will bless these gifts for your own glory. May some souls come to know you as their personal Savior because we cared enough to give. Amen.

Introduction

How should you react when disappointment comes crashing into your life? We find the answer in Job's experience. One of the most profound statements in all the Bible was made by Job when he asked, "Shall we accept good from God, and not trouble?" (Job 2:10 NIV).

Job, you are right! It is not fair to take the good of life for granted and then complain about the bad. This statement is Job's reply to his wife's suggestion about how he should respond to his troubles. Job was a good man and did not deserve what was happening to him. If anyone knew that, it was his wife. This was more than she could take. So she suggested that Job "curse God, and die" (2:9).

Job knew that all sunshine and no rain makes a desert and that we cannot have mountaintops without valleys. Job had accepted the good in life with a grateful spirit. Now he would try to endure the bad in life with a gracious spirit. He would take his losses with quietness and courage. He would not grow bitter. In his response, Job teaches us that we can conquer disappointment.

We can choose to be like clay and respond to the heat of life by letting it harden us and make us bitter, or we can choose to be like wax by letting the heat of life melt us and shape us into new patterns.

I. The options before us.

A. *The clay response.* "Then said his wife unto him, Dost thou still retain thine integrity? curse God, and die" (Job 2:9). We have all seen people make the clay response. They allow some harsh misfortune turn them to bitterness. I have seen firsthand how the clay response can corrode a human spirit.

As a young pastor, I was greatly troubled by the response of a church member who was diagnosed as having incurable cancer. After a lengthy hospital visit, I asked if I might pray for her. She said, "You can pray, but it won't do any good." Cancer was destroying not only her body but also her faith. She was choosing to make the clay response.

If we choose, we too can make the clay response, winding up as bitter and hard as Job's wife.

B. *The wax response.* I have also met people of Job's heroic spirit who simply refuse to be overcome by things that happen to them. Listen as Job speaks: "For I know that my redeemer liveth, and that he shall stand at the latter day upon the earth: and though after my skin worms destroy this body, yet in my flesh I shall see God" (Job 19:25–26). In today's idiom we would say, "When life hands them a lemon, they make lemonade." Scripture and secular history are filled with examples of such positive responses to negative experiences.

II. Examples that challenge us.

David was a lemonade maker. He wrote, "I will bless the LORD at all times" (Ps. 34:1). He had every reason to complain and become bitter. King Saul sought to kill him, his son Amnon committed adultery with his sister, his son Absalom betrayed him, and his son Adonijah tried to grab the throne just before David died.

Jesus was another lemonade maker. He was no stranger to hardship and disappointment. Again and again what he hoped for and worked hard to achieve was shattered in failure. But he never allowed these experiences to embitter him or drive him to despair. When he finally died, it was not with a whimper on his lips, but with a victorious shout.

Paul's prison epistles also challenge us. Paul must have been frustrated by his frequent imprisonments. How easy it would have been for him to become bitter and hardened. But never once did he mention the poor food, the deplorable living conditions, or the inhumane treatment of the guards. Rather, he talked about how God was using his experiences to inspire others and advance the gospel.

Some Christians have learned not to bemoan their troubles or to waste them. Rather, they have learned to turn every stumbling block into a stepping-stone. We can do the same thing if we choose to.

III. The secret that frees us.

The question could be asked, "How were all these people able to respond so creatively to hardships and disappointments? What is the secret of this resilience that enables some people to pick up the pieces and start anew, rather than going to pieces under the impact of some tragedy?"

The secret lies in how we visualize God's relation to our lives. Job's wife had a faulty view of God. She probably had been spoiled by the good life and had come to feel that God owed her a trouble-free existence. When this ended, she felt that God was acting unjustly. But Job had a different view of God. Listen as he speaks: "I have heard of thee by the hearing of the ear: but now mine eye seeth thee" (Job 42:5).

Job saw God as he is and not as one might want him to be. God does not promise us a life of ease. He does not owe us anything. He is not to blame for every trial that comes our way. The Scriptures teach us that because of God's presence, whatever happens to us will not be too much for us.

Someone rightly said that the essence of despair is relegating God to the past. We need to believe that God is still at work in the world and in our lives today. His sovereign purpose will ultimately be fulfilled.

Not everything that happens to us originates solely with God. Some events come straight from God. Others come straight from Satan or result from our own wrong decisions and are only permitted by God. God saves us through our difficulties and not from our difficulties.

Scriptures teach us that because of God's presence with us, whatever happens to us will not be too much for us. Some possibility of good will be present in these troubles. God can be counted on for this. In the most practical way, this is how we can overcome problems rather than being overcome by them.

Conclusion

Even when you feel abandoned by God, you need to remember that the feeling and the fact are not the same thing. Therefore, if in times of difficulty you feel that your prayers are not getting above the ceiling, don't worry. God can come down below the ceiling. God is not deaf; he has not abandoned us; he is not limited. He is working silently and redemptively no matter what.

So, when life comes crashing in, don't give up in despair, don't become angry at God, don't feel sorry for yourself, don't syndicate your heartaches, don't let bitterness consume you. Fight these attitudes and temptations with all your heart.

When disappointments seem to engulf you, say with Job: "For I know that my redeemer liveth, and that he shall stand at the latter day upon the earth: and though after my skin worms destroy this body, yet in my flesh shall I see God" (Job 19:25–26).

SUNDAY EVENING, APRIL 8

Title: When Faith Is Tested

Text: "And there was a famine in the land: and Abram went down to Egypt to sojourn there" (**Gen. 12:10**). "And there was a strife between the herdsmen of Abram's cattle and the herdsmen of Lot's cattle" (**Gen. 13:7**). "Then Lot chose him all the plain of the Jordan" (**Gen. 13:11**).

Scripture Reading: Genesis 12:10; 13:1–13

Introduction

Difficulties and trying circumstances do not always indicate that one is out of God's will. In fact, God may and often does design these times for our benefit. "Blessed is the man that endureth temptation [testing]: for when he is tried, he shall receive the crown of life, which the Lord hath promised to them that love him" (James 1:12). "That the trial of your faith . . . might be found unto praise and honour and glory at the appearing of Jesus Christ" (1 Peter 1:7). The testing time is a time of refining resulting in maturity and growth. One is never the same after testing. Our response to the hour of trial determines whether we have victory or defeat.

Three situations are before us in the passages under consideration. They are a *famine* in the land; *strife* between Abram's servants and Lot's servants; and the *separation* of Lot from Abram.

I. The disaster test: "And there was a famine in the land . . . the famine was grievous" (Gen. 12:10).

A. *The two alternatives.*
1. Abram can remain in the land and trust God to see him through the disaster.
2. Abram can journey to Egypt where there is pasture and plenty. This is the course he chooses. Here we see ourselves in Abram. Rationality would dictate such a decision while faith would dictate staying in the land. Egypt actually means "the house of slaves," and throughout Bible history God's people have never fared well in Egypt.

B. *Abram in Egypt: "went down into Egypt to sojourn there" (Gen. 12:10).*
Two facts are most conspicuous.
1. Abram resorted to deception and half-truth. "Say . . . thou art my sister" (Gen. 12:13). Sarai, his wife, was very beautiful. The lusting eyes of the Egyptian prince would desire her. The compromise of Abram is an indication of the price the believer must pay for compromising with the world (Egypt).
2. Abram left the altar out of his life while in Egypt. There is no mention of the altar during the sojourn in Egypt. With the altar abandoned, sacrifice, worship, and recognition of Jehovah goes begging. Upon his return from Egypt, his first activity was the reestablishment of the altar (Gen. 13:3–4).

C. *Abram's recovery (Gen. 13:1–4).*
1. He forsook Egypt: "And Abram went out of Egypt" (Gen. 13:1). At a later time in history, Moses and the people of Israel did the same thing. By faith Moses forsook Egypt, "choosing rather to suffer affliction . . . than to enjoy the pleasures of sin for a season" (Heb. 11:25, 27). Egypt represents the world system and is never an ally or a friend to God and his people.

2. Abram came to Bethel: "And he went . . . to Bethel" (Gen. 13:3). Bethel is the house of God. This would refresh his memory and revive his spirit, because it was here that "he builded an altar . . . and called upon the name of the Lord" (Gen. 12:8).
3. Abram reestablished the altar: "The altar, which he had made there at the first" (Gen. 13:4). The altar speaks of worship, communion, and fellowship with God. Abram's experience in Egypt is a vivid testimony of what happens to faith when the altar is left out.

II. The prosperity test: "And Abram was very rich in cattle, in silver, and in gold. . . . Lot also . . . had flocks, and herds, and tents" (Gen. 13:2, 5).

Prosperity is the opposite of adversity and disaster. Even so, it is likely that prosperity is a more severe test and is more difficult to overcome. It is in this sphere that the sin of covetousness raises its ugly head.

A. *Their great substance led to strife (Gen. 13:7).* By the economic gauge, these two men "had it made," but, alas, prosperity, instead of leading to contentment, often leads to friction and feuding. Contentment does not come from gain, "but godliness with contentment is great gain" (1 Tim. 6:6). The taste of prosperity often leads to a craving for more. The question is whether we possess our possessions or our possessions possess us.
B. *Their strife led to separation: "Separate thyself, I pray thee, from me" (Gen. 13:9).*
   1. Abram displays personal magnitude: "Let there be no strife . . . between me and thee" (Gen. 13:8). He takes the initiative to quell the friction.
   2. Abram recognizes their personal relationship. "We be brethren" (Gen. 13:8). Kinship should beget love and cause each to esteem the other before himself.
   3. Abram presents a totally selfless solution: "If thou depart to the right hand, then I will go to the left" (Gen. 13:9).

Abram did not contend for his rights. His giving in reveals his true character and strength and is not a sign of cowardice or weakness. He is much like our Lord Jesus who gave himself up that he might redeem us. Indeed, at a subsequent date, Abram did redeem Lot from the capture of the kings of the East (Gen. 14:16).

III. The decision or choice test: "Lot chose him all the plain of the Jordan" (Gen. 13:11).

Disaster and prosperity are not the only circumstances under which faith is tested. There may be an even more subtle tactic. Disaster may strike only once or twice in an entire lifetime or it may never come. And most of us may never experience extreme prosperity. However, each of us—young, middle-aged, or old—must face almost daily the dilemma of making choices. Life is not so much a chance as a series of choices. Right choices lead to a blessed destiny and conclusion. Wrong choices lead to peril and danger. Lot made a poor choice and lived to see the folly of his decision. He lost everything he had.

A. *Lot's motivation.*
1. He saw gain in the plain: "And Lot lifted up his eyes, and beheld all the plain of Jordan, that it was well watered everywhere" (Gen. 13:10). He did not see the warfare that was going on there (Gen. 14:4). What benefit is it to leave a family feud only to become engulfed in a horrible military conflict? Lot "jumped from the frying pan into the fire."
2. He saw grass for his cattle but did not see the loss of his family. What loneliness invades the soul of a man with a barnful of cattle and no family in his house!

B. *Limited vision led to a tragic choice: "Then Lot chose him all the plain of Jordan" (Gen. 13:11).* His choice was a result of his shortsighted, selfish vision. His choice meant two things:
1. Separation from a godly influence, Abram. "And they separated themselves the one from the other" (Gen. 13:11).
2. Alliance with the wickedness of Sodom. "He dwelled in the cities of the plain . . . pitched his tent . . . but the men of Sodom were wicked . . . exceedingly" (Gen. 13:12–13).

   Wrong choices are not without consequences. Lot is soon a victim of war. His family and goods are taken and plundered (Gen. 14:14, 16). Last but not least he loses his cattle, his wealth, and most of his family in the overthrow of Sodom (Gen. 19:25–26).

C. *Abram in contrast to Lot (Gen. 13:14–18).*
1. The Lord directs Abram to lift up his eyes in every direction (Gen. 13:14). This is quite in contrast to Lot, who lifted up his own eyes (v. 10).
2. Abram in the hills is more blessed of God than Lot in the plain.
3. Abram builds an altar at Hebron, while Lot never builds an altar in Sodom.

Conclusion

Our response to testing is pivotal. A wrong response may weaken or damage the life of faith, while a proper response may result in new strength and added blessings. God has a purpose in trials, and a right response to them will result in clearer vision and understanding of the nature and power of God.

WEDNESDAY EVENING, APRIL 11

Title: Look on the Field

Text: "I tell you, lift up your eyes, and see how the fields are already white for harvest" **(John 4:35 RSV)**.

Scripture Reading: John 4:31–38

Introduction

Our text describes Jesus's compassion and ministry to a fallen woman who was living a life of despair. He crossed racial barriers, national barriers, and traditional barriers to bring God's blessings into her life. She was so affected by his ministry that she forgot what she had come to the well for and departed immediately into the city to tell others about the Messiah whom she had come to know. This experience in a Samaritan city among people despised by the Jews was intended by our Lord to prepare his disciples for a future ministry to those who normally were considered outside the circle of God's concern. Perhaps our Lord spoke the words of this text as he saw the Samaritans, who believed because of the woman's testimony, coming out to get acquainted with him for themselves.

It is interesting to note that Jesus describes these people in terms of wheat fields that are "already white for harvest." That means that they are in peril of perishing unless someone reaps them immediately. Oats and wheat are ready for harvest when they reach a golden yellow color. If not harvested at the proper time, the grain will turn white before it rots. Jesus saw the Samaritans as being in great peril, and he urged upon his apostles an attitude of compassionate concern.

In the words of our text, which we should memorize and quote to ourselves from time to time, we are reminded of the perils to which the unsaved are exposing themselves as long as they do not come to Jesus Christ as Savior.

I. The unbeliever faces the peril of being lost from God forever.

Jesus Christ came as the expression of God's love so that he might rescue people from being lost forever. "God so loved the world that he gave his only Son, that whoever believes in him should not perish but have eternal life" (John 3:16).

II. The unbeliever faces the peril of being a complete failure in the here and now as well as in the hereafter (Mark 8:38).

No one likes to lose in an athletic contest. No one likes to go into bankruptcy. No one likes to fail in the living of life. The greatest failure that people can experience is the failure to come to know God through faith in Jesus Christ as Lord and Savior. Though a person may become a millionaire and occupy a position of great prominence on this earth, that person is a tragic failure if he or she is lost for eternity.

III. The unbeliever faces the peril of missing heaven and spending eternity in a place prepared for the devil and his angels.

    A. *To miss heaven would be a loss of indescribable proportions.*

    B. *To be an intruder into a place prepared for the devil and his angels and that for eternity would be a fate too terrible to describe (Matt. 25:41).* It is not the will of the Father God that any person miss heaven and spend eternity in the abode of demons. It is God's will that all people turn from evil and come in faith for mercy, for forgiveness, and for the gift of eternal life.

Conclusion

The burden of these words of Jesus should impress upon us the privilege that we have of being laborers in the fields that are white unto harvest. As we help others to come to know Jesus Christ as Lord and Savior, we will receive spiritual wages from him who is the Lord of the harvest. We will be gathering fruit for the eternal life which is ours through the new birth that comes through faith in Jesus Christ (cf. John 4:36; 6:27). Our Lord is in need of more laborers (Matt. 9:37–38). Lift up your eyes and look on the fields. There is work for us to do for our Lord.

SUNDAY MORNING, APRIL 15

Title: You Can Conquer Doubt

Text: "Blessed be the God and Father of our Lord Jesus Christ, which according to his abundant mercy hath begotten us again unto a lively hope by the resurrection of Jesus Christ from the dead, to an inheritance incorruptible, and undefiled, and that fadeth not away, reserved in heaven for you, who are kept by the power of God through faith unto salvation ready to be revealed in the last time" **(1 Peter 1:3–5).**

Scripture Reading: 1 Peter 1:3–9

Hymns: "A Child of the King," Buell
          "A Mighty Fortress Is Our God," Luther
          "Standing on the Promises," Carter

Offertory Prayer: You give us so much and we give you so little. You ask for the tithe and trust us to be good stewards over the nine-tenths. What a great God you are! Our offerings are an expression of our love for you and a desire to be of service to you. May our gifts carry the good news of Jesus Christ to places we shall never go, and may they bring hope to those we shall never see. We thank you for allowing us to be partners with you in touching lives and changing people. Save us from greed that would deny us the joy of giving. In the name of Christ we pray. Amen.

Introduction

Can you honestly say, "If I died this very moment, I know that I would go to heaven?" Are you really that sure of your salvation? Many sincere Christians are not. They say, "I do not feel than I can make such a positive claim. I wish I could, but I just can't." You can conquer doubting your salvation when you learn why Christians doubt. Here are some reasons why Christians may doubt their salvation.

I. A lack of knowledge of what is involved in a salvation experience.

    A. *What is involved.*

        1. A realization that you are a sinner. "For all have sinned, and come short of the glory of God" (Rom. 3:23).

        2. Willingness to turn from your sin. "Jesus answering said unto them, 'Except ye repent, ye shall all likewise perish'" (Luke 13:2–3).

        3. Total surrender to Christ. "Believe on the Lord Jesus Christ, and thou shalt be saved" (Acts 16:31).

        The word "believe" is an action word. It involves committing yourself totally to Christ. You may walk into a sanctuary believing that a pew can hold you up. But with all your belief that it can do this, it cannot hold you up until you place your entire weight on it. So, to be saved you must do more than believe historical facts about Christ. You must act on your belief by casting yourself completely on Christ.

    B. *What you may be looking for.*

        1. The "newness" to abide. "Newness" passes on in a marriage, but love is deepened by the passing of years.

        On a hot August day you may walk into an air-conditioned building. At first you feel a marked difference. But after several minutes you become adjusted to the cooler climate. The temperature has not changed; you have just gotten used to the "newness" of the cooler climate. Paul speaks of this change when he says, "Therefore if a man be in Christ, he is a new creature: old things are passed away; behold, all things are become new" (2 Cor. 5:17).

        2. A great emotional experience. "And he said to the woman, Thy faith hath saved thee; go in peace" (Luke 7:50). Luke describes this woman as "a woman in the city, which was a sinner" (Luke 7:37). Hers was not an emotional experience; rather, it was a peaceful experience. Luke later describes Lydia's salvation experience, saying she was one who "heard us: whose heart the Lord opened" (Acts 16:14). Different people respond to the gospel in different ways. It may be a dramatic experience like Paul's or a quiet and peaceful experience like Lydia's. The main thing is that they have believed in the Lord Jesus as their Savior.

3. A life free of temptation. As Paul addresses the Christians at Corinth, he tells them that they will never be free from temptation. "There hath no temptation taken you, but such as is common to man" (1 Cor. 10:13). If Satan can't keep you from being saved, he will use temptations to make us as miserable as possible.

4. A life of perfection. "My little children, these things write I unto you, that ye sin not. And if any man sin, we have an advocate with the Father, Jesus Christ the righteous" (1 John 2:1). John is saying that our goal is never to sin, but when we do, we are to turn to Christ, who will intercede for us.

II. A lack of knowledge of God's promises.

A. *His promise to save by faith.* John the Baptist said, "He that believeth on the Son hath everlasting life" (John 3:36). The one and only way Christ saves is by our belief in him!

B. *His promise to keep us saved.* Christ asserted, "I give unto them eternal life; and they shall never perish, neither shall any man pluck them out of my hand" (John 10:28). Christ could not have made a clearer statement. He promises to keep us saved!

C. *His promise never to forsake us.* God's promise to Joshua was, "I will be with thee; I will not fail thee, nor forsake thee" (Josh. 1:5).

D. *His promise to claim us in heaven.* Christ assures us with these words, "Whosoever therefore shall confess me before men, him will I confess before by Father which is in heaven" (Matt. 10:32).

III. A lack of knowledge of how to grow spiritually.

Peter admonishes us to, "grow in grace, and in the knowledge of our Lord and Saviour Jesus Christ" (2 Peter 3:18). You may have seen others who have outgrown you spiritually, and therefore you have become disappointed and begun to doubt. Your doubt will vanish when you take these steps to spiritual growth.

A. *Prayer.* Christ stressed the importance of prayer. "And he spake a parable unto them to this end, that men ought always to pray, and not to faint" (Luke 18:1). As prayer removes doubt, it keeps us from fainting.

B. *Bible reading.* The psalmist wrote, "Thy word I have hid in mine heart, that I might not sin against thee" (Ps. 119:11). Daily Bible reading will keep you informed of God's will and empower you to win over sin.

C. *Worship.* Hebrews 10:25 admonishes us not to forsake the assembling of ourselves together. Worshiping with others keeps us from growing cold and losing the joy of our salvation.

D. *Christian service.* Christ assures us that, "inasmuch as ye have done it unto one of the least of these my brethren, ye have done it unto me" (Matt. 25:40). God does not expect us to burn out. But he does expect us to render "reasonable service" (Rom. 12:1).

IV. Sin within your life.

Proverbs 28:13 warns us that, "He that covereth his sins shall not prosper."

A. *Sin removes the joy of our salvation.* David cried out to God after his sin of adultery. "Restore unto me the joy of thy salvation" (Ps. 51:12). Joy only comes when we are pleasing God. Doubt comes when we are pleasing Satan. And we are very much aware of who we are pleasing.
B. *Sin prevents answered prayers.* Listen to what the psalmist learned from his own personal experience. "If I regard iniquity in my heart, the Lord will not hear me" (Ps. 66:18).
   Sin builds a wall between you and God. Confess and forsake sin, and the gates of answered prayer will open wide.
C. *Sin causes you to revert to your old ways.* Paul warns the Galatians. "But now, after that ye have known God . . . how turn ye again to the weak and beggarly elements whereunto ye desire again to be in bondage?" (Gal. 4:9).

Conclusion

My Christian friend, you can conquer doubt! There is no reason for you to doubt. See clearly what is involved in salvation. Claim God's promises. Do those things that enable you to grow spiritually. Forsake all sin. Then the abiding sense of assurance will sweep over you like a great calm over troubled waters.

Sunday Evening, April 15

Title: After These Things

Text: "After these things the word of the Lord came unto Abram in a vision" (**Gen. 15:1**).

Scripture Reading: Genesis 15:1–6

Introduction

What happens to us today is related to what happened yesterday. There is always a connecting link between history and the present. Prayer on Saturday gives power on Sunday. Worship on Sunday gives strength for Monday. The victory of one day may fortify us in the trial of the next. The adversity of yesterday may bring humility and confession today. So it is that it is "after these things" that other meaningful truths can be learned, new heights attained, new goals realized. The daily life of faith becomes both the foundation and the stepping-stone for new and greater experiences.

I. Yesterday.

"After these things" (Gen. 15:1) calls our attention immediately to the events and experiences of yesterday in the life of the patriarch Abram. Genesis 14 gives us essential details.

A. *Yesterday—Abram did something wonderful for someone else (Gen. 14:16).* His nephew, Lot, had fallen captive to the kings of the East. Abram could have reasoned that Lot brought on his own problems by his careless choices and covetous intentions (Gen. 13), and this certainly would have been true. Being godly, however, Abram risked personal danger against great odds and at much sacrifice to rescue his nephew from capture and likely premature death.

B. *Yesterday—Abram, with Melchizedek, embraced God at Salem in a true spiritual experience of praise and worship (Gen. 14:18–20).*
1. God's praise is lifted up. "Blessed be the most high God" (Gen. 14:20).
2. God's tithe is given up. "And he gave him tithes of all" (Gen. 14:20).
   These experiences and relationships prepared Abram for tomorrow's fears and weaknesses. Abram was always, except while in Egypt, a man of the altar (Gen. 12:8; 13:4, 18). The benefits of yesterday's altar are realized in today's needs.

C. *Yesterday—Abram refused the world's spoils for greater riches (Gen. 14:22–23).* Just as Abram embraced God through a meaningful experience of worship and giving, he recognized God in his refusal of Sodom's substance. Christians must ever realize that there are appropriate things to embrace and other things that are to be refused.

There is another side to this truth. Yesterday's experiences may become fetters rather than stepping-stones if we cling to them and do not have fresh experiences with God each day. "Forgetting those things that are behind, and reaching forth unto those things which are before" is Paul's admonition (Phil. 3:13). What does he mean? Obviously the intent of this passage is to remind us that yesterday's failures are not to hinder us with today's opportunities. Likewise, yesterday's successes are not to lull us into inactivity through a sense of false security.

II. Today (Gen. 15:1–6).

A. *We have a need today for protection and provision: "Fear not, Abram: I am thy shield and thy exceeding great reward" (Gen. 15:1).* The coward is afraid before the battle, the hero after the battle is over. The prophet Elijah (1 Kings 18) displayed courage against the false prophets of Baal but was gripped with fear before the ruthless Jezebel.

B. *We have a need today for the Word of the Lord to come to us: "The word of the LORD came unto Abram" (Gen. 15:1).* Such is better than

Melchizedek's blessings and far better than Sodom's offer of the spoils of war. Each day against the background of needs, fears, and doubts, there is nothing more assuring and more fortifying than the Word, which is alive, penetrating, and powerful.

C. *We have a need today for divine protection: "I am thy shield" (Gen. 15:1).* The shield of faith is part of the whole armor of God. It enables its bearer to quench the fiery darts of the wicked one (Eph. 6:16). Since it is satanic strategy to hurl darts at believers, we need a constant shield of protection.

D. *We have a need today for divine provision: "I am . . . thy exceeding great reward" (Gen. 15:1).* The whole is greater than its parts is a true mathematical formula. Abram was rich even though he refused to appropriate to himself the spoils of war. The greatest wealth is God himself. Paul wrote of our divine supply of riches: "My God shall supply all your need according to his riches in glory by Christ Jesus" (Phil. 4:19). The psalmist in poetic praise wrote, "God is the strength of my heart, and my portion for ever" (Ps. 73:26). God is our "exceeding great" reward. He is adequate, plenteous, all-sufficient. The greatest satisfaction comes from experiencing the Lord Jehovah as our portion and reward.

III. A vital faith today is all-sufficient for tomorrow.

Divine delays are not always denials. It had been ten years since Jehovah had promised Abram a true heir (Gen. 12:7; 13:6). The delay now seemed to cast a shadow of bewilderment on the patriarch.

A. *The reassurance of faith.*
   1. Faith needs correction and direction: "The word of the LORD came unto him" (Gen. 15:4). "All scripture is . . . profitable . . . for correction" (2 Tim. 3:16). Faith is nourished, grows, and develops in our relationship to the Word. "Faith cometh by hearing, and hearing by the word of God" (Rom. 10:17).
   2. Faith needs instruction: "He that shall come forth out of thine own bowels shall be thine heir" (Gen. 15:4). Abram had applied some logic and human reason to his dilemma.
   3. Faith needs encouragement: "He brought him forth" (Gen. 15:4). He brought him forth (1) to look up to the stars, (2) to look beyond the stars to the promise, and (3) to see the almighty God behind the promise. The reassurance is further amplified by the promise "So shall thy seed be" (v. 5). The three promises to Abram in Genesis are that his seed shall be as dust (13:16), as the stars (15:5), and as the sand on the seashore (22:17).

B. *The realization of faith: "And he believed" (Gen. 15:6).* The Hebrew word for faith corresponds to our "Amen." Let it be so, verily, indeed. Reassurance had led to realization and certainty. Even so, there was to be another delay of some fifteen years before the realization became a reality.

1. Abram's faith looked to the proper object. The Scriptures assert that he believed "in the LORD" (Gen. 15:6). Real faith always looks to God.
2. Abram's faith was thoroughly founded and grounded in the word of the Lord (Gen. 15:1, 4). While experience is important, such is not a good foundation for faith. The sure and solid foundation is the Word.
3. Abram's faith produced the right result. It was counted to him as righteousness (Gen. 15:6). This is the first mention of belief or faith in Genesis. Hebrews 11:4–7 indicates that Abel, Enoch, and Noah had faith. This is, however, the first full-orbed faith, because it embraced the true seed, Christ (Gal. 3:16, 29). The true seed is not Israel or the church, but Jesus Christ.

Faith in Jesus Christ was indeed the experience of Abram (Rom. 4:12, 16). The result of this kind of faith is righteousness or justification, right standing with God through Christ (4:22–24; 5:1–2).

Jacob, the grandson of Abram, was a victim of many besetting circumstances, most of which he created. Near the end of his life as he reflected on his past, present, and future, he lamented, "All the things are against me" (Gen. 42:36). Abram too was beset with fears, bewilderment, and uncertainty, but "after these things," the word of the Lord came to him and he *believed* God. This is the victory that overcomes—even our faith.

Conclusion

Each day is a new day of experiences and events. Our response to them determines whether we mature like Abram. It is indeed wonderful if these experiences and events result in our being more like our Lord. May we grow up in him.

WEDNESDAY EVENING, APRIL 18

Title: Witnesses for Jesus Christ

Text: "But you shall receive power when the Holy Spirit has come upon you; and you shall be my witnesses in Jerusalem and in all Judea and Samaria and to the ends of the earth" **(Acts 1:8 RSV)**.

Scripture Reading: Acts 1:1–11

Introduction

We should let the words of our text from Jesus's lips dwell in us richly so that we might be reminded daily of what our task is and what our opportunity is as followers of Jesus Christ. In this particular passage, our Lord describes our mission in terms of witnessing.

I. The witness of eyewitnesses: "You are witnesses of these things" (Luke 24:48).

Our Lord first issued this Great Commission to those who were "eyewitnesses" of his mighty redemptive acts. The apostles had seen with their eyes the many miraculous things Jesus had done. With their eyes they had seen him crucified, they had seen the empty tomb, and they had seen his resurrected body. They were eyewitnesses to his life, to his love, and to his ministry. They were also "earwitnesses" in that they had heard the Sermon on the Mount and his many comments along the road of life. As eyewitnesses and as earwitnesses, their testimony was unique. Not a single living person today can be a witness in exactly the same manner as the early disciples.

II. The testimony of voice witnesses.

Primarily our Lord was saying to his disciples that their mission would be to give their personal testimony. They would communicate to others what they had seen, heard, and experienced in their own heart and life.

III. Modern-day witnesses for Jesus.

Like the disciples, we can testify only of that which we have experienced personally. If we would be effective witnesses for our Lord, we must simply relate to others what we have experienced as a result of our study of the Word of God and in prayer, worship, faith, and obedience. As we give our personal testimony to others, the Holy Spirit uses it to do a divine work in their hearts.

A. *Notice where the early disciples were to begin their witnessing—in Jerusalem.* They were to give their testimony in Jerusalem where Jesus Christ had been crucified and had risen from the dead. They were to give their testimony in this place where his opposition was concentrated. It was their task to communicate to the people of this city that Jesus Christ had come to be their Savior.

B. *Notice where they were to continue with their witness—in all Judea and Samaria and to the ends of the earth.* No one was to be left out, ignored, or considered outside the concern of God's loving heart. Everyone was included. Our Lord's great worldwide program of redemption includes all people of all nations.

Conclusion

How long has it been since you have given your personal testimony concerning what Jesus Christ means to you? How long has it been since you have told others about the joy that has come to you through faith and faithfulness and obedience? To remain silent when you have an opportunity to give a testimony that would encourage others is a sin against our Lord, against others, and against self.

Let's become more talkative for our Lord. Let's go about from place to place sharing the good news of what God has done for us in Jesus Christ. We must be his witnesses if the message is to be communicated.

SUNDAY MORNING, APRIL 22

Title: You Can Conquer the Guilt of Sin by Being Born Again

Text: "Jesus answered and said unto him, Verily, verily, I say unto thee, Except a man be born again, he cannot see the kingdom of God" **(John 3:3)**.

Scripture Reading: John 3:1–16

Hymns: "Ye Must Be Born Again," Sleeper
"There Is a Fountain," Cowper
"Nothing But the Blood," Lowry

Offertory Prayer: Almighty God, our Father, we pray that in today's service we may witness an outpouring of your Holy Spirit. May the Savior who died for us, rose again, and ever lives to make intercession be lifted up in order that people might look to him and be saved. Please remove through forgiveness the impurities of our lives that we may be the kind of people whose prayers can be answered. We bring our offering to you that we may have a part in your work. Receive it and use it according to your will to do your work in this world. We pray in Jesus's name. Amen.

Introduction

Most scholars agree that Nicodemus's visit to Jesus came during the first Passover of our Savior's ministry shortly after his baptism and his subsequent brief visit to Galilee. The reason for his coming by night could have been that he feared to be seen with Jesus but was, more likely, because both of them were busy men and they met by appointment. Nicodemus was, in all probability, one of the most moral men in Judea. The phrase "a ruler of the Jews" probably signifies that he was a member of the Sanhedrin, the official ruling body of the Jews. Jesus told Nicodemus that he needed a new birth. If a man such as Nicodemus needed a new birth, no one among us can claim to be saved by personal merit. One of the outstanding evangelists during the early years of American history preached often on the text "Ye must be born again." One day someone asked him, "Why do you preach on this subject so often?" He replied, "Because ye must be born again."

I. What is the new birth?

To answer this question, we should, first of all, begin negatively. One is not born into this world as a Christian. Physical birth does not bring us into the kingdom of God. The New Testament speaks of those who "received him" as becoming "the sons of God" and then says concerning them that they "were born, not of blood, nor of the will of flesh, nor of the will of man, but of God" (John 1:12–13). Even though children are born into the best Christian family possible, they cannot become citizens of God's kingdom upon the merits of their parents. Thus Christianity is not transmissible nor inheritable, something that can be passed on from parent to child. We are not seeking to minimize the importance of a Christian home. How fortunate are children born into homes where Christ is honored! But all children must come to a period in their life when they personally receive Jesus Christ as Savior through repentance of sin and faith in the person of Jesus Christ.

The new birth is divine and complete. As a divine change, it is God's work. We do not educate ourselves to the point of understanding the process and thus receive it upon that basis. The most mature Christian never completely understands the redeeming work of our Savior nor the transforming work of the Holy Spirit. We accept in faith and may progressively understand some things about God's work, but we never actually understand the divine change that comes to us when we surrender to the Savior.

The new birth is also a complete change in that one does not come to Jesus halfway and keep part of himself uncommitted to Christ. An old cliché says, "It doesn't take much of a man to be a Christian, but it takes all there is of him."

II. Why do we need the new birth?

Several reasons exist as to why we need the new birth. First, the Word of God says so. This would be enough, without any other reasons, for one who accepts the Bible as the Word of God. Other factors enter in, however, and demand that we be born again. God's nature requires a new birth. He is perfect righteousness, and in order to have fellowship with him, we need to enter into his presence uncondemned. Moreover, our own nature requires a new birth. We are sinners and can never find fulfillment in life without a transforming experience to bring peace to our soul regarding our spiritual condition.

The one fact that underlies all others about humans is that they are sinful persons. People are sinners because of birth, choice, and practice. Some people have difficulty in accepting the fact that we are born in sin, but the Bible plainly teaches this fact. When Adam sinned, he poured poison into the human race. Theologians speak of the "Adamic sin," meaning the sin we inherited from our father, the first man on earth.

Also, we are sinners by choice. When we come to the place where we can decide, we invariably choose to sin. Whether we call this the weakness of our human nature or a tendency inherited from our forefathers, we are sinners by choice. We then become sinners by practice. As the years pass, we find it easier to sin than to do right unless we are changed by a supernatural act that gives us a desire to act righteously.

The result of sin is guilt. Even a person who has not become a child of God knows right from wrong because God's revelation has come to him through other means. The feeling of guilt intensifies, and more guilt feelings arise. The new birth experience is the only cure for this situation.

III. What will the new birth do for us?

No one illustration or figure of speech is sufficient to describe all that happens when sinners come to Christ. They are "washed in the blood of Jesus," and they "pass from death unto life." They "become children of God," and they are "saved," "justified from their sins," and "made new creatures in Christ." All of these phrases describe the change that comes both in our status before God and in our personal life.

The guilt of past sins is taken away in the new-birth experience. Jesus Christ, when he died on the cross, did for us that which was necessary to secure a pardon for the guilt of our sins. When we come to Christ in repentance and faith, God removes the accumulated guilt of our past transgressions. He remembers them against us no longer and buries them in the deepest part of the sea. Again, these are figures of speech, for he also says that he separates our sins as far as the east is from the west. The point of all these statements is that God has dealt with the guilt of our sin in the atoning work of Christ on the cross.

Even the guilt of our future sin is covered by the blood of Christ. Some people find it hard to accept the fact that our future sins are forgiven in the new-birth experience. Some have said, "If I believed that, I would sin all I want to, because I would know that I was already forgiven." That is not the point. We are justified from the guilt of our sin, but we also are transformed by the Holy Spirit and no longer have the same attitude toward sin. Repentance means "to change one's mind concerning sin," and, therefore, to think as Jesus thinks with reference to it. Born-again people don't want to sin. If, however, they do sin and then repent and ask forgiveness, the personal experience with Christ as Savior whereby they became born-again Christians takes care of their guilt.

IV. How do we secure the new birth?

The New Testament points out two things that are necessary for becoming a Christian. First, we must repent of our sin. This means that we are genuinely sorry for every sin we have ever committed and sincerely will forsake sin. As said before, we have a new attitude toward sin. Second, we must receive Jesus Christ by faith as personal Savior. The Bible does not command us to follow Jesus in order to be a Christian, but rather to receive him in order to become a Christian. We follow Jesus after we receive him as Savior.

Conclusion

The message Jesus gave to Nicodemus was perhaps the most basic lesson he taught anywhere during his ministry. All calls to righteous living are based on the fact that we have become new persons. Any verse of Scripture in the New Testament that seems to teach salvation by good deeds should be examined in the light of the passages that make it clear that salvation comes on the basis of God's grace through our repentance and faith. Growth is important, very important! But we grow only after we are born. The new birth comes by a personal acceptance of God's Son as our personal Redeemer, Savior, and Lord.

SUNDAY EVENING, APRIL 22

Title: A Distinct Voice but Disguised Hands

Text: "And Jacob went near unto Isaac his father; and he felt him, and said, The voice is Jacob's voice, but the hands are the hands of Esau. And he discerned him not" **(Gen. 27:22–23)**.

Scripture Reading: Genesis 27:6–25

Introduction

The struggle between Jacob and Esau began at birth. Jacob was the second of the twins to be born, but came from his mother's womb with his hand on his brother's heel (Gen. 25:26). The twins' parents showed partiality to them. Isaac loved Esau and Rebekah loved Jacob (v. 28). The separation between Jacob and Esau was furthered when Esau came home from a hunt faint and weary. Jacob, seizing the opportunity to gain power over his brother, bartered him out of his birthright with some lentil stew (vv. 31–34).

The story before us is one full of deception, deceit, cunning, lying, and even daring. In reality it was all so unnecessary. The Lord Jehovah had revealed to Rebekah before the birth of her twins the destiny of each, "the elder shall serve the younger" (Gen. 25:23).

Isaac is defiant of God's will in his proposal to give the blessing to Esau. Had he forgotten, or was he stubborn? The mother likewise displays the flesh as she devises and deceitfully plans to secure the blessing for Jacob. Jacob complies with her schemes and resorts to bold lying. Isaac is aware of the plot as he feels his son and says, "The voice is Jacob's voice, but the hands are the hands of Esau."

I. Nature does not fully equip us for spiritual perception.

Isaac was now 137 years of age. Certainly he was old enough to have learned.

A. *Isaac had a good sense of taste: "[Jacob's] mother made savory meat, such as his father loved" (Gen. 27:14).* Appetite and desire control us. A son so often is like his father. Esau was controlled by appetite (Gen. 25:32, 34) just as Israel in the wilderness had hungered for the cucumbers, the melons, the leeks, and the onions of Egypt. Esau longed to satisfy the desires of his flesh and in the process missed God's blessing.

B. *Isaac could feel: "Come near, I pray thee, that I may feel thee. . . . And he felt him" (Gen. 27:21–22).* Isaac, though old, had not experienced a stroke or paralysis. His sense of feeling was as good as his appetite and taste. "Feeling" is the opposite of faith. Much of religious experience is based on feeling; however, it is faith that pleases God. "We walk by faith, not by sight" (2 Cor. 5:7). Feelings are conditioned by environment, nature, and circumstances. Faith is conditioned by its object, God. Feelings are governed by the natural, while faith puts us in touch with the eternal.

C. *Isaac could hear: "The voice is Jacob's voice" (Gen. 27:22).* Isaac, though old, was not deaf—he could hear well. It is one thing for vibrations and sounds to course the eardrum; it is quite another thing to perceive or understand. The classic example is Job. Through his agony, suffering, and pain, his friends bombarded his ears with theology. In Job 38 God begins to speak and Job begins to hear with understanding—"I have heard of thee by the hearing of the ear: but now mine eye seeth thee" (Job 42:5).

D. *Isaac could smell: "And he smelled the smell of his raiment" (Gen. 27:27).* Smell, hearing, feel, taste—Isaac possessed each of these natural endowments. But nature is so inadequate to equip us. We need the divine dimension.

E. *He could not see: "And his eyes were dim, so that he could not see" (Gen. 27:1).* Even had Isaac possessed 20/20 vision, there were deeper things that he could not see. It is always so with the flesh. Nicodemus was wonderfully equipped by nature. He was a ruler, well educated, a man of moral and ethical refinement, and very religious, but he could not "see" the kingdom (John 3:3). We must be born from above to see that which is above and beyond us.

II. Following nature and instinct creates complications.

A. *In the case of Isaac.*
   1. Isaac certainly was aware of God's will concerning his children. Genesis 25:23 sets forth God's plan. Isaac's plan to reverse the divine order came not from ignorance as much as from self-will and appetite.
   2. Isaac could not properly calculate. He thought he was going to die (Gen. 27:2). (Though 137 years old, he was to live yet another 43 years.) This led him to take things into his own hands. Such action discredits and obviates the plan and will of God.

B. *In the case of Rebekah.*
   1. She devised a scheme (Gen. 27:8–10). The old policy that the end justifies the means is the controlling motive behind her plot. She resolved to accomplish by means that were not in God's plan what God already had purposed. The point is

obvious: It is much easier to "run and do" than to "wait and see." The scheme accomplished much of what she hoped, but left the family fractured.

2. She resorted to deception (Gen. 27:15–16). Jacob dressed up in Esau's clothes, and Rebekah put goatskin over his neck and hands. Her plot was beautifully contrived, thoroughly planned, and well executed, yet Isaac still recognized Jacob's voice. Cover-up and disguise have also been favorite tricks of Satan.

C. *In the case of Jacob.* Jacob concurred readily with his mother in the deception. He even went beyond her strategy and resorted to bold lying. A lesser sin is the foundation for a greater one. "I am Esau thy firstborn," he said to his father. Asked by his father where he got the venison, he said, "The LORD thy God brought it to me." This type of lying still persists. How often people say, "The Lord told me to do it," when the Lord has not spoken.

D. *In the case of Esau.* Early in life this man's character was indicated by his appetites, emotions, and desires. Esau's emotions are first reflected by his weeping. There comes a time when it is too late to weep. Sorrow is most often the result of a misspent life. Esau's weeping turned to hate and the desire for revenge. The seed bed of hate is a prelude to murder. So Esau desired to "kill" his brother Jacob (Gen. 27:41).

Conclusion

This entire episode took place because Isaac was blind. All of his other natural abilities were good, but blindness permitted the drama of evil, deception, intrigue, and hate to inspire. Is this not true for us? Moral and spiritual blindness leads us down paths that oppose God's will for us.

WEDNESDAY EVENING, APRIL 25

Title: Hope for Sinners

Text: "I have not come to call the righteous, but sinners to repentance" **(Luke 5:32 RSV).**

Scripture Reading: Luke 5:7–32

Introduction

Our Lord was confronted daily by those who felt that their lives were completely acceptable to the Father God. They thought they were superior to those around them and saw no need for spiritual changes in their lives. There was nothing our Lord could do for them (see Luke 18:9–14). If you are perfectly satisfied with your spiritual condition, there is little the Lord can do for you. If you are content with yourself as you are, you have achieved a position comparable to that of the self-righteous Pharisees.

I. Our Lord came to save sinners.

   A. *The angel declared that Jesus would deal with sinners (Matt. 1:21).*
   B. *John the Baptist declared that Jesus would deal adequately with humankind's sin problem (John 1:29).*
   C. *Luke declared that Jesus came to seek and to save that which was lost (Luke 19:10).*

II. Jesus identified with sinners (Luke 15:1–2).

Luke alone records the three great parables of the lost sheep, the lost coin, and the lost son. These parables describe God's sorrow over and compassion for the lost. He grieves like a shepherd with a lost sheep, like a woman with a lost coin, and like a father with a lost son. In each of these parables Luke describes the joy of the Father God and of his angels when sinners repent.

III. The call to repentance.

Jesus came into the world to change the hearts and minds of people. He is able to change the heart of a person when that person becomes willing to change his or her mind about God, sin, and self. If you are willing to accept change and if you are willing to cooperate with Jesus Christ to bring about changes in your life, then there is great hope for you.

Repentance is much more than the initial experience of the convert as he or she turns from a life of wickedness to a life of faith and obedience. It is a continuing experience in which we let the mind of Jesus Christ become our mind. It is a continuing experience in which we let the Holy Spirit subjugate the flesh and produce within us the fruit of the Spirit.

If you are among the number who consider themselves as being righteous, there isn't much the Lord can do for you. If you are willing to recognize and admit your spiritual poverty and your need for the grace of God— congratulations! Jesus will help you.

Conclusion

Jesus did not come primarily to minister to those who have achieved success and who feel they have arrived. He came to minister to those who recognize their need for help. Congratulations to you if you are overwhelmed with an awareness of spiritual poverty and if there is within you a real hunger to become the kind of a person God wants you to be!

SUNDAY MORNING, APRIL 29

Title: You Can Conquer Unhappiness

Text: "What happiness for those whose guilt has been forgiven! What joys when sins are covered over! What relief for those who have confessed their sins and God has cleared their record" **(Ps. 32:1–2 TLB)**.

Scripture Reading: Psalm 32:1–11

Hymns: "All That Thrills My Soul," Harris
"He Keeps Me Singing," Bridgers
"This Is the Day," Garrett

Offertory Prayer: Our heavenly Father, we desire to obey your command to go unto all the world and preach the gospel to every creature. Yet we realize that this mission will be made possible only by our faithful stewardship and our prayers. Therefore, the tithes and offerings we bring today are an expression of the sincerity of our commitment to obey your command. We thank you for allowing us the privilege of being partners with you in reaching the lost. Ever let us experience the joy of giving. In the name of Jesus we pray. Amen.

Introduction

A fable is told of a mature cat's noticing a kitten chasing its tail. Asked the cat, "Why are you chasing your tail so?" Responded the kitten, "I have learned that the best thing for a cat is happiness, and happiness is my tail. Therefore, I am chasing it, and when I catch it, I shall have happiness."

The old cat replied, "I too have paid attention to the problems of the universe. I too have judged that happiness is in my tail. But I have noticed that whenever I chase after it, it keeps running away from me, and when I go about my business, it just seems to follow me wherever I go."

What about this matter of happiness? What are you pursuing in hopes of attaining it? In many ways, ours is an unhappy world. How can we be happy in an unhappy world? The answer is found in Psalm 32. We can be happy in an unhappy world because of the following:

I. Forgiveness.

The psalmist proclaims, "What happiness for those whose guilt has been forgiven!" (Ps. 32:1 TLB). There is no greater "blessedness" or "happiness" than to experience the forgiveness of God. God forgives our transgressions by literally carrying them away. When we feel God lifting the load of guilt from us, we know a level of happiness that can be known no other way. When God forgives our sins, he covers our sins. We are warned that we cannot cover our sins. "Whoever conceals their sins does not prosper, but the one who confesses and renounces them finds mercy" (Prov. 28:13 NIV).

Robert Robinson, author of *Come, Thou Fount of Every Blessing*, lost the happy communion he had once enjoyed with the Lord; he drifted back into a life of sin. Hoping to reclaim the happiness, he decided to travel. In the course of his journeys, he became acquainted with a Christian young lady. She asked him what he thought of a hymn she had just discovered. To his astonishment, it was none other than his own composition. He tried to evade her question, but she continued to press for a response. Suddenly he began to weep. With tears streaming down his cheeks, he said, "I am the man who wrote that hymn many years ago. I would give anything to experience the happiness I knew then." Although greatly surprised, the young lady reassured him that the "streams of mercy" mentioned in his hymn still flowed. Mr. Robinson was deeply moved. Because of his turning his "wandering heart" to the Lord and accepting God's forgiveness, he once again entered into the happiness he had lost so many years ago!

II. Honesty.

David confessed, "There was a time when I wouldn't admit what a sinner I was. But my dishonesty made me miserable and filled my days with frustration. All day and all night your hand was heavy on me. My strength evaporated like water on a sunny day until I finally admitted all my sins to you and stopped trying to hide them. I said to myself, 'I will confess them to the Lord.' And you forgave me! All my guilt is gone!" (Ps. 32:3–5 TLB).

  A. *About the person you are.*

   Don Williams, a Presbyterian minister, recalls attending his first Alcoholics Anonymous meeting with a friend. He said each member would introduce himself or herself with these words: "I am [name], and I am an alcoholic." The minister asked, "What would happen in the church if we all used the same level of honesty to introduce ourselves? What would happen if we said, 'I am Don, and I am a sinner'? Pretense would be gone. Honesty about ourselves would return, and happiness would flood our lives."

  B. *About the sins you have committed.*

   David said, "I acknowledge my sin" (Ps. 32:5). He did not say "my temperament" or "my weakness." As David was honest about his personal sins, he was relieved of the cover-up that had overwhelmed him with sorrow. Now, rather than trying to cover his sins, he allowed God to cover them for him. Be specific about your sins. Force yourself to face up to the sins you have glossed over in the past. You must call your sins by their right name and quit them.

III. Trust.

  A. *In the forgiveness of God.* In Psalm 32:5 David asserted that his forgiveness was past. He said, "You forgave the guilt of my sin" (NIV). David accepted God's forgiveness as an accomplished fact.

  B. *In the protection of God.* David painted a picture of God's protection. When the raging floods come, you will not be swept away. God will keep you secure in himself. He is your "hiding place."

   During World War II, one of our large planes took off from Guam and headed for Kokura, Japan. The sleek B-29 turned and circled above the cloud that covered the target for half an hour, then three-quarters of an hour, and finally for fifty-five minutes until the gas supply reached the danger point. With one more look back, the crew headed for the secondary target. Upon arrival, they found the sky clear. "Bombs away!" and the B-29 headed for home.

Weeks later an officer received information from military intelligence that chilled his heart. Thousands of Allied prisoners of war had been moved to Kokura one week before the suspended bombing! "Thank God," breathed the officer, "thank God for that cloud." The city that was hidden from the bomber was a prison camp, and thousands of Americans are now alive who would have died but for that cloud that rolled in from a sunlit sea. The secondary target that day was Nagasaki. The bomb intended for Kokura was the world's second atomic bomb!

You can be happy in an unhappy world when you trust in the protection of God.

C. *In the instruction of God.* "I will instruct you (says the Lord) and guide you along the best pathway for your life" (Ps. 32:8 NLT).

Following God's instruction will allow us to live the best possible life. Within God's will there is happiness. Outside God's will there is sadness. God's instruction saves us from folly. In 32:9–10 we are told we are not to be like a horse or mule who needs a bit or a bridle for control. Rather, we are to be responsive to God, obedient to his Word, and eager to walk in his ways. Trusting in the instruction of God always opens the door to God's mercy. "For thou, Lord, art good, and ready to forgive; and plenteous in mercy unto all them that call upon thee" (Ps. 86:5).

Trusting in God's instruction produces abiding joy. "Be glad in the LORD, and rejoice, ye righteous; and shout for joy, all ye that are upright in heart" (Ps. 32:11).

Conclusion

The story is told of a king who was suffering from depression and unhappiness. He was advised by his astrologist that he would be cured if the shirt of a happy man was brought to him to wear. People went out to all parts of the kingdom seeking such a person. After a long search, they found a man who was really happy, but he did not possess a shirt.

You can be happy in an unhappy world because of forgiveness, honesty, and trust!

SUNDAY EVENING, APRIL 29

Title: A Vision of God

Text: "When Jacob awoke from his sleep, he thought, 'Surely the LORD is in this place, and I was not aware of it.' He was afraid and said, 'How awesome is this place! This is none other than the house of God; this is the gate of heaven'" **(Gen. 28:16–17 NIV)**.

Scripture Reading: Genesis 28:11–22

Introduction

A vision of God is always the result of a revelation from God. Isaiah's vision came as Jehovah showed himself as the Lord of the temple. Job's vision was a result of Jehovah's revelation of himself as Creator. John's vision on Patmos was a result of the self-revelation of Jesus Christ as the risen and living Lord.

I. The place of vision is significant (28:10–19).

Jacob was now at Bethel (the house of God) and on his pilgrimage to the north.

A. *The place was a definite one: "And he lighted upon a certain place" (v. 11).* God is always immanent in every place but not always recognized in every place. Special times and circumstances make it necessary for God to reveal himself in definite ways at specific places.

Jacob was alone, with no doubt a real sense of guilt. Fears well up in his mind each step of the journey. He was wondering not only about the present but also about the future. In times like these, it is always good to light upon a certain place, Bethel, the house of God.

An authentic vision must have an authentic source—God, not man or nature. Likewise, a vision is only as meaningful as the beholder's perspective and understanding of it. Throughout the Bible, as God reveals himself and man beholds the vision, there is a vital change in the recipient—Job confesses and repents, Isaiah serves, Daniel prays, and John is comforted. Visions vary in form, but their source and result are essentially the same. Always the vision brings one closer to the reality and presence of God.

B. *The place was filled with the realized presence of Jehovah God: "Surely the Lord is in this place" (v. 16).* Once in seminary days I recall a young student returning to campus for a chapel engagement. With dramatic emphasis she insisted that the person who prayed for the chapel service not pray for the presence of God. This startled me until she explained that we should pray that each would recognize the presence of God. God is always present, but we do not always recognize that. It was so with Jacob: "Surely, the Lord is in this place, and I was not aware of it."

C. *The place was appropriately named: "And he called the name of that place Bethel" (v. 19).* A name gives identity and enables us to remember. The certain place now becomes a particular place. Certain events happen at specific places, and when we see the place we remember the event. Once I was riding through the countryside of my boyhood with my father. He too grew up in the same area. On numerous occasions he would point to a specific place by the side of the road and relate to me a definite event that happened on that place. For Jacob, this certain place was the house of God (Bethel) where he had had a definite life-changing experience. Have you ever met God in a certain place resulting in a vital experience that changed your life?

II. The particulars of the vision were most revealing (Gen. 28:12–15).

A. *The instrument of communication was a ladder (v. 72).* Jacob's ladder is not his to climb; it is to remind. It is God coming to him in grace. Jacob is deceitful, a liar. God comes to us on his ladder while we are sinners. Grace does not consider what we deserve so much as what we need. Always it is God who is seeking us. What a blessed thing then is his ladder of grace when he comes to us when we are unwilling and unable to come to him.

B. *The revelation of God met specific needs (vv. 13–15).*
   1. It brought reassurance in a time of doubt (v. 13). It was nothing unique for people in Jacob's time to dream, but what was unique was that Jehovah made himself known as the "Jehovah God of Abraham and Isaac." This enabled Jacob to realize that he was in position for God's blessing.
   2. It brought a reaffirmation of the promise (vv. 13–14). The realization of the presence of God may be comforting or it may be distressing. To Jacob it was both.
      a. The presence of God is security: "I will keep thee" (v. 15).
      b. The presence of God is guidance: "I will bring thee again" (v. 15).
      c. The presence of God is comfort: "I will not leave thee" (v. 15).

III. The response to the vision was unusual (Gen. 28:16–22).

A. *The initial response was physical and emotional.*
   1. Jacob was awakened from his sleep (v. 16). The vision was, to say the least, an awakening. A vision of the Almighty should always result in a quickening and an awakening of our intellect and spirit.
   2. Jacob was afraid in the place (v. 17). So many people testify that an experience with God brings ecstasy, joy, and happiness. This was not true here and is hardly ever true in the Bible. When sinful humanity comes face to face with a holy God, there is a terrible awareness of sin and need. Such was the experience of Isaiah the prophet and Job the patriarch.

B. *The next response was practical and demonstrative.*
　　1. The stone upon which Jacob lay his head became a special memorial (v. 18). Sometimes that which is hard and rough becomes to the memory a thing of beauty and meaning.
　　2. The place is identified (v. 19). It is the house of God where people meet with God.

Conclusion

This is the first of seven encounters and visions that Jacob was to have with God. It is enough that we conclude that throughout life there is a constant need for new understanding, new visions, and greater revelation of God to our hearts. May it be so!

MAY

■ Sunday Mornings

Conclude the series "More Than Conquerors" on the first Sunday. From Mother's Day through Father's Day, use the theme "Christ in Marriage and Family Living." Christ is greatly concerned about the problems facing modern families. The Bible and the Holy Spirit provide us with insight and guidance for dealing with the tensions that threaten wholesome family living. This series is interrupted by a special message on the Holy Spirit on Pentecost Sunday, May 20.

■ Sunday Evenings

Continue to base the messages on the lives and experiences of the great patriarchs as they are revealed in the book of Genesis. "The Way of Faith" is the theme.

■ Wednesday Evenings

Complete the series "The Words of Jesus Christ."

WEDNESDAY EVENING, MAY 2

Title: Someone Is at the Door

Text: "Behold, I stand at the door and knock; if any one hears my voice and opens the door, I will come in to him and eat with him, and he with me" **(Rev. 3:20 RSV).**

Scripture Reading: Revelation 3

Introduction

The New Testament holds many beautiful word pictures of our Lord. Matthew presents the picture of him seated on the mountainside in the midst of his disciples teaching them the great principles of his kingdom. Mark paints a picture of Jesus as a worker, a doer, an achiever. He is the Savior who ministers to the needs of others. Luke brings to us a picture of the Christ who is concerned about people of different nationalities and cultures. He describes Jesus as being concerned about the oppressed and the outcast.

Our text presents one of the most beautiful pictures of Jesus in the Bible. It is a verse used often in evangelistic sermons, for it describes God in Jesus Christ taking the initiative to meet undeserving, needy sinners. Instead of people seeking God, God comes in Jesus Christ seeking sinners in order that he might forgive them and give them an abundant life. God does not wait for people to come to him; he searches for people like a shepherd searching for lost sheep.

These words describe how the living Christ wants to come into hearts, bringing the blessings of God and a banquet feast for the soul. He is not satisfied with merely looking in as a spectator.

Jesus spoke these words as a conclusion to the seven epistles to the churches of Asia Minor. He is saying to those who are professing believers that he stands at the front door of their lives eager to make his presence known in all situations. Have we shut him out through irreverence, carelessness, forgetfulness, lack of faith, or lack of obedient cooperation?

I. Christ stands at the door wanting to come in to our times of sorrow (cf. John 11).

At times when sorrow invades our family circle, some of us almost forget the difference that Jesus Christ has made by his resurrection from the dead. Open the door and let him come in to the sorrows and the griefs in your life that he might prepare for you a banquet.

II. Christ stands at the door to come in to help you in your times of weakness and need (Phil. 4:13).

Paul let Christ come into all the situations of life. He discovered that through the help Christ brought, he could adjust himself to the most adverse of circumstances rather than letting circumstances destroy him. By God's grace we can do the same today.

III. Christ stands at the door wanting to answer our questions and perplexities.

Following Jesus's death on the cross and his resurrection from the tomb, many questions perplexed the minds of his disciples. We are not the only ones who have been disturbed and troubled. The early disciples were made of flesh as we are. They stood in need of God's guidance and help. We read that following Jesus's resurrection during a time when the disciples were filled with confusion, that Jesus himself came and stood among them. The risen, living Christ had come to impart information and consolation to their distressed minds and hearts. He wants to do the same today.

Conclusion

Many of us have missed the tremendous impact of this precious promise because we have interpreted it in an evangelistic context. We have thought of it as being a description of the activity of our Lord in his quest to enter the hearts of the lost. The truth is that it contains a description of our Lord's desire to come into all of the situations in our lives. Let him come in.

SUNDAY MORNING, MAY 6

Title: You Can Conquer Worry

Text: "Trust in the LORD with all thine heart; and lean not unto thine own understanding. In all thy ways acknowledge him, and he shall direct thy paths" **(Prov. 3:5–6).**

Scripture Reading: Proverbs 3:5–10

Hymns: "God Will Take Care of You," Martin
          "Great Is Thy Faithfulness," Chisholm
          "Just When I Need Him Most," Poole

Offertory Prayer: Our Heavenly Father, we worship you through the gifts we bring today—gifts that represent life itself. Let our lives be so lived that the cares of the world and the deceitfulness of riches will not distract us. Take our offerings and use them to carry the good news of Jesus Christ to the uttermost parts of the earth. We love you because you first loved us. These gifts are but our response to your abiding love. We offer this prayer in the name of our Lord and Savior, Jesus Christ. Amen.

Introduction

Doctor Charles Mayo of the Mayo Clinic said, "Worry affects the circulation, the heart, the glands, and the whole nervous system. I've never known a man who died from hard work, but many who died from stress."

Metropolitan Life Insurance Company once circulated a leaflet on fatigue. It said, "Hard work by itself seldom causes fatigue which cannot be cured by a good night's sleep. Worry, tenseness, and emotional upsets are the three biggest causes of fatigue."

Evangelist Vance Havner once said, "Worry is like a rocking chair. It will give you something to do, but it will get you nowhere."

In Luke 10 we read the story of Jesus coming by the house of his friends Mary and Martha. Verses 38–39 tell us that "as Jesus and his disciples were on their way, he came to a village where a woman named Martha opened her home to him. She had a sister called Mary, who sat at the Lord's feet listening to what he said" (NIV). Martha was in the kitchen preparing a meal. Every once in a while she glanced over her shoulder and saw Mary doing absolutely nothing. Finally, she could no longer handle her sister sitting while she exhausted herself with kitchen duties. "Martha was distracted." She said to Jesus, "Lord, don't you care that my sister has left me to do the work by myself? Tell her to help me!" (v. 40 NIV).

Notice Martha's reaction. She assumed that Jesus didn't care and blamed Mary for being irresponsible. "My sister has left me to do the work by myself." She tried to work things out her own way. "Tell her to help me!" How often we react in the same manner! Jesus's response was, "Few things are needed—or

146

indeed only one. Mary has chosen what is better, and it will not be taken away from her" (v. 42). He is saying, "Martha, you need to get your priorities straight. It is not necessary that we have a four-course meal." "Worry" means to be pulled apart in different directions.

I. How can you conquer worry?

The answer is found in Proverbs. "Trust in the LORD with all thine heart; and lean not unto thine own understanding. In all thy ways acknowledge him, and he shall direct thy paths" (Prov. 3:5–6).

There are four words of action in this passage. They are "trust," "lean not," "acknowledge," and "direct (thy paths)." The first three are commands. They represent our responsibility. Our responsibility is to trust and not to lean on our own understanding and to acknowledge God. The first three verbs are saying we have to do the first part ourselves.

The fourth verb is a promise. It represents God's responsibility, "And he shall direct thy paths." In other words, don't get into God's business; just do your part, and God can be trusted to do his part.

To learn how to conquer worry, you must focus on several significant terms. They are as follows:

A. *"Trust."* This calls for total dependence and submission. When I trust in him with all my heart, I take my past, my present, and my future and say, "God, it is all yours."

B. *"Heart."* We are commanded to cast all of our cares on him, holding back no areas of our lives—not our minds or emotions. We are to give him everything!

C. *"Understanding."* This is speaking of our own limited perspective. The Hebrew text makes it even clearer: "Upon your own understanding do not lean." It means don't turn first to your own limited viewpoint. When you run into a stressful situation, don't first look to yourself and ask, "How am I going to solve this problem?"

D. *"Lean."* This means we are not to put our weight on ourselves. When Samson regained his strength, he leaned against the center pillars that held up the temple. He literally put everything he could—all of his energy—on those pillars. The same terminology is used here. We are not to lean on our own strength and understanding, but on God.

E. *"Acknowledge."* We are to recognize God. Why? Because "God is our refuge and strength, a very present help in trouble" (Ps. 46:1).

F. *"Make straight."* "And He will make your paths straight" (Prov. 3:6 NASB). God will go before us, preparing the way, removing all barriers. In the Hebrew there is a feeling of intensity, of God going before us in stressful situations and, with great intensity, removing all barriers.

147

II. Three observations.

A. *This promise is for stress-filled people today.* You may say, "But Pastor, you have no clue where I am. You have no idea of the worries and burdens and anxiety and stress that plague me." And you are right. I have no clue. I wish I did. But God does. If you walk out of this building today with worry and stress still a part of your life, it is because you have not trusted and acknowledged God and relied on him.

B. *God will do his part only if we do our part.* We must trust, lean not onto our own understanding, and acknowledge him. The responsibility is on us. Our responsibility is to trust him and give him our worries. But instead, we take on the responsibility of carrying the worry ourselves.

Charles A. Tindley wrote a hymn with these words:

> *Take your burden to the Lord and leave it there.*
> *If you trust and never doubt, He will surely bring you out.*
> *Take your burden to the Lord and leave it there.*

The psalmist admonishes us to "Cast your cares on the LORD and he will sustain you" (Ps. 55:22 NIV).

C. *God can handle all areas of our lives.*

D. You may say, "Wait a minute—all areas of my life?" That's right, all areas. Not some areas, not most areas, but *all* areas of your life. Do you see the word "all" twice in this promise? Trust the Lord with what? "All" of your heart (v. 5). And in "all" your ways (v. 6).

How do we apply this passage to our lives? Simple: in all your ways recognize God, and he will smooth out your path, removing all unnecessary obstacles.

Conclusion

Think of the most stress-filled area of your life. Maybe it is your job, your family, or a strained relationship with some person. Focus on it. Now take that worry that is eating you like a rapidly growing cancer, and leave it with Jesus.

As a popular chorus of years past goes,

> *Learning to lean, learning to lean,*
> *I'm learning to lean on Jesus.*
> *Finding more power than I ever dreamed;*
> *I'm learning to lean on Jesus.*

Beginning today, lean hard on Jesus. The good news is that Christ can handle your problems. If you really love him, put all of your trust and all of your worries on him and see what he can do.

SUNDAY EVENING, MAY 6

Title: Face-to-Face with God

Text: "And Jacob called the name of the place Peniel: for I have seen God face to face, and my life is preserved" **(Gen. 32:30)**.

Scripture Reading: Genesis 32:24–32

Introduction

Twenty years had elapsed since Jacob had fled from home in Beersheba, where his life had been threatened by his brother, Esau. These years had been years of acquisition—flocks, herds, wives, children. Even so, something still haunted the patriarch. His memories of home, fears, guilt, and his unhappy experiences with Laban left him unfulfilled.

Sooner or later we all must face up to our fears, opponents, and desires. These cannot always be evaded, nor can we escape them. There is ever a tendency to feel that a new environment with new people and new situations will enable us to forget the past and live better. However, fears, guilt, emotions, and dispositions seldom are changed and less seldom eradicated by moving to another place. The prodigal's problem was not with his place (home) but with his person (self). His new companions, circumstances, and environment contributed nothing to his well-being. It was his homecoming, facing up, that brought both remedy and solution.

Jacob was now coming home, and he was to learn three important lessons: what happens *before*, *when*, and *after* one comes face-to-face with God.

I. Before one comes face-to-face with God.

Jacob had had prior experiences with God at Bethel (Gen. 28:19–21), where he had learned the presence of God, and also at Mahanaim (32:2), where he had learned the power of God. The experience at Peniel (32:30) would teach him the abiding fellowship of God with his people. Certain things made this experience necessary.

    A. *Before we come face-to-face with God, we may learn that new scenery and new circumstances do not change our situation very much.* A change of environment seldom if ever delivers us from opposition and difficulties. After all, most problems are within, and to move to a new location is only to relocate and not to relieve the problem.

    B. *The flesh (human nature) principle asserts itself, resulting in the eclipse of faith.*

        1. Jacob could plan and scheme better than wait and pray. This is always the principle of the flesh that wants to do God's work in man's way.

        2. Jacob's prosperity outdistanced his spiritual devotion and growth into faith (Gen. 30:37–43).

C. *Fears arise and faith subsides.* Jacob had lived in fear. He feared the wrath of his brother, Esau, earlier, and now he feared the encounter with his brother, whom he had not seen for twenty years (Gen. 32:7). Many fears are created. Jacob's scheming, tricks, and strategies now haunted him. We fear the law because we are guilty of some crime. We fear the truth because of a lie. We fear the light because of a sin committed in the dark. Fears and guilt that arise from sin are poison to faith.

D. *Imaginations run rampant and may be worse than the reality.* Jacob imagined what would happen to his flocks, his family, and himself (Gen. 32:7–8). He had no way of knowing what his brother would do after twenty years; however, he imagined that Esau's wrath would still be at fever pitch. In reality this was not true, as is seen in Genesis 33:4.

Just as Jacob imagined things, so do we invent problems that do not exist. We find abnormal growth in the body and we imagine a malignancy; a pain in the chest and we imagine a heart attack. So it is, before we come face-to-face with God, we live in the mental atmosphere of exaggerated imaginations that far outdistance reality.

E. *Being alone creates a situation in which we may come face-to-face with God.* "And Jacob was left alone" (Gen. 32:24).
   1. There are external distractions such as family and responsibilities.
   2. There are internal distractions such as fear, worry, and guilt.

God's purpose is to enable our minds and hearts to stay on him. "Thou wilt keep him in perfect peace, whose mind is stayed on thee; because he trusteth in thee" (Isa. 26:3).

II. When we come face-to-face with God.

It is said of Moses that no prophet since him was ever so intimate with God: "There arose not a prophet since in Israel like unto Moses, whom the LORD knew face to face" (Deut. 34:10).

A face-to-face relationship with God is a heart-to-heart fellowship before God. Before we face our friend or enemy, we need this holy intimacy. Certain things need to happen and will happen when we come face-to-face with him.

A. *Jacob experienced a new character. His name was changed from "Jacob," one who is tricky, to "Israel," a prince with God (Gen. 32:27–28).* Heretofore, Jacob had lived up to the meaning of his name. He had been a shrewd operator, scheming, plotting, planning. To some extent this continued, but it was not as pronounced as when he came face-to-face with God.

B. *Jacob experienced a new power: "For as a prince hast thou power with God" (Gen. 32:28).* Each new spiritual experience brings a realization of God's power in our lives.

Zechariah the prophet grappled with the problem of the restoration of Judah after the Babylonian desecration. Humanly the task was unattainable, but God was able to bring from the impossibility a reality because it is "not by might, nor by [human] power, but by my spirit, saith the LORD" (Zech. 4:6).

C. *Jacob experienced a new blessing: "And he blessed him there" (Gen. 32:29).*

It often is out of a crisis experience that the choicest of God's blessings emerge. The prophet Jeremiah, as he reviewed in his mind the destruction of the holy city, Jerusalem, was awed by the condition of the city and its people. How could such a scene produce hope? Because "it is of the LORD's mercies that we are not consumed, because his compassions fail not. They are new every morning" (Lam. 3:22–23).

Everything God purposes and accomplishes in life for his people is designed to bless them. His ways may be strange and past our finding out, but he designs to bless.

D. *Jacob had a new experience in learning.*
  1. He learned that God's plan is better than man's way. Human plans, strategies, and methods are unnecessary, because it is God who works in us.
  2. He learned that God's providence is what is needed: "I have seen God face to face, and my life is preserved" (Gen. 32:30).

So it is. Each time one comes face-to-face with God, there is likely a new change in character, a new power within, a new blessing, and a new experience of learning.

III. After we come face-to-face with God.

Throughout the Bible as people have experienced a deeper experience with God, the emotional impact has been different. Isaiah came face-to-face with God and saw his sin and the sins of the people. Job came face-to-face with God and repented of his ignorance. John, on Patmos, came face-to-face with the living Christ and was struck with fear. The impact on Jacob left him limping because his thigh (center of strength) was withered.

A. *Jacob learned that divine strength is adequate in human and physical weakness.* The apostle Paul too learned this lesson: "Therefore I take pleasure in infirmities . . . for Christ's sake: for when I am weak, then am I strong" (2 Cor. 12:10).

B. *Jacob learned that those who opposed him were under the control and direction of God.* In contrast to what Jacob anticipated, Esau's hate toward him (Gen. 27:41) was turned to embracing, kissing, and weeping (33:4). "When a man's ways please the LORD, he maketh even his enemies to be at peace with him" (Prov. 16:7).

C. *Jacob's experience shows us that the deeper experiences with God can soon be forgotten.*
  1. Jacob, not many days after his experience, resorted to his old way of tricks and scheming (Gen. 33:1).
  2. Jacob settled in Succoth (Gen. 33:17), which was out of God's will (see Gen. 31:13).

How readily we may see that yesterday's experiences are easily forgotten or are not sufficient for today's needs. Each day we must come face-to-face with God. Just as the body needs a new supply of food for each day, so we need fresh experiences with God. Likewise, we are not to forget the lessons learned yesterday.

Conclusion

The details of coming face-to-face with God may vary, but the need for coming face-to-face with him is always apparent. When we face God, we see our sins and his grace, and we experience his change in our hearts. May we this day come face-to-face with him!

WEDNESDAY EVENING, MAY 9

Title: The Lord's Promise to Return

Text: "And when I go and prepare a place for you, I will come again and will take you to myself, that where I am you may be also" (**John 14:3 RSV**).

Scripture Reading: John 14:1–6

Introduction

The words of our Scripture reading are among the most precious that Jesus spoke. With great profit we can memorize this entire passage and let these words of Christ dwell in us richly, instructing us, comforting us, and encouraging us.

The great truth of this passage is the promise of the Lord to return for those who trust him and love him. He says, "I will come again."

There are almost three hundred specific promises in the New Testament concerning the return of Jesus Christ to the earth. Let us give consideration to a number of the different ways in which the Lord comes again.

I. He comes the first time at the moment of conversion (Rev. 3:20).

The Lord Jesus Christ comes to live in the hearts of those who receive him as Lord and Savior (cf. John 1:12; Gal. 2:20; Col. 1:27). Becoming a Christian is infinitely more than making a decision to turn from a life of evil. It is letting Jesus Christ come into the innermost being that he might live out his life in the soul of the believer.

II. He comes to us in the time of need (Matt. 25:31–40).

Many of us seemingly are unaware that those who are in desperate need present to us an opportunity to render a ministry to the Christ. We need to visualize the coming of Christ to us in the form of those who are unfortunate and in need of his ministries of love through us. May the Lord forgive us for being blind to his presence in those who suffer and for being deaf when cries of distress fall upon our ears.

III. He comes to us in the time of worship (Matt. 18:20).

When we come to the house of prayer and worship, we often anticipate seeing family, friends, and neighbors. There are times when we are so intensely aware of the presence of other human beings that we do not concentrate on having an experience with the living Lord who has promised to return and to meet with those who come together in his name.

The Old Testament contains the promise of his first coming. The New Testament, as well as the Old Testament, contains many promises about his second coming. These words from the lips of our Lord speak to us concerning his contemporary comings to be with us when we worship. Let us allow this promise to dwell in us richly.

IV. He comes to us in the pathway of obedience (Matt. 28:18–20).

In these words, our Lord gives to us the precious promise of his abiding presence. To claim this promise, we must be in the pathway of obedience. It is the testimony of those who have given themselves in obedience to the Great Commission that they have experienced his living presence along the pathway of life. If you would find him as a contemporary today, give yourself without reservation to a life of loving obedience in witnessing about God's love.

V. He will return again in victory.

The most glorious event in the future will be the victorious return of Jesus Christ as King of Kings and Lord of Lords. At that time the living saints will rise to be with him. The saints who have already moved into the abode of the dead will be resurrected and will enter the house not made with hands eternal in the heavens. The battle with sin will be over. Death will be destroyed. The new heavens and the new earth will become a reality, and we will worship God without hindrance or limitation. We will experience life as God meant for it to be from the very beginning.

Conclusion

Our Lord promised to return at the end of the age. In the meantime, there are many promises that he made for us in this life. Let us let these great words of promise dwell in us richly and give us the guidance and the help our Lord wants us to have day by day.

Sunday Morning, May 13

Title: Helping Mothers to Be Good Mothers

Text: "Her children rise up and call her blessed; her husband also, and he praises her" **(Prov. 31:28 RSV)**.

Scripture Reading: Proverbs 31:26–31

Hymns: "O Blessed Day of Motherhood!" McGregor
"Break Thou the Bread of Life," Lathbury
"Breathe on Me," Hatch

Offertory Prayer: Heavenly Father, thank you for the abundance of gifts you have bestowed on us. We would remind ourselves that you are the giver of every good and perfect gift. We come bringing monetary gifts for use in advancing your kingdom's work. Accept these tithes and offerings as tokens of our desire to be totally involved in your work of rescuing people from the slavery of sin. Through Jesus Christ our Lord we pray. Amen.

Introduction

The writer or collector of Proverbs brings this tremendous book to a close with a fabulous classic description of a great woman who is also a good wife and mother. These words may have come from the mother of a king as she gave him guidelines concerning his future wife (Prov. 31:1).

A wife of noble character is declared to be worth far more than rubies (Prov. 31:10) and is worthy of the praises of both her children and husband. On Mother's Day it would be easy for us to become sentimental as we think about our mothers, but it would be much more profitable for us to make a contribution toward helping mothers to be better mothers.

Women should not feel slighted if someone were to declare that it is no great feat to simply give birth to a baby. The great feat deserving of praise comes as a mother becomes a good mother, providing her children with guidance and encouragement and leading them toward maturity and independence.

I. The great woman, the good mother, does more than give birth to a baby.

   A. *She is described as trustworthy (Prov. 31:11).* The good mother is one whose character is such that she can be depended on. She is reliable and responsible. Her husband can put confidence in her, and her children know her to be dependable.
   B. *She is described as benevolent (Prov. 31:12).* Marriage is seen as a partnership in which each spouse seeks to make a positive contribution toward the well-being of his or her companion and children.

154

The good mother is good to her husband and good to her children. She knows how to spell the word *love* with the letters G-I-V-E and H-E-L-P.

C. *She is described as industrious (Prov. 31:31).* It is significant that in the pre-Christian era, the great woman and the good mother is described as one who was not completely confined to the household (cf. vv. 16, 18, 24). She is described as one whose work continues from sun up to sun down (v. 27).

D. *She is described as having a good self-image (Prov. 31:23).* Modem psychology has emphasized that to be happy in life, we must have a good self-image. The woman who holds herself in low esteem will not be able to relate positively and constructively to others. The good mother is described here as having a good self-image: "Strength and dignity are her clothing, and she laughs at the time to come" (Prov. 31:25). In his book *What Wives Wish Their Husbands Knew About Women,* Dr. James Dobson declares on the basis of many seminars, questionnaires, and much personal counseling that "low self-esteem was indicated as the most troubling problem by the majority of women in the modern world." He declares that many factors combine to give the modern mother a low evaluation of her role, and this contributes to an attitude of low self-esteem. To overcome this peril, the modern mother needs to realistically evaluate herself, and she needs to be recognized and appreciated by her husband.

E. *She is described as being compassionate (Prov. 31:20).* She is compassionate toward her husband, children, and to those outside the family circle.

F. *She makes constructive use of her tongue (Prov. 31:26).*
   1. Proverbs has much to say about the use of the tongue.
   2. The tongue can be used as a knife to destroy.
   3. The tongue can be used as a soothing oil to heal our injuries.
   4. The tongue can be used to encourage the spirit like the notes of a trumpet are used to arouse people to action. A good mother should be a cheerleader to encourage her children as they face the pressures of growing toward maturity in a difficult and dangerous world.

II. Helping mothers to be better mothers.

A. *The wife must begin by helping herself to be a good mother.*
   1. Consider yourself and make certain that you are the good gift of God to your husband. The wise man said, "He who finds a wife finds a good thing, and obtains favor from the LORD" (Prov. 18:22 RSV). The gifts of God are always good. God wants to help you be one of his best gifts to your husband,

the father of your children. Only you can make certain that you are in reality God's good gift to your husband.

2. Be the real gift of God to your children. Your children need more than a biological source for their origin in the person they call mother. For you to treat yourself other than a gift of God to your children, and to consider your children less than God's gifts to you, is to open the door to great harm to the emotional well-being of your children. Every child deserves the right to be wanted, accepted, and appreciated.

You can begin the process of becoming a good mother if you will accept your children as gifts and as a trust and responsibility given to you by God, and if you will determine that at all times you will be God's good gift to your children.

B. *The husband has much to contribute toward helping his wife become a good and great mother.*

1. Accept your wife as a precious gift from God. You chose your wife to be your companion and the mother of your children. She needs your help, your support, your encouragement, your partnership. Accept her and treat her as the gift of God to your heart and life.

2. Love your wife as Christ loved the church so sacrificially that he was willing to give himself for it on the cross (Eph. 5:25–27). While it is romantic love that often draws a man and a woman together and leads to marriage, there must be sacrificial love toward each other if they are both to be the good parents their children need and deserve.

3. Love your wife as you love your own body (Eph. 5:28–33). The biblical concept of marriage is a one-flesh relationship. Husband and wife are seen as a union of two personalities into one. Paul declares that no man has ever hated his own flesh, but nourishes it and cherishes it. And even so, a man is to love his wife, who is the mother of his children.

4. Treat your wife with reverence, respect, and courtesy (1 Peter 3:7). Peter declares that a man is responsible to God for the manner in which he relates to his wife. If he mistreats her, he will disrupt his fellowship with God and will be unable to have his prayers answered. The apostle is declaring that a man is responsible for helping his wife to be a good wife and a good mother.

5. Be grateful for your wife (Prov. 31:28). We have a healthy and wholesome opinion of ourselves when we see respect in the eyes of others and hear words of appreciation from their lips. According to Dr. Dobson, modern wives are in desperate need of this contribution toward their well-being.

6. Pray for your wife. She needs your help. She needs the Lord's help. Lift her up before God's throne of grace and ask him to help her with all her problems and with all her needs.

C. *Children have much to contribute toward helping their mother become a good and great mother.*

1. Be thoughtful toward your mother. Be considerate of her as a person. Do not be unkind to her or take her for granted.
2. Become someone that your mother can be proud of and grateful for. Guard against conducting yourself in such a manner as to embarrass your mother.
3. Be grateful for your mother. Do not hesitate to express appreciation and praise to your mother for all the many things she does to make your life meaningful and purposeful.
4. Be helpful to your mother. She has many responsibilities and duties, and you can be helpful to her by doing all you can to take care of yourself and your own things.

Conclusion

God wants to help mothers to be better mothers. Jesus Christ came to be the Savior of mothers because mothers are sinners like the rest of us.

If you are a young girl, you need Christ in your heart if you would be the best possible wife and the best possible mother of your children who someday will be born.

If you are already a mother and do not have Christ in your heart, then let me encourage you to invite him to come in today. He wants to be your Savior, your teacher, and your helper.

Be assured that whatever your problems are and whatever your needs may be, Jesus Christ wants to minister to you and minister through you to your children. Choose this day to cooperate with him.

SUNDAY EVENING, MAY 13

Title: Back to Bethel

Text: "God said unto Jacob, Arise, go up to Bethel, and dwell there: and make there an altar unto God, that appeared unto thee when thou fleddest from the face of Esau thy brother" **(Gen. 35:1)**.

Scripture Reading: Genesis 35:1–15

Introduction

Some thirty years had passed in the life of Jacob since he first came to Bethel. His first visit was on the occasion of his flight from his brother's wrath. The intervening years had been filled with the drama of fear, marriage, children, deceit, travel, and return to the land of Canaan.

I. The call (Gen. 35:1).

God's call to Jacob to return to Bethel after thirty years could not help but arouse precious memories. He could recount the details of the original experience (Gen. 28) with profit. Who of us does not delight to contemplate our earlier experiences, especially those that have blessed and enriched us on the journey.

A. *Jacob would remember the significance of the name of the place.* Bethel means "the house of God" (Gen. 28:17)—not that God is confined to any one place, but certainly his presence was known in this place. God, of course, is not confined to the walls of a church building, but for many of us, his presence and power are experienced in a more profound way in his house.

B. *Jacob would remember the altar at Bethel.* The altar would remind him of worship, sacrifice, and giving. There is no reference to Jacob building an altar at any place during his journeys over the intervening thirty years. Much of his spiritual declension may have resulted from this neglect. It is at the altar where we often experience God's presence and where we are reminded of our responsibility to him.

C. *Jacob would remember his fears and the divine reassurance.* His first visit to Bethel was a unique occasion, for he was in flight from the wrath of his enraged brother Esau (Gen. 35:1). It was here that the divine reassurance came to him, "I will not leave thee, until I have done that which I have spoken to thee of" (Gen. 28:15).

D. *Jacob would remember the vows he made at Bethel during his initial visit.* Vows are no better than the character of the one making them. No doubt Jacob was sincere in his declaration that the Lord would be his God, but we must have more than intent—we must have commitment. The recall of the vow will serve to remind Jacob of his impotence and of God's omnipotence.

II. The preparation (Gen. 35:2–6).

Sin unforsaken and unforgiven is always a barrier to fellowship with God. Jacob's response to God's call for him to return to Bethel is a reminder of this truth.

A. *Idols must be forsaken: "Put away the strange gods that are among you" (Gen. 35:2).* In Jacob's case these were the teraphim brought from Laban's household in Paddan Aram. In our case it may be other things such as pleasures, worldliness, or wealth. God is not pleased with rivals that claim our attention, devotion, and service.

B. *The unclean must be cleansed: "And be clean" (Gen. 35:2).* The plaintive cry of King David was, "Create in me a clean heart, O God." The psalmist answers the question of who may come into the presence of the Lord. It is those who have "clean hands."

C. *The policy of separation must be followed: "And change your garments"* *(Gen. 35:2).* Defilement comes from contamination. For some time Jacob and his household had dwelt in Shechem where they had become defiled.

D. *The altar must be rebuilt: "I will make there an altar unto God" (Gen. 35:3).* This statement reflects Jacob's obedience to the divine direction already given him.

III. The revelation (Gen. 35:6–15).

The call having been issued and obeyed results in a realization and a revelation from God.

A. *God's will is obeyed in the rebuilding of the altar (Gen. 35:7).*

B. *To obey God's will does not remove Jacob from trials and sorrows.* No sooner is he at the right place doing the right thing than deep sorrow comes to him and his family at the death of Rebekah's nurse. We learn that sorrow is not always a punishment for sin. It is in sorrows that life is mellowed, trained, and becomes fruitful (see Rom. 5:3; 8:35–37).

C. *God appears to Jacob for the purpose of blessing him (Gen. 35:9–12).*

   1. God recalls with Jacob his changed name. It is easy to forget meaningful experiences of yesteryear. How good God is to remind us and help us to remember!
   2. God reveals himself to Jacob as the Almighty.
   3. God reminds Jacob of his responsibility. He is to be fruitful and multiply.
   4. God renews with Jacob the covenant made with Abraham.

IV. The memorial (Gen. 35:14–15).

On his first visit to Bethel, Jacob used a stone as a pillow. On this occasion stones are used as pillars. The pillow is for rest, the pillar for remembrance.

Conclusion

Places were very important in the life and experience of Jacob, and they are important to each of us. We are enriched when we remember the place where we met God, for as we remember the place, we remember the event. May we ever recall for our spiritual profit the places where we have met with God.

WEDNESDAY EVENING, MAY 16

Title: The Proof of Love

Text: "If you love me, you will keep my commandments" **(John 14:15 RSV).**

Scripture Reading: John 13:34–35

Introduction

In the words of our text, our Lord gives us a universal guideline for the proving of our love for him. He boldly declares, "If you love me, you will keep my commandments." John declared in his first epistle, "We love, because he first loved us" (4:19).

I. Do you love the Lord?

Some find it difficult to love God because they have a warped concept of his nature, his character, and his purposes. God has been misrepresented to them. They see him as something other than the object of their supreme love.

The psalmist wrote a psalm that gives expression to the abundance of love that was in his heart for God. It begins, "I love the LORD, because . . ." (Ps. 116:1).

   A. *We should love the Lord because he first loved us.*
   B. *We should love the Lord because he came to seek and to save us from the consequences of sin.*
   C. *We should love the Lord because he has given us the gift of forgiveness.*
   D. *We should love the Lord because he has given us the gift of eternal life.*
   E. *We should love the Lord because he has planted within us his divine Spirit.*
   F. *We should love the Lord because he has given us meaningful work to do and promised us resources with which to accomplish it.*
   G. *We should love the Lord because of the home he is preparing for us beyond this life (John 14:1).*

II. The proof of love: "You will keep my commandments."

The commandments of our Lord are not burdensome and galling. They do not impoverish us and bring about defeat in our lives. They are good and benevolent in their outcome, and they grow out of God's love for us and his plan to enrich our lives.

   A. *Jesus's first and greatest commandment is to love God and to love our fellow human beings.* This calls for a persistent attitude of goodwill toward others and for the giving of the supreme devotion of our heart to our God.
   B. *Jesus has commanded us to practice forgiveness toward those who sin against us.*
   C. *Jesus has commanded us to stay in dialogue with the Father God as we journey through life and as we seek to give ourselves in service.*
   D. *Jesus has commanded us to busy ourselves at the task of winning disciples as we go about from place to place (Matt. 28:18–20).*

Conclusion

The way to prove our love for the Lord is by joyfully delighting in obedience to his loving commands. The more we love him, the more gladly we will give ourselves to a life of trusting obedience.

SUNDAY MORNING, MAY 20

Title: Five Great Functions of the Holy Spirit

Text: "In him you also . . . were sealed with the promised Holy Spirit, which is the guarantee of our inheritance until we acquire possession of it, to the praise of his glory" **(Eph. 1:13–14 RSV)**.

Scripture Reading: Ephesians 1:1–14

Hymns: "God, Our Father, We Adore Thee," Frazer
"Great Is Thy Faithfulness," Chisholm
"O Love of God Most Full," Clute

Offertory Prayer: Holy Father, with a generous and forgiving heart, you have related yourself to us in grace and mercy. We thank you for cleansing us from sin and accepting us into your family. We thank you for commissioning us as your servants and as your ministers to others. We pray for your grace to be at work in our hearts, and we pray for the gift of faith that will enable us to give ourselves with total unselfishness in service to you and in a ministry of helpfulness to others. Bless the gifts we bring today as symbols of the gift of ourselves to you. In Jesus's name. Amen.

Introduction

God is a Spirit, and they who worship him must worship him in Spirit and in truth. That God is a Spirit means that he is not tangible and visible and physical and limited. We worship him with our spirit, and this worship is manifested in our actions.

In his epistle to the Ephesians, Paul makes much of the relationship of the Holy Spirit to the individual believer and to the congregation of believers in the church. He makes five great assertions concerning the functions of the Holy Spirit in the life of each believer and in all believers collectively. These five great assertions can warm our hearts and challenge us to both worship and witness more effectively.

I. The gift of the Holy Spirit is the seal of God's ownership: "Were sealed with the promised Holy Spirit" (Eph. 1:13).

Paul spoke to the Corinthian Christians in a similar manner (2 Cor. 1:22).

A seal was used during the days in which the apostle Paul wrote for a number of different functions.

A. *The seal was a sign of ownership.* Paul declares that the gift of the Holy Spirit that comes in the moment of conversion is a specific sign indicating God's ownership of us as individuals. This includes all that we are and all that we ever will have and be.

B. *The Holy Spirit is the mark by which we are identified as children of God.* He who does not have the Spirit of God does not belong to God and is not

161

a child of God. The presence of the Holy Spirit within us will identify us to other believers as being members of the family of God, and those who possess this gift of the Spirit will become known to us as the children of God though our beliefs about various matters may differ.

C. *God's brand on us is inward and spiritual.* The Holy Spirit comes into the deepest zone of our being and begins the work of God. God works from the inside to manifest his presence in an external manner through the life, love, and lips of his children.

Each one who has been redeemed by the blood of Jesus Christ is now God's property. We belong to the Creator God by his right of creation, providential care, and redemption (Ps. 24:1).

II. The gift of the Holy Spirit is the "earnest" of our inheritance: "Which is the guarantee of our inheritance until we acquire possession of it, to the praise of his glory" (Eph. 1:14).

The word translated "guarantee" is a word that comes from the business world and from the language of economics. This word refers to the deposit that is made on a purchase guaranteeing that the purchaser is committed to completing the business transaction.

A. *The Holy Spirit is God's "earnest money."*
B. *The Holy Spirit is God's "first installment" on us.*
C. *The Holy Spirit is God's "guarantee" that he will complete his work of redeeming us completely.*
   1. It is the Holy Spirit who brings about the beginning of God's good work within us. In this experience we receive salvation from the penalty of sin, which is death (cf. Phil. 1:6).
   2. It is the Holy Spirit who continues the process of saving us from the practice of sin (Phil. 2:12–13). This process begins at the moment of conversion and continues without ceasing until either the Lord Jesus returns or until death claims us.
   3. It is by the power of the Holy Spirit that God will eventually raise us from the dead and complete the great salvation he has provided for us through Jesus Christ (Phil. 3:20–21). This thrilling truth is stated even more explicitly in Paul's epistle to the church at Rome (Rom. 8:11).

III. The Holy Spirit is to aid us in our prayer life: "For through him we both have access in one Spirit to the Father" (Eph. 2:18 RSV).

A. *It is the Holy Spirit who invites us into the throne room of our Father God.* While some may look upon prayer as a duty to be performed or a habit not to be broken, we would be closer to the truth if we saw our prayer efforts as but a response to the invitation of the Holy Spirit to come to the heavenly Father.

B. *The Holy Spirit is to be our guide as we pray (Rom. 8:26–27).* He helps us with our inadequacies and intercedes for us according to the will of God. This should greatly encourage us not only to practice the habit of prayer but also to be bold in our prayer life.

IV. By the work of the Holy Spirit we are built into the temple of the Lord.

We become the dwelling place of God (Eph. 2:22). Paul sought at all times to encourage believers to recognize that God is not just a vague blur that dwells in the distance somewhere. Instead, in Spirit he has come to dwell within our hearts.

A. *Have you failed to recognize that your body has become the dwelling place of the Holy Spirit (1 Cor. 3:16; 6:19)?* Our Lord promised that the Holy Spirit would come to dwell within us forever. It is not necessary for us to pray for him to come to us. He has already arrived. We need to recognize and respond to his presence.

B. *In John's description of the New Jerusalem, he pictures God as dwelling with people (Rev. 21:3).* In the Holy Spirit, God has already come to dwell in the heart of each believer and collectively in the church. This should excite and encourage us.

V. The Holy Spirit is eager to strengthen each of us in the inner person: "That according to the riches of his glory he may grant you to be strengthened with might through his Spirit in the inner man" (Eph. 3:16).

A. *Strength of body is of tremendous importance.*

B. *Strength of mind is of immeasurable significance.*

C. *Strength in the inner person is of supreme importance if we are to live a victorious life.*

1. Without the strength of the Lord, there is no way by which we can overcome Satan's strategies (Eph. 6:10).

2. Our Lord gave his disciples a task that is impossible to accomplish using human resources alone. Consequently, he promised the power of the Holy Spirit to enable us to accomplish the task (Acts 1:8).

The precious Holy Spirit came that he might be to us the source of strength, wisdom, guidance, and help we need. We must recognize him and respond to him with faith and with an attitude of joyful cooperation.

Conclusion

If you have not yet received Christ as your Lord and Savior, the Holy Spirit would call you this day to faith in him. The Holy Spirit will effect this miracle of the new birth within your heart when you make a response of genuine commitment to him in faith. The Holy Spirit will impart to you the very nature of God, and he will come to dwell within you to accomplish the work of God and to fulfill the will of God in your life.

God has given his Son to be your Savior. God will give you his Spirit that you might grow in the realm of the Spirit and achieve success in doing the will of God in your life. He invites you to come to him today.

SUNDAY EVENING, MAY 20

Title: Hard Knocks and a Right Response

Text: "And they took him, and cast him into a pit: and the pit was empty" (**Gen. 37:24**).

Scripture Reading: Genesis 37:3–8, 11, 23–25

Introduction

Few people walk across the pages of the Old Testament with such majesty and distinction as Joseph. Into one life was distilled the rich graces of faith, hope, and love.

What contrasts also are evident in his life! At one moment he is a prophet, the next he is a victim of his prophecy. At one moment he is a prisoner, the next he is in command of the economic and political affairs of Egypt. Early in life he is hated by his brothers; later in life he is honored by his brothers. One thing was constant: The Lord was with Joseph, and Joseph obeyed, followed, and served the Lord throughout his many eventful years.

I. Joseph hated, envied, and conspired against (Gen. 37).

A. *Joseph faced problems at home.*

1. It all began at age seventeen. Joseph's brothers, with the exception of Benjamin, were all older than he. Obviously their morals and behaviors were subpar. It is difficult for a young man to grow up in the environment of evil brothers and yet maintain his honor, decency, and dignity. Joseph was a dreamer, and his dreams were prophetic.

2. He was hated by his brothers. The hatred stemmed from two sources—what Joseph did and what he said.

   a. The brothers hated him because he was the object of his father's love (Gen. 37:4).

   b. The brothers hated him because of his dreams (Gen. 37:5, 8).
      Our problem is not that we may be hated, but how we respond to it. Joseph is a good example. He did not retaliate, complain, or throw in the towel and quit because he was hated.

3. His brothers envied him (Gen. 37:11). Envy is the disposition of one who desires to be like the object of envy without paying the price.

4. His brothers conspired to kill him (Gen. 37:18). The lurking sins of hatred and envy eventually break out into vicious behavior and open hostility. The flagrant sins often are entertained in the mind before they are openly demonstrated.
5. His brothers stripped him of his coat (Gen. 37:23). This was no ordinary coat. It was a prized possession made by his father.

Joseph, then, early in life was hated, envied, conspired against, and stripped of his beautiful garment. In such an environment, what could a man do?

B. *The right response to opposition.*
   1. Joseph learned to listen, be quiet, and meditate. Observe that in all his trying experiences recorded in Genesis 37, there is no mention of verbal response to his brothers or of hostile retaliation toward them.
   2. Joseph obeyed his father (Gen. 37:14ff.).

II. Joseph in the pit (Gen. 37:24).

Until this moment, the animosity of the brothers was primarily emotional and verbal. It now broke out into volatile action revealing the sinfulness of human nature. Jesus taught this truth: "For from within, out of the heart of men, proceed evil thoughts . . . murders . . . wickedness . . . all these evil things come from within, and defile the man" (Mark 7:21–23). This is the second bitter jolt Joseph experienced.

A. *Some things he could have thought.*
   1. Is this what it is like to serve and honor God?
   2. Why me, Lord? I have done nothing to deserve this.
   3. If in my youth my fortunes are thus, what of the remainder of my life?
B. *Some things he must have thought.*
   1. Trials and difficulties are God's opportunities for revealing his power and providence.
   2. The answer to life's problems is not in the temporal, but in the eternal.

III. Joseph in Egypt as a slave (Gen. 37:28, 36).

A. *His status.* Joseph was nothing more than a common slave in Potiphar's house in Egypt. The series of hard knocks seemed to persist. First, he was hated by his brothers, then he was cast into the pit, now he was in Egypt as a slave.
B. *God's response to Joseph's position (Gen. 39:2).* In whatever circumstance, Joseph was faithful to his superiors, and his work prospered because the Lord was with him.
C. *Some New Testament truths that Joseph learned in Old Testament times.*

1. God's purposes may be frustrated, but they never fail.
2. The law of the harvest prevails though it may be slow.
3. God honors those who honor him.

Conclusion

How do we respond to hard knocks? Some of us may become bitter, vindictive, or retaliatory. Others may adopt a philosophy of resignation to them, while some may run and evade them. Some may seek relief through drugs, alcohol, or even suicide.

Our need is to learn from Joseph's experience that hard knocks are sure to come, that these may be blessed experiences through which God is working out his purpose. It is the crushed blossom that sends forth the sweetest fragrance. Righteousness will ultimately win; evil cannot.

WEDNESDAY EVENING, MAY 23

Title: The Promise of Spiritual Power

Text: "But you shall receive power when the Holy Spirit has come upon you; and you shall be my witnesses in Jerusalem and in all Judea and Samaria and to the end of the earth" **(Acts 1:8 RSV)**.

Scripture Reading: Acts 1:6–11

Introduction

The disciples of our Lord were human even as we are today. They had an imperfect grasp of spiritual reality and were in desperate need of divine instruction. This is evidenced by their inquiry concerning power and authority just before our Lord's ascension. We hear them asking, "Lord, will you at this time restore the kingdom to Israel?" (Acts 1:6 RSV). They were vitally interested in having the authority to administer governmental affairs and bring about a better economic and political situation for their nation. Even at this point, after much teaching by our Lord, they continued to have a material and political concept of what the kingdom of God ought to be.

Our Lord responded to their question concerning political power by declaring that they would receive spiritual power, the energy of God, for the accomplishment of God's work in the world.

The precious promise of our text contains some of the words of Jesus Christ that we should let dwell in our minds and hearts continually. We can rest assured that it is a part of the Father God's plan for us that we have the divine energy and strength for the doing of his will in the world today.

I. Pentecost means that power is available.

The divine event that took place on the Day of Pentecost was of tremendous significance then. The church, made up of a few Galilean peasants, was divinely authenticated and identified as the people of God through whom God was to carry on his redemptive purpose. On the Day of Pentecost, the church became the one body of Jesus Christ and was empowered to do the work of God in the world.

A. *The early believers received the power of a new insight and understanding of the death and resurrection of Jesus Christ.*
B. *The early believers received the power of a new courage that gave them boldness and a sense of authority in witnessing to the mighty works of God.*
C. *The early believers received the power of a new conviction of the lostness of people and of their need for Jesus Christ as Savior.*
D. *The early believers received the power of a new energy that vitalized them for the task that was confronting them.*

II. The power of the Holy Spirit is needed today.

Our Lord promised divine power to his church that then was and that now is.

A. *The power of the Holy Spirit is absolutely necessary if we would overcome evil.* There is evil within us and about us, and our only hope of being able to put to death the sins of the flesh and to experience the fruit of the Spirit is through the power that comes from God.
B. *The power of the Holy Spirit is absolutely necessary if we would overcome the power of our adversary the devil (Eph. 6:12; 1 Peter 5:8).* Many of us seemingly are unaware that we have a deadly enemy who is seeking to bring about our spiritual destruction. Jesus was confronted by the devil on many occasions, and his disciples through the ages have been hindered and hurt by him. In this modern day of sophistication, we need to recognize that the devil is not always dressed in red and carrying a pitchfork.
C. *The power of the Holy Spirit is necessary today because of the magnitude of our task.* Our Lord commissioned his disciples to be his witnesses. We are to witness in our Jerusalem—our own hometown—and among those who are about us. We are to be witnesses in Samaria— among those whom we have considered enemies and among those from whom we have been alienated because of prejudice. We are to be witnesses to our Lord in Judea. We have a relationship even to the state in which we live. We are to be witnesses for our Lord to the uttermost part of the earth. As followers of Jesus Christ, we need to have a heart of concern that is big enough to include the whole world. This calls not only for a warm heart and a tongue that is willing to verbalize to those about us the mighty works of God, but it also calls for a total stewardship of our resources that each of us might have a part in the world mission enterprise.
D. *The power of the Holy Spirit is absolutely necessary to aid us in our spiritual growth.* Paul wrote to the Galatian Christians and focused

on the fruit of the Spirit (5:22–23). To examine the fruit of the Spirit is to discover a verbal portrait of Jesus Christ. The Holy Spirit has come to dwell within us that he might reproduce within us the character and the spirit of our precious Lord.

Conclusion

Is the Holy Spirit a reality in your life? Are you aware, as a believer, that your body is the literal dwelling place of the Holy Spirit and that you are a shrine of the Holy Spirit? If you would experience his power, you must believe in his presence within you.

If you would experience his power, you must have faith to believe in the benevolent purposes of the Holy Spirit. The Holy Spirit does not come to make a religious fanatic out of you. He comes and abides that he might bring to fulfillment the potential beauty and fragrance that Christ can produce in a person's life. To experience the power of the Holy Spirit, we must respond to him and cooperate with him as he seeks to lead us in service to God and to others. The promise of the Lord concerning the availability of spiritual power is a word that we need to let dwell in us richly.

SUNDAY MORNING, MAY 27

Title: Guidelines for the Prevention of Divorce

Text: "For I hate divorce, says the LORD the God of Israel" **(Mal. 2:16 RSV)**.

Scripture Reading: Matthew 19:3–8

Hymns: "Great Redeemer," Harris
           "I Love Thy Kingdom, Lord," Dwight
           "Wonderful, Wonderful Jesus," Russell

Offertory Prayer: Holy Father, today we thank you for the beauty of springtime and for the joy of being able to see growing things about us. We thank you for the hope of a harvest that will come as a result of the planting season. Lord, we thank you today for the privilege of being able to bring tithes and offerings into your treasure that we might cooperate with you in redemptive activity through the church and through the missionary outreach program. Bless these offerings to the end that many will come to know Jesus Christ as Lord and Savior. In his name we pray. Amen.

Introduction

It has been declared that America's greatest danger today is the disintegration of homes. A divorce is the public and legal declaration of the disintegration and death of a home. Dr. David Mace, a specialist in marriage and family problems, has declared that something catastrophic is happening to marriage and the family in the United States and that no one seems to be doing anything about it. Statistics reveal that in many areas, more divorces are being recorded in the divorce courts than there are marriages being recorded in the county clerk's offices.

Divorce is no respecter of persons. It is invading every strata of our national life. Would it be possible for you to secure insurance against a divorce in your marriage? Many who find themselves experiencing this agony today never dreamed it would happen to them. What are you doing to avoid the possibility of divorce in your home? Do you understand and are you striving for the ideal in family relations in your marriage? Are you aware that there are many besetting problems that must be faced by almost all families if they are to achieve success? Do you recognize that there are certain dangers to family relationships that must be avoided at all costs? Are you seeking solutions to the existing problems?

The church should be involved in a ministry of divorce prevention. We who are members of the church must exercise a redemptive ministry toward those who have experienced the heartbreak and the agony of divorce. In compassion we need to pray for, support, and encourage those who have undergone this traumatic experience.

I. Help for the young and the unmarried.

Parents, pastors, and the church need to do all they can to help young people prepare for marriage. We can offer several suggestions to those who are unmarried that could provide some guidance for them and help them avoid a marriage that may later end in divorce.

    A. *Young people should recognize that marriage is for adults.* This is not a put down for the young. It is a recognition that marriage carries with it great responsibilities. Those who marry young greatly increase their chances of experiencing the heartbreak of divorce due to their immaturity at the time they entered into the relationship. All statistics indicate that it is better to reach emotional maturity before entering into the responsibilities of marriage.

    B. *Young people should recognize that romantic attraction alone does not guarantee happiness or ensure success in marriage.* Romantic attraction may be nothing more than the chemical reaction of a male to a female and vice versa. Romantic attraction is essential for a good marriage, but there must be much more than romantic attraction if the marriage is to be fulfilling through the years.

    C. *Young people should recognize that marriage is a part of God's plan for life.* This decision should be a matter of earnest prayer for guidance. If a young couple can enter their marriage making vows in the presence of God, invoking his blessings upon their actions, and asking for his help, their chances for success will be greatly increased.

    D. *Young people should recognize that happiness in marriage will be determined largely by the degree to which both of them simultaneously work for success.* It cannot be emphasized too much that while some may

want to use the letters S-E-X to spell the word *love,* a better way to
spell it is with the letters W-O-R-K. Success in marriage is never
automatic or accidental. It is more than the gift of God. It is the
achievement of a couple who diligently desire success and dedicate
themselves to achieving it in this most basic of human relationships.

II. Guidelines for the married.

Some discord is inevitable in every marriage. There is no such thing as a
perfect marriage, because such would involve the marriage of a perfect man
to a perfect woman, and they would have to relate to each other perfectly.

As said earlier, we must guard against assuming that success in marriage
will be accidental or automatic. There is no absolute guarantee that you can
avoid the heartbreak of a domestic tragedy. Marriage involves two people
and, thus, is by its nature a risk. There are some guidelines, which if followed
simultaneously by both spouses, can prevent the tragedy of divorce.

A. *Recognize and respond to your responsibility to God for the well-being of
your marriage (1 Peter 3:1–7).* It is interesting to note the emphasis
placed on responsibility in the Bible rather than on the rights and
privileges of those who choose to participate in marriage. The
responsibilities of the wife to her husband and of the husband to
his wife are emphasized forcefully (Eph. 5:21–33).

B. *Continue to work at bringing joy into the life of the one whom you
have chosen as a companion (Acts 20:35).* When our Lord spoke of
the habit of giving, he was not thinking primarily in terms of
bringing a tithe and an offering to the house of the Lord. He was
articulating a philosophy of life that works most effectively in the
marriage relationship. We receive happiness and joy only if we
have the capacity, disposition, and determination to give joy into
the life of the other.

C. *Accept the imperfections in your companion and pray for God's forgiveness
and grace to help.* Scripture says that all of us are sinners (Rom. 3:23).
This includes the finest woman and the best man among us. Each of
us is a fallen creature in need of full redemption in every area of our
life. If you would experience happiness in marriage, you must accept
the humanity, the fallenness, of your companion and pray for God's
grace and help both for your companion and for yourself.

D. *Practice forgiveness as the technique for dealing with mistreatment in marriage
(Matt. 18:21–22).* In no area of life is forgiveness for mistreatment
more necessary than in marriage. To forgive is to repudiate the right
to retaliate. It is to choose to refuse to cultivate feelings of hostility. It
is a deliberate decision to restore warm feelings.

E. *Be as courteous and accommodating to each other as you would be to your
best friend (Matt. 7:12).* If husband and wife would treat each other

as they treat their best friends, it would contribute greatly toward their happiness in marriage.

Conclusion

If the unmarried and those who are already married would not only avoid the heartbreak and tragedy of divorce but also find abundant life, they must put Christ at the center of their lives. So trust him in all your ways and depend on him for guidance and help. Seek to please him in all that you say, do, and think.

SUNDAY EVENING, MAY 27

Title: When Temptation Strikes

Text: "And it came to pass, as she spake to Joseph day by day, that he hearkened not unto her, to lie by her, or be with her" **(Gen. 39:10)**.

Scripture Reading: Genesis 39:1–12

Introduction

In recent years, science has discovered ways to immunize against typhoid fever, polio, the flu, measles, mumps, chicken pox, and a number of other viruses. We may use precautions against disease, accidents, and illness, and avoid them. During the winter months we may take flight to warmer climates to avoid cold weather. An inmate incarcerated in prison may through strategy, planning, and skill escape the institution. If people are repulsive to us, we may devise various methods to avoid them.

Evade, avoid, and *escape* are common words in our daily experiences. There is one thing that we cannot evade, avoid, or escape—*temptation*. It is the common experience of the young, the middle-aged, and the old.

Joseph gives us one of the best examples of how to prepare for temptation, how to behave when tempted, and how to benefit from the hour of trial (Gen. 39).

I. Let us prepare for the moment of temptation.

We all know about the hurricane season when torrential rains and terrifying winds lash the coastal areas. Much energy is expended by those in a hurricane's path to board up their homes and find a safe refuge. Likewise, there are things we may do to help us weather the trying time.

A. *We can maintain a daily walk with the Lord wherein we are conscious of his living presence (Gen. 39:2–3, 21, 23).* Four times in Joseph's experience it is said that "the LORD was with Joseph."

The Lord is always present, but it is most important that we realize it. There are certain things one just wouldn't do in the presence of others. But what about in God's presence?

171

B. *A daily faithfulness to our Lord in ministry and service will fortify us in the hour of adversity.* Exercise makes muscles strong. As a slave in Potiphar's house, Joseph "served him" (Gen. 39:4). As an inmate in Egypt's prison, "the keeper of the prison committed to Joseph's hand all the prisoners that were in the prison" (Gen. 39:22). Regardless of the circumstance, Joseph was always faithful to his master. A life that is filled with good things leaves little or no room for the intrusion of evil things.

C. *Daily development of character and growth in grace will make us strong (Gen. 39:6).* Throughout the passage these things are said of Joseph: "He was a prosperous man," "The LORD blessed the Egyptian's house for Joseph's sake," "But the LORD was with Joseph, and shewed him mercy," and "The LORD made it to prosper."

   Most planes carry reserve supplies in case of emergency. Growth in the grace of the Lord is the Christian's reserve in the hour of emergency. This needs to be done before the hour of trial; it is too late when trial comes.

D. *A life that is a blessing to others is not likely to falter in the hour of trial:* "And the LORD blessed the Egyptian's house for Joseph's sake" (Gen. 39:5). Even evil people may be blessed when associated with the righteous. As the righteous bring blessings to the wicked, they are storing up reserves in their life against temptation.

E. *A life saturated daily in the Word of God can face the testing times with triumph.* Jesus was tempted by Satan in the early days of his ministry, but each time he repulsed Satan by using the Word of God. May we hide God's Word in our heart so that we may not sin in the hour of trial.

II. Let us make the appropriate response to each temptation.

A. *We may say "no" as did Joseph:* "But he refused" (Gen. 39:8). It was the refusals of Moses in Pharaoh's house that helped him to identify with his people and serve the Lord. Joseph could not commit adultery with Potiphar's wife because it would be a sin against God.

B. *A responsible person must realize that his or her behavior must be honorable:* "He hath committed all that he hath to my hand" (Gen. 39:9). Privilege and opportunity place one under heavy responsibility. The apostle Paul, because of what Christ had given him, felt this responsibility and declared, "I am debtor" (Rom. 1:14).

C. *We must realize that submission to temptation is sin against God:* "How can I do this great wickedness, and sin against God?" (Gen. 39:9).

D. *Avoid flirting with trouble:* "He kept out of her way as much as possible" (Gen. 39:9 TLB).

E. *We can retreat from temptation:* "He . . . fled, and got him out" (Gen. 39:12). Throughout the Scriptures we are admonished to flee from and shun temptation. When we play with fire, we are likely to get burned.

III. Let us learn the nature and course of temptation.

A. *Temptation is nearly always an appeal to desires.* Potiphar's wife cast her eyes of desire upon Joseph. Had Joseph responded in like manner, he would have been overcome. Desires are the forerunners of behavior. If desires are holy, actions are likely to be holy.

B. *Temptations, in one form or another, are continuous and persistent.* Potiphar's wife spoke to Joseph day after day (Gen. 39:10). Christians must put on the whole armor of God so that they may effectively stand against the persistent attacks of Satan.

C. *The righteous, though innocent, may suffer from temptation.* The circumstantial evidence presented by Potiphar's wife appeared to be conclusive. However, the evidence did not support the truth. As a result of circumstantial evidence, Joseph was cast into prison.

IV. Let us be aware of the benefits of temptation.

A. *Temptations may be the wings on which the faithful child of God rises to honor.* It was from trial that Joseph came forth as prime minister of Egypt. "If God be for us, who can be against us?"

B. *Evil cannot win; righteousness will always be triumphant.* God's promise is that he will honor those who honor him.

C. *Temptations refine the dross and reveal character.* The inner life comes to the surface in the hour of trials. Joseph's convictions, character, and true nature came to the surface. His temptation became the opportunity he needed to "show his stuff."

Conclusion

Temptations are certain to come. We need to constantly be preparing so that we may be fortified against the deluge. Response to temptation determines victory or defeat. "Blessed is the man that endureth temptation: for when he is tried, he shall receive the crown of life, which the Lord hath promised to them that love him" (James 1:12).

WEDNESDAY EVENING, MAY 30

Title: A Word of Triumph

Text: "Fear not, I am the first and last, and the living one; I died, and behold I am alive for evermore, and I have the keys of Death and Hades" **(Rev. 1:17–18 RSV)**.

Scripture Reading: Revelation 1:12–18

Introduction

Today's text is one of the greatest sayings that ever fell from the lips of our Lord. John, the beloved apostle, had been exiled to the Isle of Patmos during the Roman emperor's persecution of Christianity. He had issued an imperial policy whose purpose was to eradicate Christianity from the face of the earth. It seemed as if this policy might be successful. John, the beloved, had been exiled and separated from those dear to him. Being in the Spirit on the Lord's Day, he received this vision of the triumphant, living Lord who spoke to him words of assurance and hope.

I. A vision of the resurrected Christ.

   A. *The vision described in Revelation 1 portrays Jesus Christ as alive from the dead, triumphant over sin, death, and the grave.*

   B. *John and all of the other believers toward the end of the first century of the Christian era stood in great need of this vision of the Christ who would be eternally victorious over all world situations.*

   C. *This experience John had, in which the living Christ came to him, assured him that Jesus Christ was spiritually present with him in sovereign power.*

   D. *This experience assured John that Jesus Christ would be ultimately victorious over the present tragic world conditions.*

II. The meaning of the resurrected Christ.

   A. *The resurrection identified Jesus Christ as the powerful Son of God.*

   B. *The resurrection of Christ vindicated Jesus of Nazareth as being all he had claimed to be.*

   C. *The resurrection of Jesus Christ liberated him from the limitations of his humanity and made it possible for him to be everywhere at all times with his followers.*

III. The meaning of this vision and these words for today.

   A. *The words from the risen Christ can do much to take away our fear of death.*

   B. *These words from the risen, living Christ can assure us that Jesus Christ is always with us.*

   C. *These words from the living Christ can assure us that indescribable spiritual energy is available to those who trust him and follow him in a life of faithful obedience.*

Conclusion

The risen Christ said, "Fear not." With Christ as our Savior and Lord revealing to us the love of God, we should not be afraid of God. Nor should we be afraid of the future, of death, or of eternity. Let us write Christ's precious words on the walls of our heart. Let us allow this precious promise to make an impact on our lives for the glory of God and the good of others.

SUGGESTED PREACHING PROGRAM FOR THE MONTH OF

JUNE

■ **Sunday Mornings**

Continue "Christ in Marriage and Family Living" through Father's Day. On the following Sunday begin the series "God's Plan of Salvation," based on texts from Paul's letter to the Romans.

■ **Sunday Evenings**

Continue with "The Way of Faith," a series based on the spiritual experiences of the great characters of the book of Genesis.

■ **Wednesday Evenings**

Begin a series of biographical studies titled "Witnesses from the Past Speak to the Present."

SUNDAY MORNING, JUNE 3

Title: The Practice of Forgiveness in Family Relations

Text: "Take heed to yourselves; if your brother sins, rebuke him, and if he repents, forgive him; and if he sins against you seven times in the day, and turns to you seven times, and says, 'I repent,' you must forgive him" **(Luke 17:3–4 RSV)**.

Scripture Reading: Luke 17:1–4

Hymns: "Saved, Saved," Scholfield
"Standing on the Promises," Carter
"My Faith Looks Up to Thee," Palmer

Offertory Prayer: Holy Father, thank you for offering to us the gift of forgiveness through repentance and faith in the Lord Jesus Christ. Thank you for eternal life through Christ and for your indwelling Spirit. Thank you also for your precious promises. Today we come bringing the praise of our lips, the love of our hearts, and the gifts of our hands for your glory and for the advance of your kingdom. Accept these tithes and offerings and bless them to the end that others will experience your goodness and grace. Through Jesus Christ. Amen.

Introduction

All human beings are mistake makers. We all are imperfect creatures. We sin against God, ourselves, and others. Parents mistreat their children. Married partners mistreat each other. Children mistreat their parents.

Children within the family mistreat each other. All members of the family circle stand in need of practicing the teachings of our Lord concerning forgiveness.

All human beings are mistreated. Each of us will experience injury and injustice at the hands of others. Some of us have been abused by our parents. Some of us have been terribly mistreated within the bonds of marriage. Some parents have experienced painful and repeated injury at the hands of their children. Some are in pain and agony because of the stupidity or selfishness of a brother or a sister.

How will you deal constructively with injury and mistreatment? What is your method of dealing with mistreatment at the hands of family members?

If we are professing Christians, we are obligated not only to listen but also to heed the teachings of Jesus Christ at this point. Jesus suggested, recommended, and requires that we use a forgiving spirit and attitude in dealing with the injuries that are inflicted upon us by others.

I. Consider the possible methods you have for dealing with mistreatment.

A. *You can resort to retaliation.* You can be vindictive, and you can seek to secure revenge. You can strike out and return evil for evil, blow for blow, contempt for contempt, and insult for insult.

B. *You can suppress your hostility as a result of being mistreated by others.* To suppress hostility is to let it smolder within you. Suppression will eventually create a volcanic explosion. It will contribute to an attitude of hate that will poison your whole system and create a cancer within your mind and emotions.

C. *You can resort to a self-destructive retreat into self-pity.* When we experience mistreatment at the hands of others, if we do not retaliate, if we do not suppress our hostility, we may resort to self-pity, and this can lead to discouragement, despair, and depression as black as midnight.

II. Consider Jesus's method for dealing with mistreatment.

One of the final sayings of our Lord from the cross reveals his personal method of dealing with mistreatment at the hands of others: "Jesus said, 'Father, forgive them; for they know not what they do'" (Luke 23:34 RSV).

A. *To forgive is to reject the right to retaliate, to strike back, to return evil for evil.* Joseph provides us a remarkable Old Testament example of a brother forgiving the injury he had experienced at the hands of his brothers (Gen. 50:15–21).

B. *To forgive is the deliberate decision on the part of the injured not to harbor hostility toward the one who inflicted the injury.*

C. *To forgive is to deliberately decide to return good for evil, to restore a broken relationship, to reestablish a shattered fellowship.*

D. *To forgive is to restore a warm relationship.* To forgive is to relate to the other person in terms of what is highest and best for the one who has mistreated you.

E. *Forgiveness and forgetfulness are not one and the same thing.* Forgiveness must be repeated over and over every time the injury is remembered (Matt. 18:22). By insisting on the repetition of forgiveness, our Lord was seeking to insure us against the self-destructive effects that are certain to come toward the person who refuses to practice forgiveness.

Conclusion

The practice of forgiveness toward others is based on our pre-forgiveness by our Father God. Paul said, "And be kind to one another, tenderhearted, forgiving one another, as God in Christ forgave you" (Eph. 4:32 RSV). He repeated these words of encouragement to the saints at Colossae (Col. 3:12–13).

God's forgiveness of us is hindered if we do not forgive those who sin against us. To refuse to be forgiving means that our prayers will go unanswered (Matt. 6:13–14). When we refuse to be forgiving, we cooperate with the devil as he seeks to establish a beachhead within our life from which he can work out his purposes in us and through us (2 Cor. 2:10–11).

It is never easy to be forgiving toward those who have sinned against us. Somehow in the grace of God, if we will tarry in Gethsemane and recognize the tremendous price Jesus Christ paid that we might experience forgiveness, we will find the help we need to be forgiving toward those who have been unkind and who have brought injury into our hearts and lives.

To be forgiving is not a price we pay for the privilege of being forgiven; it is a condition we must meet in order to receive forgiveness. Let us ask our Father God to give us the grace to be forgiving toward all who have sinned against us in order that we might experience the joy of his forgiveness.

SUNDAY EVENING, JUNE 3

Title: After the Storm—the Sunshine

Text: "Pharaoh said unto Joseph, See, I have set thee over all the land of Egypt" (**Gen. 41:41**).

Scripture Reading: Genesis 41:37–46

Introduction

Joseph had experienced thirteen difficult years. He had been a victim of his brothers' evil design and had been cast into a pit. From the pit he became a slave in Potiphar's house. Through the deceit and craft of Potiphar's wife, he was cast into prison. While in prison he interpreted the dreams of the king's butler and baker, but when the butler was set free, he forgot about Joseph.

These events happened when Joseph was in the bloom of young manhood. Most young men would have ended in despair, but Joseph kept on serving. He served his father obediently, Potiphar's house faithfully, the prison keeper and prisoners loyally. In this manner Joseph really was serving God and learning obedience through suffering.

At this point in Joseph's life the clouds began to pass away, the sunshine appeared, and in the midst there was a rainbow. After humiliation came exaltation. From the darkness of the dungeon, Joseph moved suddenly to the delights of the palace.

Has there ever been in all history another who moved suddenly from prison to prime minister? God himself enabled Joseph to suddenly emerge from the storm into the sunshine. Joseph's sudden promotion was no accident. Certain factors in his life led to this moment of exaltation. We shall look at these factors now.

I. Joseph knew that God was in control of his creation.

A. *He knew that God gave the answer: "God shall give Pharaoh an answer" (Gen. 41:16).* People have sought answers to their problems through various media throughout the centuries—through science and technology, education and learning, wealth and possessions. None of these can offer all the answers. God, unfortunately, is usually the last resort for people searching for answers to their problems.

B. *He knew that God revealed himself and his ways to man: "God hath shewed Pharaoh what he is about to do" (Gen. 41:25).* There is hardly a more sublime fact in the Bible than the truth that God reveals himself and his ways to us. His self-disclosure is an evidence of his love and concern for his creation. He is knowable, and his desire for us is that we might know him. Jesus Christ, his Son, is the true revelation, and all who see him may see the Father. If God is knowable, he is personal.

C. *He knew that God was able and would accomplish his purposes: "It is because the thing is established by God, and God will shortly bring it to pass" (Gen. 41:32).* Skeptics often question the power and authority of God. In the case of Egypt, God had ordained seven years of plenty and seven years of drought. He would surely bring it to pass.

The shadows in Joseph's life now began to turn to sunshine, for he understood that God provides the answers, makes himself personally known, and would bring to pass that which he had purposed. These are the truths that provide foundation, give assurance, and enable us to live in victory.

II. Joseph's inner and personal life honored and pleased God.

A. *He was filled and possessed by the Spirit of God: "Can we find such a man as this, in whom is the Spirit of God?" (Gen. 41:38 RSV).* It is amazing that a pagan ruler and his servants would recognize this.

The most telling and revealing aspect of our lives is that which comes from within. The filling of the Spirit is for the purpose of enabling us to give witness to our Lord. Even Pharaoh and his servants became aware of the mighty acts of God through Joseph's Spirit-filled life. Joseph knew that God had given him the wisdom to interpret dreams and thus reveal the purposes of the Almighty, but it is most convincing that Pharaoh himself testified that "God hath shewed thee all this."

Because Joseph was filled with the Spirit of God, Pharaoh saw that which "was good" (Gen. 41:37). The Spirit, indeed, produces and brings forth that which is good. It is thus the inner life of Joseph that enables the Egyptians to know—to some degree—the living God.

B. *He was discreet and wise: "There is none so discreet and wise as thou art" (Gen. 41:39).* The source of all true wisdom is God (see Prov. 1:7; 9:10; James 3:17). Why was Joseph wise? Was it because of educational advantages in Egypt? There is but one answer: He was a man in whom was the Spirit of God. We are wise when our lives are controlled by the Spirit.

C. *He became a worthy leader and ruler: "Thou shall be over my house" (Gen. 41:40).* God will never permit his creation to be dominated by evil, though evil is present. It is the righteous who will inherit the earth. The inner qualities of Joseph's life qualified him to be a wise and discreet leader. The sun, so long obscured by conspiracy, slavery, imprisonment, and forgetfulness, now begins to shine.

III. Joseph's circumstances reveal the sunshine.

A. *He was in authority over all Egypt: "I have set thee over all the land of Egypt" (Gen. 41:41).* What a change in circumstances from his past thirteen years! One day Joseph was a prison inmate; now he was in authority over all Egypt. It is even as the man of God said to Eli the priest, "Them that honour me I will honour" (1 Sam. 2:30).

B. *He was arrayed with kingly adornments (Gen. 41:42).*
   1. A ring on his hand signified his authority.
   2. The linen on his body signified his identity.
   3. A chain on his neck signified royalty.

C. *He was given preeminence: "And he made him to ride in the second chariot" (Gen. 41:43).* The clouds now gave way to sunshine. We have heard it said that might makes right, but in this case it was right that made might.

IV. Joseph's performance reveals the sunshine.

Two things are prominent during the next fourteen years. Joseph gathered up food for storage during the seven years of abundance, and during the following seven years he dispensed the food to drought-stricken Egyptians (Gen. 41:47–57).

A. *God's wise servants will always need to store up before they can give out.* We can only impart that which we have received. The apostle Paul recognized this principle when he wrote to the Corinthians, "I delivered unto you the first of all that which I also received" (1 Cor. 15:3). His desire for the Roman Christians was that he might impart to them some spiritual gift, but one can hardly impart that which he has not first appropriated to himself. What we store up in the plenteous years makes us adequate for the lean years.

B. *God's wise servants should always dispense that which they have received.* The Dead Sea is dead because it is always receiving the waters of the Jordan but never giving out. Life was spared and blessed in Egypt because Joseph dispensed to the needy in the time of their distress. Is your life a channel of blessing? It is to the extent that you receive and impart.

Conclusion

Joseph's faith in God plus the reality of God in his inner life were two factors that brought the sunshine into his life. In the midst of exaltation and promotion, he remained faithful to his stewardship. When God is real to us and we are faithful to him, we need not despair. The sun will shine.

WEDNESDAY EVENING, JUNE 6

Title: Abel: The Man of Respect

Text: "And Abel, he also brought of the firstlings of his flock and of the fat thereof. And the LORD had respect unto Abel and to his offering" **(Gen. 4:4)**.

Scripture Reading: Genesis 4:1–8

Introduction

Abel is the first name recorded in Hebrews 11, the chapter referred to as the hall of faith. There is a lesson for twentieth-century Christians from a man such as Abel.

I. Consider who Abel was.

A. *His name must have meaning.* Even though most Bible characters' names have meaning, we cannot always determine the meaning with accuracy. There are two possibilities as to the meaning of Abel. His name may mean "breath" or "vapor," which is suggested by his brief existence. It also may mean "shepherd" or "herdsman," suggesting his occupation.

B. *Abel and his brother, Cain, represent the two fundamental pursuits of civilized life.* Cain was a farmer and Abel a keeper of livestock. Each of these is a noble occupation and is essential in modern-day living. It was what Abel did with his livelihood in relation to God that made the difference.

II. Consider some facts about Abel's offering.

A. *To discuss Abel's assets, it is almost impossible not to discuss Cain's faults.* In this discussion, the focus is on Abel and not Cain. Therefore, there is need to discipline oneself in seeking the positive and eliminating the negative. One never finds oneself right with one's heavenly Father on the faults of someone else, but on his or her own personal relationship to God.

B. *How did Abel receive a testimony of righteousness?* Since he was the first man to receive divine approval, it is significant for all humankind to take notice. He had no established precedent to follow, no example to emulate. He offered his offering out of a heart that was right with God. He is also the first example of what faith can do when one exercises it. Hebrews says, "By faith Abel offered unto God a more excellent sacrifice" (11:4). His faith was quality and not just quantity.

C. *This man Abel still speaks (Heb. 11:4).* This is some kind of legacy. Abel's action stimulates action in others. His action testifies how faith is rewarded, how one can be in favor with God forever.

Conclusion

The best reason for studying a man like Abel is to learn some lessons. What are some of these lessons? We should consider the offerings we bring to God day by day. For any kind of material offering to be acceptable, we must offer ourselves first. Another lesson we can learn from our Scripture reading is that when a Christian dies physically, he or she still speaks. May that truth spur us on to make sure our lives speak the right things.

SUNDAY MORNING, JUNE 10

Title: Who Is Responsible for Christian Home Life?

Text: "Be subject to one another out of reverence for Christ" (**Eph. 5:21 RSV**).

Scripture Reading: Ephesians 5:21–6:4

Hymns: "God, Our Father, We Adore Thee," Frazer
"I Would Be True," Walter
"God, Give Us Christian Homes!" McKinney

Offertory Prayer: Holy Father, today we thank you for family blessings. We are grateful for the blessings you have bestowed upon us through our parents, through our faithful spouses, and through our children. We give ourselves to you again today, and we bring the fruits of our labor in the form of tithes and offerings. We ask that you receive them and bless them to the end that your kingdom will come in the hearts and homes of people everywhere. In Jesus's name. Amen.

Introduction

Something tragic is happening to marriage and family living in America. Millions of marriages are ending in divorce. This is a tragedy of indescribable proportions for everyone involved.

Who is responsible for this national tragedy? We cannot hold the government or the school systems responsible for the breakup of marriages. To what degree is the church responsible through neglecting to teach and preach the truths of God concerning this most important of human relationships? To what degree are the parents of previous generations responsible for the marital tragedies of the present?

In the final analysis, we must come to the individual family unit and recognize that the husband, wife, and children each have a definite responsibility for the welfare of home life.

I. We are responsible to Christ for our home life.

"Be subject to one another out of reverence for Christ" (Eph. 5:21). The apostle Paul encourages us to respond to the truth that we are responsible to our Lord for the manner in which we relate to each other in family relationships.

   A. *The home is of divine origin (Gen. 1:27–28).* Marriage is a provision of God for humankind's well-being. Marriage is God's remedy for human loneliness and incompleteness (Gen. 2:18–23). God made us "male and female." He made us for each other.
   B. *The Bible contains divine laws to safeguard the home.* This truth is emphasized in the Ten Commandments.
      1. The fifth commandment concerns the relationship of children to their parents (Ex. 20:12).
      2. The seventh commandment sets forth the sacredness of sex and insists on the preservation of sexual purity (Ex. 20:14; cf. v. 17).

There is a mutual or reciprocal responsibility among the members of the family according to the plan and purpose of God.

II. The New Testament contains guidelines that point toward wholesome and creative family relationships.

As we face the high challenges of our Lord and the apostles, most of us will recognize our failures and our need for forgiveness.

   A. *A guideline for both husband and wife (Eph. 5:21).* The husband and the wife live under the grace, guidance, and judgment of our Lord. It is the divine plan for us that we adjust ourselves to each other as husbands and wives in a creative and healthy relationship that is mutually beneficial. We cannot mistreat our companion in marriage without having to deal with a just and righteous Lord. God in all his grace will assist us as we seek to work together in love and faith and helpfulness.

B. *Guidelines for the wives.* There are two in our Scripture passage.

    1. "Wives, be subject to your husbands, as to the Lord" (Eph. 5:22). If this verse is taken out of context, it seemingly discriminates against the wife. This is not the intention of the writer. In Christianity we all stand as equals before God. Paul declared to the Galatians, "There is neither Jew nor Greek, there is neither slave nor free, there is neither male nor female; for you are all one in Christ Jesus" (3:28).

    2. "Let the wife see that she respects her husband" (Eph. 5:33). Such verses have been used to justify domination rather than to encourage devotion. Paul is not giving husbands a right to dominate and to be tyrants over their wives.

        Our Scripture passage is dealing with the problem of individual self-assertion and insistence on private personal rights within the union of marriage. Paul is suggesting that in the relationship of marriage, the wife is to recognize her husband as the "president of the corporation" and to adjust herself to this fact. It has been said that the so-called democratic family, which may be either headless or two-headed, often leads to confusion and disappointment. The subordination of the wife to the husband is to be voluntary, and the reverence she gives to her husband is to be deserved by him.

C. *Guidelines for husbands.* Two guidelines are suggested for husbands.

    1. The husband is to love his wife as Christ loved the church (Eph. 5:25). The word translated "love" does not refer to sexual love. It refers to the sacrificial, self-giving love illustrated by Christ when he died on the cross for the church. Sacrificial love that gives of itself without reservation is absolutely essential for successful family relationships. It should characterize all family members.

    2. The husband is to love his wife as he loves his own body (Eph. 5:28–30). From the viewpoint of Scripture, marriage is a "one-flesh" relationship. Both the husband and the wife are to be as concerned about the well-being of their companion as they are their own "flesh and blood." From God's viewpoint, the husband-wife relationship is a one-flesh relationship, and Paul affirms, "No man ever hates his own flesh, but nourishes and cherishes it, as Christ does the church, because we are members of his body" (Eph. 5:29–30 RSV).

D. *Guidelines for children (Eph. 6:1–3).* Children are encouraged to live in obedience to parents. This is because God has appointed parents to be the teachers, guides, and correctors of their children. This is the divine order. Children who choose to disregard parental guidelines expose themselves to great danger.

Young people, if you are at war with your parents, you need to recognize that you are walking on thin ice. You need to recognize that you are close to a precipice over which you could plunge to your own destruction.

Parents are not perfect. Parents are not always right. Because they are human, they make mistakes. In most instances they sincerely desire what is best for their children, and in many instances they have a better concept of what is best for their children than those children have for themselves.

Conclusion

Invite Christ Jesus to come into your home life and be Lord of the husband-wife relationship and parent-child relationships. Let Christ assist you with problems that disturb you and the questions that upset you. Seek to please Christ in the attitude you take and in the activities in which you engage. Deliberately seek to serve Christ in your family relationships. Be a witness for Jesus Christ and share with the members of your family your experiences with God's love and grace and what you observe him doing in the hearts and lives of others.

Each of us is responsible, at least to some degree, for the well-being of the home of which we are a part. God wants to help us and will if we will let him.

SUNDAY EVENING, JUNE 10

Title: All These Things Are Against Me

Text: "Me have ye bereaved of my children: Joseph is not, and Simeon is not, and ye will take Benjamin away: all these things are against me" (**Gen. 42:36**).

Scripture Reading: Genesis 42:36–38

Introduction

There is a vivid contrast between the father, Jacob, and his son, Joseph. Jacob came near to the end of his life lamenting, "All these things are against me." Joseph came to the end of his life in the flush of victory saying, "But as for you, ye thought evil against me; but God meant it unto good" (Gen. 50:20). Both had experienced tragedy, travail, and temptation. For one these had become stones about his neck, for the other they had become stones upon which to step.

Why did Jacob end up annoyed while Joseph ended up assured? Why was the one bothered and baffled while the other was buoyant and brave? Why was one confused, the other composed, one dejected and disgusted, while the other distinguished and dynamic? These contrasts are not accidents but outcomes. While some problems are unavoidable, others often are created.

A young contractor working in his father's firm was given the assignment of building a house. The younger partner decided to use inferior and less expensive materials in the structure, thinking that the profits then would be greater. Upon completion of the building, he was told that the house was a gift in which he would then live. The young man had to live in and with that which he had put into the house.

Is this not the point between Jacob and Joseph? They were so close in kinship but so far apart in that which each incorporated in his life.

I. The ultimate in life is much a result of what is initial.
  A. *The character and nature of Jacob's early life.*
    1. Jacob entered the world with his hand on his brother's heel. This is an omen of his innate nature or desire to cause his brother to fall. Such a spirit is contrary to the way of faith. Such an attitude early in life is certain to incur retribution, causing one to end up with the lament, "All these things are against me."
    2. Jacob resorted to deceit and lying in his youth. The boys were hardly grown before Jacob, in complicity with his mother, through deceit, craft, and manipulation, cheated his brother Esau out of his blessing. Even prior to this he had swindled Esau's birthright away from him. By divine law, what one sows he will reap. Early in life Jacob sowed treachery, sham, and fraud. At harvest time he could only exclaim, "All these things are against me."
  B. *The advantages of Jacob.*
    1. Before Jacob was born, he was the object of divine love (Rom. 9:11–13). Advantages mean little unless there is a proper response.
    2. He was the one to whom God had intended the divine inheritance (Gen. 27:28; 28:13). Even God's gifts must be received by faith rather than human procurement.
    3. He was wealthy (Gen. 30:43; 31:18). By the world's standards Jacob was successful. His wealth failed to bring peace to his heart, however.

Because Jacob was an object of God's love, an heir of God's promise, and a man of wealth, we would think that he would come to the end of his life rejoicing, but to the contrary, he ended up with a mournful dirge, "All these things are against me."

II. Problems are more complex when imaginations run rampant.
Many of the perplexing situations we face are compounded by ignorance of the truth and a vivid imagination that goes beyond reality.

A. *Jacob thought that Joseph's and Simeon's absence had resulted in their death: "Joseph is not, and Simeon is not" (Gen. 42:36).* This, to be sure, was not the case. In reality both were much alive.

Job's misunderstanding of the nature and ways of God added terror to his dilemma. A victim of tradition, he came to a false conclusion—namely, that loss of health, property, and family was evidence of divine disfavor. Once Job learned the sovereignty and greatness of God, his problems disappeared.

Jacob exclaimed, "All these things are against me," but they were not nearly so pronounced as his imagination had led him to believe.

B. *False conclusions about the past may lead to inaccurate forecast of the future: "And ye will take Benjamin away" (Gen. 42:36).*

The present often is colored by the past. One false notion becomes a base of operations for yet others. One of the tricks human nature plays on us is that the dreadful experiences of yesterday are bound to confront us today or tomorrow. Those thus convinced will conclude with Jacob, "All these things are against me."

III. The contrasts in Joseph's life make the difference.

Joseph was a dreamer in his youth while Jacob was a schemer. Jacob practiced deception toward his family while Joseph prepared for deliverance. Jacob defrauded his father but Joseph demonstrated devotion to his. The outcome was demonstrative. Jacob ended up in the throes of depression while Joseph reflected dignity. The older of the two exhibited discouragement and distress while the younger became a diplomat.

A. *Joseph's disadvantages were his opportunities.*
    1. He was envied by his brothers. This could have provoked Joseph to a spirit of retaliation, but he lived in the calm confidence that God had a purpose for all his trials.
    2. He was cast into the pit by his brothers. This could have caused him to question or doubt the goodness of God, but it became the occasion in his life through which God could show himself mighty in Joseph's behalf. Man's extremities are God's opportunities.
    3. He was a slave in Egypt. This could have been a cause for loneliness and dejection. However, Joseph was aware that God was with him even in a foreign land and among a strange people. As a slave he served God and his fellow humans faithfully.
    4. He was the victim of a falsehood by Potiphar's wife. Even in the moment of temptation, Joseph became an example of morality and purity. He could not become a victim of illicit sex and sin against God.

5. He was in prison for many days. This could have resulted in despair. "What's the use of serving God?" he might have asked, but he continued to serve and wait.

Few people have ever been subjected to more sinister designs than Joseph. Trials were but the road to triumph, his adversities were the means for advancement, and his opposition became his opportunity. Thus, Joseph ends up exclaiming, 'Ye thought evil against me, but God meant it unto good."

B. *Joseph's character counts.* It is important to have things for God. It is even more important to do things for him. But it is most important to be something for God. Character is the basis for possessions and deeds.

   1. Joseph was faithful. There seems never to be the slightest deviation from this principle. He was faithful to his father, his brothers, and even his masters in Egypt.

   2. Joseph was fruitful. Seemingly everything he did, regardless of the circumstance, was rewarded. Just as the Lord Jesus increased in favor and stature with God and man, so did Joseph.

   3. Joseph was forgiving. Men of lesser stature would not have demonstrated this principle as did Joseph.

The person who dares to live like Joseph in faithfulness and forgiveness will be fruitful.

Conclusion

Many of us are beaten and bruised by the vicissitudes of life. Two factors enable us to overcome: our ability to make the right response to testings and the ability to appropriate the resources available to us in time of need.

WEDNESDAY EVENING, JUNE 13

Title: Enoch: The Man Who Walked with God

Text: "Enoch walked with God: and he was not; for God took him" (**Gen. 5:24**).

Scripture Reading: Genesis 5:18–24

Introduction

Enoch is presented in the Bible as a man who was translated, or taken from this life, without death. He was translated not meritoriously, but by faith (Heb. 11:5).

I. Enoch walked with God (Gen. 5:24).

A. *To walk with God, we must move in the divine direction.* Everything is moving. Everything is in transition. For Christians to become what they are intended and/or hope to be, they have to move in a godly direction.

B. *To walk with God we must be in agreement with God.* Amos 3:3 says, "Can two walk together, except they be agreed?" Agreement means no controversy, acting in the will of God. Those who are in agreement with God have repented and confessed their sin. They are then bound with the purpose, passion, and power of God.

C. *To walk with God there must be mutual trust.* Enoch trusted God and God trusted Enoch. There was no doubting or suspicion on the part of one for the other.

D. *To walk with God we must be in step with him.* We cannot run ahead of God and still walk with him. Neither can we lag behind and walk with him. We must be in step with him.

II. Enoch pleased God (Heb. 11:5).

A. *What are some essentials to pleasing God?* We must be accepted by him (Gen. 4:4). Each person is accepted by God through faith. Faith enables us to submit to God's will. We are accepted by God when we live, move, and act according to God's will.

Also, the manner of doing God's will must be pleasing to him. As followers of the Lord Jesus, we are to be humble (1 Cor. 15:11), sincere (Isa. 38:3), and cheerful (2 Cor. 8:12; 9:7).

B. *There are two summary statements in regard to pleasing God.* To please God we must walk before him in uprightness and obedience. We also must respond to God's overtures and trust his guidance.

III. Enoch was translated (taken from this life) by God, and his translation was done by faith (Heb. 11:5).

Faith is twofold (Heb. 11:6).

A. *We must believe in the existence of God.* Faith is the only thing that puts God in his proper place and man in his proper place as they relate to each other. Faith is surrender to God and resting on him. Faith wills what God wills and lets God have his way. No amount of work will compensate for lack of faith. To refuse to believe God is to make him out a liar.

B. *We must believe that God is a rewarder of those who seek him.* Enoch's reward was translation. He was changed from one place to another and was not overcome by death. This is the Christian's reward, for God has "rescued us from the dominion of darkness and brought us into the kingdom of the Son he loves" (Col. 1:13 NIV).

IV. Enoch prophesied (Jude 14).

Walking with God precedes service. Prophesying is a service. Enoch lived in a trying and difficult day. He had faith and was of service. He then was rewarded.

Conclusion

Let's make the presence of God our one desire and his will our one choice. Let's make God's help our one trust and his likeness our one hope.

SUNDAY MORNING, JUNE 17

Title: Helping Fathers to Be Good Fathers

Text: "When Enoch had lived sixty-five years, he became the father of Methuselah" **(Gen. 5:21 RSV)**.

Scripture Reading: Genesis 5:21–24

Hymns: "Breathe on Me, Breath of God," Hatch
        "Jesus Saves," Owens
        "Saved, Saved," Scholfield

Offertory Prayer: Holy Father, thank you for being our heavenly Father. Thank you for the love, mercy, and strength that comes to us through this relationship. We come today to love you and to praise you. In our lives we would fulfill your purpose for us. We would live worthy of this relationship and encourage others to trust in you. Because you have given so much of yourself to us, we come today giving portions of ourselves to you in the form of offerings. These offerings indicate our desire to belong completely to you and to be useful in your loving work. Through Jesus Christ we pray. Amen.

Introduction

What is a father? To some he is a biological incidental. To some he is an economic necessity. And to some a father is simply the responsible party. The root meaning of the word *father* is "the source or prototype." The father is "that one from whom I get my strength." Fortunate indeed is the family who has the privilege of growing up to maturity under the influence of one who personifies integrity and goodness and all those graces of character that God wants to see nourished and flourishing.

I. God can help you be a good father.

As a father you are potentially the child's finest teacher about God. When teaching his disciples how to pray, Jesus taught them to address the Eternal One as "Our Father which art in heaven." This statement was a great compliment to the father of the home in which Jesus was born and grew to maturity. It also provided insight into the character of God.

II. Christ will help you be a good father.

There are many illustrations in the New Testament of fathers who came to Jesus in need of his help and he responded affirmatively.

A. *An official whose son was ill came to Jesus in his distress (John 4:46–54).* Jesus met a need in the life of the son which the father could not supply. Christ will make a contribution through you to your children if you will but come to him and let him do his work of grace and power in your life.
B. *A ruler of the synagogue came to Jesus on behalf of his daughter who was at the point of death (Mark 5:21–24).* Our Lord responded immediately to this father's plea for help and demonstrated his miraculous power by restoring the daughter to life because of the father's great faith (Mark 5:35–43). We can be assured that our Lord wants to help us when death comes or crises confront us.
C. *Matthew records the plight of a father whose child was a helpless epileptic (Matt. 17:14–20).* With faith in his love and his power, we need to come to Jesus Christ that he might help us as we seek to minister to the needs of our children.

III. The Holy Spirit will help you to be a good father.

Many are frightened at the thought of the Holy Spirit being at work in their hearts and lives. We must not be frightened away from making a personal response to the Holy Spirit because of the exorbitant claims of some.

A. *You became the dwelling place of the Holy Spirit at the moment of your conversion (1 Cor. 3:16; 6:19–20).* God in the Holy Spirit took up his dwelling in your innermost being to do the work of our gracious God within you on a day-by-day basis. Do not remain in ignorance concerning the indwelling presence of the Holy Spirit.
B. *The Holy Spirit is seeking to reproduce within you the character and the personality of Jesus Christ (Gal. 5:22–23).* The fruit of the Spirit described by Paul is a verbal portrait of the character of Jesus Christ. The gifts of the Spirit are for all the children of God.

Do not neglect to make a personal response to God's great gift to you, his Holy Spirit. Do not seek to fulfill your responsibilities as a father without letting the Holy Spirit be your help.

IV. You can give good gifts to your children (cf. Matt. 7:9–11).

Our Lord used the earthly relationship between a father and his children to describe the relationship between God and his children. He speaks of the fact that an earthly father seeks to give only good gifts to his children. He will not deliberately give that which is harmful and destructive.

A. *Give to your child a good name (Prov. 22:1).* Perhaps the finest gift you can bestow upon your child is a character and an example and a heritage of which he or she can be proud.

B. *Give to your child a humble faith (Heb. 11:6).* A genuine faith is described in terms of sincerely believing with all your heart that God is real and that he is a rewarder of those who diligently seek him.
C. *Give to your child love.* Be available. Give time. Express appreciation for your child. Do not be stingy with praise. Help your child to accept and to appreciate self. Give your child a positive, optimistic perspective toward life and toward people.

Conclusion

Parents can help their sons become good fathers someday. Win your sons to Jesus Christ and teach them so that someday they can be worthy fathers to their children.

A wife can help her husband be a good father. A man cannot be the father his children deserve and need without the sympathetic support and cooperation of a good wife. Put your faith in God and seek to help your husband be the best possible man he can be.

The church can and must help fathers to become better fathers. The church must provide opportunities for enriching family relationships and improving the quality of home life.

Each father must help himself to become a good father. In the final analysis, you are responsible for the kind of father you are to your children. Let Christ come into your heart to help you. Let the Bible assist you in becoming a good father and make much of prayer. And let the church have a vital place in your life that you might be a better father.

SUNDAY EVENING, JUNE 17

Title: The Memorable Moment

Text: "So it was not you that sent me hither, but God: And he hath made me a father to Pharaoh, and lord of all his house, and a ruler throughout all the land of Egypt" **(Gen. 45:8).**

Scripture Reading: Genesis 45:1–15

Introduction

Events vary as to the imprint they make on our minds. Joseph's revelation of himself to his brothers and their subsequent reconciliation with one another was doubtless memorable. Emotions often make indelible imprints. Joseph could not restrain his tears nor hide his love. The brothers could not forget their guilt, and their conscience now came to the surface in the awful moment of truth. It was indeed a memorable moment. For Joseph the moment was one of revelation and reconciliation; for the brothers it was a moment of recollection and repentance. Such never occur without leaving their imprint.

I. The moment was memorable because of discovery.

History is filled with events we call discovery. The discovery of America, the North Pole, the moon—each of these was a memorable event. A scientist was once asked, "What is the greatest discovery you ever made?" His reply was, "That I was a great sinner and Jesus Christ was a great Savior."

A. *Joseph makes himself known to his brothers (Gen. 45:1–5).* For fifteen years they had been separated. Time has a way of erasing the past, even wickedness and guilt. The sudden disclosure of Joseph, in a moment, brought recall. The brothers remembered their wicked design toward their estranged brother.

   1. We see Joseph's compassion. His emotional outburst of weeping was an evidence of this. It was our blessed Lord Jesus who likewise wept tears of compassion over an estranged city, Jerusalem (Luke 19:41). It is a great moment in life when we are able to shed tears of compassion over those who have ill-treated us and sought to do us harm.

   2. We see Joseph's initiative. He did not delegate the responsibility of making himself known to others. This is much like our Lord, who himself came personally to this earth to make himself known. We may learn as much from what Joseph did not say and do as from what he did.

      Joseph did not chide his brothers or remind them of their evil deeds toward him. He could have said, "I told you so," but he refrained. He could have gotten revenge, for now the brothers were at his mercy. He could have displayed through the years a cynical spirit that God does not seem to intervene when his people suffer. He could have shown defiance. Love and compassion do not behave that way.

      It is indeed a great moment when a man takes the initiative to forgive and then is graciously disposed toward those who have mistreated him.

   3. We see Joseph's forgiveness. How like the Lord Jesus was Joseph in this display. Indeed, it is a grand moment when the innocent takes the initiative to love and forgive his enemies.

B. *The brothers discover their sins.* The discovery was new, but the sins were old. It is always a memorable experience when a man comes face to face with his sins. For Isaiah it was a moment of renewal, for Job it was a moment of repentance, for the prodigal it was a moment of restoration.

The goodness of God has a strange way of helping us remember the forgotten, uncover the hidden, and we must come face-to-face with that which we have ignored.

II. The moment was memorable because of testimony (Gen. 45:6–9).

Joseph recalled the trials of his life. He saw the pit into which he was thrown by his brothers. He remembered the years of slavery into which he was thrust by his brothers. Doubtless he reflected on the diabolical scheme of Potiphar's wife resulting in his being cast into prison. He may even have recounted that hour when he interpreted the butler's dream and thought that his hour of deliverance had come. Joseph could see the hand of God in all of these trials.

In Genesis 45:5–9 Joseph used God's name four times when recounting for his brothers what God had done. Each divine activity reflected the hand of God on behalf of his people. Joseph testified about how the God of the covenant had brought good out of evil and shown himself mighty.

A. *Joseph's testimony shows God's absolute control over all creatures and events.* "For God did send me before you to preserve life" (Gen. 45:5). The plots, the pit, the dungeon—all were the designs of humans, but likewise were in the purpose and plan of God. Thus Joseph's millstones about his neck had become stepping-stones on which he might walk the path of victory and success.

B. *Joseph's testimony shows that while God may be slow to our thinking, he is always sure.* It is one thing to be aware of God's ways in history; it is quite another to wait patiently for his timing.

C. *Joseph's testimony makes us aware that the Bible ascribes the actions of people both to themselves and to God.* The God of providence is able to direct even the evils of men so that they serve his ultimate purpose. The pagan king Cyrus, according to Isaiah's prophecy, was God's servant as was the arrogant Nebuchadnezzar.

D. *Joseph's testimony shows that God's hand is always moving long before it is revealed.* This was true in the incarnation and death of Jesus Christ.

E. *Joseph's testimony helps us to see how God can triumph over evil and cause his plans to succeed.*

III. The moment was memorable because of the accomplishments (Gen. 45:9–15).

A. *It brought reality and the fulfillment of Joseph's early dreams.* These dreams had been the cause of the brothers' envy and hate. Now that which was mere prophecy was fulfilled. The father and brothers were dependent on and subservient to the lordship of Joseph.

B. *It was a display of God's salvation.* Man cannot live by bread alone; neither can he live efficiently without it. The wisdom bestowed on Joseph enabled Joseph to be in the role of savior.

C. *It effected a reconciliation after fifteen years of estrangement.* The embracing, the kissing, the tears are all eloquent testimonials that the family was now one. What joy and emotion swells within the heart when that which was lost is found!

D. *It proved that appearances often are deceptive.* Let us recall the blood-splattered coat the brothers had brought to their father, Jacob. Jacob's conclusion based on appearance caused him to lament, "Joseph is dead." But not so, Joseph was alive. How often we too are victimized by appearances and uncertain evidences that lead us to wrong conclusions.

Conclusion

This moment in Joseph's life served to reconfirm to both him and his brothers that the hand of God is always at work in each life. Joseph's policy of waiting in faithfulness and serving in loyalty is a worthy example. We may be assured that God's timing is always wise, even though some anguish may be ours until that time.

A thread of truth throughout the Bible that God will vindicate the righteous is never more evident than in this memorable moment in Joseph's experience. May we learn from him to trust, to wait, to serve. God is always at work.

WEDNESDAY EVENING, JUNE 20

Title: Noah: The Man Who Built the Ark

Text: "Noah found grace in the eyes of the LORD" **(Gen. 6:8)**.

Scripture Reading: Genesis 6:5–22

Introduction

Many faithful followers of Christ long to see a real spiritual awakening. They feel that times are corrupt, something like they were during the days of Noah. They pray and wait for God to intervene. Lessons can be learned from Noah that will inspire Christ's followers in times like these.

I. Consider Noah and his times.

A. *Consider the man.* There are two sources from which information is gained—Hebrews 11 and the Old Testament.
1. Hebrews says Noah was warned by God (Heb. 11:7)—that is, God revealed his purpose to Noah. Noah was moved with godly fear as God talked with him. He prepared an ark and, by doing so, condemned the world. His radical obedience condemned the unbelief and disobedience of those around him. Peter says that Noah was a preacher of righteousness (2 Peter 2:5).
2. The Old Testament gives three characteristics of Noah. He was a just, or righteous, man (Ezek. 14:14). He was perfect in his generation. This means he was mature and sound in judgment. He also walked with God as Enoch did.

194

B. *Consider the times.* It was a wicked time. Genesis 6:5 says, "God saw that the wickedness of man was great in the earth, and that every imagination of the thoughts of his heart was only evil continually." The wickedness was so bad that God regretted having made man (Gen. 6:6; cf. v. 11).

II. Consider some lessons to be learned.

A. *People are to take God at his word.* At times, humanly speaking, doing what God says to do may appear foolish, because it may be contrary to what everyone else does or thinks, and it may mean giving up normal activities. To everyone comes a choice. We must listen to and obey the word of God, or we must disregard it. We must live as if the word of God is important or as if it is unimportant.

B. *God's people are not to make decisions based on the mockery of others.* This probably was the hardest thing Noah had to accept. He was mocked and ridiculed by the masses who thought that building an ark was stupid. Radical Christians today face the same ridicule.

C. *There are some dangers of being genuinely Christian.* The world will not understand. The people of the world will call you a fool. You will be mocked and will face hard times.

D. *Righteousness is by faith, not by works.* Paul says that we are saved by grace through faith and not of works (Eph. 2:8–9). No person can be good enough in his or her own rights. We must have saving faith. James says that good works come in conjunction with faith (James 2:17).

Conclusion

In our day when there is so much violence, corruption, and ungodliness, the Lord is looking for people who will do right. May all Christians pattern their lives after Noah, who was godly and faithful in wicked times.

SUNDAY MORNING, JUNE 24

Title: Proud of the Gospel

Text: "I am not ashamed of the gospel of Christ: for it is the power of God unto salvation to every one that believeth; to the Jew first, and also to the Greek" (**Rom. 1:16**).

Scripture Reading: Romans 1:1–17

Hymns: "God of Grace and God of Glory," Fosdick
"We've a Story to Tell," Nichol
"Heralds of Christ," Copenhaver

Offertory Prayer: Our heavenly Father, we thank you that you are the God of grace and glory. For the revelation of your righteousness and love revealed in the gospel, we praise you. The love that sent Jesus to die for our sins is beyond our understanding but not contrary to it. Forbid that we should ever be ashamed of the gospel of Christ. Grant that we may so live that the Christ of the gospel will not be ashamed of us. We pray in Jesus's name. Amen.

Introduction

The gospel is the good news from God about God's plan of salvation. The greatest treatise ever written on the gospel is the letter of the apostle Paul to the Romans. Paul wrote of "my gospel" (Rom. 16:25) in contrast to the false gospels of the Judaizers and the antinomians. It was his gospel by experience and by revelation. Paul was sure that his gospel was the gospel of Christ, and he was proud of the gospel, for it is the power of God unto salvation for everyone who believes. "God's Plan of Salvation" according to Paul will be the theme of the next several morning messages.

Paul dictated this letter to the Romans to Tertius, his secretary (Rom. 16:22), from the home of his host, Gaius (Rom. 16:23; 1 Cor. 1:14), in Corinth. Phoebe, a deaconess of the church at Cenchrea, carried it on her journey to Rome (Rom. 16:1–2). Paul probably would have been surprised at the idea that the letter would one day be counted as part of the sacred Scriptures. However, he would have rejoiced to know that it would profoundly influence succeeding generations to acceptance of the grace of God.

I. The occasion and purpose of the letter.

Paul had never been to Rome. Many times he had intended to go but had been hindered (Rom. 1:13). It is amazing how many of the Christians there he knew personally. Priscilla and Aquila he had known well in Corinth (Rom. 16:3–4; Acts 18:1–3). In Romans 16:5–15 he mentions more than a score of persons by name, some his relatives. Some had become Christians before Paul. Some had been his fellow prisoners. All roads in the empire led to Rome. It is probable that some of those converted at Pentecost carried the gospel to Rome. It is even more probable that the Christians who were dispersed by the great persecution following the death of Stephen may have gone to the capital city. From Paul's conversion about AD 35 until the writing of this letter in about AD 57 or 58 during a three-month stay in Greece (Corinth) just before Pentecost (Acts 20:2–6), he had preached vigorously in Europe and Asia. Many of the persons contacted in his ministry now lived in Rome.

Not only did Paul know many Christians, but he prayed for them by name. Only God could know about his secret prayer life, so the apostle calls God to witness that he always remembered them by name whenever he prayed (Rom. 1:9). We are reminded that Jesus prayed for Peter by name (Luke 22:31–32). Praying for people by name develops goodwill.

When Jesus in grace saved Paul, he also called him to be an apostle (or missionary) to all people. Paul's calling was to lead people of all nations to obedient faith in Jesus Christ (Rom. 1:5; Acts 9:15–16; 22:14–15). Among those whom Jesus Christ had effectually called out of sin into salvation were these believers in Rome who are called saints, as indeed are all saved people. A saint is one who is separated to God and whom God has claimed as his own possession. As Paul wrote in later years to Titus, "He [Jesus] gave himself for us, to rescue us from all wickedness and make us a pure people who belong to him alone and are eager to do good" (Titus 2:14 GNT).

The saints at Rome seem to have had more than one church. Some worshiped in the home of Priscilla and Aquila (Rom. 16:5). Romans 16:14–15 suggests two other worshiping congregations. The letter is not addressed to the church in Rome but "to all in Rome who are loved by God and called to be his holy people [saints]" (Rom. 1:7 NIV).

It was natural for Paul to want to renew fellowship with the Christians whom he knew at Rome. The good report that had come to him—indeed, that had spread throughout the whole world—concerning the faith of the saints at Rome made him eager to go to them (Rom. 1:8). However, Paul had a deeper reason for wanting to visit Rome. God had given him a fruitful ministry among the Gentiles. His delay in coming to them sooner had been because so many unsaved were at hand to be won that he could not find it in the will of God to pass them by.

Conditions had now changed. As soon as he could go to Jerusalem with the offering for the poor Christians (Rom. 15:25–26), he planned to go to Rome. He expected his presence to be a blessing, and he expected to be fruitful. He expected also to receive a blessing from them. What blessed fellowship believers have (Rom. 1:11–12; 15:24)! The most mature Christian can be blessed by Christian fellowship.

Paul wanted to preach the gospel where it had not been preached. Beyond Rome was Spain. He purposed in the will of God and with the assistance of the Roman saints to go on to Spain (Rom. 15:24–28). He had prayed "that somehow by God's will I may now at last succeed in coming to you" (Rom. 1:10 RSV). He wrote, "And I am sure that, when I come unto you, I shall come in the fulness of the blessing of the gospel of Christ" (Rom. 15:29).

Paul did go to Rome, but not as he had expected. He was arrested at Jerusalem, and after imprisonment in Caesarea, he was sent to Rome as a prisoner in chains. In the providence of God he was able to do more for the extension of the kingdom than if he had gone as a free man (Phil. 1:12ff.; Acts 28:30–31).

Paul probably had just written the letter to the Galatians in which he defended salvation by grace against the Judaizers and the antinomians. Perhaps he feared that these enemies of the gospel would get to Rome before he did. He wrote this letter to the end that his readers might be established in the faith (Rom. 1:11) and have an accurate understanding of the gospel of God.

II. The Gospel of God.

A. *God had promised the gospel by his prophets in the Holy Scriptures (Rom. 1:2; Matt. 1:22).* Jesus proclaimed this in Luke 24:25–27, 44–48.

B. *The gospel concerning his Son, Jesus Christ our Lord, "who as to his earthly life was a descendant of David, and who through the Spirit of holiness was appointed the Son of God in power by his resurrection from the dead: Jesus Christ our Lord" (Rom. 1:3–4 NIV).* This is the answer to the puzzling question Jesus asked the Pharisees in Matthew 22:41–44.

C. *The gospel reveals the character of God as righteous and proclaims the salvation that God has in grace provided so that sinful persons can have peace with him (Rom. 1:17).*

D. *The gospel is for all humankind.* There are no limitations of race nor of culture (Rom. 1:13–15; John 3:16; Gal. 3:26–29).

E. *Salvation is received by faith.* Those justified by faith experience the power of God in making them new people. They have new life that is eternal both in quality and in duration.

Conclusion

One who has been saved is under obligation to witness to others. It is an obligation of love to the Savior. Refusal to acknowledge a debt does not discharge it. The believer's debt extends to all people. The Greeks called all others barbarians because their speech sounded like *bar-bar.* They thought themselves above others. The Jews classed all others as Gentiles. Christ died for all people. We are obligated to witness to all people (Acts 1:8). Let us say with Paul, "I am debtor" (Rom. 1:14). The only way to discharge the debt is to proclaim the gospel. God does not demand more than his disciples can supply. Let us say with Paul, "So, as much as in me is, I am ready" (Rom. 1:15).

When Paul wrote, "I am not ashamed of the gospel of Christ," he was really saying, "I am proud of the gospel." The gospel rightly understood is in accord with the character of God. If there is anything in the gospel of which we are ashamed, the fault is in our understanding of the gospel and not in the gospel.

Can you say, "I am debtor, I am ready, I am not ashamed"?

SUNDAY EVENING, JUNE 24

Title: Facing the Final Enemy

Text: "The last enemy that shall be destroyed is death" (**1 Cor. 15:26**).

Scripture Reading: Genesis 50:24–26; Hebrews 11:21–22

Introduction

The book of Genesis begins with a garden but ends with a coffin in Egypt. Between these two circumstances is the entrance of sin into the human race. Humankind's final enemy is not sin but death caused by sin.

Throughout the book of Genesis we see people struggling with the vicissitudes of life. Abraham struggles with doubt, Isaac with his family, Jacob with his carnal efforts to seize what God has already promised, and Joseph with envy, hate, conspiracy, and imprisonment. While their struggles were different, their common enemy was the same—death.

It is like a song: the stanzas are different but the chorus is the same. "Then Abraham . . . died in a good old age" (Gen. 25:8). "Isaac gave up the ghost, and died" (35:29). "Jacob . . . yielded up the ghost" (49:33). "Joseph died . . . and he was put in a coffin in Egypt" (50:26).

While death is universal, it is not final. Two little words sweep into the mind like a fresh breeze on an intolerable day: faith and hope. These two truths enabled the patriarchs to live victoriously and face death triumphantly.

I. Facing an inevitable fact.

"And Joseph said unto his brethren, I die" (Gen. 50:24).

A. *Death is universal.* "It is appointed unto men once to die," the writer of Hebrews tells us. In Adam all die. "So death passed upon all men" (Rom. 5:12). Death is no respecter of persons. We would like to think that those with excellent qualities like Joseph's could evade death, but not so. Death is the last enemy, and every person must face this foe. Joseph's acknowledgment, "I die," is the testimony of us all.

B. *Death is inevitable.* Science, technology, and sociology have combined their talents to evade death, but medicine, health care, dieting, and caution will never enable us to escape the inevitable.

C. *Death is an appointment that God has with people.* "It is appointed unto men once to die, but after this the judgment" (Heb. 9:27). There is no evasion and no cheating with this appointment. Joseph's testimony, "I die," is the testimony of each person.

II. Forecast of the future.

"God will surely visit you" (Gen. 50:24). This forecast, to be sure, did not come to pass in the life span of Joseph's brothers. History tells us that the divine visitation occurred over three hundred years later.

A. *The divine visitation was an emancipation.* The book of Exodus reminds us of the rigors and hard bondage of Israel especially near the end of the more than four hundred years in Egypt. The land of Egypt is always a symbol of bondage and death. At no time in history did God's people fare well over a prolonged period in Egypt. It is always God's purpose to deliver from sin and bondage. The foremost revelation of this fact is the death of Jesus on the cross.

B. *The divine visitation was a redemption.* The book of Exodus (chap. 12) shows us how Israel was redeemed by the mighty hand of God through the shedding of blood. It is through the shedding of blood that sins are remitted.

C. *The divine visitation looked forward to a consummation.* God will not only "bring them out," but he will also "bring them in." It is a wonderful thing to experience deliverance from the penalty of sin; it is equally glorious to live in the light of that redemption. That which removes the sting of death is redemption in and through the death of Jesus Christ.

III. The final request.

"And ye shall carry up my bones from hence" (Gen. 50:25). People today, for the most part, give little heed to the sanctity of the human body. Perhaps we need to remember that according to the apostle Paul the body is the temple of the Holy Spirit. Also the body, though vile, is to be raised a glorious body. Likewise, the natural body is to be raised a spiritual body. Joseph, though not living in New Testament light, had enough revelation to believe in the resurrection.

A. *The request indicates Joseph's faith in God.* Hebrews 11 has a list of the Old Testament heroes of faith, including Joseph. Of him it is said, "By faith Joseph, when he died, made mention of the departing of the children of Israel; and gave commandment concerning his bones" (v. 22). Faith is not only the victory that overcomes the world, but it is also the believers' disposition that enables us to embrace God through and beyond the experience of death.
B. *The request indicates Joseph's hope in the resurrection.* In many ways Joseph's request reveals New Testament truth. Paul, in the greatest teaching on the resurrection, says, "If in this life only we have hope in Christ, we are of all men most miserable" (1 Cor. 15:19).
C. *The request was honored by the children of Israel.* In the course of the Exodus, we are reminded that "Moses took the bones of Joseph with him" (Ex. 13:19).

IV. The coffin is not final.

"And they embalmed him, and he was put in a coffin in Egypt" (Gen. 50:26). This is a unique contrast to what is said concerning the death of Abraham, Isaac, and Jacob: They were "gathered to [their] people" (Gen. 25:8; 35:29; 49:33 NIV). The grand goal of redemption is to gather all God's people unto Jesus Christ. The apostle states this clearly: "In whom we have redemption . . . that in the dispensation of the fulness of times he might gather together in one all things in Christ" (Eph. 1:7, 10). "Thanks be to God, which giveth us the victory through our Lord Jesus Christ" (1 Cor. 15:57).

Conclusion

Because of what God has done in Christ to provide our redemption, we need not be overcome by the last enemy. In Christ there is hope; in the resurrection there is victory. Let us walk and live in the light of victory!

WEDNESDAY EVENING, JUNE 27

Title: Abraham: The Father of a New Spiritual Race
Text: "In thee shall all families of the earth be blessed" **(Gen. 12:3)**.
Scripture Reading: Genesis 12:1–4

Introduction

Abraham has been referred to as the "father of faith." A study of this man will reveal him as an illustration of the personal character of Israel's religion.

I. Abraham's call was the beginning of his usefulness.

A. *It was a straightforward call.* Scripture does not tell how Abraham's call came about. In all probability it was an inner compulsion. Genesis 11:31 tells of Abraham leaving Ur and going to Haran. But this was not all the way; it was only a stop-off. The promises of God would never have been realized had Abraham not gone the full distance of the call. Genesis 12:1–4 tells of Abraham's call to Canaan.

B. *A call is a decisive event in any life.* Each person's call is distinctive. In the Bible, God calls some people with an audible voice. Others have visions. Still others have the sensation of a certain touch or taste. But each has a call not to be doubted and a compassion from which there is no escape.

C. *Abraham's call was to leave home and kindred and go to an unknown land.* It was a call to act in faith. His obedience to the call made him a great intercessor for others (Heb. 11:8–10).

II. Certain outstanding characteristics of Abraham made him great.

A. *He was obedient.* First Samuel 15:22 says, "To obey is better than sacrifice, and to hearken than the fat of rams." Abraham's obedience was the launching pad for usefulness.

B. *He was unselfish.* For one to be useful in God's work, unselfishness is a must. Genesis 13:9 gives the scriptural account of this characteristic in Abraham. It also is found in other men of the Bible, such as Joseph, Moses, Jonathan, Daniel, and Paul.

C. *He was courageous.* It is difficult to picture Abraham in war. However, Genesis 14:14 tells the story. "When Abram heard that his relative had been taken captive, he called out the 318 trained men born in his household and went in pursuit as far as Dan" (NIV).

D. *He was benevolent.* Great men of contemporary times, as well as of history, have had this characteristic. Genesis 14:20 tells of Abraham giving his tithe. Tithing is a badge of love and loyalty.

III. Outstanding events in Abraham's life contributed to who he was.

A. *He made mistakes.* He lied about Sarah being his wife (Gen. 12:11–13) and sought to aid the Almighty with a personal plan (Gen. 16:3). He had sex with Hagar in an effort to help God fulfill his promise of an heir.

B. *He made strong intercessory prayer (Gen. 18:23–24).* Most people who have accomplished big things for God have had this experience at one time or another. One must be concerned enough about others to be a person of Abraham's caliber.

C. *He underwent a very severe test (Gen. 22:1–2).* Tests are essential in determining moral character. Abraham was tested, stood the test, and has been a legend for others in hearing God's voice, obeying the command, and receiving the reward.

IV. Modern disciples can glean some lessons from Abraham's life.

A. *God uses weak and sinful people in his work.* No perfect people are available. He wants all his children to strive for perfection (Matt. 5:48). The word for perfect in Matthew is better rendered in modern terminology as "mature." Mature people can fall and get up again and be used.

B. *Tryon Edwards said, "If we make God's will our law, then God's promise shall be our support and comfort, and we shall find every burden light, and every duty a joy" (Tryon Edwards,* The New Dictionary of Thoughts, Standard Book Company, 1960, 726).

George Truett said, "To know the will of God is the greatest knowledge. To do the will of God is the greatest achievement."

Conclusion

God has a plan for each of his children, and he communicates that plan to those who are sensitive to his leadership. When they carry out God's plan, they become great in his eyes.

Suggested preaching program for the month of

JULY

■ **Sunday Mornings**

Continue with "God's Plan of Salvation," a series based on texts from Paul's letter to the Romans. God's plan of salvation is a program of redemption that touches every area of life. We need to enlarge our concept of the great salvation God has provided for us.

■ **Sunday Evenings**

Our beliefs matter much. The doctrines that grip us serve as the skeletal structure for a strong faith. Doctrinal messages center around the theme "Vital Doctrines for Victorious Living."

■ **Wednesday Evenings**

Complete the series of biographical and character studies using the theme "Witnesses from the Past Speak to the Present."

SUNDAY MORNING, JULY 1

Title: The Universal Necessity of Salvation

Text: "Now we know that what things soever the law saith, it saith to them who are under the law: that every mouth may be stopped, and all the world may become guilty before God. Therefore by the deeds of the law there shall no flesh be justified in his sight: for by the law is the knowledge of sin" **(Rom. 3:19–20).**

Scripture Reading: Romans 1:18–3:20

Hymns: "Holy, Holy, Holy," Heber
         "Free from the Law, O Happy Condition," Bliss
         "Out of My Bondage, Sorrow, and Night," Sleeper

Offertory Prayer: Heavenly Father, author of liberty, we gratefully acknowledge the blessings provided by this wonderful country, including the right to worship you in accord with the dictates of our own conscience. For all who have lived and died for freedom, we thank you. We pray your blessings on all who occupy places of public trust. May they first be your servants and then the servants of the people that the blessings of liberty may be provided for all and denied to none. We thank you for Jesus who died and rose from the dead to set us free from the bonds of sin and death. Amen.

Introduction

The only person without conviction of his or her sin is one without a conviction of the holiness of God. The gospel reveals the righteousness of God (Rom. 1:17). It tells us that the righteous God reacts against sin. "For the wrath of God is revealed from heaven against all ungodliness and unrighteousness of men" (Rom. 1:18). Ungodliness is impiety against God; unrighteousness is injustice against people. God's wrath is not rage nor loss of temper, but his righteous indignation against sin.

The conclusion is that no person, either Jew or Gentile, is without sin, "for all have sinned, and come short of the glory of God" (Rom. 3:23). No one in the judgment can say, "I have not sinned. I am good enough to go to heaven." Note today's text, Romans 3:19–20. Paul in Romans 1:18–2:16 first showed this to be true in the case of the Gentiles who had not had the Mosaic law; then in Romans 2:17–3:8 he proved it to be true in the case of the Jews.

I. The case of the Gentiles (Rom. 1:18–2:16).

    A. *The reason for their condemnation (Rom. 1:18–2:5).*

        1. God had given them sufficient light.

            a. They had the inner light of conscience which the Creator has given to every person. "Because that which may be known of God is manifest in them; for God hath shewed it unto them" (Rom. 1:19). Compare John 1:9: "That was the true light, which lighteth every man that cometh into the world." The Gentiles did not have the law of Moses and the prophets as did the Jews, but they did have the inner light placed in every person by the Creator, which indicates that God is holy and that every person ought to do right. "For when the Gentiles, which have not the law, do by nature the things contained in the law, these, having not the law, are a law unto themselves: Which shew the work of the law written in their hearts, their conscience also bearing witness, and their thoughts the mean while accusing or else excusing one another; in the day when God shall judge the secrets of men by Jesus Christ according to my gospel" (Rom. 2:14–16).

            b. They had the outer light of God's revelation of himself in nature. "For the invisible things of him from the creation of the world are clearly seen, being understood by the things that are made, even his eternal power and Godhead; so that they are without excuse" (Rom. 1:20).

        2. They had sinned against the light they had (Rom. 1:21–32). These verses catalogue their sins as ingratitude, idolatry, homosexuality, and all kinds of actions that were not fitting. The crowning condemnation was that they willfully sinned

against God. "Who knowing the judgment of God, that they which commit such things are worthy of death, not only do the same, but have pleasure in them that do them" (Rom. 1:32). See a similar condemnation in John 3:18–21.

3. Condemning others is no excuse for one's own sin (Rom. 2:1–2). Those who know enough to condemn the sins of others have established the basis of judgment on which God can judge them. If they know that some actions are sin for others, they know that they are sin for themselves. Others' badness does not excuse those who note it. God will judge all people according to the truth.

4. People are also foolish to think that because God delays punishment, that punishment will be forgotten (Rom. 2:3–5). God delays judgment in the hope that sinners will repent. If people are impenitent and continue to sin, then for every sin they will receive added penalty. Every trespass and disobedience will receive a just recompense of reward (Heb. 2:2).

B. *God's judgment is righteous (Rom. 2:6–16).*

1. "Shall not the Judge of all the earth do right?" (Gen. 18:25). Abraham's question is valid. God is righteous. He will be true to his character.

2. "[God] will render to every man according to his deeds" (Rom. 2:6). This includes heart attitude. Compare Jesus's statements in Matthew 16:27 and Revelation 22:12. These statements do not conflict with Romans 3:20 nor with Ephesians 2:9. Works of the law in the latter passages refer to actions such as legal and ceremonial obedience to the law apart from the right heart attitude. If the heart is not right, no amount of good deeds can form a basis on which one can claim to have earned salvation.

3. "God does not show favoritism" (Rom. 2:11 NIV). God does not favor one person over another. Jews and Gentiles will be treated alike. All will be judged on the basis of the light they had. In addition to all the light the heathen had, the Jews also had the advantage of the law of God revealed through Moses and the prophets. The Jews first in privilege will be first also in responsibility. Paul's double meaning to the word *law* is tricky in Romans 2:14–16. Law in the ultimate sense means God's will for any person or thing. The heathen did not have the Mosaic law, but they did have a partial revelation of God's law (will) written in their hearts sufficient for their judgment. No one has lived up to the light he or she has. All have sinned. Anyone who is saved will be saved by the grace of God on the basis of the atonement of Jesus Christ.

Those who hastily conclude that Paul and Jesus teach that the merits of Christ's atonement can be applied only to those who have consciously believed in Jesus Christ have come to a conclusion that casts a cloud on God's justice. Most would agree that somehow God's salvation applies to infants and children who have not come to the years of discretion—even to the infants of the heathen. The Scriptures clearly teach that Abraham, Isaac, Jacob, and other Old Testament saints are saved. God's salvation provided in Christ was applied to them without their understanding how. Do not Romans 2:7, 10, and 15 leave open the hope that of the Gentiles who did not know about God's salvation, some who with open hearts responded to the light God gave them will be saved by Jesus even though they did not know him?

II. The case of the Jews (Rom. 2:17–3:8).

A. *Outward religion is of no avail without a right heart (Rom. 2:17–3:2).* The Jews had been designated as God's chosen people. They had the law and were the religious teachers of the world. They had all the light the Gentiles had plus the advantage "that unto them were committed the oracles of God" (Rom. 3:2).

The religious leaders did not follow the light they had. They had disobeyed the law they taught. What a severe indictment of the chosen people that instead of bringing the heathen nations to God, "the name of God is blasphemed among the Gentiles through you" (Rom. 2:24). Circumcision, the sign given to Abraham, was of no avail unless the people were truly yielded to God. No outward ceremony could replace a right heart.

B. *God condemns them justly (Rom. 3:3–8).* All the reasons for the condemnation of the Gentiles apply to the Jews. The Jews had the additional advantage of the revelation of God's will through Moses and the prophets. Added light brings added responsibility. "To the Jew first, and also to the Gentile" was true both in privilege and in responsibility. The basic truth is that God is righteous. He will deal justly with every person.

Conclusion

All persons are under sin (Rom. 3:9–23). In Romans 3:9–18 the apostle compiles a chain of Scripture quotations to describe the depraved condition of both Jews and Gentiles. The will of God in the law has revealed that the whole world stands guilty before God. As a mirror tells us that our face is dirty, so the law reveals that "all have sinned, and come short of the glory of God" (v. 23). As the mirror is powerless to wash the face, so the law has no power to save.

Sinners have no power to save themselves. Only God can forgive sins.

If any sinner is ever saved, it must be by the salvation God provides. God does not want to punish sin. He wants to save. He has provided a way for sinful people to be justified (made right) with himself. The good news about what God has done to provide salvation is the gospel. The nature of God's salvation will be the theme next Sunday morning.

SUNDAY EVENING, JULY 1

Title: The Blessed Book

Text: "All scripture is given by inspiration of God, and is profitable for doctrine, for reproof, for correction, for instruction in righteousness" **(2 Tim. 3:16)**.

Scripture Reading: 2 Timothy 3:14–17

Introduction

Of all the books ever written, none is more interesting than the Bible. No other book contains such a variety of history, philosophy, love stories, war stories, drama, poetry, and informal letters. The Bible tells about a man who lived for 969 years (Gen. 5). The Bible speaks of a donkey that spoke (Num. 22). It tells about a man with a bed 13^1/$_2$ feet long and 16^1/$_2$ feet wide. It also tells of how the sun stood still (Josh. 10). The Bible relates the gruesome incident of how a woman killed a man by driving a spike through his skull (Judg. 4). In Judges 20 there is mention of seven hundred left-handed men. In 2 Samuel 14 we find the story of a man who got a haircut once a year, and the waste weighed 6^1/$_4$ pounds. The Bible tells in 2 Samuel 21 about a man born with twelve fingers and twelve toes. In 2 Chronicles we read of a father with eighty-eight children. Needless to say, the Bible is an interesting book.

Infinitely more important than its interest is the fact that the Bible is a book needed for living. It is the sourcebook for Christian belief. It is a means of confronting the living Christ. Let us look at some great truths of this blessed book.

Infinitely more important than its interest is the fact that the Bible is a book needed for living. It is the sourcebook for Christian belief. It is a means of confronting the living Christ. Let us look at some great truths of this blessed book.

I. The Bible is a divinely prepared book.

The Scripture is not just another great literary work. It is a literary miracle. The Bible holds no peer. A group of writers did not sit on a committee and plan the sixty-six books of the Bible. Rather, more than forty different writers and editors worked on the Bible over a span of sixty generations.

A. *The Bible is a divine production.* Paul said, "All scripture is given by inspiration of God" (2 Tim. 3:16). The word *inspiration* is a compound of two Greek words that could be translated

"God-breathed." This means that in some miraculous manner, God led in the production of the Bible.

Through the years scholars have sought to describe how God inspired the Bible. There are such theories as plenary-verbal, naturalistic, mechanical, and dynamic. No theory is adequate that limits inspiration to insight and illumination. One has to include the miraculous moving of God.

B. *The Bible reveals human personality.* God used human beings to write the Holy Bible. The authors were farmers, shepherds, tentmakers, tax collectors, physicians, governors, kings, and fishermen. In the divine preparation, God did not rob the various writers of their distinctive styles or personalities.

Seeing the humanity in the preparation of Scripture increases the Bible's pertinence. The Bible did not fall from the sky. Instead, God inspired various human authors in diverse life situations. This makes the Scripture pertinent to life on earth.

II. The Bible is a uniquely preserved book.

Hundreds of literary works have been preserved. Libraries contain copies of Plato's *Republic* and Homer's *Iliad* and *Odyssey*. Yet to read the story of how the Bible has been uniquely preserved is thrilling.

A. *The Bible has been preserved throughout antiquity.* The Bible's 3,500-year history is miraculous. It has defied the ravages of time and survived thousands of scribal copyings and translations. Beginning with the work of Moses around 1,400 BC and continuing with John's letter to the seven churches (Revelation), the Bible has been uniquely preserved. To think of the thousands of copies made and the primitive writing material makes the preservation nothing short of a miracle.

B. *The Bible has been preserved during attacks.* Even when the books of the Bible circulated individually, opponents sought to destroy them. The Syrian despot Antiochus Epiphanes destroyed all the Old Testament books he could find. The Roman emperor in AD 303 decreed the burning of all Scriptures. In 1229 a Catholic synod in Toulouse, France, forbade the laity to own a Bible.

Though ungodly people have sought to destroy the Bible, we have it today. It has been uniquely preserved through the years of attack. As Peter said, "The word of the Lord endureth for ever" (1 Peter 1:25).

III. The Bible is a thoroughly proven book.

The test of any book is its durability. Can a book stand the test of time? Can a book accomplish a purpose in today's world? The Bible has been proven through the years. It has stood the test of time. It accomplishes results in today's world.

    A. *The Bible is true to its purpose.* God did not inspire human authors to write a textbook on science or history. He inspired human authors to disclose his will for human beings. To make the Bible a textbook on science abuses the original intent of Scripture. Furthermore, there is history in the Bible, but these facts are not the final purpose. The Bible confronts people with God. Through the years the written Word has proven adequate to confront people with the living Word.

    B. *The Bible stands under the assault of skeptics.* Voltaire, the noted French infidel, once boasted, "One hundred years from my day there will not be a Bible in the earth except one that is looked upon by an antiquarian curiosity-seeker." Two hundred years later a first edition of Voltaire's works sold in Paris for eleven cents. On the same day, the British government paid the Soviet government five hundred thousand dollars for an ancient biblical manuscript, the *Codex Sinaiticus*, which dates back to AD 350.

    The Bible stands today having withstood the attack of scoffers through the years. Many in our modem generation do not bother to discover the durability of Scripture. Some deny the historicity, scoff at the miraculous, and seek to prove the Bible erroneous. But God's Word can stand the test.

IV. The Bible is an especially pertinent book.

Paul said that the Bible is "profitable for doctrine, for reproof, for correction, for instruction in righteousness" (2 Tim. 3:16). No book is more pertinent to life today than the Bible.

    A. *The Bible teaches us the first step of faith.* Paul said to Timothy, "From a child thou hast known the holy scriptures, which are able to make thee wise unto salvation through faith which is in Christ Jesus" (2 Tim. 3:15). The Scriptures opened Timothy's spiritual eyes to his need of a Savior. The Bible discloses the need and the means of a life in Christ.

    B. *The Bible leads us in future steps.* Salvation begins with a step of faith, but it continues in a walk with the Lord. Paul told Timothy that the Bible pertained to his progression in the Christian life. It is profitable for "doctrine," which means the instruction we need for living.

    The Bible is profitable for "reproof." Throughout the life of a Christian, false steps need to be corrected. Restoration is essential. Therefore, the Bible is profitable for "correction." Not only does the Bible convict us of wrong, but it also helps to correct us. It instructs us "in righteousness."

Wherever you touch life, the Bible is especially pertinent. It helps us with self-improvement, with interpersonal relationships, and with our fellowship with the Lord.

Conclusion

Many books confront you in this "Gutenberg galaxy." No other book can mean more to you than the Bible, for when you listen to or read the Bible, you will encounter the living Christ.

WEDNESDAY EVENING, JULY 4

Title: Jacob the Supplanter Transformed into Israel the Prince of God

Text: "Thy name shall be called no more Jacob, but Israel" (**Gen. 32:28**).

Scripture: Genesis 32:24–32

Introduction

Jacob is a classic example of how the Lord deals with people who are loaded with imperfections. He shows how the Lord uses such people to accomplish much in his program. All who are weak and sinful can take heart after such a study.

I. A brief biography of Jacob is essential in understanding his contribution.

Jacob was born a twin to Esau. His parents were Isaac and Rebekah. He was a gift of God. He tricked his brother out of the family birthright and tricked his own father into blessing him. In turn, his father-in-law cheated him out of wages and gave him the wrong daughter to be Jacob's wife. After many years of trials, heartache, disappointments, and anxieties, he died in Egypt, the father of twelve sons by whom the twelve tribes of Israel were named.

II. Jacob had some inherited characteristics worth noticing.

A. *Some were from parents.* From his father he inherited deceit and cowardice, which stem from unbelief. From his mother he inherited shrewdness, initiative, and resourcefulness.

B. *Some were from beyond the family circle.* He acquired from early teaching a firm conviction of the value of what God had promised, and this became his supreme ambition for himself and his children.

III. Jacob had a divine transformation.

It started with a combination of natural endowments but passed through a course of divine tuition and issued in the triumph of grace. This transformation took place in three schools.

A. *The school of sorrow.* Jacob suffered long exile and disappointment. He went through the valley of passions, of greed, anger, hate, lust, and envy of others. These resulted in perplexity and bereavement.

B. *The school of providence.* The Lord taught Jacob to rely on divine power and guidance and to accept God's will. This led to a realization of divine nearness and faithfulness. Jacob's God did this through alternate giving and withholding, danger and deliverance, and good and evil.

C. *The school of grace. God was with Jacob to bless.* The changes that took place in Jacob's life were divinely ordained and were for his ultimate good.

Conclusion

There are some truths to learn from Jacob's life.

1. We learn that we reap what we sow. Jacob was deceitful in his relationships with his father, Esau, Laban, and others. He reaped the bitterness of having to flee from home and of being deceived by Laban. He did not use good judgment regarding affection for his children, and he reaped heartache.

2. We learn the lesson of God's grace. Jacob prayed in times of crisis, and God delivered him. Grace is not related to merit.

SUNDAY MORNING, JULY 8

Title: The Nature of God's Salvation

Text: "But now the righteousness of God without the law is manifested, being witnessed by the law and the prophets; even the righteousness of God which is by faith of Jesus Christ unto all and upon all them that believe" (**Rom. 3:21–22**).

Scripture Reading: Romans 3:19–31

Hymns: "Amazing Grace," Newton
              "Grace Greater Than Our Sin," Johnston
              "Whiter Than Snow," Nicholson

Offertory Prayer: Holy Father, your will is holy as you are holy; your will is loving as you are love. We thank you that you are more interested in our salvation than in our damnation. From the slavery of sin you have provided the freedom of salvation. We thank you for freedom from the penalty of sin and for freedom as your children to live in accord with your will as revealed through our Lord Jesus Christ. Grant that we may accept the lordship of Jesus Christ and grant to every person here the greatest possible freedom within his lordship. In Jesus's name we pray. Amen.

Introduction

The most important consideration for any person is his or her relationship to God. Are you saved or lost? If judgment were today, would you be with the sheep on God's right hand, destined for eternal life, or with the goats on the left hand, destined to eternal destruction?

No one will be saved on the basis of his or her sinlessness. No one will be saved by good deeds or by religious ceremonies. (Read again Rom. 3:19–20.) "For there is no difference: For all have sinned, and come short of the glory of God" (Rom. 3:22–23). Paul does not mean that all are equally sinful. The best man is not good enough to earn salvation. The worst man is not so bad that God cannot save. A person on the top of Mount Everest and another near the Dead Sea are thousands of feet apart in altitude, but there is no difference in their ability to reach the stars. Neither has the ability. There is no difference in that all need salvation and in that all are powerless to save themselves.

God would be just to keep every person from heaven and to punish everyone in accord with the magnitude and willfulness of his or her sins; but God is love. His purpose is not to condemn but to save. How can the righteous God be just and justify unrighteous persons? The love, righteousness, wisdom, and power of God are all revealed in the gospel. Humankind's sinful state was God's opportunity for mercy. "For God hath concluded them all in unbelief, that he might have mercy upon all. O the depth of the riches both of the wisdom and knowledge of God! how unsearchable are his judgments, and his ways past finding out!" (Rom. 11:32–33). Let us inquire as to the nature of God's salvation.

I. A salvation from God.

"But now the righteousness of God without the law is manifested" (Rom. 3:21). Righteousness is used to describe the character of God, as in Romans 1:17, but also to designate the salvation he provides, as in Romans 2:21. As we shall see, by righteousness, Paul means both justification and sanctification.

If sin is against God, then it follows that only God can forgive sin. Sin is a breach of right relationship with God. Only God can restore this right relationship. The gospel of God for which Paul was set apart as a missionary is the good news from God as to how sinners can be put in right relationship to God.

II. A salvation witnessed by the Law and the Prophets.

"But now the righteousness of God without the law is manifested, being witnessed by the law and the prophets" (Rom. 3:21). It was never God's intention that persons should be saved by keeping the Mosaic law. The law revealed to people their sinful condition. The law pointed to the need of a Savior, but the law was powerless to save (Rom. 3:20; Gal. 3:21–29; Galatians probably was written shortly before Romans). However, the Old Testament did bear witness to God's purpose to save through the one anointed for that purpose— the Messiah. Jesus interpreted for his disciples the revelation of God in the

Law and the Prophets concerning himself as the Messiah (Luke 24:26–27, 44–48). Read the sermons in Acts and you will see that the apostles under the leadership of the Holy Spirit developed that which Jesus had taught them.

III. A salvation without distinction of persons (Rom. 3:22–23).

The gospel is for all persons. There is no distinction of sinners; all sinners need salvation. There is no distinction of culture (Rom. 1:14), gender (Gal. 3:28), or races; Greek and barbarian, Jew and Gentile all need salvation and have it offered to them on the same basis—by faith (Rom. 1:5, 14–16)."To every one that believeth" is an invitation for everyone to believe.

IV. A salvation grounded in the atoning death of Jesus (Rom. 3:24–26).

A. *The death of Jesus secured a real redemption.* "Being justified freely by his grace through the redemption that is in Christ Jesus" (Rom. 3:24). A ransom was the price paid to free a slave. The slave then was bound to the new owner. If the new owner graciously set him free, he was redeemed from slavery. Jesus had done everything necessary to redeem sinners from the bondage of sin. "For even the Son of man came not to be ministered unto, but to minister, and to give his life a ransom for many" (Mark 10:45). God, as an act of free grace, justifies (declares just and sets right) and redeems (sets free) those who have faith in Jesus.

B. *The death of Jesus was propitiatory.* "Whom [Christ Jesus] God hath set forth to be a propitiation through faith in his blood" (Rom. 3:25). In Old Testament times when people sinned they offered a sacrifice that they hoped would expiate the sin and propitiate God. The more thoughtful persons seemed instinctively to realize that these offerings were at best symbolic and had no inherent power to forgive sin (Gen. 22:8; Ps. 51:16; Mic. 6:6–7). "For it is not possible that the blood of bulls and goats should take away sins" (Heb. 10:4). God has provided an appropriate sacrifice: "the Lamb of God, which taketh away the sin of the world" (John 1:29; cf. Matt. 26:26–28; John 3:26; Gal. 4:4–6; et al.).

C. *The death of Jesus manifests God's righteousness and forbearance (Rom. 3:25–26).* God's plan of salvation must conform to his character. Since God is just, his plan of salvation must be just. Does God really hate sin if he justifies sinners? The answer is in the cross. "For he hath made him to be sin for us, who knew no sin; that we might be made the righteousness of God in him" (2 Cor. 5:21). Is God just in allowing sins before the coming of Christ to go unpunished? The answer is that God in forbearance has allowed time for repentance; also, every sin either before the cross or subsequent to the cross will either be covered by the atonement of Christ or receive its just recompense of reward. God in his wisdom has designed a way to be just to himself and to justify every person who believes in Jesus. "Mercy and truth are met together; righteousness and peace have kissed each other" (Ps. 85:10) at the cross. Hallelujah!

Conclusion

God's salvation excludes human boasting. It is not on the basis of keeping the law or doing good works. It is not something one could buy or merit. Salvation is God's free gift; so to him belongs the glory (Rom. 3:27–28; 6:23; Eph. 2:8–9).

Salvation is open to all persons on the same basis—by faith. On the assumption that there is only one God (Ex. 20:1–3; Deut. 6:4–5), it follows that God is the God of all people, both of Jews and Gentiles. This one God has revealed that he has only one way of salvation, and that is salvation by faith.

Those saved by faith in Jesus are now his voluntary bond slaves. They are under constraint to do the will of God as revealed in Jesus. Just as the Mosaic law was fulfilled in Jesus, so the demands of the moral law are not canceled, but are fulfilled in believers' union with Christ. They are now children of God through faith in Christ Jesus, and as children, they desire to please their heavenly Father.

"For Christ's love compels us, because we are convinced that one died for all, and therefore all died. And he died for all, that those who live should no longer live for themselves but for him who died for them and was raised again" (2 Cor. 5:14–15 NIV).

SUNDAY EVENING, JULY 8

Title: God Is Alive!

Text: "My soul thirsteth for God, for the living God" **(Ps. 42:2)**.

Scripture Reading: Psalm 42:1–11

Introduction

At various times we think God is far removed from us. The author of Psalms 42 and 43 felt that way. Reading both of these psalms yields the conclusion that the author once led pilgrims in procession to God's house. Now he is in serious trouble. He has been exiled from Jerusalem and the temple and tormented by enemies. The psalmist longed to know God.

Various circumstances make us long for the living God. Like a deer longing for flowing streams in the dry season, so the psalmist longs for God. When we study the Bible, we can learn many truths about the living God.

I. God is real.

Many people deny the existence of God. Philosopher Bertrand Russell wrote a defensive work entitled *Why I Am Not a Christian* to deny the existence of God. Though we may not conclude philosophically that God does not exist, we may doubt God's existence during some of life's trying experiences.

A. *The Bible affirms the reality of God.* The Bible records the deeds of God and reveals his character.

B. *Logic affirms the reality of God.* Through the years, traditional arguments have been presented for the existence of God. The four traditional logical presentations are the ontological, the cosmological, the teleological, and the moral. These logical truths will not prove the existence of God, but they will affirm the world's need for God.

C. *Experience affirms the reality of God.* When you experience the God revealed in Scripture, you know the reality of God. Logic can be challenged, but the change that God makes in a person's life defies challenge. One of my favorite theologians is an anonymous blind man. Listen to his theology after Jesus healed him: "One thing I know, that, whereas I was blind, now I see" (John 9:25).

II. God is great.

The psalmist longed for God, for he knew that God was alive. He knew something of his greatness, but he wanted to know more of the grandeur and glory of God. Humankind never exhausts the truths about God. Each day we can learn more about him, and the more we know, the more we rejoice in his greatness.

A. *God is powerful.* Nothing can compare to the awesome power of God. God spoke and the world came into being. With his creative hand he formed human beings, and he infused them with the breath of life. Not only did he create the universe, but he also has power to sustain it.

B. *God has supremacy.* The God revealed in Scripture has absolute supremacy. The world and its affairs are in his control. Satan seeks control over the affairs and destiny of humankind, but God has absolute supremacy over Satan. Paul said, "And having spoiled principalities and powers, he made a shew of them openly, triumphing over them in it" (Col. 2:15). Jesus defeated Satan by dying on Calvary. John records how Jesus has ultimate supremacy over the evil world: "And the devil that deceived them was cast into the lake of fire and brimstone, where the beast and the false prophet are, and shall be tormented day and night for ever and ever" (Rev. 20:10). Only God is great, for he has absolute supremacy.

C. *God does not change.* God is great because he never changes. He does not think or react capriciously. He has a continuous settled disposition against sin. He also has a constant, unfailing love toward sinners. James said, "Every good gift and every perfect gift is

215

from above, and cometh down from the Father of lights, with whom is no variableness, neither shadow of turning" (James 1:17). You can always count on God to be the same way he has always been.

III. God is knowable.

The psalmist longed for God, for God had made himself known. The psalmist desires to know God more. He wants to go to the temple and be admitted as a worshiper to the presence of God. For those of you who long to know God, you can know him, for he makes himself known.

A. *God made himself known on stone tablets.* In the history of Israel, God made himself known on Mount Sinai on two stone tablets on which he wrote the Ten Commandments. These commands reveal God's righteous will for people. God desires that people honor him with priority, sovereignty, sincerity, and sanctity (first four commandments). He also demands that they honor and respect other human beings and their property (last six commandments). On these stone tablets God reveals himself as a God of law and order.

B. *God made himself known on the sand.* He made himself known supremely in the life and ministry of Jesus Christ. The episode of Jesus's confrontation with the adulterous woman and her accusers furnishes us a truth about God (cf. John 8:1–11). The Pharisees had caught a woman in the act of adultery. They tested Jesus to see what he would do with the law, which commanded that the woman be stoned. In an unusual gesture, Jesus wrote on the ground. Then he said, "He that is without sin among you, let him first cast a stone at her" (John 8:7). Evidently something that Jesus wrote on the ground convicted the Pharisees, for all the accusers left. Someone has said that Jesus wrote the sins of the Pharisees. From this story we learn that God does not desire to condemn anyone, but seeks their highest good.

C. *God made himself known on a piece of wood.* He made himself known when Jesus died on the cross. On a rough piece of wood Jesus disclosed his love for humanity. "But God commendeth his love toward us, in that, while we were yet sinners, Christ died for us" (Rom. 5:8).

IV. God is able.

The psalmist longed for God. He knew that God was real, that he was great, and that he was knowable, and he also knew God's ability.

A. *God is able to give strength during the troubles of life. God is alive, and many have experienced his strength during the vicissitudes of life.* Paul found that God was able to strengthen him during trouble. The psalmist said, "God is our refuge and strength, a very present help in trouble" (Ps. 46:1).

B. *God is able to deliver from temptation.* When the solicitation for evil is the strongest, our God can deliver. "There hath no temptation taken you but such as is common to man: but God is faithful, who will not suffer you to be tempted above that ye are able; but will with the temptation also make a way to escape, that ye may be able to bear it" (1 Cor. 10:13).

C. *God is able to deliver from the fear of death.* He causes people to be able to face the future without fear. Listen to Paul's confidence in the face of death: "For I know whom I have believed, and am persuaded that he is able to keep that which I have committed unto him against that day" (2 Tim. 1:12). God can deliver you from the fear of death.

Conclusion

Irrespective of the philosophies of the time, God is alive. The God of the ages wishes to be alive and active in your life.

WEDNESDAY EVENING JULY 11

Title: Moses: The Leader and Lawgiver of Israel

Text: "Come now therefore, and I will send thee unto Pharaoh, that thou mayest bring forth my people . . . out of Egypt" **(Ex. 3:10)**.

Scripture Reading: Exodus 3:1–10

Introduction

Some have referred to Moses as the greatest man, other than Jesus, who ever lived. It also has been said of him that he was the greatest man among mere men in the history of the world. Because of Moses's importance, it behooves every student of the Word to make a study of him.

I. The background and early life that led up to Moses's call are of significance.

A. *Moses was born at a time when Pharaoh had issued an order that all newborn male children should be put to death.* The Egyptians were afraid of the Israelites and sought to destroy them. God led the midwives to disobey Pharaoh and allow the baby boys to live.

B. *Moses's mother played an important role in his life.* Even though she had been ordered to throw her son in the river, she recognized Moses as a fine child and thus defied the order (Ex. 1:22; 2:2–3). After Moses was found by Pharaoh's daughter, his biological mother became his nurse (2:5–10). This is a good lesson for all on the influence of a mother.

C. *Some events in Moses's early life made a tremendous impact.* Moses elected not to be called the son of Pharaoh's daughter and instead chose to share ill treatment with the people of God, thus identifying with the slave class rather than with the princes of the empire. He was thought to be a nobody rather than the ruler of Egypt. After fleeing from Egypt, Moses was left to mellow and mature by God's providence.

From these experiences, we can learn the importance of decisions.

II. The preparation of Moses for the task God had for him was of vital importance to his usefulness.

This preparation was threefold.

A. *He had spiritual training.* He was trained by his mother and sister to have faith in God and in God's promises to his nation. And he was taught to live a godly life.
B. *He had academic and cultural training.* Moses was trained by the princes of Egypt and was considered an Egyptian. Thus, he had princely education and became learned in the wisdom of the Egyptians.
C. *He had geographical and leadership training.* Moses became associated with the man who later became his father-in-law. This man taught him good judgment. While caring for his father-in-law's herds, Moses also became familiar with the desert over which he was to lead the people.

Two lessons are to be gleaned from these experiences: God prepares his people for the tasks he calls them to do, and he can turn seeming tragedies into victories.

III. Moses's call was the heart of his usefulness.

A. *This call was the most appalling commission ever given to mere man.* It was the commission to a solitary man to go back home and deliver his people from a dreadful slavery at the hand of the most powerful nation on earth.
B. *This call came from a God who is not new, but is the God of the fathers (Ex. 3:6).* In the call, Moses recognized that his God entered into the struggle of his people and that God works through people (Ex. 5:10).
C. *Moses responded to this call with four excuses.* He questioned whether he would be equal to the task (Ex. 3:11). What was his authority (v. 13)? Would the people believe him (4:1)? Was he a capable enough speaker (v. 10)? Each time, Moses's God was equal to the occasion.

IV. The response to the call was a response of faith.

A. *Moses found his true and living God more than capable of dealing with the various gods of the Egyptians.* This is seen in the ten plagues.

B. *Moses found as he responded in faith that God used him to deliver his people from bondage.* He also became the instrument by whom the Ten Commandments were given.

Conclusion

Moses was a mere man, but God called him to a gigantic task. He obeyed his Lord, was used of his Lord, and was blessed by his Lord. This is a true lesson for all of us in listening to the voice of God and doing what he says.

SUNDAY MORNING, JULY 15

Title: Salvation by Grace through Faith Illustrated

Text: "Now to him that worketh is the reward not reckoned of grace, but of debt. But to him that worketh not, but believeth on him that justifieth the ungodly, his faith is counted for righteousness" (**Rom. 4:4–5**).

Scripture Reading: Romans 4

Hymns:　　"Have Faith in God," McKinney
　　　　　"The Solid Rock," Mote
　　　　　"Jesus Paid It All," Hall

Offertory Prayer: Heavenly Father, we thank you for the witness of the Holy Spirit with our spirits that we are children of God. Our regeneration and desire to serve are evidences to us of our justification and forgiveness. For the sins that mar our sense of fellowship, we beg forgiveness. For the union with you which no one can break, we give you eternal praise, through our Lord Jesus Christ. Amen.

Introduction

Paul developed the need for salvation in Romans 1:18–3:20. He expounded the nature of God's salvation in Romans 3:21–31. Now in Romans 4 he illustrates salvation by grace through faith primarily in the case of Abraham and secondarily in the case of David.

I. Significance of Abraham, Father of the faithful (Rom. 4:1–8).

A. *"What then shall we say that Abraham, our forefather, discovered in this matter?"* (Rom. 4:1 NIV). What light can we get from his salvation? Was he saved by faith or by works? If any person could have been made right with God by good works, surely Abraham was that person. However, the account of his conversion in Genesis 15:6 reads, "Abraham believed God, and it was counted unto him for righteousness" (Rom. 4:3). "A man who works is paid: his wages are not regarded as a gift, but as something that he has earned" (Rom. 4:4 GNT). Abraham had many good works of which to boast, but his good works had nothing to do with his right relation to God.

His faith was imputed (a bookkeeping term that means to place on one's account) for righteousness. When God imputes righteousness to believers on the credit side of the ledger, he also debits their trespasses, for "God was in Christ, reconciling the world unto himself, not imputing their trespasses unto them" (2 Cor. 5:19).

B. *Salvation then is not something one earns.* If earned, salvation would be a payment of debt rather than a gift of God's grace. We could boast of ourselves rather than of God. Boasting is excluded. All have sinned, and only God can forgive sin. All of one's good works cannot merit nor obtain forgiveness.

C. *Salvation is the gift of God.* Only God could have provided a way by which he could "justify the ungodly." If God offered his salvation only to those who were good enough or who earned it, then no one could be saved, but since he offers his salvation to sinners on the basis of faith, then there is hope for all people.

D. *David understood this great truth.* In Psalm 32:1–2 (quoted here from Rom. 4:6–8) he describes the happy condition of the person "unto whom God imputeth righteousness without works, saying, Blessed are they whose iniquities are forgiven, and whose sins are covered. Blessed is the man to whom the Lord will not impute sin."

II. Abraham's experience illustrates that salvation is not dependent on ceremony (Rom. 4:9–25).

Abraham was saved before he was circumcised. The account of the former is in Genesis 15 and the latter in Genesis 17. This is Paul's very astute observation. Perhaps no one else had noticed this fact.

A. *Since Abraham was saved before circumcision, this rite was not essential to his salvation.* He was saved not as a Jew, but as a human being. Whether one is Jew or Gentile has nothing to do with one's salvation. As God is one and is God of both Jews and Gentiles, he has only one plan of salvation for both Jews and Gentiles. The condition is not that one become a Jew or submit to some ceremony, but that one have faith (Rom. 3:26–31). Some Jewish Christians found it difficult to accept the salvation of the Gentiles without their becoming Jews. Certain men from Judea came to Antioch, where Paul and Barnabas and others were having a very successful ministry among the Gentiles, and caused great dissension by saying, "Except ye be circumcised after the manner of Moses, ye cannot be saved" (Acts 15:1). This resulted in the conference of Paul and Barnabas with the apostles and elders at Jerusalem in which they reached full agreement that both Jews and Gentiles are saved by grace through faith without circumcision. The interesting account is in Acts 15 and Galatians 2.

B. *Paul further affirms that Abraham "received circumcision as a sign, a seal of the righteousness that he had by faith while he was still uncircumcised.* So then, he is the father of all who believe but have not been circumcised, in order that righteousness might be credited to them" (Rom. 4:11 NIV). The ceremony was a sign and seal of the reality. Apart from the reality, it was nothing (recall Rom. 2:25–29). This is true of all religious ceremonies, as, for example, baptism and the Lord's Supper. They are signs and seals of great spiritual realities but do not have any saving value per se.

C. *What a theological bombshell it was when Paul interpreted the promise to Abraham in Genesis 12:1–3 to refer to the sons of Abraham who have faith like Abraham's rather than to the sons of Abraham who were circumcised and kept the Mosaic law.* "For the promise, that he should be the heir of the world, was not to Abraham, or to his seed, through the law, but through the righteousness of faith" (Rom. 4:13; read also vv. 14–16). Paul had already amplified this view in Galatians 3 (a letter he wrote just before Romans). Paul's conclusion is that the promise to Abraham is fulfilled in Christ and in those of all races who come to God through faith in Christ (Gal. 3:14–16). This promise was given to Abraham 430 years before the law was given to Moses, so it is impossible that the law of Moses should cancel the promise to Abraham (vv. 17–18). Paul's conclusion is, "For ye are all the children of God by faith in Christ Jesus. For as many of you as have been baptized into Christ have put on Christ. There is neither Jew nor Greek, there is neither bond nor free, there is neither male nor female: for ye are all one in Christ Jesus. And if ye be Christ's, then are ye Abraham's seed, and heirs according to the promise" (vv. 26–29).

Jesus affirms this interpretation. When Zacchaeus was saved, Jesus said to him, "This day is salvation come to this house, forsomuch as he also is a son of Abraham" (Luke 19:9). Zacchaeus had been a son of Abraham according to race since his birth, but now he had become a son of Abraham according to the promise by his faith.

Conclusion

Paul, James, and Jesus agree. James 2:14–26 seems to disagree with Paul. The apparent disagreement is cleared up when one notes that Paul and James use the same key words but with different meanings. Paul refutes the error that one can be saved by good works apart from the atoning death of Christ. James refutes the error that one can be saved by faith in Jesus Christ without this faith issuing in a changed life that will bring forth the fruit of good works.

1. James calls himself "a servant . . . of the Lord Jesus Christ" (James 1:1) and writes of "our Lord Jesus Christ, the Lord of glory" (2:1). There is no disagreement with Paul here.

2. At the Jerusalem conference, James agreed with Paul that the Gentiles did not have to become Jews before they could become Christians.
3. For Paul, faith is active. Alleged faith that does not issue in action is not faith at all. For James, faith is more than intellectual assent. If there is no action, the faith is dead faith (James 2:14–20). Faith that issues in action is live faith. James's "live faith" equals Paul's "faith." James's "dead faith" is for Paul no faith at all. Paul, James, and Jesus would all agree that the faith that saves is more than intellectual assent. It issues in regeneration and life change.

For Paul, works are meritorious deeds, ceremonial acts such as circumcision, tithing, fasting, and keeping of Mosaic laws, which one might erroneously trust for salvation (see "not of works," Eph. 2:9). Paul does, however, use works in the sense of obedience or the fruit of faith (as in "created in Christ Jesus unto good works," Eph. 2:10). James uses works as the kind of good life that evidences faith. Paul, James, and Jesus would all agree that one cannot be saved on the basis of good deeds or ceremonies. All would agree that the saved person will bring forth good fruit, some a hundredfold, some sixtyfold, some thirtyfold.

For Paul, "justify" is the judicial act of God by which one is declared to be free from the penalty of sin and is set right with God. For James, "justify" is more the proof in the eyes of one's peers that one's faith is genuine. Jesus used "justify" in both senses; for example, Paul's usage in "I tell you, this man went down to his house justified rather than the other" (Luke 18:14), and James' usage in "Wisdom is justified of all her children" (Luke 7:35). Jesus, Paul, and James would agree that Abraham was justified (saved) by faith (live faith) and then justified (proved) it by his works.

SUNDAY EVENING, JULY 15

Title: A Giant Step for God

Text: "The Word became flesh and made his dwelling among us. We have seen his glory, the glory of the one and only Son, who came from the Father, full of grace and truth" **(John 1:14 NIV)**.

Scripture Reading: John 1:1–14

Introduction

On July 20, 1969, Neil Armstrong was the first man to set foot on the moon. His first statement was, "One small step for man, one giant leap for mankind." To be sure, this was a gigantic step in the progress of science.

Another giant step for humanity occurred nearly two thousand years earlier in the obscure Middle-Eastern village of Bethlehem. It was a giant step for both humanity and God when Jesus came to earth. One of the most fascinating studies we can make is to learn more of Jesus in his visit to earth and his ministry to humanity. Let us notice three important facets of the life and ministry of Jesus Christ.

I. His incarnation.

One of the greatest facets of Jesus Christ is that he is the God-man. He is fully God and fully man. God came to earth and lived in human flesh. This has to be the greatest step in recorded history.

A. *The incarnation implies that God knows man.* Since God became man in Jesus Christ, we know that God knows humankind. During World War II, Lawrence of Arabia sought to cast his lot with the Allied army. They said to him, "If you would lead us, you must eat the same food we eat, find shelter in the same tents in which we dwell, accept the same risks that we accept, meet the same difficulties that we meet, live the same life we live, and live it better than we do." Jesus Christ identified completely with humankind. He walked, talked, and lived in Palestine as a human being.

Because God became flesh, he knows our problems. Jesus experienced physical and mental needs. The author of the letter to the Hebrews stated Jesus's identity beautifully: "For we have not an high priest which cannot be touched with the feeling of our infirmities; but was in all points tempted like as we are, yet without sin" (4:15). Jesus knew what it was like to be human.

B. *The incarnation implies that Jesus reveals God.* Even though God became flesh, this did not rob him of deity. Jesus was the Son of God. As we study Jesus's life, we immediately conclude, "Jesus is more than a man." His character reflects his deity. He refused every solicitation to sin and denied every temptation to a self-centered ministry. Every disclosure of Jesus's character affirmed that he was the Son of God.

Jesus's miracles reflect his deity. He demonstrated power over the world of nature when he calmed a stormy sea and changed water into wine. He disclosed his deity when he demonstrated his ability to restore health to the sick, sight to the blind, hearing to the deaf, mobility to the paralyzed, and life to the dead. Jesus also exhibited his divine power when he took authority over demons.

The nature of Christ's personhood is a mystery. How God could become man and be fully God and fully man is a paradox. But the Incarnation implies that Jesus of Nazareth understands the human plight and is thoroughly capable of revealing God's nature.

II. His dedication.

Another great facet of Jesus Christ is his dedication to God and humanity. The greatness of a person can be measured by his or her degree of dedication.

No other person compared to Jesus's obedience to the Father's will and to Jesus's service for humanity.

A. *Dedication means obedience to the Father's will.* Whatever the Father wanted Jesus to do, Jesus obeyed. From the outset of his ministry, Jesus determined to do the Father's business. When Mary and Joseph sought him in the temple, Jesus said, "Didn't you know I had to be in my Father's house?" (Luke 2:49 NIV). In the wilderness, Satan tempted Jesus with three attractive proposals, but Jesus chose to obey his Father's will. Throughout Jesus's life, he continued to obey his Father, even to the extent of dying on a cross. The greatness of the Master can be seen in his unfailing commitment to the Father's will.

B. *Dedication means a service to the needs of people.* Jesus sought to minister to people where they hurt. He announced the intention of his ministry in a temple sermon at Nazareth: "The Spirit of the Lord is upon me, because he hath anointed me to preach the gospel to the poor; he hath sent me to heal the brokenhearted, to preach deliverance to the captives, and recovering of sight to the blind, to set at liberty them that are bruised. To preach the acceptable year of the Lord" (Luke 4:18–19). Jesus then fulfilled the announcement in a ministry completely dedicated to others.

III. His exaltation.

When Jesus entered human history, it was a giant step for God and a tremendous benefit to humanity. He did not remain in a physical body on earth. After his shameful death on Calvary, Jesus was exalted. One cannot study the full ministry of Jesus without looking at the Lord's exaltation.

A. *The resurrection of Jesus Christ exalts the Lord.* Reading the bitter details of the cross causes one to flinch. No one has ever died a more cruel death than crucifixion. Death is final for all other leaders. Indeed, the disciples thought that their masterful teacher and miracle worker had been silenced forever. But Scripture records that God raised Jesus from the grave. Death could not hold its prey. Not mentioning the glorious resurrection of Jesus Christ leaves the account incomplete. The glory of Jesus can be seen in his glorious resurrection.

B. *The reign of Jesus in glory continues to exalt his glory.* The story of Jesus's life and death is not to be perpetuated as an ancient story. He is a living Lord ruling over the affairs of history at this present moment. "Wherefore God also hath highly exalted him, and given him a name which is above every name: That at the name of Jesus every knee should bow, of things in heaven, and things in earth, and things under the earth; and that every tongue should confess that Jesus Christ is Lord, to the glory of God the Father" (Phil. 2:9–11). Jesus reigns at the right hand of the Father.

Conclusion

God has taken many steps for humankind. He took a giant step when he stepped through time and space to come to rescue humankind. He wants you to take one step toward him in faith that will lead to a walk with him.

WEDNESDAY EVENING, JULY 18

Title: Joshua: The Soldier of the Lord

Text: "And Moses said unto Joshua, Choose us out men, and go out, fight with Amalek: tomorrow I will stand on the top of the hill with the rod of God in mine hand" **(Ex. 17:9)**.

Scripture Reading: Exodus 17:9–16

Introduction

Ordinarily when character studies are made of Bible personalities, Joshua is not one who is used. But this man, whose name means the same as Jesus, is worthy of a Christian's consideration. His name means "deliverer" or "savior."

I. Joshua is known as the minister of Moses (Ex. 24:13).

   A. *Joshua was commissioned by Moses (Ex. 17:9–13).* When the Amalekites warred against Israel, Moses commissioned Joshua to be his leader. Joshua was to choose the men and fight the battle. This is the passage of Scripture that tells about Aaron and Hur holding up Moses's arms.

   B. *Joshua accompanied Moses when he received the Ten Commandments from God (Ex. 24:13).* At the end of the forty days and during the descent from the mountain, Joshua discovered chaos in the camp as the people worshiped a molten calf. Joshua was a faithful servant and had a sensitive spirit.

   C. *Joshua was trusted by Moses in a place of responsibility (Ex. 33:11).*

   D. *Joshua was faithful to Moses (Num. 11:28).* Eldad and Medad were critical of Moses. When Moses needed a friend, it was Joshua who stood by him.

   E. *Joshua was Moses's successor as the leader of Israel (Deut. 31:23).* Scripture shows that a bond existed between these two great men. Often a person's usefulness is determined by how he stands by a friend.

II. Some outstanding events in Joshua's life gave evidence of the supernatural.

   A. *He saw the waters of the Jordan River part and his people walk through on dry ground (Josh. 2:10).* As a follower of God and a leader of Israel, Joshua took the initiative and our Lord blessed.

B. *An angel of God appeared to him outside the walls of Jericho (Josh. 5:13–15; 6:2–5).* At a crucial time in Joshua's leadership career, he needed a special message from God. Because of his closeness to God and desire to serve his Lord, the angel appeared and gave him assurance.

C. *He saw the walls of Jericho fall flat (Josh. 6:12–21).* When the Lord has a task to perform, he has a plan to do it. When he has a task and a plan, he uses people to expedite them. Joshua was obedient to his heavenly instruction and was victorious for his Lord.

III. Joshua had three positions of prominence.

A. *He was the minister of Moses and became his successor.* Joshua is a good example of being faithful where he was, and he was rewarded with greater responsibility.

B. *He was one of the twelve spies sent out to investigate Canaan.* Because of Joshua's closeness to his Lord and his faith in God, he believed the land could be taken. He was able to see and understand God's plan.

C. *He was the leader of the people when they entered the Promised Land.* This was bound to have been a happy day for Israel. They had forty years of slavery and forty years of wandering in the wilderness. Joshua led them and rejoiced with them.

IV. Certain characteristics in Joshua's life were similar to those of other great men.

He was a faithful and loyal friend. He had strong faith, deep consecration, and unfaltering obedience. He was able to make clear, concise decisions.

Conclusion

Men and women who desire to be useful people in kingdom work can learn from this man Joshua. He was at the right place at the right time with the right attitude. As a result, he was a winner all the way.

SUNDAY MORNING, JULY 22

Title: Rejoice in God

Text: "Not only so, but we also rejoice in God through our Lord Jesus Christ, through whom we have now received our reconciliation" **(Rom. 5:11 RSV)**.

Scripture Reading: Romans 5:1–11

Hymns: "Hallelujah! What a Savior," Bliss
"Sunshine in My Soul," Hewitt
"Crown Him with Many Crowns," Bridges

Offertory Prayer: Heavenly Father, with joyful hearts we acknowledge the peace that passes all understanding that you have given to those who love you. Flood our hearts with the assurance of your love. Grant that we may live for you here and live with you in joyful fellowship forever. In Jesus's name. Amen.

Introduction

Jesus's beatitudes describe the Christian life as a happy life (Matt. 5:1–12). Jesus said, "I am come that they might have life, and that they might have it more abundantly" (John 10:10). Abundant life overflowing in satisfaction is the normal experience of dedicated Christians. For example, how many unhappy missionaries do you know?

Paul exulted in the blessings of his salvation. Romans 5:1–11 reads like a hymn of joyful praise.

I. Rejoice in peace with God (Rom. 5:1–2).

A. *Before salvation, there is no peace.* "There is no peace, saith the LORD, unto the wicked" (Isa. 48:22). "For the wrath of God is revealed from heaven against all ungodliness and unrighteousness of men" (Rom. 1:18; read again 3:19–23). "For the wages of sin is death" (Rom. 6:23). "He that believeth on the Son hath everlasting life: and he that believeth not the Son shall not see life; but the wrath of God abideth on him" (John 3:36). "O death, where is thy sting? O grave, where is thy victory? The sting of death is sin; and the strength of sin is the law" (1 Cor. 15:55–56). The anticipation of death and judgment is fearful for one who is not saved.

B. *After salvation there is peace.* "Therefore, since we have been justified through faith, we have peace with God through our Lord Jesus Christ" (Rom. 5:1 NIV). When we are justified, we do have peace with God. We are saved from the wrath to come (v. 9). "There is therefore now no condemnation to them which are in Christ Jesus" (8:1).

However, the justified person may not fully appropriate and enjoy the peace he or she has. A troop transport ran into a storm the first night at sea. Experienced sailors on the ship went about their tasks with little fear. Hundreds of young men spending their first night at sea were very frightened. Their safety did not depend on their fears but on the seaworthiness of the ship and crew. Christians may be saved but not experience the joy of full assurance. Paul's exhortation is not "Let us get peace" but "Let us enjoy the peace God has for us."

C. *Peace is more than a cease-fire.* Peace means harmony with God. "By whom also we have access by faith into this grace wherein we stand" (Rom. 5:2). The figure is that of being ushered into the presence of royalty or of entering into a temple through the grand entrance door. Through the door Jesus ushers the justified one into the presence of God. As Paul develops later in the Roman letter, God never justifies sinners whom he does not also regenerate. The redeemed stand in God's presence unafraid because God has given them a standing in grace, their sins are forgiven, they have eternal life, they have been adopted as God's children, and the Holy Spirit has sealed them unto the day of redemption (Eph. 1:13–14; 4:30). Let us rejoice!

II. Rejoice also in tribulations (Rom. 5:3–4).

A. *The exhortation is not to rejoice because of tribulations, but rather when they come to find joy in them.* Jesus said, "These things I have spoken unto you, that in me ye might have peace. In the world ye shall have tribulation: but be of good cheer; I have overcome the world" (John 16:33). The Christian does not know what the future holds, but he has faith in God who holds the future. "We know that in everything God works for good with those who love him, who are called according to his purpose" (Rom. 8:28 RSV).

B. *The Christian believes that God can use tribulations to build character.* God deals with us as with children. He loves us too much not to build character in us. (Read Heb. 12:5–11.)

   1. "Tribulation worketh patience" (Rom. 5:3). Synonyms for patience are fortitude, steadfastness, and endurance. The quality is not passive but active. It describes the person who is unswerved from deliberate loyalty to faith by even the greatest trials and sufferings.

   2. Patience works experience, or character. Refined metal is that which has been purified by fire and has stood the test. Because of the test, the metal is pure. It could not have been purified without the fire. Do you not know those of Christian character who were refined by the fires of tribulation? They have a character they could not have attained any other way.

   3. Experience works hope. Those who have found God true in experience have hope for God's continued goodness. Their experience confirms that of earlier believers. "Our fathers trusted in thee: they trusted, and thou didst deliver them. They cried unto thee, and were delivered: they trusted in thee, and were not confounded" (Ps. 22:4–5). These Christians are sure that God will not disappoint them. Paul's hope became brighter with the passing of the years. In the last letter from his pen written from the Roman prison to Timothy, the aged apostle wrote, "For the which cause I also suffer these things: nevertheless I am not ashamed: for I know whom I have believed, and am persuaded that he is able to keep that which I have committed unto him against that day" (2 Tim. 1:12). In

the shadow of martyrdom, experience works hope: "For I am now ready to be offered, and the time of my departure is at hand. I have fought a good fight, I have finished my course, I have kept the faith; henceforth there is laid up for me a crown of righteousness, which the Lord, the righteous judge, shall give me at that day: and not to me only, but unto all them also that love his appearing" (2 Tim. 4:6–8).

III. Rejoice in God the Father through whom we have reconciliation (Rom. 5:2; 6:11).

"Rejoice in hope of the glory of God" (Rom. 5:2). The preacher at a union service had already announced his subject and had read the Scripture when he suddenly became ill and could not preach. The congregation turned to my father who, from the subject and Scripture already announced, preached a magnificent sermon. I was only a boy, but to this day I recall how proud I was of my father. How much more should we exult in hope of the glory that God has and will bring to his name. His glory is manifest in creation. "The heavens declare the glory of God; and the firmament sheweth his handiwork" (Ps. 19:1). Far more than in nature his glory is manifested in grace: "God's love has been poured out into our hearts through the Holy Spirit, who has been given to us" (Rom. 5:5 NIV).

God's love is beyond human understanding. Scarcely for a righteous man (one without sympathy) would anyone die; perhaps for a good man (one with sympathy) someone would have the courage to die. But when we were without strength, when we were sinners, when we were enemies of God, God commended his love toward us in that Christ died for us. If God loved us when we were enemies, now that we are reconciled to God, our final salvation is as sure as his eternal existence.

Conclusion

Let us continue to exult in God through our Lord Jesus Christ, by whom we have received reconciliation. In Romans 3:27 Paul asks, "Where is boasting then? It is excluded." The boasting that is excluded is the boasting about oneself. It is not wrong to boast about God. In fact, it is right and proper. Hallelujah! What a Savior!

SUNDAY EVENING, JULY 22

Title: The Abundant Energy Resource

Text: "Verily, verily, I say unto you, he that believeth on me, the works that I do shall he do also; and greater works than these shall he do; because I go unto my Father" **(John 14:12)**.

Scripture Reading: John 14:12–31

Introduction

When God's people depend on human strength and knowledge, an energy crisis can develop in the church. God's people need to realize that God is present with his people as an unfailing supply of power for his people.

When the apostles heard Jesus speak of his death, they panicked, thinking that Christianity was finished. But Jesus taught of a greater ministry. He promised a continuous supply of energy in the power of the Holy Spirit. Let us notice the promises that Jesus gives of the Holy Spirit.

I. The Holy Spirit will be a personal presence.

A. *The personal presence of Jesus meant much to the disciples.* Think of the times when Jesus was not present. When a storm arose on the sea, the disciples were alarmed, for Jesus was not present. His presence later strengthened these frightened men. Think of the frustration of the disciples who sought to heal a man's son while Jesus was on the Mount of Transfiguration. The personal presence of Jesus later made a difference.

B. *Jesus promised a continued personal presence.* "And I will pray the Father, and he shall give you another Comforter, that he may abide with you forever" (John 14:16). The word "another" comes from the Greek word that means "one of the same kind." This meant that the Holy Spirit would be a presence to them of the same nature of Jesus Christ. Comforter means "someone called alongside to help you." This says that the Holy Spirit would be beside us throughout life to help us.

C. *The personal presence of the Holy Spirit can revolutionize our churches.* The Holy Spirit is not some impersonal force or energy. The Holy Spirit is a person who wishes to abide with us.

II. The Holy Spirit will be a helpful teacher.

A. *The teaching ministry meant much to the disciples.* In the solitude of Galilean and Judean hillsides, Jesus taught great truths about the kingdom of God. No greater teacher ever lived than Jesus of Nazareth. The disciples wondered how future followers would learn the great truths of the kingdom of God.

B. *Jesus promised a continuous, helpful teacher.* "When he, the Spirit of truth, comes, he will guide you into all the truth" (John 16:13 NIV). Jesus taught the disciples many matters, but in some cases the disciples did not understand. The Holy Spirit would continue Jesus's teaching. After Jesus's resurrection, the Holy Spirit taught the disciples about the meaning of the cross and the universality of the gospel.

C. *The helpful teacher can revolutionize our churches.* The Holy Spirit will lend balance in the church by guarding believers from false and/ or faddish teachings.

III. The Holy Spirit will be an authoritative guide.

A. *Jesus served as a guide to the disciples.* He chose the twelve apostles and lived with them for three years. He told them what to do and where to go. He acted as a guide for life. The disciples would miss his leadership.

B. *Jesus promised an authoritative guide for life's moral decisions.* He said the Holy Spirit would "bring all things to your remembrance, whatsoever I have said unto you" (John 14:26). He promised that the Holy Spirit would live in believers and guide them into the likeness of Christ's character. The Holy Spirit can lead Christians in every circumstance of life.

C. *The authoritative leadership of the Holy Spirit can revolutionize our churches.* There is a revolt against authority today. An energy crisis will develop when we fail to follow the Spirit's direction. Churches can be led in the right direction when they depend on God's leadership.

IV. The Holy Spirit will be a dynamic resource.

A. *Jesus was a great resource for the disciples.* He worked alongside them to help and encourage them. Often the disciples were discouraged and Jesus cheered them. When they needed wisdom and strength, Jesus was available to offer a suggestion or to help with a task. The disciples would miss the dynamic resources of the Master.

B. *Jesus promised a continued resource.* The word *Comforter* has numerous meanings. It could mean someone who helps with a legal battle, an encourager of soldiers engaging in warfare, or one who gives expert advice. All of these meanings are applicable to the work of the Holy Spirit.

Conclusion

The disciples thought that when Jesus died, there would be a serious energy shortage. Jesus assured them of greater power and greater works. After the death, resurrection, and ascension of Jesus Christ, the Holy Spirit came to abide with God's people. A great supply of energy was available for the early church, and that same energy supply is still available today. No congregation needs to suffer an energy shortage. God is ready to bless our churches today with his presence and power.

WEDNESDAY EVENING, JULY 25

Title: Jethro: The Man with Sound Advice

Text: "I will give thee counsel, and God shall be with thee" (**Ex. 18:19**).

Scripture Reading: Exodus 18:13–27

Introduction

Jethro is an obscure biblical character in comparison to many of prominence. Usually when character studies are made, students seek out the names of
those in the limelight and those who have made the headlines. But the headline
person is not always the one who makes the greatest contribution. Sometimes
it is the one behind the scenes who does the most. Jethro is such a character.

I. The name Jethro has some significance.
   A. *The meaning is "excellence."* This probably is Jethro's official name.
      The meaning of the word shows the stature of this man.
   B. *He also is identified by other names.* He is called Reuel (Ex. 2:18)
      and Raguel (Num. 10:29). These probably are his proper names,
      meaning the same thing.
   C. *He is better known as Moses's father-in-law.*

II. The Scriptures tell of some special events in Jethro's life.
   A. *Exodus 2 tells of Jethro's first experience with Moses.* It is here that one
      finds that he was a priest, that he had seven daughters, and that
      he was concerned with the welfare of his daughters. He gave one
      daughter, Zipporah, to Moses in marriage.
   B. *Exodus 4 tells of Jethro's response to Moses.* Upon Moses's request to go
      to Egypt to deliver his people, Jethro said, "Go in peace" (Ex. 4:18).
   C. Jethro had to have a sympathetic ear to even listen to Moses. He
      also had to have concern for those in slavery.
   D. *Exodus 18:13–27 tells of his advice to Moses after the deliverance.* This is
      the heart of all that is known about Jethro.
   E. *Exodus 18:6–7 tells of Jethro's response over Moses's success.* He "rejoiced
      for all the goodness which the LORD had done" (Ex. 18:9).

**III. Jethro's characteristics are what make him of interest to Bible
students.**
   A. *Jethro had the ability to discern.* He recognized a problem. He saw that
      what Moses was doing was not good for Moses nor for the people,
      and he was able to see beyond the problem to a solution. There is
      far too much emphasis in our day on problems rather than on the
      efforts to solve them.
   B. *He was a sensitive family man.* This sensitivity made him aware of needs.
      Because of a concern for his daughters, he noticed that they returned
      too quickly from drawing water. In giving Zipporah in marriage to
      Moses, he recognized a man of worth. He had a happy relationship
      with his daughters, grandchildren, and son-in-law (Ex. 18:6–7).
   C. *He was concerned about and had a compassion for people.* When he realized
      someone had helped his daughters, he inquired about him. When
      Moses requested permission to go to Egypt, he granted the request.

D. *He walked close to God.* This is the most important quality of all. From this characteristic comes others such as discernment and sympathy. This relation to God enabled him to perform the duties of a priest satisfactorily.

Conclusion

The man who becomes great because he is in the shadow of true greatness is one to be studied. One who can work beside one of notoriety and prominence without jealousy is to be admired. Jethro was such a man.

SUNDAY MORNING, JULY 29

Title: Blessings Brought by Christ

Text: "Therefore as by the offence of one judgment came upon all men to condemnation; even so by the righteousness of one the free gift came upon all men unto justification of life. For as by one man's disobedience many were made sinners, so by the obedience of one shall many be made righteous. Moreover the law entered, that the offence might abound. But where sin abounded, grace did much more abound" **(Rom. 5:18–20)**.

Scripture Reading: Romans 5:12–21

Hymns: "I've Found a Friend," Small
            "He Is Able to Deliver Thee," Ogden
            "He Is So Precious to Me," Gabriel

Offertory Prayer: Our heavenly Father, the height, the depth, the width, and the length of your love is beyond our understanding. Much more than we know or can imagine, you are worthy of our praise. Your love reaches beneath the most wicked person. It is wide enough to include all races of people in all places. It is high enough to draw us unto you. Wonder of wonders that you would love us enough to save us and then trust us enough to use us. In your grace is our confidence and salvation. Forgive us of our sins. Lead us by your Spirit. Help us to do your will and to find joy in the doing of it, for Jesus's sake. Amen.

Introduction

Peter, in writing about "our beloved brother Paul," indicated that Paul's epistles contain "some things hard to be understood, which they that are unlearned and unstable wrest, as they do also the other scriptures, unto their own destruction" (2 Peter 3:16). One of the passages of Paul that Peter found hard to understand must certainly have been Romans 5:12–21, which is the Scripture passage for consideration in this sermon. Modern interpreters without exception find the passage difficult. Some theologians have adopted Augustine's conclusions about original sin and have declared, "There are infants in hell not a span long" because of Adam's sin.

Some propositions are wrong even though they seem to be supported by Scripture. Theological conclusions that contradict God's justice and love simply cannot be correct. Many competent theologians deny Augustine's doctrine of original sin and do not believe that Paul teaches it in this passage or elsewhere.

It is a good rule of interpretation that the obscure Scripture passages should be interpreted by the plain. Erroneous and harmful conclusions result when the plain teaching is subordinated to some fanciful interpretation of an obscure text. In this message we hope to let Paul interpret himself.

The general theme is clear: The blessings that have come to the race through Jesus Christ are much more wonderful than the evils that have come to the race through Adam.

I. Adam's sin and ours.

"Wherefore, as by one man sin entered into the world, and death by sin; and so death passed upon all men, for that all sinned" (Rom. 5:12). This sentence was not completed. Paul probably intended to write: "so also by one man righteousness entered into the world, and life by righteousness."

The reference, of course, is to the account of Adam's sin and banishment from the garden of Eden as recorded in Genesis 3. Adam and Eve, before their sin, had fellowship with God and were immortal. Sin broke the bond of fellowship between them and God. The sentence of death was executed on them in that they became mortals, but more importantly, they died in the spiritual sense that they were driven from fellowship with God in the garden of Eden. At the time of executing the sentence, God promised a Savior of the seed of the woman who would crush Satan (Gen. 3:15). An altar symbolic of the provision God would make for the forgiveness of their sins was placed at the east entrance of the Garden and was guarded by cherubim with flaming swords to keep open the way back to the tree of life. The record does not tell us whether Adam and Eve availed themselves of the provision God made for their salvation. We hope they repented and accepted the atonement God provided by his grace.

All of Adam's posterity have been mortal. All have inherited the tendency to sin. All "by nature" follow the bent to sin. As naturally as water seeks a lower level, all people naturally sin. "All we like sheep have gone astray; we have turned everyone to his own way; and the LORD hath laid on him the iniquity of us all" (Isa. 53:6). Sheep by nature tend to go astray. A cat or a dog may find its way back home, but not a sheep. It is the nature of sin to seek one's own way rather than God's way. Isaiah affirms that people are sinners by nature and sinners by practice; but God has laid on Jesus, the Suffering Servant, the sins of all of us, and he bears them away.

All of Adam's posterity are "dead in trespasses and sins" (Eph. 2:1). Dead people cannot resurrect themselves. Only God can give them new life. We cannot save ourselves, for salvation is of God.

II. Are we condemned for Adam's sin?

A. *"For that all have sinned" (Rom. 5:12) is the key passage.* Did Adam's posterity sin in Adam? Augustine, misled by the Latin translation, understood Paul to say, "In whom all sinned," and developed the theory that the whole race was seminally present in Adam. The federal theory held that God made a covenant with Adam as the representative of the whole race. Others have maintained that Paul believed in the solidarity of the family or race to the extent that the sin of one is the sin of all. All of these theories are unworthy of Paul and certainly unworthy of God.

B. *A growing group of modern theologians understood Paul's "For that all have sinned" to mean that individually the posterity of Adam has sinned.*

   1. Paul makes a valid distinction between sin and guilt (although he does not use the word *guilt*). "For until the law sin was in the world: but sin is not imputed when there is no law" (Rom. 5:13). Impute means to charge to one's account. Guilt is not charged when there is no knowledge of right or wrong. For example, a toddler found a lighter and set a fire. The toddler had sinned in that the action was wrong. Guilt was not imputed because the baby did not know the law. The law of Moses made God's law (i.e., his will) clearer "that the offence might abound" (Rom. 5:20). Why then did death reign from Adam to Moses? Because humankind always has had some knowledge of God. Recall Paul's argument in Romans 1:18–20 that the Gentiles had knowledge of God because of God's revelation in nature, and in Romans 2:14–16 because of God's revelation in human nature.

   2. Paul compared and contrasted Adam and Christ in bold, sweeping lines without noting exceptions. If from "Therefore as by the offence of one judgment came upon all men to condemnation" (Rom. 5:18) we draw the conclusion that all are condemned for Adam's sin apart from personal participation, then logically from "even so by the righteousness of one the free gift came upon all men unto justification of life" (Rom. 5:18) we might conclude that all are saved apart from repentance and faith. We know both of these conclusions are false because of what Jesus and Paul have taught elsewhere.

Conclusion

"Where sin abounded, grace did much more abound" (Rom. 5:20). Whatever the disabilities because of human relations to Adam, the blessings in Christ are much more.

"The wages of sin is death" (Rom. 6:23), but the sinner need not stay dead. "The gift of God is eternal life through Jesus Christ our Lord" (Rom. 6:23).

As light can overcome darkness, eternal life can overcome death. "The Word was the source of life, and the life brought light to men. The light shines in the darkness, and the darkness has never put it out" (John 1:4–5 GNT).

This is the message: Where there was sin and guilt, there is justification and forgiveness; where death, there is eternal life; where sin reigned bringing death, grace reigns through righteousness unto eternal life by Jesus Christ our Lord.

SUNDAY EVENING, JULY 29

Title: Whatever Became of Sin?

Text: "And Nathan said to David, Thou art the man" **(2 Sam. 12:7).**

Scripture Reading: 2 Samuel 12:1–14

Introduction

The name Karl Menninger is synonymous with the practice of psychiatry. Through the years Dr. Menninger has sought to analyze and to solve world problems with the application of psychiatry. In his book entitled *Whatever Became of Sin?* he seeks to look into the worldwide problem of gloom, apprehension, depression, and discouragement. He traces many of these results to the problem of sin. Menninger calls for a universal recognition of sin as a prevention against self-destruction.

The word *sin* has almost disappeared from the vocabulary of most people. Though the word no longer prevails, the sense of guilt remains in the hearts and minds of people. Perhaps we need to look again at the idea of sin. It means rebellion against God, estrangement from a loving God, and missing the mark a holy God intends. It is a tragedy when the discussion of sin disappears from our thinking.

Almost any story in the Bible could furnish a text for the subject of sin. The incident of David's rebellion against God gives numerous insights into the matter of sin.

I. Whatever became of the reality of sin?

Months after David's departure from God's will by committing adultery with Bathsheba and planning the death of her husband, he suffered the torment of guilt. Evidently he would not face the reality of sin in his life. Nathan confronted him when he said, "Thou art the man!"

People experience serious guilt problems because they are unwilling to face the reality of their sins. Some try to evade the fact of sin, while others try to rationalize the prevalence of sin.

    A. *Observation teaches us the reality of sin.* One only has to look at the news headlines to admit the reality of a rebellion against God. The political scandals, the atrocious crimes against people, and the abuse of property testify to the reality of sin. Drive through a city, and you will learn that people believe in sin: police officers abound, jails incarcerate criminals, car owners arm their cars with alarms, armed guards roam school hallways, and security guards and cameras watch over department stores and malls. As you look about, you will see many more evidences of the universal belief in sin.

B. *Experience teaches us the reality of sin.* A close introspection into our own personal lives will convince us of sin's reality. Our thoughts convince us that we do not think as God wants us to think. Studying our speech reveals our lack of concern for other people. Our actions reflect that most of life's concerns center in ourselves.

C. *The Holy Spirit teaches the reality of sin.* Jesus taught that one prominent ministry of the Holy Spirit would be to teach the reality of sin. "When he comes, he will prove the world to be in the wrong about sin and righteousness and judgment" (John 16:8 NIV). The Holy Spirit confronts people with the reality of sin.

Though we might not have committed the atrocious acts of David, we need to be confronted with the reality of our sins. Few people are willing to recognize and deal with their rebellion against God.

II. Whatever became of the regret over sin?

Nathan confronted David with the reality of his rebellion. When David acknowledged his sin, he had deep regret. Anytime one confronts sin seriously, profound regret will result.

A. *Regret comes because sin hurts God.* God has a high intention for humankind. When we fail to live in accordance with God's will, God is deeply hurt. What was the predominant feeling of God when David sinned? God was not angry. He was deeply troubled. His mood was one of profound sorrow. Sin wounds the heart of God.

B. *Regret comes because sin destroys self.* God allows people the privilege of either accepting or rejecting him. People can rebel against God and destroy themselves. We can look at numerous examples in biblical history and in contemporary life to see how sin destroys selfhood. Samson knew the regret of self-destruction.

C. *Regret comes because sin impairs human relationships.* Sin separates you from a harmonious relationship with other human beings. Families divide, nations fight, and community groups are alienated from each other. Sin against another human being should bring regret because of the seriously impaired relationships.

Looking into some of the psalms penned by David (Pss. 32 and 51) yields the conclusion that David regretted his sin. A genuine sorrow over sin is the need of our day.

III. Whatever became of the repentance from sin?

David saw the reality of his rebellion. It brought profound regret to him, but godly sorrow led him to repentance. He repented and committed his life anew to the Lord.

   A. *Repentance has a supreme place.* Nathan was God's appointed prophet to call David to turn in God's direction. The job of the Old Testament prophets was to turn people to God. Then Jesus came preaching a message of repentance. Today preachers call people to move in the direction of God.

   B. *Repentance has profound meaning.* Repentance does not mean to acknowledge your rebellion and to regret it. No, it means to change your mind to the extent that you will change directions. It means to turn from selfishness to commitment to the Lord.

   C. *Repentance produces wonderful results.* When David repented, his life moved in a new direction and took on new meaning and significance. Repentance removes the guilt of sin and affords a new life in Jesus Christ.

Conclusion

When I travel to New Orleans, Louisiana, I travel frequently on a bridge over Lake Pontchartrain that is almost twenty-four miles long. At various intervals, there are crossovers called "turn-a-rounds." Each time I see these signs, I think that throughout life, there are opportunities to turn life around by repenting. How about you—do you need to turn and go in God's direction today?

AUGUST

- **Sunday Mornings**

    Complete the expository messages based on Paul's letter to the Romans using the theme "God's Plan of Salvation."

- **Sunday Evenings**

    Complete the series of doctrinal messages with the theme "Vital Doctrines for Victorious Living."

- **Wednesday Evenings**

    Continue the series "Witnesses from the Past Speak to the Present."

WEDNESDAY EVENING, AUGUST 1

Title: Elijah: Mighty in Prayer

Text: "[Elijah] . . . prayed earnestly that it might not rain: and it rained not on the earth by the space of three years and six months" **(James 5:17)**.

Scripture Reading: 1 Kings 17:8–24

Introduction

Several instances in the Bible tell of a person praying for the dead to be raised and seeing them restored to life. Elijah is one of those who raised the dead through the power of God. He is a good example of a praying man.

I. Elijah was a person just like us (James 5:17).

A. *He had some weaknesses.* For some reason, he was not able to reflect on his victories to offset his fears. He had many spiritual fears. Elijah was not as wise as he should have been in caring for his physical needs, and he succumbed to discouragement (1 Kings 19:3–4). He was not infallible in his judgment (v. 14).

B. *He used his strengths to carry him in spite of his weaknesses.* Elijah was a fearless reformer. He challenged King Ahab and was victorious (1 Kings 18:17–40). He was able to control the weather at times (James 5:17). He performed many miracles, such as restoring life to a child (1 Kings 17:22), multiplying a widow's oil and meal (v. 14), slaying men by fire (2 Kings 1:10), and dividing the waters of the Jordan (2:8).

239

II. Elijah provides many lessons on prayer for today.

    A. *Each of us must face self-doubts.* There is much about prayer that no one understands. To claim to have all the answers is to be dishonest with oneself and with others. Since no one knows all there is to be known about prayer, we have much to learn, and growing in knowledge requires self-discipline. It is not easy.

    B. *Elijah challenges each individual and each church to pray more.* It is much easier to read and talk about prayer than it is to do it.

    C. *We should have a planned prayer program or schedule.* Churches should devise a prayer program that will involve the membership in all kinds of prayer. Individuals should plan a time and place for praying and have a definite prayer list for guidelines.

Conclusion

Prayer is the most vital link Christians have with their God. Each child of God should use this opportunity as Elijah did for the honor and glory of God, for his or her own spiritual development, and for the good of all society.

SUNDAY MORNING, AUGUST 5

Title: The New Attitude of the Saved Person

Text: "But now being made free from sin, and become servants to God, ye have your fruit unto holiness, and the end everlasting life. For the wages of sin is death; but the gift of God is eternal life through Jesus Christ our Lord" **(Rom. 6:22–23)**.

Scripture Reading: Romans 6:1–7:6

Hymns: "More Love to Thee, O Christ," Prentiss
           "Redeemed, How I Love to Proclaim It," Crosby
           "O Happy Day That Fixed My Choice," Doddridge

Offertory Prayer: Father, we desire to cooperate with you, the infinite potter, who is even now working with the clay of our lives to make us useful and beautiful. Forgive us of our sins of omission, of commission, and especially of disposition. May we neither be afraid of death nor of life knowing that the former shall not hold us and that the latter is in your providential keeping. Help us to be sons and daughters of you both now and in eternity, bringing glory to your name, through Jesus Christ our Lord. Amen.

Introduction

In the first five chapters of Romans, Paul deals primarily with what God does *for* the saved person in justification and redemption. The emphasis in chapters 6, 7, and 8 is on what God does *in* the saved person in sanctification.

Some in Paul's day did not understand salvation by grace through faith. If one who is saved is justified from all sins, has eternal life, has come out from under condemnation, and will not again enter into condemnation, then, they erroneously argued, could not one get saved, live wickedly, and still go to heaven? They alleged, 'Your salvation is not fair. It pronounces sinners just and sets them free to sin as they please." They argued, "If God is glorified in the salvation of sinners, then the more sin he forgives, the more glory he receives, so shouldn't we sin as much as we can in order to bring more glory to God in our salvation?" Some even said, "After salvation we should continue to sin that God's grace may abound in forgiveness."

I. "What shall we say then? Shall we continue in sin that grace may abound?" (Rom. 6:1).

Paul's reply is a horrified, "God forbid. No! No!"

A. *The whole purpose of God is to save from sin.* It is unthinkable that the holy God would provide a salvation that winks at sin and allows saved people to go on willfully sinning. Note these Scriptures: "And she shall bring forth a son, and thou shalt call his name JESUS: for he shall save his people from their sins" (Matt. 1:21). "For the Son of man is come to seek and to save that which was lost" (Luke 19:10). "[Jesus] gave himself for us, that he might redeem us from all iniquity" (Titus 2:14). A woman who wanted to divorce her husband in order to marry another man admitted it was wrong. Her husband had given her no valid grounds. She said to her counselor, "Couldn't I go ahead and do it, and then ask God to forgive me?" That is a cheap view of grace indeed, to which we as well as Paul reply, "God forbid. No!"

B. *God's purpose in salvation is also to bring many people to glory (see Heb. 2:10).* Christ gave himself for us not only to save us from sin but also to "make us a pure people who belong to him alone and are eager to do good" (Titus 2:14 GNT). By his very nature, God is holy. He hates sin and would not provide a salvation that encouraged sin.

C. *The nature of salvation is such that justification and regeneration always go together.* God does not remove the penalty without changing the heart attitude of the one redeemed. "Not by works of righteousness which we have done, but according to his mercy he saved us, by the washing of regeneration, and renewing of the Holy Ghost" (Titus 3:5). David prayed correctly, "Wash me thoroughly from mine iniquity, and cleanse me from my sin" (Ps. 51:2), but also, "Create in me a clean heart, O God; and renew a right spirit within me" (Ps. 51:10). Saved people will not be as good as Jesus but will strive to be. They grow toward perfection. When they fall, they fall toward Jesus. "How shall we, that are dead to sin, live any longer therein?" (Rom. 6:2).

The conditions for salvation are repentance and faith. Repentance means a change of mind that issues in a changed life.

241

People come to believe about sin as God believes. They therefore hate it and turn from it. People come to believe as God believes and turn to God as revealed in Jesus Christ. Turning from sin as a way of life is repentance; turning to God is faith. God does not make any mistakes. When he sees repentance and faith, he saves. When he saves, he both justifies and regenerates. The greatest assurance saved people have is that they want to do God's will. Those who claim to be Christians but who keep on willfully sinning are deceivers or are deceived. So wrote John, "If we say that we have fellowship with him, and walk [the tense means keep on walking willfully] in darkness, we lie, and do not the truth: But if we walk in the light, as he is in the light, we have fellowship one with another, and the blood of Jesus Christ his Son cleanseth us from all sin" (1 John 1:6–7).

D. *Illustrated by baptism (Rom. 6:3–14).* If in Romans 6:34 we translate the preposition "into" correctly as "with reference to," we will be saved from the grave error of baptismal regeneration. The reality is that Christ died, was buried, and was raised up by the glory of the Father. In his death, Jesus, the Messiah, the Son of God, provided the atonement for our sins. (See again Rom. 3:24–26; 4:24–25; 5:8–11; and many others.) When we repent and believe on Jesus, God saves us. The old life dies and we are justified. The Holy Spirit so changes our moral disposition that Jesus says we are "born again," or "born from above," and Paul writes, "Therefore if any man be in Christ, he is a new creature: old things are passed away; behold, all things are become new" (2 Cor. 5:17).

These great truths are pictured in baptism, in which act of obedience new Christians are able to confess publicly that they believe Jesus died, was buried, and rose again. In baptism believers picture that the old life is dead and buried and that they are new creatures in Christ.

The living of the new life for Christ will not be automatic. Temptation will not cease. In fact, it probably will intensify, but as Paul explains in Romans 8, new Christians have been aligned with a God who will not allow them to be defeated. The Holy Spirit, who before the sinner's conversion was on the outside, convicting of sin and inviting to salvation, has now come on the inside. From the throne rooms of Christians' hearts, the Holy Spirit will help them gain victory over sin and become more like Jesus. Because believers have a part in this, Paul turns to exhortation in Romans 6:12–14.

II. Shall we sin because we are not under the law but under grace?

Again Paul answers, "God forbid. No!"

A. *This is illustrated by a change of masters (Rom. 6:16–23).* Before salvation, people are slaves to sin. Obeying the lusts of sin, we yielded the members of our bodies to iniquity and uncleanness of which we are now ashamed. In the providence of God we heard the gospel and accepted Christ. Christ became our new master. Redeemed people have no obligation to the old master. That relationship is dead. We are now the voluntary slave of our new master. There is no middle ground. We are either slaves to sin or slaves to Christ. This slavery to Christ is such freedom that Paul apologizes for using the illustration, saying, "I speak after the manner of men" (Rom. 6:19). It is a service of joy, the fruits of which are holiness and eternal life. Christians are sons, not slaves. We serve out of love rather than out of fear. When the prodigal son returned home and was received as a son, he did not have to work for wages or because of fear. But do you not think that he outworked all of the servants because he loved his father?

B. *This is illustrated by the laws of marriage (Rom. 7:1–6).* The death of one partner in marriage frees the other to contract a new marriage. The old, unregenerate person died when saved by Christ. The union with sin is dead. The new person is free to marry Christ, as it were, and bring forth fruit unto God.

Conclusion

This then is the conclusion of the whole matter: "For the love of Christ constraineth us; because we thus judge, that if one died for all, then were all dead: And that he died for all, that they which live should not henceforth live unto themselves, but unto him which died for them, and rose again" (2 Cor. 5:14–15). The only law for Christians is to do the will of our heavenly Father. All of the Law and the Prophets is summed up in love for God. The person who serves for love need not worry about the law, for all that the law enjoins and much more is included in filial love.

SUNDAY EVENING, AUGUST 5

Title: Born Again

Text: "Marvel not that I said unto thee, Ye must be born again" **(John 3:7)**.

Scripture Reading: John 3:1–15

Introduction

Nicodemus was a great man in Israel. He was an educated rabbi, a member of the Sanhedrin. Outwardly he was a morally respectable man, but his heart was hungry, for the meticulous keeping of laws failed to satisfy him. When Nicodemus heard of Jesus, he visited him, and Jesus spoke to him about a new birth.

People today long for a new birth, a chance to start over. Let us notice the various facets of being born again.

I. The mandate of new birth.

When Nicodemus visited Jesus, he opened the conversation with diplomacy. Nicodemus acknowledged that Jesus had performed mighty works of God. Jesus changed the conversation from complimentary matters to an entirely new direction. Jesus shared with Nicodemus the mission and passion of his ministry. He gave the mandate of the new birth.

A. *The new birth is essential for one to see the kingdom of God.* "Verily, verily, I say unto thee, Except a man be born again, he cannot see the kingdom of God" (John 3:3). Birth is a means by which life is renewed. The human race would perish if babies were not born. Jesus emphasized that a birth from above was necessary before one could see the kingdom.

Nationalistic attachment will not allow a person to see the kingdom. Nicodemus could not be a part of the kingdom by being a Jew. He needed a birth from above.

The word "see" here could mean "to experience" (cf. John 8:51; Luke 2:26). Therefore, when Jesus spoke of seeing the kingdom, he could have meant experiencing the kingdom.

B. *The new birth is essential to enter the kingdom of God.* "Verily, verily, I say unto thee, Except a man be born of water and of the Spirit, he cannot enter into the kingdom of God" (John 3:5). Nicodemus thought he was inside the kingdom. He thought that being born a Jew and being obedient to the law were his legitimate means of entry. But Jesus said that was not enough; Nicodemus had to be born again to enter the kingdom of God. The term "born again" (*anothen*) could be translated "born from above." Jesus emphasized that the point of entry into the kingdom is a birth from God.

When you go to a football game, you need a ticket for entrance. You cannot enter the stadium and enjoy the game without one. To enter the kingdom, you must be born again. Jesus said, "Marvel not that I said unto thee, Ye must be born again" (John 3:7).

II. The mystery of the new birth.

Jesus explained the mystery of the new life with two analogies. The first analogy is one of birth. It describes the mystery of a new beginning wrought by God. The second analogy is one of the wind. It describes the mystery of how God puts his Spirit into a person.

A. *The idea of a new birth was not unheard of by the Jews.* When a proselyte came into Judaism, he was regarded as reborn. All the old connections of his life were broken. But Nicodemus was not aware of a birth from above. He had to allow God to begin life over again for him.

When we open our lives to God, we allow God to change us. Jesus Christ works a change in us. Therefore, it is through him that we are reborn. He enters into our lives and begins the process of change. No one can really understand or explain this mysterious process.

B. *The mystery of the new birth is compared to the wind.* After using the birth analogy, Jesus then used the wind as analogous to the new life. Jesus spoke to Nicodemus about the wind. We can see it, hear it, and feel it, but we cannot determine its origin. Yet we can see the evidence of the wind with the blowing of branches. There are many matters about the wind that we cannot understand, but the work of the wind is evident.

We cannot understand exactly how God works. Yet we cannot deny the powerful effect of the Spirit of God in our lives. The most convincing proof of Christianity is a life changed by the power of Jesus Christ.

III. The means of the new birth.

Jesus made the means of the new birth explicitly clear. He related the Old Testament story recorded in Numbers 21:4–9. The Israelites complained that they had left Egypt, and so God punished them with serpents. The people cried for mercy, and God instructed Moses to make an image of a serpent and to erect it on a pole in the midst of the camp. Those who looked upon the serpent would be healed. This story teaches us the valuable lesson of looking to Christ for our salvation.

A. *God provides the remedy for plagued humanity.* Homemade remedies would not heal the bitten Israelites in the wilderness. As unusual as his instructions seemed, God told the people to look at the brazen serpent on the pole and they would be healed. They had to depend totally on God for their healing.

God provides a remedy for humankind's sin in Jesus Christ. Human remedies cannot bring new life to people. The new birth begins with the recognition that God provides the remedy for sin.

B. *Humankind must depend on God's provision.* Even though Moses put a brazen serpent on a pole, the people had to look. Some may have refused to look. Others may have searched for other remedies. But those who looked represented those who depended on God's remedy.

People who wish to be born again must open their lives to God. "God so loved the world, that he gave his only begotten son, that whosoever believeth in him should not perish, but have eternal life" (John 3:16). The only way new life can begin is by opening our lives to Christ and depending on him.

Conclusion

Your life can take on new meaning if you will open it to Christ. Being born again may seem mysterious, but you will see the evidence in your life.

WEDNESDAY EVENING, AUGUST 8

Title: Gideon: The Big Little Man
Text: "The LORD is with thee, thou mighty man of valour" **(Judg. 6:12)**.
Scripture Reading: Judges 6:11–16

Introduction

Gideon referred to himself as poor and the least in his father's house, but God called him a mighty man of valor. By human standards Gideon was hardly known at all, yet God used him to do what no other person would do.

I. The book of Judges is a book of cycles and gives a background to Gideon.

A. *The cycle starts with sin.* The people of Israel did evil in the sight of God by following after other gods, such as Baal and Ashteroth.

B. *The cycle continues with God's punishment.* The Lord gave them up. He allowed and/or sent an oppressor upon them. In such cases, the punishment was generally in proportion to the severity of evil. The Midianites, in the case of Gideon, acted the part of tyrants.

C. *The cycle moves along with the cry to God for help.* When the evildoers came to realize their evil deeds, they then looked to God for help.

D. *The cycle ends with God answering the prayer.* The Lord responded to their prayers in two ways in this particular case. He sent a prophet who gave instructions and made it possible for their faith to move and work (Judg. 6:7–10), and he sent a liberator—Gideon.

II. God gave Gideon a specific call.

A. *When the Lord has a task to perform, he has a person for the task.* Gideon had already distinguished himself as a resistor of the Midianites, and God called him a man of valor. Gideon had proved himself an industrious person. He was making the most of circumstances. He also was a man who was trained in humble duty and disciplined in common tasks. Therefore, he was in the frame of mind and of such character that he was called to deliver Israel (Judg. 6:14).

B. *The Lord called Gideon in two ways.* First, he called him by an angel (Judg. 6:11). Second, the Lord spoke to him (Judg. 6:14).

C. *The call came in two steps.* Gideon first was to destroy the altar of Baal and set up the altar of God (Judg. 6:25). In order for the God of Israel to do his work, he must find faith and courage among his people. Then Gideon was to deliver his people from the hands of the Midianites.

III. All calls foster a reaction, and Gideon's was no exception.

A. *He raised two questions.* He wanted to know why all that had happened to his people had happened if the Lord was with his people (Judg. 6:13). Then he raised the question, "Wherewith shall I save Israel?" (v. 15). What could a man like Gideon do?

B. *He put his Lord to the test (Judg. 6:17).* He prepared an offering of a young goat and unleavened bread for the altar, and the Lord consumed it (vv. 19–22). Then Gideon put out a fleece. One time only the fleece was wet with dew, and another time only the fleece was dry. The Lord responded to Gideon's request, and Gideon knew his Lord was calling.

Conclusion

God gave Gideon specific instructions about what to do. When Gideon obeyed, his Lord delivered the Israelites according to his promise.

SUNDAY MORNING, AUGUST 12

Title: A Person's Intense Struggle against Sin

Text: "But now we are delivered from the law, that being dead wherein we were held; that we should serve in newness of spirit, and not in the oldness of the letter" (**Rom. 7:6**).

Scripture Reading: Romans 7:4–25

Hymns: "Yield Not to Temptation," Palmer
"My Soul, Be on Thy Guard," Heath
"Saviour, More Than Life to Me," Crosby

Offertory Prayer: Our heavenly Father, we thank you that you have made us immortal souls endowed with the capacity for fellowship with you. You have created us spiritual, responsible beings in your own image with the capacity of becoming your sons and daughters. Grant that your courage of love in creating us as persons may be rewarded by our filial response. Open our minds to know your will. Empower our wills to do your will. Forgive us our debts as we forgive our debtors, and lead us not into temptation, but deliver us from evil. For yours is the kingdom, and the power, and the glory, forever. Amen.

Introduction

"So God created man in his own image, in the image of God created he him; male and female created he them" (Gen. 1:27). Humans are spiritual beings, as is evidenced by self-conscious thought, speech, the knowledge of right and wrong, and a conscience that tells us we ought to do the right. We all are immortal souls responsible to God for our choices. This is our most precious and perilous possession.

We must make moral choices for which we are accountable to God. Life is a stewardship. There is no way by which we can cease being stewards, so we determine by our choices whether we will be good or bad stewards. The parable of the talents in Matthew 25:14–30 illustrates this great truth.

Life is not lived in a vacuum. Everyone is born into a world in which forces for good and for evil are operating against each other and are competing for control of every person. Genesis 3:15 names these forces as God and Satan. The battle will be fierce, but the promise is that the seed of the woman (the Messiah) will crush the serpent's (Satan's) head. There is no doubt about the outcome of this perpetual battle: God will win. The battlefield of this earthly life is the arena where each one decides whether he or she will win with God or be defeated by Satan.

I. The great battle (Rom. 7:7–25).

Romans 7:7–25 is almost certainly autobiographical. Devout expositors of the Bible divide sharply over whether Paul is describing his personal struggle before or after his conversion. The statement, "I am carnal, sold under sin" (Rom. 7:14), seems to indicate before salvation; yet how could an unsaved person write, "For I delight in the law of God after the inward man" (Rom. 7:22)? In fact, the battle for the soul of a person begins early and continues through all of one's life. When we get to heaven, we will ask Paul about some of these difficult statements. In the meantime, we shall emphasize some truths that seem apparent.

A. *The antagonists in this great battle are God and Satan and all the persons and forces used by either side.* God the Holy Spirit (also called Spirit of God and Spirit of Christ) seeks to possess people by leading them to salvation and to a spiritually minded attitude whose end is eternal life. Satan seeks to control through the carnal mind, or flesh, by which Paul seems to mean the unregenerate part of a person that is in opposition to God and has not been renewed by the Spirit of God. Read carefully Romans 8:3–9. Note that flesh in this context does not mean the part of the body that covers the bones, but rather the unregenerate nature. When Paul writes, "They that are in the flesh cannot please God" (Rom. 8:8), he does not mean that a human being cannot please God, but rather that no matter what we do in the way of good deeds, we cannot be pleasing to God unless we yield to God's will as revealed by the Holy Spirit. "But ye are not in the flesh, but in the Spirit, if so be that the Spirit of God dwell in you. Now if any man have not the Spirit of Christ, he is none of his" (Rom. 8:9). The context then is between the Spirit and the flesh. In his letter to the Galatians (written probably just before Romans), Paul described the battle in very clear terms (see 5:16–25).

248

B. *The law of God versus the law of sin.* Throughout the whole discussion of this terrible battle, these two oppose each other. Law of God is a synonym for the will of God. As Paul has already argued, the law of God is revealed in nature (Rom. 1:18–21) and in a person's moral consciousness (2:14–16). The law of sin is anything that falls short of God's law. Thus, sin is everything other than God's will. The word that Paul uses throughout for sin is a word that means "to miss the mark." It may be represented by an archer shooting at a target. He may fall short, shoot beyond, or miss on either side. To miss the target, which is God's will, is sin.

II. The purpose of God's law is:

A. *To reveal sin and to make sin appear exceedingly sinful.* A wall of a building may appear to be perpendicular until one drops a plumb line. In childhood we become conscious of right and wrong. Almost simultaneously with the development of self-consciousness, we come to know that we ought to do right, that God is holy, and that God's will is right and good. As we mature, we find that some of the practices we have been following without any twinges of conscience are wrong. In Romans 7:7–11 Paul illustrates with the matter of covetousness. Before he knew the commandment "Thou shalt not covet," he thought that he was alive—that is, right with God—because he did not know the law and felt no condemnation for it. When he learned the law, he, as it were, died—that is, felt estranged from God—because the law brought his sense of sin to life. Before Paul became a Christian, he persecuted Christians. He thought that he was doing God's will. When he saw the light of God's law (will) revealed to him by Jesus on the Damascus road, he knew he had been the chief of sinners. God forgave Paul because he had persecuted the Christians ignorantly and in unbelief.

"What shall we say then? Is the law sin? God forbid. Nay" (Rom. 7:7). Is the plumb line a bad thing because it reveals that the building is out of plumb? No. The plumb line serves a useful purpose yet has no power to correct the fault in the building. In a similar way, the law has no power to save. It points out the need of the sinner for a Savior.

B. *To lead to the Savior.* God never intended that people should be saved by keeping the law. From Genesis 3:15 to the present, God has planned that sinners would be saved by accepting his provision of salvation as a gift of his grace. Before Christ came, sinners were saved on the promise of what God would do. Symbols of the atonement were provided looking forward to Christ's death on Calvary's cross. Since Calvary, the symbols of baptism and the Lord's Supper have pointed back to Calvary. God has only one way of salvation. We may confidently affirm that he will never have but one way of salvation. All who ever have or ever will be saved will be saved by the atonement for sin that God has provided through Jesus Christ. Jesus said, "I am the way, the truth, and the life: no man cometh unto the Father, but by me" (John 14:6).

Paul may have been referring to an ancient custom of tying the body of the one murdered about the neck of the murderer, when he cried out, "O wretched man that I am! who shall deliver me from the body of this death?" (Rom. 7:24). He is aware that he is dead in trespasses and in sins. He has no power to save himself. "The wages of sin is death" (Rom. 6:23). His good impulses are so feeble that there is no hope for him to keep God's perfect law, but he sees ultimate victory rather than defeat as he answers, "I thank God through Jesus Christ our Lord" (Rom. 7:25). The victory is in Jesus. Paul discusses this at length in Galatians 3:21–29. "Wherefore the law was our schoolmaster to bring us unto Christ, that we might be justified by faith" (v. 24). The pedagogue, translated "schoolmaster," was the tutor or guardian of the child until he or she came to maturity.

Conclusion

The law is good. It is God's method of revealing his will. God's will is in harmony with his nature, which God's law also reveals. The law awakens our conscience and pricks our heart with our need of the Savior.

The law is fulfilled in Jesus. "For Christ is the end of the law for righteousness to every one that believeth" (Rom. 10:4). The law has accomplished its purpose for us when it leads us to salvation in Jesus.

The law of God as symbolized in the worship of the Old Testament was fulfilled in Jesus. No other priest is needed, for Jesus is the High Priest. No sacrifice is needed, for Jesus is the Lamb of God. No prophets are needed, for Jesus is the Word of God. All of the moral and ethical precepts of the law are fulfilled in Jesus.

Those who try to be right with God by obeying all of the precepts of the law are like slaves who serve because of hope of reward and fear of punishment. Those under grace in Christ are children who serve out of love (see Rom. 8:14–18).

"Now we are delivered from the law, that being dead wherein we were held; that we should serve in newness of spirit, and not in the oldness of the letter" (Rom. 7:6).

SUNDAY EVENING, AUGUST 12

Title: The Marvel of Being Human

Text: "What is man, that thou art mindful of him? and the son of man, that thou visitest him? For thou hast made him a little lower than the angels, and hast crowned him with glory and honour" **(Ps. 8:4–5).**

Scripture Reading: Psalm 8:1–9

Introduction

For centuries the question "What is man?" has been considered. Humanity comes in various sizes, colors, and temperaments. The world is inhabited by different yet similar people who speak various types of languages. People live all kinds of lifestyles. Some ride camels while others fly jets. Some dress in business suits while others wear animal skins. A casual observer cannot help but marvel over the question "What is man?"

Answers vary. The physician would describe man as a physical being of blood, bones, and muscles with a digestive apparatus that grinds food, adds chemicals, and transmits energy. The psychiatrist would define man as a being complete with an id, ego, and superego. The philosopher would major on the mind of a person. The most effective resource for the answer to the question about man is the biblical revelation. Let us discover what the Bible says about man.

I. The dignity of man.

We can understand the dignity of man when we understand that man is a creation of God.

    A. *Man is a creature of dust.* Humankind has a unity with the rest of creation. God formed man from the dust of the ground. We have bodily systems and characteristics much like those of other animals, and our physical bodies are not evil in themselves. God made us as biological creatures for whom he has a purpose. To be happy, we must follow God's purpose. We were created to serve God with all we are. Good and evil may use the body, but evil does not have its source from biological drives.

    B. *Man is a creature of a divine image.* Even though man is a creature of dust, he is unique in that he is made in the image of God. God breathed into man the breath of life, and this makes him different from other created order. No animal spends its life in pursuits unrelated to survival.

    A part of the divine image of God in man is man's freedom. God grants to people the privilege to determine what kind of beings they will be. A dog is controlled by environment and heredity, but a man can determine his character, lifestyle, and habits.

II. The depravity of man.

No biblical study of humankind would be adequate without a look into the depravity of man. Humankind has fallen from God's intended dignity.

A. *Man misused his freedom.* God created one pair, Adam and Eve, who lived in perfection and innocence with only one prohibition. God told them not to touch one particular tree. Tempted by the serpent, Eve was attracted to the fruit of the tree and could not resist the temptation. Her husband joined in her rebellion, and their fellowship with God was disrupted.

We all have the freedom to choose whether or not we will sin. Satan tempts us all, and when we give in to him and disobey God, guilt results. Because of the universal prevalence of sin, the history of humanity is stained with the misuse of freedom.

B. *Man abused God's good gifts.* With the abuse of God's greatest gift of freedom, people proceed to abuse God's other gifts. Human depravity can be seen in what people do to the world God gave them. They abuse natural resources and use them for selfish purposes. Human depravity can be seen further in what people do to other human beings. The depths of injustice of one human being to another reflects the tragic abuse of God's gift of other people.

III. The duty of man.

What is our main duty? The key, according to the biblical revelation, is found in our relationships. We fulfill God's intention by forming and maintaining proper relationships.

A. *Man has a relationship to his Creator.* We fulfill our duty in life by a proper relationship to God. The essence of humanity is the interaction of God and man. Our duty to God is to worship and ascribe honor to him. We fulfill part of this duty when we recognize that God is the Creator and we are the created. Another duty of man to his Creator is obedience. Those who worship God obey his wishes. We fulfill our duty and high purpose for life by doing whatever the Lord commands.

B. *Man has relationships to the world and to the inhabitants of the world.* We fulfill the duty of life in a proper relationship to the world. God gave humankind dominion over the earth. Everything is given to us for our use—not our misuse. Throughout the Scriptures there are many references to conservation.

Moreover, we fulfill our duty by a proper relationship to the inhabitants of the world. God prescribed love and justice as the norms for an ideal social life. Whenever we base our relationships on love and justice, our duty will be fulfilled. As we love mercy, live justly, and walk humbly with God, we will find meaning in life.

Conclusion

To really know man, we need to look at *the Man,* Jesus, our example. When we know Jesus Christ, we know what we should be.

WEDNESDAY EVENING, AUGUST 15

Title: Isaiah: The King of the Prophets
Text: "Here am I; send me" **(Isa. 6:8)**.
Scripture Reading: Isaiah 6:1–12

Introduction

Four men were sitting in an outer office waiting to be interviewed by a man who wanted to hire a telegraph operator. Two of the four talked while they waited, and a third read a magazine. Suddenly the fourth man got up, walked to the door marked "Private," and went right in. A few minutes later he emerged with a smile because he had the job.

Why did he get it? Because he knew how to listen. Inside the office, the boss had been tapping out a code message. It said, "The first man to read my message and come into my office, will get the job."

Isaiah is a good example of a man who listened to God and was used by God.

I. The conditions of the time when Isaiah was called makes the listening even more important.

A. *Economically, it was a time of prosperity.* A number of people had become rich, and large estates were growing. Luxuries from abroad were plentiful, and friendly foreign relations led to the adoption of customs that were contrary to God's law. The land was full of silver and gold.

B. *It was a time of military strength and agricultural prosperity.* Isaiah saw that complacency came as a result of satisfaction with military strength and material wealth. People did not feel a need for dependence on God. Religious devotion was little more than formality, and the people were being taught by religious leaders who were devoid of understanding.

II. How did Isaiah receive a call under such circumstances?

A. *He saw the Lord.* He saw the Lord as holy and exalted. God was set apart from humanity but desired to draw near to people.

B. *He heard a pronouncement of sin in his own life and that of his nation.* Once Isaiah realized just how sinful he was, he experienced the cleansing power of God. This cleansing enabled him to hear God's voice. These two—cleansing and hearing—are great needs today.

C. *He heard a voice seeking a person to send into a sinful world.* This distinctive call led to a submission to God's will for his life and therefore to the label "The King of the Prophets."

253

III. What kind of ministry did Isaiah have that merited such a title?

A. *It was a prolonged ministry.* Isaiah's ministry lasted forty years, from his youth into old age. He observed many changes and had his endurance and enthusiasm tested, but his message remained the same. It was marked with confidence in the midst of frustration.

B. *It was constantly in his own community.* Isaiah walked and talked among his own people, making himself and his children a sign to the people. His children bore significant names to indicate the importance of his message. He walked the streets for three years in the wretched garb of a captive.

C. *It was a proclamation of salvation.* Isaiah kept saying that one day salvation would come, but the people would not heed.

Conclusion

Isaiah teaches loud and clear that we can live righteous lives in the time of affluence. When we do, we can hear God's voice and be obedient to him. Isaiah also taught the lesson of endurance and persistence in the same place.

Sunday Morning, August 19

Title: The Christian's Ultimate Triumph

Text: "For I reckon that the sufferings of this present time are not worthy to be compared with the glory which shall be revealed in us" **(Rom. 8:18)**.

Scripture Reading: Romans 8:1–30

Hymns: "Mighty God, While Angels Bless Thee," Robinson
"The Kingdom Is Coming," Slade
"Stand Up, Stand Up for Jesus," Duffield
"I Am Thine, O Lord," Crosby

Offertory Prayer: Holy and loving heavenly Father, you have made us, redeemed us, and sealed us. We are yours. We believe that you work all things together for good for those who love you. Help us to bear your chastening. Grant that through the tests and sufferings of this present pilgrimage, we may grow more like you. Give us the faith to believe even when we do not see that your purposes for us are good, and that the end will be unto your glory. In Jesus's name. Amen.

Introduction

When by repentance and faith we accept Jesus Christ as Lord and Savior, God does some wonderful things for us.

1. *We are justified.* God counts us as righteous (see Rom. 3:24–28). The penalty of our sin is completely removed forever. "There is therefore now no condemnation to them which are in Christ

Jesus" (8:1). The law that the Holy Spirit gives eternal life to those who believe in Jesus has overcome the old law that "the wages of sin is death" (Rom. 6:23; see 8:2).

2. *We have peace with God and are exhorted to enjoy it.* "Since we have been justified through faith, we have peace with God though our Lord Jesus Christ" (Rom. 5:1 NIV).

3. *We are regenerated.* "Therefore if any man be in Christ, he is a new creature: old things are passed away: behold, all things are become new" (2 Cor. 5:17).

4. *We are children of God.* The Holy Spirit of God is now residing in us to give guidance and help. Saved people purpose to let the Holy Spirit have control. They do not "walk after the flesh"—that is, do not willfully follow the desires of the unregenerate nature. They now "walk after the Spirit." "For if ye live after the flesh, ye shall die: but if ye through the Spirit do mortify the deeds of the body, ye shall live. For as many as are led by the Spirit of God, they are the sons of God" (Rom. 8:13–14).

5. *We have eternal life.* Before salvation when we were "carnally minded," the end was death. Now that we are saved, we are "spiritually minded" and the end is life and peace (see Rom. 8:6–7). No matter how many good things unsaved people may do, they cannot please God. Nothing is right unless the heart is right: "So then they that are in the flesh cannot please God" (v. 8). God promises in a most wonderful way that redeemed people have eternal life, and that having come out from under condemnation, they will never return to condemnation. "Verily, verily, I say unto you, he that heareth my word, and believeth on him that sent me, hath everlasting life, and shall not come unto condemnation; but is passed from death unto life" (John 5:24). This is Jesus's solemn promise. "My sheep hear my voice, and I know them, and they follow me: And I give unto them eternal life: and they shall never perish, neither shall any man pluck them out of my hand" (10:27–28).

6. *We are sealed by the Holy Spirit.* "Now he which stablisheth us with you in Christ, and hath anointed us, is God; who hath also sealed us, and given the earnest of the Spirit in our hearts" (2 Cor. 1:21–22). The king's seal stamped the document as authentic. The earnest money was the down payment to assure the fulfillment of the contract. God's Holy Spirit in believers' hearts is the seal of our salvation and the pledge that God will bring us to glory. "When we cry, 'Abba! Father!' it is the Spirit himself bearing witness with our spirit that we are the children of God, and if children, then heirs, heirs of God and fellow heirs with Christ, provided we suffer with him in order that we may also be glorified with him" (Rom. 8:15–17 RSV).

I. The battle with sin continues.

A. *One would expect that a saved person for whom the Lord has done so much would be released from all suffering and would be free from the battle with sin.* The actual fact is far otherwise. Jesus said, "In the world ye shall have tribulation: but be of good cheer; I have overcome the world" (John 16:33). The battle with sin may even be intensified after one becomes a Christian. The saved man purposes to do God's will, but Satan trips him up. In Galatians, Paul wrote, "Brethren, if a man be overtaken in a fault, ye which are spiritual, restore such an one in the spirit of meekness; considering thyself, lest thou also be tempted. Bear ye one another's burdens, and so fulfil the law of Christ" (6:1–2).

B. *The difference between an unsaved person who deliberately sins and a Christian who slips into sin is as different as death and life, but it is difficult to get the saved person to see the distinction and almost impossible to get the unsaved person to see it.* John makes the distinction clearly in 1 John 1, where he is writing about the fellowship of believers with the Father through Jesus Christ. Fellowship means sharing, partnership, participation; hence, it is a synonym for salvation. "If we say that we have fellowship with him, and walk in darkness [the tense means to continue to walk as a way of life], we lie, and do not the truth: But if we walk in the light, as he is in the light, we have fellowship one with another, and the blood of Jesus Christ his Son cleanseth us from all sin" (1 John 1:6–7). On the other hand, "if we claim to be without sin, we deceive ourselves and the truth is not in us" (v. 8 NIV). No person who follows sin willfully is saved. No saved person is as good as Jesus. Every person slips up. The apostle Paul himself made it clear that he had not attained the sinless state. To the Philippians he wrote: "Not as though I had already attained, either were already perfect: but I follow after, if that I may apprehend that for which also I am apprehended of Christ Jesus. Brethren, I count not myself to have apprehended: but this one thing I do, forgetting those things which are behind, and reaching forth unto those things which are before, I press toward the mark for the prize of the high calling of God in Christ Jesus" (Phil. 3:12–14).

The test of Christians is not that they live without sin, but that they sincerely purpose to do so, and that when they discover they have sinned, they confess and ask forgiveness. "If we confess our sins, he is faithful and just to forgive us our sins, and to cleanse us from all unrighteousness" (1 John 1:9).

II. God deals with you as with sons (Heb. 12:7).

A. *Union or fellowship with Christ is so strong that no person or thing can break it.* Christ deals with believers as a loving father deals with his children. When children do wrong, they do not cease to be their fathers' children. They continue as children, albeit disobedient ones. We are justified once for all. The fellowship cannot be broken, but the joy of fellowship is so fragile that the least unconfessed sin will destroy it. For this reason, Jesus taught Christians to pray, "Forgive us our debts" (Matt. 6:12). Debts are, of course, personal obligations unfulfilled—that is, sins.

B. *The heavenly Father loves his children too much to see them go on in sin without doing something about it.* He convicts them of sin. He chastises them, as the author of Hebrews wrote so eloquently in Hebrews 12:5–11. His providences (which seem to us both good and bad) are designed to turn backsliders from the error of their way.

C. *The heavenly Father wants his children to grow in grace and knowledge.* He desires them to produce the fruits of righteousness, to do good works that will glorify him. The Holy Spirit is present in believers to assist them.

Conclusion

Salvation is past, present, and future. At our conversion we were justified, regenerated, and adopted as God's children, given eternal life, and sanctified in the primary sense that God sealed us as his own possession.

Since conversion, salvation has been a continuing process of sanctification in the secondary sense that the Holy Spirit has been cooperating with us to make us more like Christ and to lead us to obedience.

In the future, salvation will be complete when we are glorified. Freed from the penalty of sin in justification, progressively freed from the dominion of sin by our progress toward sanctification, when we see Jesus, we will be freed from the presence of sin. "Beloved, now we are the sons of God, and it doth not yet appear what we shall be: but we know that, when he shall appear, we shall be like him; for we shall see him as he is" (1 John 3:2).

At the end of the age, the bodies of the redeemed will be raised, glorified, and made like Christ's raised and glorified body (see Rom. 8:11, 23–24; Phil. 3:20–21). The redeemed of all ages now glorified will be at Christ's right hand. Not one will be missing. Some of the saved will have great reward and some will have little reward, as Paul explains in 1 Corinthians 3:6–15.

Are you saved? Will you share in the eternal kingdom of our God?

SUNDAY EVENING, AUGUST 19

Title: Satan Is Real

Text: "Put on the whole armour of God, that ye may be able to stand against the wiles of the devil" (**Eph. 6:11**).

Scripture Reading: Genesis 3:1–15; 2 Corinthians 4:4

Introduction

The idea of Satan has virtually disappeared from the beliefs of many people. Our world of rationalism has dismissed the idea of a devil. Perhaps the reason for the denial of the devil comes from humanistic concepts of Satan. He has been pictured wearing a red suit, carrying a pitchfork, and having horns and a forked tail.

Where did such ideas originate? One thing is sure, you cannot find this description of Satan in the Bible. These weird descriptions of the devil come mainly from medieval theology, the writings of John Milton, and imaginative artists of the Middle Ages.

Satan is real. One has only to be aware of the immense power of evil to be assured of Satan's reality. There are atrocious crimes committed in our world that can be attributed neither to man nor to God. The first report of Satan's activity came from a garden. Since his initial spotting, you can trace his murderous, malignant footsteps through the pages of history.

To understand Satan, we must know him for what he really is. We can know the nature and work of Satan by a close study of the Bible, for Scripture gives ample insights into his reality.

I. Satan has personality.

Satan is not just a figment of someone's imagination. Wherever the Bible presents Satan, it seems that he has personality traits.

  A. *Satan has personal qualities.* In reading two biblical accounts of Satan's presence, we can see his personal qualities. When Satan came to Eve, he talked with her. Then when Satan encountered Jesus in the wilderness, he talked and reasoned with the Master. From these two accounts we can deduce that Satan has intellect and will.

  B. *Satan's personality is revealed by his names.* In the Bible a person's character is reflected in his or her name. The Bible uses many names for the leader of evil: devil, Satan, Beelzebub, evil one, serpent, dragon, murderer, father of lies, angel of light, and many others. Let us notice what kind of person Satan is by looking at two of his names. First, the name Satan means adversary or opposer. Wherever you find Satan, you will find one in malicious opposition to God. Second, the name devil means slanderer or false accuser. The devil seeks to slander the good name and character of God. Studying Satan's other names would yield an adequate description of the kind of being he is.

II. Satan has a purpose.

Satan's purpose can be seen by a study of the Bible names. Wherever you encounter the devil in Scripture, he is seeking to hinder the work of God.

A. *Satan seeks to prevent repentance.* He tries to keep people from opening their lives to Jesus Christ. Paul said, "The god of this world hath blinded the minds of them which believe not, lest the light of the glorious gospel of Christ, who is the image of God, should shine unto them" (2 Cor. 4:4). Satan uses various procedures to prevent belief or trust in Jesus Christ.

B. *Satan seeks to hinder growth and commitment to Jesus Christ.* After one becomes a Christian, Satan is not finished. There remains a constant battle of the flesh and Spirit. Satan seeks to prevent people from obeying God's will. He tempted Jesus Christ with three attractive proposals. In the early church he often caused disturbances. On one occasion Paul said, "Wherefore we would have come unto you, even I Paul, once and again; but Satan hindered us" (1 Thess. 2:18).

III. Satan has procedures.

To accomplish his purposes, Satan uses crafty procedures. In our text Paul warned the Christians against the "wiles of the devil." Christians need to be aware of the tactics of the tempter.

A. *Satan uses distortion.* Paul said, "Lest Satan should get an advantage of us: for we are not ignorant of his devices" (2 Cor. 2:11). The word "devices" could mean sophisticated reasoning. He first gets people thinking in a distorted and doubting manner. In the case of Eve's encounter with Satan, she thought that she would become like God by following the satanic suggestion. No more attractive, plausible proposals could have been presented to the Messiah than the three presented to Jesus. Satan's procedure is to distort the truth.

B. *Satan uses detraction.* Satan always comes disguised to detract a person from obeying God's will. "But every man is tempted, when he is drawn away of his own lust, and enticed" (James 1:14). Though Satan is not mentioned in this verse, his procedure can be seen. He seeks to get humankind away from God with the detractive elements of the world. We need to be aware of Satan's cunning devices to draw us away from fellowship with God.

IV. Satan has power.

A casual observation of life about you will convince you of Satan's power. He is called "the prince of this world." Yet we need to understand the biblical facts about Satan's power.

A. *Satan has a designated time for power.* Jesus Christ defeated Satan on the cross. Paul said, "And having spoiled principalities and powers, he made a show of them openly, triumphing over them in it" (Col. 2:15). John described the procedures that persecuted Christians used to defeat Satan: "And they overcame him by the blood of the Lamb, and by the word of their testimony; and they loved not their lives unto the death" (Rev. 12:11). Satan has only a limited season. Between Jesus's resurrection and the Lord's final return, Satan has power.

B. *Satan has a designated day of doom.* God has marked a day on the calendar when the complete overthrow of Satan will be manifested. When the Lord comes for the final consummation of history, Satan's doom will be pronounced.

When I was a boy, I read Hardy Boys mysteries. This series related the stories of two boys, Joe and Frank, whose father was a detective. Often Joe and Frank tried to solve cases. In each story these boys would get in tight places with criminals. Every time I would come to these situations in the book, I would turn to the final chapter to see if they were alive. In every case they would be safe with their family in the final chapter. Then I would read the account of the criminals' capture of the boys with enjoyment. I knew how matters would end.

Christians know how the world will end. We can read the last chapter: "And the devil that deceived them was cast into the lake of fire and brimstone, where the beast and the false prophet are, and shall be tormented day and night for ever and ever" (Rev. 20:10).

Conclusion

Satan is real. He opposes God. You need to get on the more enjoyable side of life, the Lord's way. Give your life to the Lord, and Satan will be defeated.

WEDNESDAY EVENING, AUGUST 22

Title: Joseph: A Just Man

Text: "Then Joseph her husband, being a just man . . ." **(Matt. 1:19)**.

Scripture Reading: Matthew 1:19–25

Introduction

One of the greatest compliments that can be given a person is that he or she is just—that is, right with God and with fellow humans. Joseph was that kind of man, as evidenced by his actions. He conducted himself nobly in a very difficult situation.

I. Joseph was subjected to some unusual trials.

A. *Most of the time attention is focused on Mary as this passage is read.* Much discussion is built around the feelings and emotions of Mary when she was told by the angel that she would give birth to the Christ child.

B. *Love can be tried.* In the beginning of this test, Joseph had no message from God. He only had Mary's word, and this would have been hard to believe. Thus, he was thrown into a very difficult dilemma. He was genuinely perplexed. He loved Mary and wanted to believe her, but he did not see how this could be possible. One can almost hear him say, "Mary, I love you. I want to believe you, but you just can't fool me this way. I'm sorry." He could not wholly believe nor wholly disbelieve.

II. Joseph had to take action one way or the other.

A. *He was a just man and he loved Mary.* A truly just person does not take a stern approach based only on the letter of the law. This is not the way the Lord deals with people, and it is not the way the Lord's people are to deal with their fellow humans.

B. *His love was tempered with mercy and compassion.* Joseph's feelings toward the one he loved and wanted as a wife would not let him bring Mary into the danger of shame and death. Being the kind of person he was, he decided to act kindly. He would put her away privately.

This is a great lesson for those whose marriage ends in divorce. It needs to be done graciously and kindly.

III. Joseph had an angel appear to him and clarify the whole matter.

A. *He thought on these things (Matt. 1:20).* One can be assured Joseph prayed. It was misery to mistrust and also misery being in doubt about the right path to take. Whenever children of God find themselves with such a difficult decision, prayer is the only solution.

B. *He was not left permanently in this perplexing situation.* The Lord will never leave his children in such straits. In time the Almighty clears up doubt and teaches what we ought to do. But such situations must be dealt with prayerfully.

C. *God sent his angel, his messenger (Matt. 1:20).* God sends messengers to bring a message of love or to guide and undergird when one turns to him with all of his or her heart. The Lord used the angel to calm Joseph's fears, remove his doubts, and to enable him to rejoice—rejoice in his love for Mary and rejoice in his relation to Jesus.

Conclusion

Joseph was a just man. Therefore, when he found himself in a trying situation, he knew what to do. He did not panic or go into a temper tantrum. He quietly turned to his God, found the answer, and filled the role of a great man in Jesus's life.

SUNDAY MORNING, AUGUST 26

Title: More Than Conquerors

Text: "Who shall separate us from the love of Christ? shall tribulation, or distress, or persecution, or famine, or nakedness, or peril, or sword? . . . Nay, in all these things we are more than conquerors through him that loved us" **(Rom. 8:35, 37).**

Scripture Reading: Romans 8:31–39

Hymns: "O Love That Wilt Not Let Me Go," Matheson
"Faith Is the Victory," Yates
"Come to the Savior Now," Wigner

Offertory Prayer: You, O God, are holy. Your cause is right and just. You, O God, are all powerful. Victory is sure with you. You, O God, are omniscient. Your way is best. You, O God, are love. In this confidence we live knowing that no one and no thing can separate us from your love. Forgive us, lead us, guard us from all enemies; keep us for yourself forever, we ask in Jesus's name. Amen.

Introduction

Our Scripture reading, Romans 8:31–39, presents the climax of Paul's great exposition of God's plan of salvation in the first eight chapters of Romans. The theme here is that the battle of life is to live victoriously.

The immediate battle for Paul and those to whom he wrote was persecution. Nero, that "combination of mud and blood," was already on the throne in Rome. Only a few months later he would saturate the bodies of Christians with oil and drive his chariot by the light of their burning bodies. It was dangerous to be a Christian. To say "Lord Jesus" instead of "Lord Caesar" often meant to sign one's death warrant. The beasts of the arena were fed on Christian flesh. When Paul asks, "Who shall separate us from the love of Christ? shall tribulation, or distress, or persecution, or famine, or nakedness, or peril, or sword?" he does not speak figuratively but literally. Daily, men and women faced those terrors for the name of Jesus.

While we do not have the same problems Paul faced, we do fight enemies peculiar to our age that tend to separate people from Christ.

I. Some enemies Christians face.

A. *Christians must fight against secularism.* How vastly different is the modern mechanized life of today from the simple frontier life of our forefathers. With unhurried steps they tramped through God's woods, slept under God's sky, drank from God's springs, and ate that which nature provided by God's providence. Today we sleep on man-made beds in man-made houses, eat canned food and drink tap water, step out on man-made sidewalks, drive man-made cars under smoke-filled skies to man-made factories to handle man-made tools to produce man-made products. People are so busy that they have little time for thinking. So involved are they with making a living that making a life becomes secondary. The battle of this age is against a materialistic view of life that exalts might before right, money before family, position before people, and greed before God.

B. *Christians must fight against skepticism.* We live in an age of new truth. Scientific investigation and research are daily discovering undreamed of facts about the universe. It is an era of transition. In every field of thought, change is taking place. Ancient formulations in theology, as in science, have been found inadequate. Many whose faith rested on false premises are skeptical as to life's ultimate issues. Our faith rests in the integrity of Jesus Christ. He is "the Truth." We are not afraid of truth. We are afraid of half-truth. Jesus has nothing to fear from honest investigation. The light of honest, critical study will but reveal more of the genuine beauty of the divine character of the Son of God.

C. *Christians must fight against pessimism.* The news media tells every day of those who have not found life worth living. War budgets mount. Children are taught to hate and kill. Liquor and drugs have a stranglehold. The Christian family and the whole system of Christian ethics are subject to constant attack. Man's inhumanity to man makes countless thousands mourn. It is impossible to be optimistic without faith in God.

D. *Every Christian must battle sin.* Sin unforgiven means death. As the preceding messages have proclaimed, God saves sinners when they are willing to repent and believe. God the Holy Spirit abides in Christians to help them overcome sin. Anything other than God's will is sin, and sin must go. "No man can serve two masters" (Matt. 6:24). We battle against that which would keep us from giving our hearts to God. How Jesus hates sin! Could words be more graphic than these? "Wherefore if thy hand or thy foot offend thee, cut them off, and cast them from thee; it is better for thee to enter into life halt or maimed, rather than having two hands or two feet to be cast into everlasting fire. And if thine eye offend thee, pluck it out, and cast it from thee; it is better for thee to enter into life with one eye, rather than having two eyes to be cast into hell fire" (Matt. 18:8–9). Jesus is saying that if sin be as dear to you as your arm, or foot, or eye, cut it out. How God hates sin! As the mother loves the child but hates the disease that would claim the child's precious life, so God hates sin but longs to reclaim the sinner.

One vacationing in the mountains tells that his party was engaged in watching an eagle soaring majestically above the highest peaks. Monarch of the air was he! Suddenly his great wings folded and the bird fell with a thud to the distant mountain. Such an unusual occurrence caused the party to make the journey of some hours to find the bird. They found the eagle had clutched a weasel in his talons, which during the flight had drained the eagle's life's blood from its breast. So secret sin will do to you if you try to clutch it to your bosom. Sin must go, else there can be no victorious living.

II. The victory is in Christ.

"We are more than conquerors through him that loved us" (Rom. 8:37). The victory is in Christ alone because:

A. *In Christ one is on God's side.* "If God be for us, who can be against us?" (Rom. 8:31). In a battle with the lines drawn so sharply—Christ versus Satan, the will of the Spirit versus carnal flesh, good versus evil, godliness versus ungodliness, holy living versus immorality, living at one's best versus living at less than one's best—can anyone doubt which is God's side? During the Civil War, one of Lincoln's aides is reported to have asked the great leader, "Mr. Lincoln, are you sure that God is on our side?" Lincoln replied, "I am not so much concerned, sir, as to whether God is on our side as I am concerned as to whether we are on God's side." Victorious living is to find out what God is doing and to do it with him.

B. *In Christ one is justified.* "Who shall lay any thing to the charge of God's elect? It is God that justifieth. Who is he that condemneth? It is Christ that died, yea rather, that is risen again, who is even at the right hand of God, who also maketh intercession for us" (Rom. 8:33–34). No one can condemn a person whom God has justified on the basis of Jesus's atonement. In heaven Jesus intercedes for us. He pleads not our righteousness but his own (see Rom. 5:1–2; 8:1–2; Heb. 4:14–16).

C. *In Christ one has the Holy Spirit for guidance (Rom. 8:15–16), for overcoming sin (vv. 4–13), and for help in praying (vv. 26–27).* A little boy was overheard as he prayed. He had remembered father, mother, and sister, and now desired to ask God's blessings on the candy man down the street who had been especially kind to him. The little boy couldn't remember his name, so he prayed, "God, bless the candy man. You know, Lord, the one who walks this way." And getting up from his knees, he limped across the room in imitation of his friend. I think that God heard him although he could not frame the words. How good to know that when we pray and cannot frame the words, God the Holy Spirit and God the Son are interceding for us according to God's will.

III. The assurance of victory is in Christ's love.

In our text, Romans 8:35, 37, Paul exhausts his vocabulary in an effort to state that nothing past, present, or future, in heaven, earth, or hell can ever separate us from God's love revealed in Christ. Human love may waver; God's never. Trusted friends may betray; God abides sure. No person ever came to the end of life saying, "I trusted in Jesus. I served him, but in my hour of greatest need he failed me."

Jesus pledges in John 10:27–30 that he will not let us go. If all the demons in hell should try to snatch the weakest Christian from the fold of the Great Shepherd, they could not do it. "I am the good shepherd, and know my sheep, and am known of mine. As the Father knoweth me, even so know I the Father: and I lay down my life for the sheep" (John 10:14–15). The proof of God's love is in the cross. If God "spared not his own Son, but delivered him up for us all, how shall he not with him also freely give us all things?" (Rom. 8:32).

Conclusion

The victory is in Jesus Christ. Trust him. He invites you to come. "Him that cometh to me I will in no wise cast out" (John 6:37), he assures. Trust God. Trust Jesus. If Jesus Christ be true, it matters everything; if Jesus be false, nothing matters.

A story is told of a father and his young son walking the streets of London one winter day. The lad was proudly wearing a new overcoat. Sleet had left the streets very slick in places. The little fellow came to a slick place. Out went his feet and down he fell. Getting up, he wiped the slush from his new coat, and putting out his hand, he said, "Daddy, let me hold your hand." They came to another slick place. Out went his feet. He held on for a moment and then down he went, falling harder than before. This time he arose wiping the slush from his coat and a tear from his eye. He then reached up and said, "Daddy, you hold my hand." On they went. Coming to another slick place, out went the lad's feet, but the strong grasp of his father's hand held him fast.

You cannot walk alone. You cannot hold on to God. Let go, and let God hold on to you.

SUNDAY EVENING, AUGUST 26

Title: One of Christ's Greatest Promises

Text: "If I go and prepare a place for you, I will come again, and receive you unto myself; that where I am, there ye may be also" **(John 14:3)**.

Scripture Reading: John 14:1–6

Introduction

Jesus made many claims that gave people a right to expect many blessings. Time will not allow a complete enumeration of the Lord's promises. Think of only a few. Jesus pledged rest (Matt. 11:28–30). He pledged that everyone who came to the Lord would be accepted by him (John 6:37). And he promised to live with his followers forever (Matt. 28:19–20).

One of Jesus's most precious promises is about the future. Jesus promised to return to earth and to claim his people. His return often is called the Second Coming. Christians need to look often at the Lord's promise of his return to the earth.

I. The prediction of Jesus's return.

How can one be certain that Jesus will return to earth? The Bible says so.

A. *Jesus promised his future return.* No words could be more specific than "I will come again" in John 14:3. Jesus assured his disciples that he would return from death and also return after the Resurrection in a glorious consummation of history.

Jesus spoke of his final return both in parables and in his teachings. In Luke 12:39–40 he referred to a house owner whose house had been invaded by a thief. He compared the sudden, unexpected visit of the thief to his final return. Jesus said, "Be ye therefore ready also: for the Son of man cometh at an hour when ye think not" (Luke 12:40). A study of the parables will yield the conclusion that Jesus predicted a final, victorious return to earth.

B. *Angels predicted the return of the Lord.* Angels are used as messengers by God throughout the Bible story. Their message is true and should be heeded. Immediately after Jesus's ascension, an angel predicted Jesus's return. "This same Jesus, which is taken up from you into heaven, shall so come in like manner as ye have seen him go into heaven" (Acts 1:11).

C. *The apostles predicted Christ's return.* Part of the grand treasures of Holy Scriptures are the inspired writings of the apostles. This includes Paul. All of the apostles wrote of the final return of the Lord to earth. Listen to John: "Behold, he cometh with clouds; and every eye shall see him, and they also which pierced him: and all kindreds of the earth shall wail because of him. Even so, Amen" (Rev. 1:7). Listen to Peter: "Wherefore gird up the loins of your mind, be sober, and hope to the end for the grace that is to be brought unto you at the revelation of Jesus Christ" (1 Peter 1:13).

II. The purpose of his coming.

Without a doubt, Jesus promised his return. We cannot doubt the certainty, but we might wonder why he is coming.

A. *Jesus will return for vindication.* He will support his people's faith. Notice the Lord's words "receive you unto myself that where I am, there ye may be also." Through the long, troublesome course of history, God's way has been rejected and ridiculed. When Jesus returns, he will vindicate his righteousness.

Jesus will reward his people. "And when the chief Shepherd shall appear, ye shall receive a crown of glory that fadeth not away" (1 Peter 5:4). Jesus will reward his followers with a greater quality of life.

B. *Jesus will return to resurrect the dead.* Paul said, "For the Lord himself shall descend from heaven with a shout, with the voice of the archangel, and with the trump of God: and the dead in Christ shall rise first" (1 Thess. 4:16). The word translated "rise" means "to stand up again." Jesus will return to resurrect the dead. He will make them stand up again.

C. *Jesus will return for vengeance.* Paul said, "And to you who are troubled rest with us, when the Lord Jesus shall be revealed from heaven with his mighty angels, in flaming fire taking vengeance on them that know not God, and that obey not the gospel of our Lord Jesus Christ" (2 Thess. 1:7–8). The coming of the Lord is a blessing for believers, but it will be a disaster for unbelievers.

III. The plan of his coming.

Now that we have established the certainty and purpose of Jesus's coming, we need to look at the plan of his coming. Some expositors furnish elaborate details about his return. Without speculating, let us look at what the Bible teaches about the manner of the Lord's return.

A. *The Lord will return personally.* Jesus said, "I will come again." This suggests a personal return. Paul emphasized this fact when he said, "The Lord himself shall descend from heaven with a shout" (1 Thess. 4:16). The promise of the angels indicated a personal return—"shall so come in like manner" (cf. Acts 1:11).

B. *The Lord will return unexpectedly.* No one can predict the exact date of the Lord's return. Jesus intended for his followers to look for his return at any time. He compared his return to a thief in the night. Because of the unannounced date, Christians should live each day for the Lord's return.

C. *The Lord will return victoriously.* Jesus came the first time in shame as a rejected Messiah. His final return will be with heavenly splendor as a victorious king. The drama of Revelation depicts the glorious return of the Lord.

IV. The preparation for his coming.

Since Jesus promised to return, we need to prepare. Jesus's main challenge is to be ready for his return.

A. *Everyone needs to prepare for Jesus's return.* Jesus stressed the necessity of preparation in the parable of the virgins recorded in Matthew 25:1–13. Five of the virgins chose to prepare for the wedding and five virgins did not. Those who were unprepared were not allowed to enjoy the wedding festivities.

B. *Christians need to live godly lives.* Knowing that our Lord will return challenges God's people to live in such a way that they will not be ashamed when he comes. Some Christians participate in questionable activities. If the Lord returned, they would be ashamed. Paul said, "Teaching us that, denying ungodliness and worldly lusts, we should live soberly, righteously, and godly, in the present world, looking for the blessed hope, and the glorious appearing of the great God and our Savior Jesus Christ" (Titus 2:12–13).

C. *Christians should work with zeal in light of the Lord's promised return.* They should be faithful with that which God has given them and persuade others to earnestly prepare.

Conclusion

On March 11, 1942, President Franklin Roosevelt ordered General Douglas MacArthur to leave the besieged Philippine Islands. Before MacArthur's departure to Australia, he said to the people on the Japanese-occupied islands, "I shall return." In 1944 the general walked on the Philippine island of Leyte and announced, "I have returned."

In approximately AD 33 our Lord said, "I will come again." Someday he will step to earth and say, "I have returned." Make preparation for his return by opening your life to him.

WEDNESDAY EVENING, AUGUST 29

Title: Titus: A Faithful Henchman

Text: "Titus, mine own son after the common faith" **(Titus 1:4)**.

Scripture Reading: Titus 1:1–5

Introduction

Webster defines the word *henchman* as "an attendant, squire, or page." He is a trusted follower and supporter. This is the kind of man Titus was. He was a loyal, faithful supporter and attendant of Paul. Paul called him his true son (Titus 1:4). Although the Bible does not tell a great deal about Titus, he is a good example for believers of genuine devotion.

I. What kind of man was Titus?

A. *Titus was a true companion of Paul in an awkward and difficult time.* Paul had to make a trip to Jerusalem to visit a church that was suspicious of him and thus did not trust him. Titus was the companion Paul took along under such a circumstance (Gal. 2:1).

It was said of Dundas, a famous Scotsman, by one of his friends, "Dundas is no orator; but Dundas will go out with you in any kind of weather." This was the kind of friend Titus was. This is the kind of friend each person needs and each one ought to be.

B. *Titus delivered a severe letter to the church at Corinth in the peak of trouble (2 Cor. 8:16).* Titus had a strength that enabled him to handle a difficult situation. There are two kinds of people—those who make a bad situation worse and those who bring order out of chaos and peace out of strife. Titus was the latter type.

C. *Titus had a gift for practical administration.* Paul chose him to organize the collection for the poor members of the church at Corinth (2 Cor. 8:6–10). Every church should be thankful to God for people to whom they can turn in times of trouble.

II. Titles that Paul gave Titus indicate his esteem for the faithful henchman.

A. *Paul called him his true child.* This probably means that Paul was instrumental in the conversion of Titus. It is always a joy to a Christian to have children in the Lord. The tide also indicates esteem and affection.

B. *Paul called him his brother (2 Cor. 2:13) and his partner and fellow helper (8:23).* Real evidence of spiritual growth and maturity is when a child in the faith becomes a brother in the faith. It is a great experience when one has won another to Christ and that one becomes a mature partner in ministry.

C. *Paul said that Titus walked in the same spirit with him (2 Cor. 12:18).* Because of this walk, Paul knew Titus would deal with issues as he himself would. It is a glorious thing to have a lieutenant to whom one can commit his or her work and know it will be done right. This being true of Paul's confidence in Titus, he gave him a great task. He sent him to Crete to be a "pattern" to the Christians who were there (Titus 2:7), not just to tell them what a Christian was but to show them what a Christian was.

Conclusion

There is no greater compliment that can be given a person than that he or she be asked to show others what a Christian is. This is a challenge to each follower of Christ today.

SEPTEMBER

■ Sunday Mornings

This month's theme is "Christ Meeting Our Deepest Needs." John's gospel contains some of the great claims of Jesus Christ. He is able to make these claims because of who he is and what he can do. These messages speak to believers and unbelievers alike.

■ Sunday Evenings

In addition to Jesus Christ, there are a number of great personalities who walk through the pages of the New Testament. One of the most significant of these is the apostle Peter. "Peter, the Very Human Apostle" is the suggested theme for messages based on the experiences and words of Peter.

■ Wednesday Evenings

For the balance of this year's sermons, use the theme "Jesus As Mark Saw Him."

SUNDAY MORNING, SEPTEMBER 2

Title: Jesus Is the One You're Looking For

Text: "Jesus said unto her, I that speak unto thee am he" **(John 4:26)**.

Scripture Reading: John 4:1–26

Hymns: "Tell Me the Story of Jesus," Crosby
          "Let Others See Jesus in You," McKinney
          "Make Me a Blessing," Wilson

Offertory Prayer: Our Father, we pray that you will enlarge our hearts that we may, like the Israelites of old, willingly offer our substance to you. Help us never to forget that our days on earth are only as a shadow and that here we have no abiding place. Cause us to be mindful that all things come from you. In that spirit, may we with perfect hearts offer ourselves daily to you in service. Guide us each, according to our ability, to support your work. Lead us to recognize that we are blessed not because we deserve to be blessed, but rather that we might be a blessing to others. Kindle within us the fire of your love; strengthen our weaknesses with your power; bind us closely to you that we might be bound closer to one another. Make us firm and indissoluble in unity with you. Receive this offering from us and use it to your glory and for the salvation of lost people. We pray in Jesus's name. Amen.

Introduction

After a brief ministry in Judea, Jesus, upon hearing that John the Baptist had been cast into prison, was ready to go to Galilee and begin his public ministry. If he had been an ordinary Jew, he would have gone up into the region of Jericho, cut across the Jordan into Perea, and gone north until he could turn back west across the Jordan into Galilee. The phrase "must needs go through Samaria" indicates that he had a spiritual compulsion. In his infinite wisdom, Jesus knew there was someone who needed him, and he felt a divine necessity to give the message of himself to that thirsting soul.

Jesus met this person at the well of Sychar. Although many scholars, following the Jewish method of computing time, see this incident as occurring at noon, there seems to be more evidence that John uses the Roman method in his gospel. If this be so, he met the woman in the late afternoon. We see four stages in their conversation.

I. Attracting her interest.

Jesus's request for a drink of water was sincere. It afforded him, however, an opening for offering this woman an even richer gift than she could possibly bestow on him. Whenever we do a kindness for someone, we come to take a more than ordinary interest in that person. We actually do others a favor when we allow them to be helpful to someone else. This awakens a kindly feeling toward those they help. The example of Jesus in asking the woman for a drink of water was one of the many ways in which Jesus led sinners to himself. She was astonished at his request. Although we often hear emphasized the difference between a Jew and a Samaritan as she did in the biblically recorded conversation, perhaps she was just as surprised that a man spoke to her, a woman, since this too was probably a social custom not ordinarily practiced.

Whatever the contributing factors, Jesus certainly attracted the woman's attention. He came to where she was. Had he merely set up an office in Samaria and announced his availability at certain hours, Jesus never would have been able to minister to this woman. If we are to reach people for Christ, we must be where they are, be interested in the things that interest them, and use both personal ingenuity and creativity to awaken their interest in the message we are seeking to bring them.

II. Arousing a sense of sin.

People cannot be saved without repentance. Neither can they repent until they realize they are sinners. Jesus's next step was to make this woman realize she needed a Savior. If he had charged her directly with being an immoral person, she probably would have adopted some type of defense mechanism. Thus, he did it in a very subtle way, asking her to call her husband, presumably in order that he might share in receiving this living water about which Jesus had told her. This, of course, brought to focus the fact that she was engaged in immoral practices.

One outstanding preacher said recently that what our country needs more than anything else is a renewed realization of both the fact of sin and the awfulness of it. Modern man has tried to account for sin in many ways. He has called it theological fiction and has labeled it a "pathological state deliberately fomented in the public mind by salaried representatives of religion with a view to implementing their own ends and serving their own vested interests." We cannot, however, avoid sin by merely referring to it as an "evolutionary legacy" or a "moral hangover from our alleged animal ancestry." Sin is more than "good in the making" or "the growing pains of the race." Sin is rebellion against God's standard, and the one thing we cannot do is deny that it has made havoc of God's fair earth. What a terrible thing sin is! How we need to share God's Word about sin with people so that the Holy Spirit may convict them of their guilt!

III. Avoiding an attempted evasion.

The woman made no attempt to deny her sinfulness. The inner look of the Savior had caught her off guard. She realized that she stood in the presence of one who knew all about her. On the other hand, when she realized she had been unmasked, she tried to evade the issue by raising a theological discussion. She, as a Samaritan, had been reared in the area of Mount Gerizim. Her loyalty, therefore, was to her own heritage. She proceeded to raise a controversial matter. Which is right: to worship at Mount Gerizim in Samaria or at Mount Zion in Jerusalem?

Actually, the woman probably was more interested in changing the subject from her own sinfulness to another topic than she was in the proper place to worship. So often when we talk to lost people about their condition, they throw some irrelevant subject across the path to sidetrack us in our soul-winning efforts. I remember years ago discussing with a lady her need for a Savior. When, with the aid of the Holy Spirit, I had brought her to a point of conviction and was pressing for a decision, she replied rather flippantly, "If I ever join a church, I wouldn't join one of your denomination anyway." I had not even discussed membership in a local congregation. I was pressing for a decision about the Savior. She wanted to dodge the question of her personal responsibility to God by raising a question that was of no concern at that time.

IV. Announcing the Good News.

Firmly, yet tactfully, Jesus stuck to his task. He would not be sidetracked. Neither would he fly off the handle and lose his temper.

First, he pointed out a fact about religion. Worship is not concerned with externals but rather with spiritual matters. The place of worship is relatively unimportant. The person worshiped is what matters and also the way in which that person is understood and approached. We are as prone today as the people of Jesus's day to magnify externals and fail to recognize the spiritual nature of God. When Jesus insisted on a proper concept of deity, he was once more pressing his case on her. She made a second effort to dodge the question by saying, perhaps rather casually, that when the Messiah comes, he will tell us all about these things. She seemed to be saying that she couldn't worry about religious matters but would wait for someone to explain them to her.

At this point, Jesus was ready to announce himself to her. Plainly, yet lovingly, he told her the facts about himself. He was the Messiah! All that people had been looking for through the centuries could be found in receiving him. John did not tell us everything that occurred when Jesus announced himself to her, but the subsequent actions of the woman assure us that she received him.

Conclusion

The woman's open avowal of Christ later to the men in the city is the best proof that she received Jesus. The day in which she lived was, no doubt, like our own in that people were reluctant to openly confess that they were sinners and profess their faith in God's provision for their forgiveness. When people's hearts are changed, however, faith and love abide. The mouth is then willing to confess what the heart feels and what the will has chosen to do. Jesus had opened the eyes of this woman to a new life. Notice that "the woman then left her water pot" and went to the city. Probably she was so excited with her discovery that things that had a few moments ago seemed important now were of little consequence. When Jesus comes to a person's life, he develops a new set of priorities. Paul said that "old things are passed away, behold, all things are become new" (2 Cor. 5:17).

SUNDAY EVENING, SEPTEMBER 2

Title: The Conversion of Simon Peter

Text: "One of the two which heard John speak, and followed him, was Andrew, Simon Peter's brother. He first findeth his own brother Simon, and saith unto him, We have found the Messias, which is, being interpreted, the Christ. And he brought him to Jesus. And when Jesus beheld him, he said, Thou art Simon the son of Jona: thou shalt be called Cephas, which is by interpretation, A stone" **(John 1:40–42).**

Scripture Reading: John 1:35–42

Introduction

Simon Peter had a certain charm. He was a fascinating person with whom everyone can identify. Paul was sometimes so deep in theology that he drowns us. John the beloved was so close to the Master that we despair of attaining his nearness. But impulsive, outspoken, boastful, self-confident, sinning, confessing, forgiving Simon—of him we say, "There but for the grace of God go I." We naturally picture Simon Peter as a big, burly, rugged fisherman. He had such a big heart; he must have had a large body in which to carry it.

273

He was quick to speak, sincere, genuine, the natural leader of any group. As Simon becomes Peter, we identify with the process and discover that Master Sculptor chiseling away on our own life to release the imprisoned person that he wants us to be.

This series of sermons is really about the Lord of Simon Johnson, who so graciously, tenderly, persistently worked with him until he became Peter (we might say "Rocky") Johnson. If the Lord could do that for Simon, there is hope for every person. Sermons about the Lord's dealings with Simon Peter tell much about the beginnings of Christianity and have great practical value for Christians today.

I. Factors in Simon's conversion.

A. *The ministry of John the Baptist.* Peter and Andrew, as well as James and John, two sets of brothers from Bethsaida ("house of fish") in Galilee, were attending the revival meeting being conducted by John the Baptist on the east side of the Jordan River across from Judea at Bethany. John the Baptist identified himself as the forerunner of the Messiah who had come in the spirit and power of Elijah as prophesied in Isaiah 40:3–5 and Malachi 3:1; 4:5–6 (see Matt. 3:1–6; Mark 1:2–6; Luke 3:3–6).

   1. John preached, "Repent ye: for the kingdom of heaven is at hand" (Matt. 3:2). All people were called to prepare for the coming of the Lord by repentance from sin. They symbolized their death to sin and the remission of their sins by baptism. John warned the Pharisees and Sadducees that they would not be saved just because they were the natural children of Abraham. They must show evidence of repentance (vv. 7–9). He warned against procrastination. As a tree that does not bear fruit is cut down, so, he warned, they would he cut down by judgment if they did not bring forth the fruit of repentance (Matt. 3:10).

      John the Baptist announced that the Messiah was at hand. John's baptism had been symbolic. The Messiah would baptize with the Holy Spirit and fire (Matt. 3:11). The fire probably referred to the purifying effects of fire in separating dross from pure metal. The Messiah would separate God's people from those not his as thoroughly as the thresher separated chaff and wheat (6:12).

      When Jesus came to John asking for baptism, John hesitated. Jesus insisted, "Suffer it to be so now: for thus it becometh us to fulfil all righteousness" (Matt. 3:15). Jesus by his baptism signified that he was beginning his ministry that would culminate in his death and resurrection. At Jesus's baptism the Spirit of God descended like a dove on him and a voice from heaven identified him as the beloved "son" of Psalm 2:7 and the "suffering servant" of Isaiah 42:1 by saying, "This is my beloved Son, in whom I am well pleased" (Matt. 3:17).

This was the sign John the Baptist needed. He now boldly proclaimed that Jesus was the Messiah, the Son of God (John 1:19–34), and "the Lamb of God, which taketh away the sin of the world" (v. 29) who fulfilled Isaiah 53:7.

2. John encouraged his disciples to follow Jesus. A mountain preacher in Oklahoma, in a sermon to preachers, made these observations: first, John the Baptist knew he was not the Messiah; second, John knew who the Messiah was; third, John knew how to direct his disciples to the Messiah, to which the speaker added, "This is more than some of you preachers know."

"Again the next day after John stood, and two of his disciples; and looking upon Jesus as he walked, he saith, Behold the Lamb of God! And the two disciples heard him speak, and they followed Jesus" (John 1:35–37). "Then Jesus turned, and saw them following, and saith unto them, What seek ye? They said unto him, Rabbi, (which is to say, being interpreted, Master,) where dwellest thou?" (v. 38), which was a polite way of saying they would like a conference. "Come and see," said Jesus to them as he has answered every seeking soul. Jesus can stand investigation. He welcomes honest inquiry. He is the truth. Andrew, Simon Peter's brother, and his unnamed companion (who is almost certainly John, the brother of James, who became the beloved apostle and the author of the book of John) spent the day with Jesus. John remembered that it was about the tenth hour. He apparently used Roman time, which is our time.

3. Andrew and John became disciples of Jesus. How did Jesus win these two first disciples? Neither has left any record. Was there some divine revelation of his personality? Was there some sign such as that given to John the Baptist? Did Jesus, as he did later (Luke 24:44–48), show from the Old Testament Scriptures the prophecies fulfilled in him? We do know that life for them was changed completely that day. They testified, "We have found the Messiah" (John 1:41 RSV).

B. *Andrew brought Simon to Jesus.* "He first found his brother Simon, and said to him, 'We have found the Messiah' (which means Christ). He brought him to Jesus" (John 1:41 RSV).

1. The record probably means that, before anything else, Andrew went to tell Simon about Jesus. It may mean that he got to

Simon before John got to his brother James. The desire to see another come to know Christ is the natural desire of every saved person. Concern for the spiritual welfare of others is a good sign that one has been saved.

2. Andrew told his experience. He did not tell Simon that he ought to quit his cursing and do better. He said, "We have found the Messiah." His enthusiasm overcame any objections that Simon may have offered, and Andrew did what every soul winner would like to do: he brought Simon face-to-face with Jesus and got himself out of the way. Simon must have been impressed by the fact that Jesus knew him. "Jesus looked at him, and said, 'So you are Simon the son of John? You shall be called Cephas' (which means Peter)" (John 1:42 RSV). Cephas is the Aramaic and Peter is the Greek for "rock." Jesus saw in Simon qualities that when developed would make him worthy of the new name Peter.

II. Andrew, Simon Peter's brother.

Andrew was an ordinary man of extraordinary character. Three times in his gospel John mentions Andrew. In the first two instances he introduces him as "Andrew, Simon Peter's brother" (John 1:40; 6:8; 12:22). John is afraid that we will not recognize Andrew unless he tells us that he is the brother of the more famous Simon Peter. I imagine John introducing Andrew to Mr. Doe, who shakes hands in a perfunctory manner, a hydromatic handshake with no clutch at all. Then John says, "Andrew is Simon Peter's brother." Mr. Doe shakes more vigorously, "So you are Simon Peter's brother. I am glad to know you. I heard Simon Peter preach on the Day of Pentecost. He is a wonderful man!" How would you like to go through life as your brother's brother?

Andrew in many ways had the most difficult place in the apostles' group. He and his brother Peter, as well as James and John, were of the same village. They played together and doubtless went to school together at the feet of the village rabbi. Andrew as well as Peter, James, and John left the fishing business to give full time to the gospel ministry. For some reason, Peter, James, and John formed an inner circle from which Andrew was excluded. At the raising of Jairus's daughter, Peter, James, and John were present. On the Mount of Transfiguration, Peter, James, and John saw the Lord's transfigured glory. Andrew was with the disciples at the foot of the mountain. In Gethsemane, Peter, James, and John went with Jesus (Mark 14:32–35) while Andrew stayed behind with the others. It is not easy to see one's companions receive promotions while one is left behind. A lesser soul would have been filled with envy. Not Andrew. He seemed to know that his talents were more ordinary than his more gifted brother. It must have given him satisfaction at Pentecost and on many subsequent occasions when God used Peter so mightily, to say to himself, "I brought him to Jesus."

Conclusion

Note again some of the factors in Simon's conversion: (1) The preaching of the Word of God by a man called by God; (2) the witness of the preacher to Jesus as the Son of God, the Servant of God, the Messiah, and the Lamb of God; (3) the willingness of an inquirer to seek the truth; (4) the courageous, winsome testimony of a saved person to his experience with Jesus; (5) the concern of the religious community evidenced by attendance at the revival services.

If God in his grace can make Simon into Peter, there is hope for all of us. Who would have thought that Simon the fisherman of Bethsaida would ever be Peter the preacher of Pentecost? What hath God wrought?

Andrew, the ordinary man, was used by God to win Simon Peter. Many believers of ordinary ability have been used by God as the human instrument in the salvation of those who became more prominent in the kingdom of God than they.

WEDNESDAY EVENING, SEPTEMBER 5

Title: Jesus As Mark Saw Him

Text: "The beginning of the gospel of Jesus Christ, the Son of God" **(Mark 1:1)**.

Scripture Reading: Mark 1:1–14

Introduction

When I first entered the ministry, a friend gave me a key to the four Gospels and their varied representations of Jesus Christ. I share this insight with you. Matthew, the man with civil responsibility and access to royalty, pictures Jesus as the perfect King. Mark, an apparent minister to Peter and others, presents Jesus as the perfect Servant. Luke, a physician, depicts Jesus as the perfect Man. John, an obvious mystic of Patmos, envisions Jesus as the perfect God.

Three matters are to be considered in introducing this series of sermons on the manner in which Mark presented the person of Jesus Christ. We must note the life of Mark, the impetus of Mark (i.e., what motivated him to produce the gospel account), and the particular presentation of Mark.

I. Mark's life.

    A. *His family.* Mark was the son of a wealthy woman whose home was used by the early church (Acts 12:12). He was a nephew of the great Barnabas (Col. 4:10).

    B. *His ministry.* Though not one of the original twelve apostles, Mark was eager to identify himself as an early follower of Jesus (Mark 14:51–52). He went on a missionary journey with Paul and Barnabas but did not complete the effort (Acts 12:15; 13:13). This act caused Paul to split with Barnabas when the issue of taking Mark with them arose again (15:37–41). Mark then traveled with

Barnabas. In spite of this rift, Paul later declared that Mark was "profitable" to him (2 Tim. 4:11).

C. *His contribution.* Mark seemed to be a helper of Paul (Philem. 24) and Peter (1 Peter 5:13). A rather common tradition is that he became the first bishop of the church at Alexandria. Beyond a doubt, his greatest contribution was the writing of the gospel bearing his name.

II. Mark's impetus.

As we consider the motivations that caused Mark to record the gospel, we must understand that he was led by the Holy Spirit to write every word as he did. With this in mind, there are three factors that the Spirit of God used to direct Mark in this endeavor.

A. *Roman believers.* According to Eusebius (c. AD 310), the believers who heard the apostle Peter preach in Rome urged Mark, in that he was a follower of the apostle, to record Peter's messages. This would give them a written account of this apostle's works. Tradition maintains that Mark submitted to this pressure.

B. *Peter's message.* Mark was a companion of Peter at Rome (c. AD 61–63). The contents of the gospel of Mark sustain the concept that Mark used Peter's ministry and teachings as his chief source.

C. *Gospel's action.* Mark's gospel is often referred to as the "action gospel." Mark was eager to show the Lord as a person of action. Thus, he was brief in recording the words of the Lord. He did not give a lengthy discourse from the Lord, but this is what one would expect from the Servant—action, not words.

III. Mark's presentation.

A. *Jesus as a historical person.* Jesus is not presented as a superhuman who was quasi-historical. Rather, Mark depicts Jesus as a complete man. He had taken upon himself the total likeness of humanity. His body had natural functions (eat, 2:16; sleep, 4:38–39; hunger, 11:12; thirst, 15:36); his emotions had natural expressions (grieved, 3:5; angry, 10:14); and his mind and body had natural limitations (knowledge, 5:30; 13:32; death, 15:37).

B. *Jesus as a divine person.* Whether Mark referred to Jesus as the "Son of God" (1:1; 3:11; 5:7; 15:39) or as the "Son of man" (2:10, 28; 8:38; 9:9; et al.), the author placed him in the divine role operative among humans. Jesus conquered the infirmities of people (8:22–26 et al.), stupefied the archenemy death (5:21–42), and arrested the powers of the natural order (4:35–41; 6:48). Only God in the flesh could accomplish these feats!

Jesus also manifested the divine in that he was able to discern the hearts of people (2:8), forgive and heal people (e.g., v. 5), cross religious barriers to express his love (vv. 16–17), and declare that he was "Lord also of the Sabbath" (v. 28).

C. *Jesus as a decisive person.* Mark was not writing simply as a historian. His heart was afire with the exciting message of the Master, for the Holy Spirit was impressing him to pen words of eternal value. His readers were going to depend heavily on every word of this sacred manuscript. Thus, Mark was sharing a present experience of spiritual involvement with future believers.

This Jesus was not to be heard and subsequently forgotten. He was to be obeyed. Therefore, Mark was aware that each person hearing the account of the Master's life would be forced to make a decision. Mark saw Jesus as the object and appeal of human faith in the invitation of the ages: "Whosoever will come after me, let him deny himself, and take up his cross, and follow me" (8:34). Jesus said that he was the substance of humankind's salvation (vv. 36–38).

Conclusion

Let us allow Mark's excitement and near impatience as he presents the Servant-Lord to become part of our experience as we worship and serve Jesus Christ.

SUNDAY MORNING, SEPTEMBER 9

Title: Jesus Is the Way

Text: "Jesus said to him, 'I am the way, and the truth, and the life; no one comes to the Father, but by me'" **(John 14:6 RSV)**.

Scripture Reading: John 14:6–11

Hymns: "Joyful, Joyful, We Adore Thee," Van Dyke
"One Day," Chapman
"Have Thine Own Way, Lord," Pollard

Offertory Prayer: Holy Father, you have been so generous and kind to us. You have blessed us beyond anything we can ever merit. Today we praise you and thank you for your goodness to us. We pray that you will now give to us generous and gracious hearts as we come bringing tithes and offerings. Accept these gifts and bless them that they might be used for your glory and for the good of those in need. We pray in Jesus's name. Amen.

Introduction

The Lord Jesus Christ made some great claims and some great promises. He could make these claims and promises because of who he is and what he was going to do and because of what he can do in the lives of those who trust him as Lord and Savior and follow him as leader and teacher.

The words of our text contain one of the great claims of Jesus Christ.

Let us open our minds and hearts to the implications of Jesus's great claim, "I am the way."

Jesus Christ is the way *out*—of the difficulties and the perplexities of life that threaten us. He is the way out from under condemnation and guilt. He is the way out of failure and emptiness. He is the way out of spiritual death. Jesus Christ is the way *in*—to life and love and hope and peace. He is the way in to that which makes life meaningful and beautiful. Jesus Christ is the way *through*—an uncertain tomorrow. He is the way through the storms that threaten us and the clouds that cause the horizon of the future to appear dark. Jesus is the way *up*—to the Father and to the home above.

If we interpret the words of our text in their context, we will conclude that our Lord is making three bold declarations.

I. Jesus is claiming to be the way to the Father God—"I am the way."

There are many ways by which we can learn about God. We can study biology and that which is very minute through a microscope and discover the fingerprints of the Almighty. We can stare out into space with a telescope and see the autograph of the eternal and all-powerful Creator. "The heavens are telling the glory of God; and the firmament proclaims his handiwork" (Ps. 19:1 RSV).

While it is possible to learn about God through many different avenues of exploration and intellectual struggle, one comes to know God as Father *only* through Jesus Christ. Jesus is the way to the Father.

II. Jesus is claiming to be the truth concerning the Father—"I am the way, and the truth."

From the dawn of human history, people have wondered about the nature and character of God. It remained for Jesus Christ, the sinless, stainless, spotless Son of God, to manifest and to reveal him in all of his grace and glory (John 1:16–18).

Philip, one of the apostles, was eager that our Lord reveal the nature and character of the Father God to the apostles. Jesus reminded him, "He who has seen me has seen the Father; how can you say, 'Show us the Father'? Do you not believe that I am in the Father and the Father in me?" (John 14:8–10 RSV).

Jesus Christ was the eternal Father God with a human face, a human body with hands that served, and a human voice that spoke God's truth.

If you want to know what the true God is like, then look into the face of Jesus Christ, listen to the words that fell from his lips, and examine closely the deeds and achievements of his life.

III. Jesus is claiming to be the bringer of life from the Father—"I am the way, and the truth, and the life."

Because of sin, man has lost the life he had from God at the time of the creation. He stands in need of a new birth, a birth of the Spirit, a birth from above, that would impart to him the quality of life God wants him to have.

John declares that those who receive Jesus Christ through faith receive the power to become the children of God (John 1:12). John also declares that God so loved the world that he gave Jesus Christ to die on a cross for our sins that through faith in him we might receive the gift of eternal life (John 5:16).

Our Lord says, "He who believes in the Son has eternal life; he who does not obey the Son shall not see life, but the wrath of God rests upon him" (John 3:36 RSV). This eternal life comes through faith in Jesus Christ alone. Only Jesus Christ brings the life of God to the believer (John 5:24).

Conclusion

If you want to know the way to the Father and the truth concerning the Father and experience the life that comes from the Father, then let Jesus Christ become the Lord of your life.

SUNDAY EVENING, SEPTEMBER 9

Title: Simon Peter's Call to the Ministry

Text: "And Jesus, walking by the sea of Galilee, saw two brethren, Simon called Peter, and Andrew his brother, casting a net into the sea; for they were fishers. And he saith unto them, Follow me, and I will make you fishers of men" **(Matt. 4:18–19)**.

Scripture Reading: Luke 5:1–11 (see also Matt. 4:18–22; Mark 1:16–20)

Introduction

Andrew and Peter, John and James, Philip and Nathaniel became disciples of Jesus as recorded in John 1:35–51. They accepted Jesus as the Messiah; they heard him gladly; they accompanied him frequently; but they did not leave their secular businesses. They were laymen. Andrew and Peter, John and James were partners in the fishing business. Their business was large enough that they had at least two boats and some employees. We are indebted to John for informing us that the disciples were with Jesus at Cana in Galilee when he worked his first miracle (John 2:1–11); with him for a brief visit to Capernaum (v. 12); and with him in Jerusalem for the first cleansing of the temple at the Passover (vv. 13–25) and for his interview with Nicodemus (3:1–21). They were also with him in Samaria and marveled at Jesus's conversion of the woman by the well in Sychar (4:1–42). They arrived in Galilee and witnessed Jesus's second miracle, the healing of the son of a courtier of Capernaum. After Jesus's rejection at Nazareth (vv. 16–31), he made his new headquarters at Capernaum (Matt. 4:13–16; Luke 4:31), a city on the Sea of Galilee near Bethsaida, the disciples' fishing village.

What a wonderful privilege to be great Christian laypeople. We can make money at some honest profession, business, or trade; we can uphold high

Christian standards in business and in the community; we can serve in the church; and we can bear personal witness to Jesus without someone saying, "They're paid to do it."

One layman spoke more than he intended when he said, "We can't all be preachers; somebody has to work." It is equally true that we cannot all be laypeople; somebody has to preach. God has no source from whom to call preachers than laypeople. Let not the layperson forget it, especially when tempted to criticize the preacher.

I. The circumstances of Peter's call to the ministry (Luke 5:1–11).

A. *A multitude of people were pressing to hear Jesus preach the Word of God.* He was standing by the Lake of Gennesaret (another name for the Sea of Galilee). The fishing boats of Simon and Andrew and James and John were at the shore, and the fishermen were busy washing their nets. Jesus entered Simon's boat. At Jesus's request, Simon put out a little from the shore. Jesus sat, as was the custom of the rabbis, and taught the multitude from the boat. Peter must have been pleased that Jesus would use his boat as a pulpit from which to cast the gospel net. God can use your business too if you will loan it to him.

B. *"Launch out into the deep, and let down your nets for a draught,"* Jesus said. Simon knew the fishing business. At night was the most favorable time and near shore was the best place to catch fish. A carpenter surely didn't know as much about fishing as a fisherman. Simon answered him, "Master, we have toiled all the night, and have taken nothing: nevertheless at thy word I will let down the net" (Luke 5:5). He would grudgingly obey just to prove that there were no fish available. Simon's halting obedience was nevertheless obedience. He was not like some who dislike some command of Jesus and disobey. How complete was Simon's surprise when the net enclosed such a multitude of fish that Simon called for his partners to come help. The catch overfilled both of the boats.

C. *Simon received a needed vision of Jesus (Luke 5:8–9).* He recognized in Jesus the majesty and power of God. In the presence of deity, instinctively "he fell down at Jesus's knees, saying, Depart from me; for I am a sinful man, O Lord" (v. 8). Isaiah had the same reaction when he saw God high and lifted up and himself as a sinner in the midst of a sinning people (Isa. 6:1–7). An exalted opinion of Jesus and a humble estimate of oneself are qualities necessary for the ministry.

D. *Jesus called Simon Peter (as well as Andrew, James, and John) to leave the fishing business and to give full time to the gospel ministry.* In Luke's account, "Jesus said unto Simon, Fear not; from henceforth thou shalt catch men. And when they had brought their ships to land, they forsook all, and followed him" (Luke 5:10–11). In Mark's

282

account Jesus said to Simon Peter and Andrew, "Come ye after me, and I will make you to become fishers of men" (Mark 1:17). In similar manner he also called James and John. Their response was immediate and complete. Of Peter and Andrew we read, "And straightway they forsook their nets, and followed him" (v. 18). Of James and John we read, "And they left their father Zebedee in the ship with the hired servants, and went after him" (v. 20).

II. Glorious truths about the call to ministry.

A. *"Fear not" when God calls.* Whom God calls, he will qualify. From our human viewpoint our Lord makes some strange choices. Why would he call these fishermen rather than the religious leaders? "If a man desire the office of a bishop, he desireth a good work" (1 Tim. 3:1), but the Christian ministry as a vocation is a work to be undertaken only by the express call of God. Jesus said, 'Ye have not chosen me, but I have chosen you and ordained you" (John 15:16).

Humanly speaking, those who enter the ministry face many things that could make them fearful. Consider facing a congregation of highly educated lawyers, doctors, teachers, bankers, insurance executives, and others Sunday after Sunday. Should the preacher fear for what to say? No. Fear not. God's people have come to worship. They have come to hear the Word of God. More important than practicing law, medicine, or engineering, God's man is to deliver God's message by which people are caught for God. "Now then we are ambassadors for Christ, as though God did beseech you by us: we pray you in Christ's stead, be ye reconciled to God" (2 Cor. 5:20). Christ's promise is "Lo, I am with you always, even unto the end of the world" (Matt. 28:20).

B. *God's call is to be accepted.* Just as God's call to salvation can be rejected, so God's call to the ministry can be rejected. Some people pride themselves on holding out against God's call, but rejecting God's will is nothing to be proud of. The advice "Do not accept the call to the ministry if you can do anything else" is erroneous. The better advice: "Do not accept the call to the ministry if you can do anything else with a clear conscience." Compromise on response to the call to the ministry is reprehensible, just as is compromise on the call to salvation. One is called to forsake all and follow Jesus. Simon and his companions left a thriving fishing business. There was no turning back. Jesus said, "No man, having put his hand to the plough, and looking back, is fit for the kingdom of God" (Luke 9:62).

Dr. B. H. Carroll, founder of Southwestern Baptist Theological Seminary, spoke of his call in these moving words:

I made a solemn covenant with God, that while I lived I would never have any other business or profession or calling than to preach the gospel—to give myself wholly to that, "sink or swim, live or die, survive or perish," to turn back to any other, NEVER, NEVER, NEVER, FOREVER. I learned to see that it was a small matter if I did die. I remembered the Master's words: "He that loseth his life for my sake, and the Gospel's shall find it; and he that findeth his life shall lose it." Indeed, it might be the best for me to die. It might be the best that I should starve to death. I didn't know. Who can tell? But I was certain that whether I starved or fattened it was my duty to preach the gospel. (B. H. Carroll, *Jesus the Christ* [Nashville: Baird-Ward, 1937], 209.)

C. *The will and way of God must be sovereign for God's preacher.* Peter saw that the Lord knew all about the tasks to which he was called. It was a holy task, so he must approach it with all humility. He would win people not primarily by eloquence, knowledge, or organizational methods, but by dedication of all his talents to the Lord. He must fish for men wherever and with whatever type of net the Lord willed. Sometimes the biggest catch is just ahead. Perhaps the Lord wants his ministers to let down their nets deeper where they are than to be looking for more favorable waters in which to fish.

Conclusion

"I magnify my ministry" (Rom. 11:13 RSV), Paul said with reference to his call to be a missionary to the Gentiles. To Timothy he wrote, "And I thank Christ Jesus our Lord, who hath enabled me, for that he counted me faithful, putting me into the ministry; who was before a blasphemer, and a persecutor, and injurious: but I obtained mercy, because I did it ignorantly in unbelief" (1 Tim. 1:12–13).

The layperson in the will of God is just as important as the minister in the will of God. God needs both laypeople and ministers. The important consideration is that one be in the will of God.

An outstanding physician with an established practice conferred with a pastor about ordination to the ministry. He was a thoroughly dedicated man but did not evidence a clear call. The pastor showed him that he could serve the Lord as a Christian doctor with a wonderful witness better than as a mediocre preacher.

In Paul's marvelous figure of the church as the body of Christ in 1 Corinthians 12:12–31, he notes that the organs of the body most visible are not always the organs that are most valuable. Heart and lungs, for example, are more important than nose and ears. The minister who stands in front may not be as important as the layperson whose service is not so visible. Layperson or minister, let us be what God would have us to be and magnify our ministry for the glory of God.

WEDNESDAY EVENING, SEPTEMBER 12

Title: One Having Authority

Text: "And they were astonished at his doctrine: for he taught them as one that had authority, and not as the scribes" **(Mark 1:22)**.

Scripture Reading: Mark 1:14–28

Introduction

Mark presents Jesus as the Servant of God and humanity. A servant is a person under authority, not with authority. Even though the Servant-Messiah concept is prevalent in Mark's writing, Jesus's authority would by nature expose itself. This element in his life was necessary to gain the respect of those to whom he was to minister. Mark's emphasis on Jesus's authority is quite obvious (Mark 1:22, 27). In the first chapter of Mark we see Jesus's authority recognized, taught, and pondered by all who came in contact with him.

I. Authority recognized (Mark 1:2–13).

A. *John the Baptist (Mark 1:2–9).* John had captured the spiritual scene of the day. He was a spiritually moving force among people, yet he made it clear that he was not to be the center of attraction (John 3:30). He submitted to the Christ and cried, "There cometh one mightier than I after me."

B. *The Holy Spirit (Mark 1:10–12).* The Holy Spirit may be defined as the moving force within the Trinity (John 16:7–14). He substantiated Jesus's authority when he descended upon Jesus. Also, the voice from heaven validated Jesus as being the expression of God to man (Mark 1:11).

C. *Satan (Mark 1:13).* Satan is universally declared to be the moving force within the evil world. Yet after his onslaught on Jesus Christ, he had to submit to Jesus's authority. No one can overcome Jesus (Rom. 8:31–39).

II. Authority taught (Mark 1:14–15).

A. *Jesus in leadership position (Mark 1:14).* The text tells us that John was imprisoned. Jesus assumed the role of spiritual leader and gave the good news of the kingdom of God.

B. *The time is fulfilled (Mark 1:15).* Jesus said that he was the fulfillment of prophetic history. The time of God's unique revelation had arrived within his person. The kingdom of God was literally among humans.

C. *Repent ye (Mark 1:15).* Jesus manifested the authority to call people to repent of their sins and to accept the revealed way of God. He had to be either a madman or the Messiah to preach these words.

III. Authority pondered (Mark 1:16–42).

A. *In the manual world (Mark 1:16–22).* Peter, Andrew, James, and John had their own plans. Jesus had a task for them to accomplish, and he assumed the authority to call them to forsake all and to follow him. They submitted to this call.

B. *In the ethereal world (Mark 1:23–27).* Jesus had command over the world of angels (good spirits) (Heb. 1:6). Mark 1:27 teaches that even the evil spirits were submissive to his authority (Mark 1:27). He needed only to say, "Come out of him," and the unclean spirit obeyed.

C. *In the physical world (Mark 1:28–42).* Prior to the historical Jesus, people lived in dread of their own physical bodies and eventual death. Jesus changed this. He exposed his authority over the weaknesses and diseases of the flesh. He counteracted the decaying processes in people.

Conclusion

Jesus's authority may be challenged in one area (Mark 1:43–45). Jesus commanded the healed man to keep silent and go through proper channels to be declared "clean." The man, in his freedom of choice, selected to disobey the Lord. As a result, the ministry of Jesus was curtailed to a degree. People have the ultimate power to choose whether they will accept the authority of Jesus Christ in their lives.

SUNDAY MORNING, SEPTEMBER 16

Title: Christ the Door

Text: "I am the door; if any one enters by me, he will be saved, and will go in and out and find pasture" **(John 10:9 RSV)**.

Scripture Reading: John 10:1–10

Hymns: "O God, Our Help in Ages Past," Watts
"The Way of the Cross Leads Home," Pounds
"I Will Arise and Go to Jesus," Hart

Offertory Prayer: Our heavenly Father, we come to you with gratitude in our hearts for the extravagance of your provisions for us. You have blessed us richly in the physical realm and even more abundantly in the spiritual realm. Thank you for the glad consciousness of forgiven sin and for the joy that comes to us through the gift of eternal life. Today we come to your house and to this moment of personal dedication with tithes and offerings as symbols of our desire to live under your grace and guidance. Add your blessings to these gifts and use them for your glory. We pray in Jesus's name. Amen.

Introduction

Our Lord used common experiences as vehicles for communicating great truths about God. In writing the fourth gospel, which is evangelistic in purpose, John the beloved apostle selected a variety of events in Jesus's life along with a variety of his teachings to communicate great truths about God.

It was no accident that Jesus described himself as the Light of the World. From day to day his disciples could remind themselves that Jesus Christ was the light that dispels the darkness that disturbs and threatens life.

In speaking of Jesus as the *logos*, John used a term familiar both to Jews and Gentiles to describe Jesus Christ as the very mind of God, the language of God, the utterances of God, the conversation of God by which the eternal God was communicating with the minds and hearts of people.

John selected a statement from our Lord concerning his being the Living Bread from heaven as a means of revealing that Jesus Christ alone satisfies the deepest hungers of the human heart. John also quotes Jesus telling a woman at a well that he was the Living Water that quenches the thirst of the soul.

In John 10, the "Great Shepherd" chapter, John uses two major figures of speech from the lips of Jesus to describe his mission and ministry. Our Lord is the Good Shepherd who gathers his flock into one fold (John 10:3–4; 14:6–27). All of the sheep, be they Jewish sheep or Gentile sheep, belong in the same flock. The Good Shepherd guards his sheep from every destructive force (10:7–8, 11–15, 28–29). He also guides them into good pastures (10:3, 9–10).

In the midst of these references to our Lord's ministry as the Good Shepherd, we find also that he is the door to the sheepfold. This figure of speech was familiar to those who lived in the Middle East. The sheepfold was an enclosure in which the sheep were brought together at night for protection from their natural enemies. The shepherds took their sheep out to pasture during the day and brought them to the sheepfold at night for safety and rest. A shepherd or gatekeeper would literally make his bed in the doorway to the sheepfold. An enemy could not enter without crossing his body. A sheep could not stray during the night without crossing over the gatekeeper's body. Our Lord was declaring himself to be the way of entrance and, at the same time, saying he provides security for those who enter.

I. Christ is the door of entrance to God the Father.

This statement of our Lord likely was prompted when, after Jesus healed a blind man, the man was treated severely by those in charge of the synagogue. They cast him out because of his favorable words about Jesus. By casting him out, they were declaring themselves to be the way of entrance to God. Jesus boldly affirmed that he, rather than the religious institutions of that day, was the way to the Father God. And he continues to be the only way to the Father God today.

One can find out much about God by various methods of study and observation. We can learn something about the antiquity of God by studying the universe. We can behold the intricacy and the delicacy of his creative activity by looking through a microscope. We can observe the artistic ability of our God in the wonders of nature. But it is through Jesus Christ that we come to know God as Father.

A. *Jesus came into a world where many people thought of God only as a stranger.*
B. *Jesus came into a world in which many thought of God as an enemy.*
C. *Christ came to reveal God as the loving Father.*
D. *Christ spoke of himself as the Good Shepherd who reveals the continuing concern of the loving Father.*

In the midst of his conversation about his relationship to the people as a shepherd to the sheep, he uses the figure of the door to describe his role and function in ministry.

II. Christ is the door to real security.

"I am the door; if anyone enters by me, he will be saved, and will go in and out and find pasture" (John 10:9). To be able to "go in and out" is to be able to move about in an environment that is absolutely safe and secure. All of us are security seekers. This is true for the baby with his blanket, the businesswoman with her bank account and stock portfolio, the student seeking a college education, and the person seeking to complete an adequate insurance program. On the international level, nations seek security through armaments and alliances. One of the basic needs of the human heart is security.

A. *Jesus Christ is the doorway to security from the past.* All of us have made mistakes. Each of us is a sinner, and we all stand in need of forgiveness for the past. Only Jesus Christ can give us the security we need at this point.
B. *Jesus Christ is the doorway to security in the present.* The only real security is spiritual. It is wonderful to have good health, a quality education, kind friends, and a prestigious position, but we need to recognize that many of these things that we lean on for security are temporary and transitory. In the final analysis, our only security is in the realm of the spiritual. Jesus Christ wants to be with us in all of the crises of life to help us be secure.
C. *Jesus Christ is the doorway to security for the future.* The security that Christ offers for the future is not found in military alliances or financial success. He offers security in the grace of God and through the abiding presence of the Holy Spirit, who has promised to never leave us nor forsake us.

III. Christ is the door to perfect satisfaction.

"Go in and out and find pasture." It was the role of the good shepherd to bring the sheep into the sheepfold at the close of the day where they could rest in safety from their enemies during the night. It also was the function of the shepherd to lead the sheep out into the pastures and watering places during the day. The well-being of the sheep was dependent on the shepherd's provisions.

    A. *Through Jesus Christ we enter into an experience of the love of God and, with his help, we relate to others in terms of a persistent, unbreakable spirit of goodwill.*

    B. *In Jesus Christ we experience the joy of fellowship with other members of the family of God.*

    C. *In Jesus Christ we experience the satisfaction of the freedom to be all that God would have us to be.* He works to set us free from the forces that would hinder us.

IV. Christ is the door for any person and every person.

    A. *Christ is the door out of the confusion and chaos that sin and carelessness bring into life.* If you want to find your way out, then come to Jesus Christ, who is the door.

    B. *Christ is the door in.* No one likes to be an outsider. Jesus Christ is the door into the family of God. He is the way into abundant life and peace.

    C. *Christ is the door through.* No one knows what tomorrow holds. For some of us it will be joy, but for others of us it will be sorrow. For some it will be prosperity, while for others it may be poverty. For some it will be health, and for some it will be illness. Christ Jesus wants to help us go through whatever life brings with an attitude that is positive and constructive and benevolent.

    D. *Christ is the door up to the highest and best that people can experience.* He is the door up to our highest possible manhood and womanhood. He is the way up to true success.

Conclusion

Let Christ be your door. Today the door is open for you to enter. Come to Jesus Christ and let him be your Savior, Teacher, and Guide. Make him Lord, and you will find him to be the entrance to a full life.

SUNDAY EVENING, SEPTEMBER 16

Title: In Simon Peter's House

Text: "And Jesus said unto them, Come ye after me, and I will make you to become fishers of men" (**Mark 1:17**).

Scripture Reading: Mark 2:1–12 (parallel reading: Matt. 9:1–8; Luke 5:17–26)

Introduction

One wonders how Peter broke the news to his wife that he was quitting the fishing business to catch people for Jesus. Did they wonder, as have others who have left a good livelihood for the sake of Jesus, how they would live?

Jesus probably won her confidence just as he had won Peter's allegiance. In any case, she remained with Peter, and from 1 Corinthians 9:5 we learn that after Pentecost she traveled with him on his missionary journeys. Jesus seems to have made Peter's house his home in Capernaum.

Jesus entered Peter's home on a busy Sabbath (Mark 1:29). He had just taught in the synagogue and had also healed a man (vv. 25–28). Those in the synagogue were amazed both at his teaching and his healing. When Jesus entered Peter's house, he found Peter's mother-in-law sick in bed with a fever, "and he came and took her by the hand, and lifted her up; and immediately the fever left her, and she ministered unto them" (v. 31). That same night at sunset, just as the Sabbath ended, all the city gathered at the door bringing their sick and those possessed with demons, and Jesus healed them (see Matt. 8:14–17; Mark 1:29–34; Luke 4:38–41).

The next morning a great while before day (while Peter was still asleep), Jesus went to a desert place to pray. Peter and the multitudes found him there and said, "All are seeking thee." Jesus did not think it best to go back to Capernaum. "And he said unto them, Let us go into the next towns, that I may preach there also; for therefore came I forth. And he preached in their synagogues throughout all Galilee, and cast out devils" (Mark 1:38–39). Let your imagination dwell on Matthew 4:23–25 and Mark 1:45 to realize the magnitude of this great Galilean ministry. Of course, Peter was sharing in it all and learning from Jesus every day. After some days they returned home to Peter's house in Capernaum.

I. Four men lower a paralytic through the roof of Peter's house (Mark 2:1–4).

As soon as the word was passed that Jesus was at home, a great crowd gathered. The house soon filled to overflowing. The crowd continued to grow until there was no room for them, not even around the door. Pharisees and teachers of the law from Galilee, Judea, and Jerusalem were listening to his teaching and observing his healing miracles (Luke 5:17).

Four men came carrying a paralyzed man. His bed was probably a pallet. We assume that each man carried one corner. When they could not get him into the presence of Jesus because of the great multitude of people, they broke up the roof and let the man down in front of Jesus. The roof probably was constructed of poles covered with mud tiles or thatch. Most houses had flat roofs reached by an outside stairway, so their problem was not as difficult as Western people might imagine.

II. Parallels exist between getting this man to Jesus for physical healing and our getting people to him for spiritual healing.

    A. *Who were these four men?* History does not record their names. They had a reason to believe that Jesus could heal their friend. Had Jesus healed one of them?

We who are saved have the assurance that if the Lord Jesus saved us, he can save anyone. We have the experience of millions who called to him in sincerity and found salvation. His invitation is, "Whosoever will may come," and the promise stands, "Him that cometh to me I will in no wise cast out" (John 6:37).

B. *These men were concerned about their friend.* They knew they had no hope for his recovery unless he was divinely healed.

All people need salvation. There is no hope for spiritual healing except from the Savior. No one ought to be overlooked. Jesus related this truth by telling the story of a king who wanted his banquet hall to be full of guests. He commanded, "'Hurry out to the streets and alleys of the town, and bring back the poor, the crippled, the blind, and the lame.' Soon the servant said, 'Your order has been carried out, sir, but there is room for more.' So the master said to the servant, 'Go out to the country roads and lanes, and make people come in, so that my house will be full'" (Luke 14:21–23 GNT).

C. *These four men cooperated in the task.* All four of them were needed to bring the man to Jesus. Two of them might have brought the man to the edge of the crowd, but all four men were needed to get him into Jesus's presence. Who organized this party? Did the wife of the man call for help? We do not know, but someone had to care and had to enlist others to help.

Bringing people to Jesus is a cooperative task. Paul wrote, "I have planted, Apollos watered; but God gave the increase. So then neither is he that planteth any thing, neither he that watereth; but God that giveth the increase. Now he that planteth and that watereth are one: and every man shall receive his own reward according to his own labour. For we are labourers together with God: ye are God's husbandry, ye are God's building" (1 Cor. 3:6–9).

When Jesus fed the five thousand, he did it in orderly fashion. He had the people sit down in groups and had the disciples assist in the distribution so that no one would be overlooked. The church offers Christians a way to cooperate in orderly fashion to help get people to Jesus. The preacher, the choir, the musicians, the directors, the teachers, the ushers, the intercessors, the members—all in accord can pool their talents in orderly fashion under the leadership of the Holy Spirit to bring people to Jesus. The church has many critics, but it has no rivals in the work of helping people come to Jesus.

D. *These four men overcame opposition.* It was not a convenient time for them to come. The world will never be evangelized by people who wait for a convenient time to visit and evangelize. Did they plan to pay for the repair of Peter's roof? At least they were willing to risk having it cost them something to get their friend to Jesus. It costs to proclaim the gospel both at home and on the mission fields. It takes effort and money to overcome the difficulties. These men thought their friend was worth the effort and the cost.

III. Jesus forgave and healed the paralyzed man.

Jesus first said, "Son, thy sins be forgiven thee." Jesus knew this man, and he knew that his sickness had been the result of his sins. He knew that his primary need was for the salvation of his soul. We must not erroneously conclude that all suffering results from personal sin. John 9:3 refutes that conclusion. To say that all suffering is the result of personal sin is as false as it is cruel, and as cruel as it is false. Jesus rewarded the faith of the sinner and the faith of the four who brought him by pronouncing forgiveness. The scribes rightly reasoned, "Why doth this man thus speak blasphemies? who can forgive sins but God only?" (Mark 2:7). Jesus knew what they were thinking. He wanted them to know (especially did he want Peter to know) that he was not just a man but the Son of Man (a veiled term for the Messiah). Mark, looking through the eyes of Peter, wrote, "And immediately when Jesus perceived in his spirit that they so reasoned within themselves, he said unto them, Why reason ye these things in your hearts? Whether is it easier to say to the sick of the palsy, Thy sins be forgiven thee; or to say, Arise, and take up thy bed, and walk? But that ye may know that the Son of man hath power on earth to forgive sins, (he saith to the sick of the palsy,) I say unto thee, Arise, and take thy bed, and go thy way into thine house" (vv. 8–11).

The men glorified God and rejoiced. When Jesus told the palsied man to arise, "immediately he arose, took up the bed, and went forth before them all; insomuch that they were all amazed, and glorified God, saying, We never saw it on this fashion" (Mark 2:12).

Conclusion

When we are saved, we are happy. Several girls in a children's home made profession of faith during a Sunday school service led by a seminary student. As the young man left, one of the girls placed a hastily written note in his hands that said, "Isn't it good to be a Christian? I just had to write and tell you." Joy is "Jesus" and 'You" with "nothing" between. Many people have thanked others for bringing them to Jesus. Have you ever heard anyone say, "I'm sorry you brought me to Jesus"?

Those who bring others to Jesus are also glad. Peter must have shared in the joy of these four even though his roof was torn up.

More importantly, God rejoices when a soul is saved. Jesus said, "There is joy in the presence of the angels of God over one sinner that repenteth" (Luke 15:10). That must surely mean that God himself also rejoices.

Simon Peter was learning every day from Jesus about how to catch people for God.

WEDNESDAY EVENING, SEPTEMBER 19

Title: One Facing Attacks

Text: "Therefore the Son of man is Lord also of the sabbath" **(Mark 2:28)**.

Scripture Reading: Mark 2

Introduction

As Jesus entered Capernaum, he experienced immediate popularity among the common people. Because of this, he had to expect opposition. This chapter presents the problems he faced from the scribes (Mark 2:6, 16), the Pharisees (vv. 16, 24), and the followers of John the Baptist (v. 18, cf. Matt. 9:14). Charges were made against Jesus in the heat of malicious jealousy (Mark 2:16), scriptural misunderstanding (vv. 6, 24), and earnest heart-searching (v. 18).

He was accused in four different circumstances. He was charged with blasphemous statements, for banqueting with sinners, and for having backslid disciples. Finally, he was charged with breaking a commandment.

I. Charge of blasphemous statements (Mark 2:1–12).

A. *Man sick with palsy (Mark 2:2–5).* Friends of a man sick with palsy had brought him to Jesus. Jesus ministered to his primary needs first by saying, "Son, thy sins be forgiven thee" (v. 5).

B. *Religious opposition (Mark 2:6–7).* A clerical pride arose. The scribes knew they were not capable of forgiving sins. In their concept of God, Jesus should not have been able to do so either. Thus, they charged him with blasphemy.

C. *Response of Jesus (Mark 2:8–12).* Jesus responded to the charge by healing the man of his illness as well as forgiving him of his sins.

II. Charge of banqueting with sinners (Mark 2:13–17).

A. *Social life of Jesus (Mark 2:13–15).* Jesus was being entertained in the home of Levi, a tax collector. He desired salvation for this household.

B. *Watchdogs (Mark 2:16).* Jealous men doggedly followed his steps. They cast this charge upon him: "How is it that he eateth and drinketh with publicans and sinners?"

C. *Response of Jesus (Mark 2:17).* Jesus countered this charge by expressing the purpose of his ministry: "They that are whole have no need of the physician, but they that are sick. I came not to call the righteous, but sinners to repentance" (v. 17).

III. Charge of having backslid disciples (Mark 2:18–22).

A. *Disciples of Jesus (Mark 2:18).* Both a sincere group of John's followers and a sinister group of the Pharisees joined minds to question the seeming lack of dedication of Jesus's disciples.

293

B. *Right time (Mark 2:19–20).* Jesus taught that his followers were enjoying a time of personal pleasure with him. Their hour of sadness would come "when the bridegroom shall be taken away from them" (v. 20).

C. *Newness of life required (Mark 2:21–22).* This attack on Jesus's disciples caused him to teach in parable that his coming had ushered in a new order of life and religion. "New wine must be put into new bottles" (v. 22). One must be created anew to be able to accept the newness in Christ.

IV. Charge of breaking a commandment (Mark 2:23–27).

A. *A sabbath stroll (Mark 2:23).* The disciples of our Lord walked across a field on the Sabbath. They pulled off some of the ears of corn and began to eat.

B. *Charge of law-breaking (Mark 2:24).* The legalistic watchdogs interpreted this deed as breaking the fourth commandment. "Behold, why do they on the sabbath day that which is not lawful?" (v. 24).

C. *Purpose given (Mark 2:25–27).* Jesus repelled this attack by discerning the very purpose of the Sabbath: "The sabbath was made for man, and not man for the sabbath" (v. 27).

Conclusion

Jesus quelled these attacks by declaring that "the Son of man is Lord also of the Sabbath" (Mark 2:28). All opposition must come to naught when Jesus is recognized as Lord.

Sunday Morning, September 23

Title: Christ the Living Bread from Heaven

Text: "Jesus said to them, 'I am the bread of life; he who comes to me shall not hunger, and he who believes in me shall never thirst'" **(John 6:35 RSV).**

Scripture Reading: John 6:32–40

Hymns: "God, Our Father, We Adore Thee," Frazer
"A Child of the King," Buell
"Break Thou the Bread of Life," Lathbury

Offertory Prayer: Holy Father, on this Lord's Day we come with reverence and with an earnest desire in our hearts to worship the eternal God in spirit and in truth. Help us to open up our minds and hearts for the entrance of your truth. Cause our will to be yielding to your divine will. As we bring tithes and offerings, add your blessings and use these gifts to add to the ministries of those who seek to communicate the good news of your love to a needy world. We pray in Jesus's name. Amen.

Introduction

John, the beloved apostle, lived and ministered in the great city of Ephesus, which was a Gentile city where Greek culture was dominant. He faced the task of communicating the coming of Jesus Christ, the Jewish Messiah who was the Savior of the world.

John announced that the eternal God had entered time and space, the invisible God had become visible, the spiritual had become physical in Jesus of Nazareth, and the Creator had become a part of his own creation. He proclaimed Jesus as the very language of God in which God was seeking to communicate with people concerning himself, the nature of humanity, the purpose for life, and the meaning of eternity. John has proclaimed Jesus as the very Light of the World that dispels darkness and puts chaos to flight.

John presents Jesus Christ as the Living Bread from heaven that sustains and supports life. He is not medicine that prevents disease, cake enjoyed as a dessert, or candy enjoyed for its mere sweetness. He is the Bread of Life that is essential for life.

This great chapter concerning Jesus as the Bread of Life follows the miracle of the feeding of the five thousand. The miracles in John's gospel are parables through which Jesus sought to teach something about the life of the Spirit, the life of faith, the life of worship, and the life that leads to joy.

Our Lord met a great physical need of the hungry multitude. He used this experience on the human level to reveal divine truth on the spiritual level. Christ asserted that he came into the world on a much greater mission than that of merely satisfying the physical needs of people. He came to meet their heart and soul needs.

In his great claim to being the Bread of Life, our Lord used figurative language that identified him with the manna God gave through Moses. While God gave the manna for only a limited time, he now provides spiritual bread on a continuing basis (John 6:32). Jesus Christ, the Living Bread, continues to provide sustenance for the innermost being of those who trust him and look to him for grace and guidance in life (John 6:48–51).

I. There is great hunger in the world.

A. *There is a great physical hunger in the world today.* The population explosion has created vast multitudes in areas of the world where there is a scarcity of essentials for human existence. In some great metropolitan areas, poverty has created famine conditions. Our governments, churches, and parachurch organizations are faced with an urgent challenge to feed the hungry. These hunger conditions present every Christian with both an invitation and a commission to be of help.

B. *There is a greater spiritual hunger among the nations of the earth.* Everywhere there is a haunting dissatisfaction within people's hearts. They feel incomplete because they do not know God through Jesus Christ.

C. *Humankind is hungry today.*
  1. There is a great hunger for truth, and Jesus Christ is the truth.
  2. There is a great hunger for abundant life, and Jesus Christ is the source of that life.
  3. There is a great hunger for love, and Jesus Christ is the medium through which the love of God comes to us.
  4. There is a great hunger for forgiveness, and Jesus Christ makes forgiveness possible for us.
  5. There is a great hunger for peace among people, and as the Prince of Peace, Jesus Christ can help us to have the harmonious relationships that make for peace among people.
  6. There is a great hunger for meaning and purpose in life, and great joy can come to those who follow the purposes of Jesus Christ.
  7. There always has been a hunger for eternal life, and Jesus Christ alone can give that eternal life.

II. The food of the world does not satisfy the hunger of the soul.
  A. *A barn full of grain cannot satisfy the hunger of the soul (Luke 12:13–21).*
  B. *Pleasure alone will leave a sour taste in the mouth.*
  C. *Knowledge, as wonderful as it is, cannot satisfy the deepest hungers of the human heart.*
  D. *Power and position do not satisfy this deep hunger of the soul. Power can often be very frustrating.*

III. Christ is the Living Bread sent from heaven.
Humanity is hungry for two primary reasons.

  A. *Sin has made people hungry for God.* To live a life of no faith is like trying to satisfy thirst by drinking saltwater. It is like trying to satisfy the hunger of the stomach by feeding on sawdust.
  B. *God has created us with a hunger for himself.* God made us with a nature like his own and has placed within us a hunger that cannot be satisfied with anything except God himself.

People try to satisfy this hunger by piling up money or by studying books or by enjoying all the pleasures that the world has to offer. The God-shaped vacuum within the human soul cannot be satisfied with anything except God himself. Christ is the Bread sent from God to meet the deepest needs of the human heart.

IV. Christ is the Bread sent from heaven for all people.
  A. *Christ is the Bread of Life available to the chief of sinners.*
  B. *Christ is the Bread of Heaven available to the hungriest of the hungry.*
  C. *Christ is the Bread of Heaven available to the thirstiest of the thirsty.*
  D. *Christ is the Bread of Heaven available to the poorest of the poor.*

E. *Christ is the Bread of Heaven needed by the best of the best among us.*

F. *Christ is the Bread of Heaven who offers himself for the meanest of the mean among us.*

Christ is the Bread from heaven that makes life possible. Without bread, people could not live, and without the Bread of Life, people cannot know the life of God.

Christ is the Bread that strengthens and nourishes and makes growth and development possible. It is he who gives vitality and strength to our moral muscles.

Christ is the Bread that satisfies perfectly. Jesus declared that they who hunger and thirst after righteousness shall be filled (Matt. 5:6). Our Lord is adequate to meet every spiritual need in our lives. As we cannot live the natural life without bread, we cannot live the spiritual life without the Bread of Life.

Conclusion

Christ, as the living Bread of Heaven, is the best food upon which the soul can feed. Furthermore, this Bread is a free gift from God and is congenial to the appetites of all who will come to him.

But Christ, as the living Bread of Heaven, is beneficial only to those who eat. You must eat your own food. When our Lord speaks of his flesh, he is referring to his incarnation, his coming into the world as a visible manifestation of the love and grace of God. When he speaks of his blood, he is really speaking of his life, which was given for us. As we trust him and meditate on all that he came to do for us, and as we give ourselves in obedience to him, we feast on the living Bread from Heaven.

SUNDAY EVENING, SEPTEMBER 23

Title: Peter's Lesson on Faith

Text: "But straightway Jesus spoke unto them, saying, Be of good cheer; it is I; be not afraid. And Peter answered him and said, Lord, if it be thou, bid me come unto thee on the water" **(Matt. 14:27–28).**

Scripture Reading: Matthew 14:24–33 (parallel reading: Mark 6:45–52; John 6:14–21)

Introduction

How did Peter and the other disciples come to an intelligent understanding of Jesus and of his plans and purposes? By Jesus's self-revelation through his words and his works. The New Testament contains but a portion of all that Jesus said and did (see John 20:30–31; 21:25), but the record is sufficient for one to trace some significant steps in Peter's progress.

A. *Matthew 9:9–13; Mark 2:13–17; Luke 5:27–32.* Jesus called Levi (Matthew), a tax collector, to follow him. Matthew left all to follow

297

Jesus and gave a great feast in honor of Jesus so that his friends could meet Jesus. "And when the scribes and Pharisees saw him eat with publicans and sinners, they said unto his disciples, How is it that he eateth and drinketh with publicans and sinners? When Jesus heard it, he saith unto them, They that are whole have no need of the physician, but they that are sick: I came not to call the righteous, but sinners to repentance" (Mark 2:16–17).

B. *Matthew 9:14–17; Mark 2:18–22; Luke 5:33–39.* When some disciples of John joined the Pharisees in criticizing Jesus's disciples for not fasting, Jesus replied that it would be as inappropriate for his disciples to fast as for a bridal party to fast. In the parables of the new patch on an old garment and of new wine in old wineskins, Jesus taught that Christianity is not a patch on Judaism and that the old wineskins of Judaism cannot hold the new ferment of the gospel.

C. *In a series of controversies about the Sabbath, Jesus defended his right to heal and to do good.* John 5:1–18 records the healing of a lame man at the pool of Bethesda in Jerusalem on a Sabbath. On another Sabbath Jesus was with his disciples when they plucked ears of corn in the fields and ate (Matt. 12:l; Mark 2:23–28; Luke 6:1–5). On a third Sabbath Jesus healed a man with a withered hand in a synagogue (Matt. 12:9–13; Mark 3:1–6; Luke 6:6–11). Jesus defended his action by teaching, "And he said unto them, What man shall there be among you, that shall have one sheep, and if it fall into a pit on the sabbath day, will he not lay hold on it, and lift it out? How much then is a man better than a sheep? Wherefore it is lawful to do well on the sabbath days" (Matt. 12:11–12), and also by saying, "The sabbath was made for man, and not man for the sabbath: Therefore the Son of man is Lord also of the sabbath" (Mark 2:27–28).

D. *Mark 3:13–19; Luke 6:12–16.* After a night of prayer, Jesus selected from his disciples twelve whom he named apostles. In four accounts of the Twelve in Matthew, Mark, Luke, and Acts, the first named is Simon Peter. Peter was naturally the leader. He was first among equals.

E. *Jesus delivered the Sermon on the Mount to the twelve disciples and a great crowd (Matt. 5–7; Luke 6:12–49).* In it he proclaims the meaning of Christian discipleship. Peter and the others learn the privileges, the principles, and the requirements of the kingdom of God.

F. *Peter continued to grow as he witnessed Jesus's miracles.* These included, among others, the raising of the widow's son at Nain (Luke 7:11–17), the stilling of the tempest on the Sea of Galilee (Matt. 8:23–27; Mark 4:35–41; Luke 8:22–25), the healing of the Gadarene demoniac (Matt. 8:28–34; Mark 5:1–20; Luke 8:26–39), the healing of Jairus's daughter and of the woman who touched Christ's garment (Matt. 9:18–26; Mark 5:21–43; Luke 8:40–56), and others.

G. *The parables of Jesus about the kingdom of God were most instructive (Matt. 13:1–53; Mark 4:1–34; Luke 8:4–18).*

H. *Peter had practical experience as the disciples went out two by two preaching and healing (Matt. 9:35–11:1).* When the disciples returned, Jesus suggested that they go to a desert place on the eastern side of the Sea of Galilee for rest. While they were sailing across the lake, a great multitude of people ran around the lake on foot and were waiting for them. Jesus had compassion on them and taught them. When the day was almost over, he took the lunch of a little boy and multiplied it to feed the five thousand. The account is in Matthew 14:13–21; Mark 6:30–44; Luke 9:10–17; and John 6:1–13. Peter must have been impressed that Jesus gave God thanks for the food, that he used the disciples to serve the multitudes, that he had them sit in orderly arrangement by companies of about fifty each, and that he did not waste anything but gathered up the broken pieces that had not been eaten. This brings us to the Scripture for this sermon.

I. Jesus's strange command (Matt. 14:22–23; Mark 6:45–46; John 6:14–15).

A. *"And straightway Jesus constrained his disciples to get into a ship, and to go before him unto the other side, while he sent the multitudes away" (Matt. 14:22).* How strange his order seemed to the disciples. Jesus had just fed the five thousand. The crowds were enthusiastic. They said, "Surely this is the Prophet who is to come into the world" (John 6:14 NIV). They wanted to make Jesus king. With his miraculous power, the hated Roman conquerors could be expelled from their land and the kingdom of God established. The disciples shared the enthusiasm of the crowd. How strange that Jesus would not allow them to make him king! How strange that he should send them away!

Satan had used the crowd and the disciples to renew the temptation he had presented to Jesus in the wilderness; namely, to be a popular, political Messiah rather than to go to the cross. Jesus, as he often did, climbed a mountain to have some time alone with God in prayer. He would not be the kind of Messiah the people wanted. "His hour had not yet come" to draw the issues to a close and go to the cross.

B. *The disciples encountered strong winds and heavy seas (Matt. 14:28; Mark 6:47–48; John 6:16–18).* The darkness had come on. They continued rowing hard until the fourth, or last, watch of the night. They had made little progress. Why did Jesus not come? They were doing what he had commanded them to do. Why the storm and the difficulty when they were obeying? We are reminded of Jesus's two-day delay after he heard of the death of Lazarus (John 11:6). This delay turned out for God's glory when Jesus raised Lazarus from the dead. In this case the disciples' faith will be increased because they have been so sorely tested, but of course they could not know that Jesus was watching them from the mountain. The purpose of adversity may be to build character. God certainly brings good out of evil. Christians must learn to trust the Lord's good purposes even when life's providences are so perplexing that they do not understand.

II. The terror and the recognition (Matt. 14:25–27; Mark 6:48–50).

Jesus came to the disciples walking on the sea. They were troubled, thinking they were seeing a ghost. They were filled with the fear of the unknown, but especially with the awesome dread we mortals have of deity. Jesus called out, "Be of good cheer; it is I: be not afraid" (Matt.14:27). Part of Jesus's purpose was to reveal that God is not one to be feared with a nameless dread; he is our loving heavenly Father. If God is as Jesus, you can trust him. "Be not afraid."

III. Peter's impulsive response (Matt. 14:28–31).

Impulsively Peter replied, "Lord, if it be thou, bid me come unto thee on the water" (Matt. 14:28). Some believe that Peter was motivated by his desire to be first or by his desire to do some rash act. Is it not rather a typically impulsive response? Jesus said, "Come," and Peter walked on the water to Jesus. As long as he looked to Jesus, he did well; but when he saw the wind and the boisterous waves, he became afraid and began to sink. "Lord, save me!" he cried. Immediately the Lord stretched out his hand and caught him and said, "O thou of little faith, Wherefore didst thou doubt?"

Why do we doubt? We look at the awful circumstances around us and at our own weakness instead of focusing on Jesus's power. When we begin to think of our sins and the uncertainties of life, we begin to sink. Peter did not commend himself to Jesus. He did not enumerate his good points. He simply called out, "Lord, save me!" One's helplessness is the worthiest petition one can send to God for help.

Conclusion

With Jesus in the boat, the journey to shore was made quickly (John 6:21). When Jesus came into the boat, the wind ceased and the disciples worshiped him saying, "Of a truth thou art the Son of God" (Matt. 14:33). This was a remarkable advance in faith. They did not understand Jesus. They still thought in terms of a political kingdom, but they had learned from his teaching and his miracles that he was higher than they in character, in teaching, and in the exercise of God's power.

The disciples were learning to trust Jesus. In calm and in storm, he will not forsake his children. Through Jesus we learn that God is no nameless dread to fear, nor a ghostly apparition, but a Father to be loved who desires to bring each one to life's true destiny.

WEDNESDAY EVENING, SEPTEMBER 26

Title: One Demanding Response

Text: "For whosoever shall do the will of God, the same is my brother, and my sister, and mother" **(Mark 3:35)**.

Scripture Reading: Mark 3

Introduction

The life and ministry of Jesus Christ was so profound that those meeting him felt the need to respond to him either in love or in hate. No one met him without becoming personally involved in some kind of decision regarding the Lord. There are five decisive scenes in this chapter involving the Pharisees and scribes, unclean spirits, and Jesus's friends and family.

I. Pharisees wanted to destroy him (Mark 3:1–6).

A. *Healing ministry (Mark 3:1, 3–5)*. Jesus helped a man who had a physical deformity. The problem would not cause him to die.

B. *Spiritual spies (Mark 3:2)*. Mark indicted the pharisaical watchdogs for spying "that they might accuse him" (v. 2). Jesus is recorded as being "with anger, being grieved for the hardness of their hearts" (v. 5).

C. *Devious schemes (Mark 3:6)*. The Pharisees responded to Jesus by seeking to form an alliance with the Herodians, a nonreligious political party. Their purpose was to destroy him.

II. Unclean spirits wanted to expose him (Mark 3:7–12).

A. *Multitudes came (Mark 3:7–8)*. Multitudes were flocking to experience the ministry of Jesus (v. 10).

B. *Unclean spirits speak (Mark 3:11)*. The evil spirits intended to harm Jesus's ministry. Their pronouncement of Jesus as "the Son of God" would cause harm to him in at least two ways: He would be proclaimed an ally of his heralds (the evil spirits), and his messianic ministry would be thwarted by a premature announcement of his deity.

C. *Spirits silenced (Mark 3:12)*. Jesus immediately silenced the evil spirits. They could not disobey his demand "that they should not make him known" (Mark 3:12).

III. Friends wanted to comfort him (Mark 3:13–21).

A. *Followers organized (Mark 3:13)*. Jesus selected a few men to follow him. As these men were chosen, they came to his side.

B. *Ministry launched (Mark 3:14)*. The Lord shared with his followers three things: he gave them authority through ordination, purpose through command, and accomplishment through power.

C. *Beside himself (Mark 3:21).* The text indicates that Jesus had become so absorbed in serving others that he neglected the basic necessities of life for himself. His friends sought to restrain him, for they interpreted his concern for others as insanity. What a gross mistake!

IV. Scribes wanted to misinterpret him (Mark 3:22–30).

A. *With "loaded guns" (Mark 3:22).* The scribes came from Jerusalem with a prejudiced conclusion. They interpreted his deeds as being empowered by demons.

B. *Spiritual logic (Mark 3:23).* Jesus retorted with a very logical premise, "How can Satan cast out Satan?" (v. 23). As men of learning, the scribes could not help but detect their own inaneness.

C. *Unpardonable sin (Mark 3:28–29).* Jesus then taught one of the most sobering of all Christian doctrines, that of the unpardonable sin. Mark opined that this was taught because of their accusations (v. 30).

V. Family wanted to minister to him (Mark 3:31–35).

A. *Family concern (Mark 3:31).* One may easily imagine that the friends (v. 21) had sent word for the family to come and help protect Jesus from himself. They did come looking for him in love and concern.

B. *Work continues (Mark 3:32).* Jesus was still under the pressure of serving others when his family arrived. They tenderly called for him.

C. *"Who is my [family]?" (Mark 3:33).* The Lord was not being calloused toward his family with his question, "Who is my mother . . . ?" Rather, he was teaching that there was a greater relationship than the blood relationship.

Conclusion

Jesus declared that the greatest relationship among people is found within the realm of God's will (Mark 3:35).

SUNDAY MORNING, SEPTEMBER 30

Title: The Open Secret Concerning the Resurrection

Text: "Jesus said to her, 'I am the resurrection and the life; he who believes in me, though he die, yet shall he live, and whoever lives and believes in me shall never die. Do you believe this?'" **(John 11:25–26 RSV)**.

Scripture Reading: 1 Corinthians 15:47–57

Hymns: "All Creatures of Our God and King," Francis of Assisi
"Christ the Lord Is Risen Today," Wesley
"He Lives," Ackley

Offertory Prayer: Holy Father, we come with gratitude for the harvest of the fields and for the beauty of nature. We come thankful for the bounty of your mercy in the realm of our spirit and for all of the blessings of life.

Today we offer ourselves on the basis of your forgiving grace and redeeming power. Accept the tithes and offerings that we bring as acknowledgment of your ownership and our stewardship. May your blessings rest on these gifts to the end that others will be blessed and helped. In Jesus's name. Amen.

Introduction

John contains the touching account of Jesus's visit in the home of his friends when that home had been touched by the cold hand of death. Sooner or later the angel of death comes and knocks at the door of every home. We need to develop a plan for dealing with death.

Jesus's ministry is described in terms of his clothing himself in human flesh that he might experience death and, in so doing, destroy him who had the power of death, that is, the devil. This was not only to bring about the forgiveness of sin but also to deliver us from the fear of death (Heb. 2:14–18).

By looking at how our Lord related to those who were experiencing agony and grief over the death of a loved one, we can learn how he wants to relate to us when we are in the same situation. We can rejoice that our Savior is the same yesterday, today, and forever. He came declaring that through faith in him as the resurrection and the life, those who trust in him have the assurance of eternal life (John 14:19).

The death of one dear to us always causes us to raise questions about the fate of those who have died. It is not the will of our heavenly Father that we be in total ignorance concerning those who are asleep in the Lord (1 Thess. 4:13–18). Our God would have us live a life of confidence and cheer as we face the end of our earthly pilgrimage.

I. Our resurrection is affirmed as a revelation from God (1 Cor. 15:51–56).

The belief in the natural immortality of humanity is a Greek concept rather than a Hebrew or biblical concept. Some have let the thoughts of the Greeks concerning immortality color the Christian concept.

Paul declared to the Corinthian believers that God had revealed that which had been concealed in the past as a mystery. It was Job who articulated the question, "If a man die, will he live again?" (Job 14:14). It remained for Jesus Christ to provide the answer (John 11:25–26). Paul proclaims as a truth revealed by God through Christ that death is a defeated foe, that the grave will give up its victims, and that we will achieve final victory through our Lord Jesus Christ (1 Cor. 15:57).

II. Our resurrection is based on the wisdom and the power of God (1 Cor. 15:37–42).

Modern people, like the people of the first century, ask, "How are the dead raised? With what kind of body do they come?" (1 Cor. 15:35). Paul declares that this question is one that must be left to both the wisdom and the power of God.

    A. *He declares that God has given to each plant a body or stalk appropriate to its seed, flower, or fruit.*

    B. *He illustrates that God has given to each living creature a body perfectly adapted to its habitat.*

        1. People have been given bodies perfectly adapted for living in their habitat and performing their functions.

        2. Animals of the field have been given bodies perfectly suited for their habitat.

        3. Birds that fly through the air have been given lightweight bodies perfectly adapted for that type of dwelling and activity.

        4. Fish have been given bodies perfectly adapted for living in the water.

        5. So it will be in the resurrection. We will be given a body perfectly adapted for living in the heavenly Father's home.

    C. *Paul declares that each of the heavenly bodies has its own uniqueness and its own glory. So it will be in the resurrection of the dead.*

        1. What is sown is perishable; what is raised is imperishable.

        2. It is sown in dishonor; it is raised in glory.

        3. It is sown in weakness; it is raised in power.

        4. It is sown a physical body; it is raised a spiritual body.

III. Our resurrection is the result of the resurrection of Jesus Christ (I Cor. 15:20–26).

Our resurrection is not based on some natural immortality of humanity. It is based solidly on the fact of the resurrection of Jesus Christ. Apart from the resurrection of Jesus Christ, there is no hope of our rising from the dead and escaping from the grave.

    A. *Christ has been raised from the dead and is the firstfruits of those who have fallen asleep. This is a revelation of the purpose of God for each believer.*

    B. *As in Adam all of us became mortals, so in Christ we have the privilege of becoming immortal (1 Cor. 15:22).*

    C. *The final conquest of our triumphant Lord will be his ultimate defeat of death and his deliverance of the kingdom to God the Father (1 Cor. 15:24–26).*

Conclusion

If an unborn baby could contemplate the pain and trauma of birth, it would be with real terror that he or she faced the future. But the agony of the birth experience is necessary for the baby to enter a larger and more wonderful life.

Life is made up of a series of cycles. A baby is thrust out of the womb and placed in a cradle. The baby then becomes aware of the room and the family circle. This later enlarges to include the house and the yard and eventually church, school, the community, and the world. At some point in our human pilgrimage, the cycle begins to reverse itself, and if we live to old age, we may be limited to our home, a room in a nursing home, or possibly our bed. The death experience for the Christian, like the birth experience of a baby, is but the gateway into a larger life as we move out of our earthly tent into our eternal house, not made with hands, in the heavens (2 Cor. 5:1).

Let us be comforted and let us take courage as we approach the end of life in the faith that death is not a dead-end street, but rather it is the gateway on the horizon that permits us to enter into a life without the limitations, hindrances, and handicaps we have known here. We will dwell with God ages without end.

SUNDAY EVENING, SEPTEMBER 30

Title: Peter's Loyalty to Jesus

Text: "Then said Jesus unto the twelve, Will ye also go away? Then Simon Peter answered him, Lord, to whom shall we go? thou hast the words of eternal life. And we believe and are sure that thou art that Christ, the Son of the living God" **(John 6:67–69)**.

Scripture Reading: John 6:53–69

Introduction

There seems not to be any evidence that Peter ever doubted the super-natural character of Jesus after that first day when he accepted him as the Messiah. Peter continued to learn daily about Jesus's nature and purposes. He heard Jesus's teaching, including the parables and the Sermon on the Mount. He witnessed Jesus's miracles. He must have been profoundly affected by the feeding of the five thousand and the experience of walking on the water to Jesus.

The day after Peter's walk on water, Jesus entered a synagogue in Capernaum. The crowd was perplexed as to how and when Jesus had gone to that side of the Sea of Galilee. When they could not find him on the eastern shore, they came in larger numbers to the western shore, where they found him. They desired more miracles and wanted him to be their king. Peter and the other disciples continued to share these hopes also.

Jesus used the opportunity to give a discourse on the Bread of Life. His miracle of feeding the five thousand people had, as it were, rung the church bell of the universe to invite them to consider him as the true Bread from heaven. Just as God had given manna in the wilderness to allay the physical hunger of the children of Israel, he had now sent Jesus as the true manna for allaying the spiritual hunger of humankind. He would give his life for the sins of the world. The account is found in John 6:22–65. Jesus said, "I am the bread of life: he that cometh to me shall never hunger; and he that believeth on me shall never thirst" (v. 35). He preached that those who believed on him would also have everlasting life and would be raised up at the last day. The multitudes who thought of him as the son of Mary and Joseph were offended by his claims. When he mystically spoke of believing in him and by faith appropriating the merits of his death on the cross as "eating my flesh and drinking my blood," many then (as multitudes erroneously continue to do) took his words literally and were both puzzled and offended by them.

The crux of the problem seemed to be that the multitudes began to perceive that Jesus would not be a political leader. The more they understood him, the more they turned from him. "From that time many of his disciples went back, and walked no more with him" (John 6:66). The Twelve had noticed that, and they also were disappointed. "Then said Jesus unto the twelve, Will ye also go away?" (v. 67). The question expects a negative answer. "Then Simon Peter answered him, Lord, to whom shall we go? thou hast the words of eternal life. And we believe and are sure that thou art that Christ, the Son of the living God" (vv. 68–69).

I. To whom shall we go? This is the first question of a soul that has awakened to moral consciousness.

A. *Every person needs soul satisfaction.* There is an inarticulate longing in the heart of every person to know the Eternal and to have fellowship with him. The book of Genesis teaches that "God created man in his own image, in the image of God created he him; male and female created he them" (Gen. 1:27) and that "the LORD God formed man of the dust of the ground, and breathed into his nostrils the breath of life; and man became a living soul" (Gen. 2:7). The passage is saying that whatever likeness we humans may have to animals, there is something distinctive about us: We are made in God's image. Through Jesus, the Word of God, we have the light of reason and conscience given to us at our entering into this world. "That was the true Light, which lighteth every man that cometh into the world" (John 1:9). As Augustine so well said centuries ago, "Thou hast made us for thyself, O God, and our hearts are restless until they rest in Thee."

B. *Every person needs intellectual satisfaction.* Hogs and horses don't seem to have a philosophy of life, but people do. Our very nature compels us to think. We have to have some intellectual satisfaction to go on living. To whom shall we go?

C. *Every person needs forgiveness of sins.* Not only does every person know that there is right and wrong, but we know by experience that we have done wrong. We know that God is holy. One sick in body consults a physician. One sick in soul, bearing the weight of guilt—to whom shall he or she go?

II. To whom could we go?

To the inquiring people of Jesus's day, three main systems were open:

A. *The Sadducees were the skeptics and rationalists of the Jewish nation.* They denied immortality, angels, and the Resurrection. Shall we go to skepticism and materialism?

  1. Infidelity is too simple an answer. If there is no God, and all is mindless matter, which is the result of chance, then your thought processes are also the result of chance; hence, they cannot be trusted.

  2. Infidelity solves no problems. Skepticism does violence to the cravings of the human soul. Skepticism is a cruel mother who puts the baby to sleep with a drug rather than feed him.

  3. The life that skepticism produces does not commend it. Where are the hospitals and orphanages that it has built? What person was ever made better by the loss of his or her faith in God?

B. *The Pharisees were those who had allowed the letter of the law to take precedence over the spirit.* They became concerned with outward ceremonies, Sabbath observance, and clean and unclean regulations, rather than with the weightier matters of justice, mercy, and faith. Shall we go to ritualism?

  1. Ritualism has mistaken the outward forms for the inner content. No forms, however ancient or sacred, can save. They are symbols of the reality, and they bring to remembrance Jesus Christ and his salvation. They teach important truths, and their observance is important to obedience.

  2. No person or institution has the power to forgive sins. The church cannot save. Sin is a breach of personal relation with God. Only God can forgive sin and restore the breach of relationship.

C. *The Essenes were the ascetics of the age.* They withdrew from society and lived in separate communities. They were a prototype of monasticism. Shall we go to asceticism?

  1. It is essentially a system of seclusion, selfishness, and cowardice. A modern asceticism that would withdraw from active participation in attempting to heal humanity's hurt is as contemptible as the indifference of the priest and Levite in Jesus's parable of the good Samaritan who "passed by on the other side."

  2. Withdrawal from participation is exactly the opposite of that which our Lord desires for his disciples. Jesus prayed, "I pray not that thou shouldst take them out of the world, but that thou shouldst keep them from the evil" (John 17:15).

Conclusion

Let us go to Jesus, for he has the words of eternal life. He reveals that God is love and that God has created us with courage of love. He has made us in his own image with the power of choice, and he has also made a way for his sinful creation to be saved from our bad choices.

God has revealed himself in Jesus Christ. Jesus is the truth about God who satisfies our intellect. Jesus is the way to God who fulfills our need. Jesus is eternal life, our heart's desire. As water to a thirsty person, as food to the hungry, so Jesus is the Water of Life and the Bread of Life. He meets our need for truth, for direction, for forgiveness, for a purposeful life.

The negations of skepticism are for those who have no need for a personal God. The hypocrisies of formalism are for those who have no sin. The practice of asceticism is for those who have no sorrow, loneliness, love, nor pity. But for my needy hungry soul, there is none but Christ.

Peter had the answer and the only correct answer to the question, "To whom shall we go?" Let us go to Jesus, who is the Christ, the Son of the living God.

SUGGESTED PREACHING PROGRAM FOR THE MONTH OF
OCTOBER

■ Sunday Mornings

The mission of the church and the privilege of each individual follower of Christ is contained in the word *evangelism*. Day by day we are to share the good news about God revealed in Jesus Christ. The primary purpose for this activity is to bring about the conversion of those who have not yet believed. "Four Great Conversions" is the theme for four messages based on prominent conversion experiences recorded in the New Testament.

■ Sunday Evenings

God speaks in a variety of ways—through Jesus Christ, through the Holy Spirit, and through the written Word. The theme for these messages is "Nature Speaks of God."

■ Wednesday Evenings

Continue the study of the gospel of Mark using the theme "Jesus As Mark Saw Him."

WEDNESDAY EVENING, OCTOBER 3

Title: One Sharing Truth

Text: "And he began again to teach by the sea side: and there was gathered unto him a great multitude, so that he entered into a ship, and sat in the sea; and the whole multitude was by the sea on the land. And he taught them many things by parables" **(Mark 4:1–2)**.

Scripture Reading: Mark 4

Introduction

Society has not always looked upon the teaching profession with great favor. In times past, the position of teacher was associated with the servant class. This concept is not far removed from this fourth chapter of Mark. Jesus, as God's Servant, shares four basic truths with his followers. He led them to see the basic principles of sowing and reaping (vv. 3–20), revelation (vv. 21–25), growth (vv. 26–29), and expansion (vv. 30–33).

The first two verses of this chapter prepare the reader for these teachings. Four elements are found in the introductory verses: the servant is at work ("he taught"), there is a surge of people ("great multitudes"), a systematic approach is made ("by parables"), and a subject of study is given ("his doctrines").

I. The principle of sowing and reaping (Mark 4:3–20).

A. *"Seed" is the same (v. 3).* The implication in this passage is that the farmer used the identical "seed" in different locations. God's Word is the seed. It is the same whether it is presented in Amsterdam or Chicago.

B. *"Soil" is different (vv. 5, 7, 8).* Mark lists the places where the soil differed. Every human heart is different, yet the same Holy Spirit appeals to all.

C. *Satan is at work (v. 15).* Though Satan is at work universally, some hearts are more easily conquered than others. Those hearts given over to the "growth of God's seed"—the Word of God—cannot be touched by Satan.

D. *Savior reaps benefits (v. 20).* Two things happen when God's Word is allowed to grow in the heart: (1) the individual receives a special blessing, and (2) the Lord Jesus gets honor and glory.

II. The principle of revelation (Mark 4:21–25).

A. *God purposes to reveal (v. 21).* When God created light, he did not expect it to go unrevealed. Neither is the gospel to go unnoticed. God's plan calls for revelation.

B. *Satan tries to conceal (v. 21).* Satan will always be at odds with God. He encourages believers to place their "candles under baskets."

C. *Truth must come out (v. 22).* The nature of truth makes it impossible to keep hidden. It will be revealed in spite of human efforts.

D. *People's destiny determined (vv. 23–25).* People's destiny is determined by the way they respond to truth. God's truth is personified in the person of Jesus Christ. Consequently, people's future is determined by their response to the Christ.

III. The principle of growth (Mark 4:26–29).

A. *Sowing of the seed (v. 26).* A similar illustration is used to teach another truth. The principle of spiritual growth is the lesson at hand.

B. *Sleeping of the man (v. 27).* The fact is mentioned that even though humans go to sleep (are inactive), growth continues. God is not dependent on people to bring the increase.

C. *Springing of the seed (vv. 27–28).* The process of growth appears insignificant at first. Finally, multiplication of seed and effort is realized.

D. *Securing of the crop (v. 29).* No profit is made from any crop until the reaping takes place. This comes at the harvest, and only God is able to designate the time of harvest.

IV. The principle of expansion (Mark 4:30–33).

A. *Sown in significance (vv. 30–31).* This entire chapter uses agricultural experiences to proclaim spiritual truth. A third scene of sowing is used to illustrate yet another truth. A very small seed is planted.

B. *Godly expansion (v. 32).* Nature brings about a vast expansion of the original seed. There is no way to compare the seed and its fruit.
C. *Place of security (v. 32).* This growth is used by birds as a place of safety and shelter. God can take feeble human efforts and expand them to great usefulness.

Conclusion

After giving private instruction (Mark 4:34) and using a graphic illustration (vv. 35–39), Jesus caused his followers to search for truth by faith. This is seen in the question, "What manner of man is this, that even the wind and the sea obey him?" (v. 41).

SUNDAY MORNING, OCTOBER 7

Title: Zacchaeus

Text: "So he made haste and came down, and received him joyfully" **(Luke 19:6 RSV).**

Scripture Reading: Luke 19:1–10

Hymns: "Praise to the Lord, the Almighty," Neander
"He Leadeth Me! O Blessed Thought," Gilmore
"I Surrender All," Van DeVenter

Offertory Prayer: Father, we thank you for this beautiful and comfortable meeting place and for the equipment to facilitate effective ministry in this church. We thank you for dedicated full-time personnel to serve in the church. Thank you for the benevolent and missionary ministry of this church, with all of the committed people whose ministry we support throughout the world. We pray for them a special sense of your presence as we bring our tithes and offerings to support them. In Jesus's name. Amen.

Introduction

Some people need salvation and don't know it. Some know they need the Lord but refuse him or delay receiving him. Today we are looking at a man who knew he needed Jesus but never expected to receive him.

Because of the reputation of Zacchaeus's occupation and his own statements at the time of his conversion, Zacchaeus usually is considered a crooked businessman and corrupt politician. Zacchaeus lived in Jericho where he made his headquarters as the chief tax collector. The taxes for which he was responsible were those on imports, exports, or other special merchandising customs. Tax collecting positions were sold by the government to the highest bidders. The bidder then collected enough extra to reimburse himself and gain whatever profits he could. Generally tax collectors had a reputation for extortion and dishonesty. Luke tells us that Zacchaeus was rich, and the assumption is that he made himself rich by immoral if not illegal means.

The Hebrew people resented the Roman government, the taxes, and the tax collectors. Even if the tax collectors were Israelites, they were denied access to the religious life and blessings of the rest of the people. This explains why Zacchaeus would be surprised and the Jewish leaders would complain that Jesus would associate with and be kind to tax collectors.

It should be helpful to us to review Zacchaeus's conversion and the characteristic love and compassion of Jesus as demonstrated in this incident.

I. Zacchaeus knew he needed Jesus.

A. *He had doubts that Jesus would be willing to receive him.* He perhaps had heard about Jesus's ministry, but it would be very surprising if a Jewish religious leader would have anything to do with a tax collector. Zacchaeus is symbolic of thousands of people who know they need the Lord but seriously doubt if any help is available for them. They feel that they have gone too far and that even the Lord will not forgive them. Such people often defend themselves on the grounds that they are no worse than many church members. Or they hope that somehow they may have done enough good in their lives that God will extend to them some special concession.

    I recall a man who lived in the community where I grew up. He occasionally attended church, and he always spoke highly of church people. He was a gentleman in every sense. When talked about becoming a Christian, however, he always turned cold. Most people thought it was because in his younger days he had allegedly committed a murder, and he would rather go on unsaved than to run the risk of embarrassment by having this sin brought out in the open. Such people feel that they have somehow forfeited their right to be a Christian. They need to be shown, as Jesus showed Zacchaeus, that Jesus came to seek and to save the lost.

B. *Maybe Zacchaeus's seeking was merely curiosity, but down deep in his soul there was a subconscious desire to receive the blessings of Jesus.* He did not come openly seeking. Besides, because he was small in stature, he couldn't compete with the crowds in even getting a look at Jesus. He therefore ran ahead and climbed up a tree where he could at least get a glimpse of Jesus. Did Zacchaeus have a faint hope that this could be the beginning of a new life for himself?

C. *He demonstrated his aggressive drive.* The ambitious drive that made him a successful businessman, though dishonest, was evident as he overcame obstacles in getting to the place where he could see Jesus. He demonstrated more curiosity than pride in running ahead of the crowd and climbing a tree where the parade was to pass by. Perhaps he had little pride and self-respect left anyway. Thank God he had enough of a deep-seated and Holy Spirit–led conviction of his wrongdoings to go as far as he could.

III. Zacchaeus responded quickly and joyfully to Jesus's invitation.

I recall the closing of a revival meeting years ago. There was a man present for whom dozens had been praying all week. He was a very influential man in the community and was known to have misused his influence. I admit I had him in mind as I preached and extended the invitation. When he started moving from his position at the center of the pew, I thought I saw anger in his face. I felt some sense of guilt that maybe I had been overly anxious and had embarrassed him. He started up the aisle toward the door. Then suddenly he turned and came running down the aisle, laughter mingled with tears, as he joyfully surrendered to the Lord.

A. *Zacchaeus "made haste and came down."* He demonstrated good sense as well as excitement. Here was the offer of a lifetime. This religious leader was not scorning him, warning him, or even admonishing him for his despicable life. Jesus was extending his characteristic touch of friendship.

All religious workers should remember that we often have to make a friend before we can make a convert. With Jesus this is not mere strategy. Our Lord does love people. His heart reaches out for their loving response. Zacchaeus hurried to receive Jesus's invitation.

B. *He received Jesus joyfully.* A Jewish convert in an evangelistic service said to me when she came forward, "Is everybody this happy when he or she becomes a Christian?" While people tend to be fearful, reluctant, and defensive about receiving Jesus, once they take the first step, they are always joyful and excited.

IV. Zacchaeus demonstrated a changed life.

A. *Love for others.* He said, "Lord, the half of my goods I give to the poor." Money had been Zacchaeus's primary downfall. But now that he had committed his life to Jesus, he began to think about what he could do for others. When we receive Jesus into our life, we receive the love of Jesus into our life. Jesus not only loved his neighbor as himself but commanded his followers to do likewise. We find this impossible in our own nature, but when we receive Jesus into our lives, his love flows through us so that we can love our neighbors as Jesus loves them. This was immediately seen in Zacchaeus's commitment.

B. *Dishonesty and selfishness were replaced by integrity and benevolence.* Zacchaeus stood before the Lord and the people and said, "And if I have defrauded any one of anything, I restore it fourfold." This was more than was legally required. It was required only that he add one-fifth to what he had taken wrongfully, but he offered to restore fourfold, which was the legal requirement for a stolen sheep. He felt that he had been a thief and robber. He repented accordingly.

There is no evidence that Jesus had made any requirements in advance. Jesus does not deal legalistically with people, but offers them a new life with a new sense of values.

Conclusion

It is significant that we never seek Jesus as ardently as he seeks us. Jesus always meets us more than halfway. You may be the best person in the community or you may be so far away from the Lord you doubt that he would have any interest in you whatsoever. I assure you on the basis of every promise in God's Word that he will come into your life today if you will open your mind and heart to receive him.

SUNDAY EVENING, OCTOBER 7

Title: The Eagle Christian

Text: "But they that wait upon the LORD shall renew their strength; they shall mount up with wings as eagles; they shall run, and not be weary; they shall walk, and not faint" **(Isa. 40:31)**.

Scripture Reading: Isaiah 40:28–31; Psalm 103:5

Introduction

The eagle is the king of the birds. What the lion is to the animal world, the eagle is to the bird kingdom. No other bird compares with the eagle in superiority or power. The eagle is mentioned thirty-two times in Scripture. Isaiah said, "But they that wait on the LORD shall renew their strength; they shall mount up with wings as eagles" (Isa. 40:31). The prophet is saying that those who yield their life—who surrender their will to God—shall renew their strength. They shall mount up with wings as eagles. God promises that you and I can be eagle Christians.

What are some of the characteristics of the eagle's life?

I. Habits of the eagle.

A. *The eagle builds its nest in the clefts of the rock, in the crags of the mountains.* Job put it like this: "Doth the eagle mount up at thy command, and make her nest on high? She dwelleth and abideth on the rock, upon the crag of the rock, and the strong place" (Job 39:27–28). God promises to set us on the high places.

The psalmist spoke of "the rock that is higher than I" (Ps. 61:2). There is a rock in a high place that is a safe refuge for God's people. God has promised to put our feet on that rock—the rock of security, assurance, and safety.

B. *The second habit of the eagle is that of rising above the storms of life.* The eagle takes advantage of the wind to soar, to mount up high in the heavens. The eagle gets above the fog, the mist, and the clouds.

314

Every day dozens of people commit suicide in America. They leap out into utter darkness with a cry of hopelessness on their lips. They feel that life is a prison sentence. They lose sight of the stars. But if only they would surrender their lives fully to God, they could rise above the storms and find the peace of God that passes all understanding. David remembered this promise when life closed in for him. His home and hometown were burned to ashes. His family and families of his friends were made captives by roving bands of outlaws. But that was not all. His trials were even greater. His own men were blaming him for the catastrophe and were threatening to stone him to death.

What did David do? The Bible says, "David encouraged himself in the LORD" (1 Sam. 30:6), and his life was renewed like the eagle's. Brushing away his tears, he reorganized his men, went forth to battle, conquered his enemies, and was victorious over all. He remembered the wings God had given him and, like the eagle, rose above the storm.

C. *Think of what the eagle does about his enemies.* He simply soars up out of their reach. He puts himself between them and the sun. He flies straight into the sun, and there they lose sight of him. As we get nearer to God, Satan and our enemies cannot reach us. Satan cannot touch us if we will only direct our lives toward the Son of Righteousness, who comes to our aid with healing wings. "He that dwelleth in the secret place of the most High shall abide under the shadow of the Almighty" (Ps. 91:1).

D. *The fourth habit of the eagle is how she cares for her young.* The mates live together beside the nest and are devoted to one another. Their care for the young is a beautiful and touching picture. "As an eagle stirreth up her nest, fluttereth over her young, spreadeth abroad her wings, taketh them, beareth them on her wings" (Deut. 32:11). This verse pictures the mother eagle teaching the little one to fly. The mother eagle pushes the baby eaglet out of the nest on top of the cliff. As the little one flies downward, if the eaglet cannot fly, the mother eagle swoops down swiftly and spreads out her wings under the little one and bears it up on her wings lest its life be lost on the rocks below.

God too at times will try his people, but he does not put more on us than we are able to bear. In Exodus 19:4 the great Jehovah God speaks to the children of Israel. He recalls with them how he cared for them during the wilderness wandering. He says, "I bore you on eagles' wings" (RSV). What a beautiful and inspiring picture of God's care of his people as he led them through the wilderness. His care for them was like the mother eagle's care of her young. Sometimes they fainted along the road and sometimes they were hungry or thirsty, yet God was there to bear them up on his wings.

II. The heritage of the eagle.

A. *The eagle inherits a set of good eyes.* His eyes are very strong and can see long distances. As he flies to the heights, he looks out into the vast beyond and sees far into the distance.

God makes our lives like the eagle's life. He gives us visions of our days and our future and of the things of God. You and I can lift up our eyes to the everlasting hills and see a city foursquare and a King seated on his throne. God gives his people power to see life through his eyes. We can see sin as he sees it. We see goodness, love, and truth as he sees them. We see people as he sees people. We see our duty as he sees it. We see our opportunities and his will for our lives. Then, as we live for him and fulfill the destiny he has set for us, we can say with Paul, "Wherefore, O King Agrippa, I was not disobedient unto the heavenly vision" (Acts 26:19).

B. *The eagle inherits a longing to be free.* Eagles never flock. They select the tallest trees of the forest, the topmost crag of the mountains, and pairs live in solitude, hunting and feeding singly.

The eagle is an independent creature and does not want to be caged. He wants to be free. This is a parable of humanity's relationship with God. We long to be free. We were born to stand alone before our God. Let us never be afraid of solitude, but think of it as an opportunity to be with our Lord.

Although we are born to be free, this freedom can be lost. It can be bartered away for a mess of pottage. People can be enslaved by sin. One day a rancher saw a giant eagle swoop down in its flight and seize a snake from the plains. The eagle started to climb back to the heights. Again and again the eagle was bitten by the snake. The poison from the snake's fangs sank into the bloodstream of the eagle. The rancher watched the pitiful sight—the mighty eagle being bitten by the snake. Then he watched as the poison gradually took effect, and the mighty eagle began to go down, down until it fell lifeless to the earth. It is a parable of the life of man as he takes up sin, some evil habit, and learns the high cost of low living. The Bible says, "For the wages of sin is death" (Rom. 6:23).

C. *Further, the eagle inherits a substance on his beak that hinders him in his flight.* One day the eagle realizes he is hampered in flight by this substance. He goes to a rock and hits his beak again and again on the rock until the substance begins to flow from his beak and he is freed from it.

Likewise, by nature we humans have something within us that hinders us from soaring to the heights, from taking flights into the spiritual stratosphere. But one day we can go to the Rock of Ages and have our lives freed from the sin that hinders.

Is your load of sin hindering your life? Are you burdened down by its weight? Remember that you were made for the heights—you

316

were made for God—and you will never find satisfaction or peace until your life is yielded to him.

D. *The eagle inherits long life.* The eagle is known to live about 120 years, even in captivity. Each year the eagle sheds some of its feathers and has the appearance of youth. Naturalists say that when the eagle is one hundred years old, he sheds all of his feathers and fresh ones come so that he looks completely young again.

God, in like manner, promises to renew our youth like the eagle's. By his Spirit and power, God restores and revives our lives and returns us to the days of our youth. As Paul said, "The inward man is renewed day by day" (2 Cor. 4:16). For the Christian, then, there is not only perpetual youth, but there is immortality. We shall live forever. Victor Hugo expressed this belief when he said, "Winter may be upon my head, but the eternal springtime is in my heart."

Conclusion

Let us as the people of God wait upon the Lord—that is, yield ourselves fully to him—that our lives may be renewed like the eagle's.

WEDNESDAY EVENING, OCTOBER 10

Title: One Conquering Fear

Text: "And he said unto her, Daughter, thy faith hath made thee whole; go in peace, and be whole of thy plague" **(Mark 5:34)**.

Scripture Reading: Mark 5

Introduction

A major role of the servant in the Grecian world was to care for the children of the master. The passage of Scripture under consideration portrays Jesus as the Servant of God given over to the task of conquering fear in the lives of believers.

Jesus and his followers were on a mission that took them through the country of the Gadarenes, then to Decapolis, and back across the Sea of Galilee (Mark 5:1, 20–21). They were confronted with the awesome fear of demon possession, physical death, and an incurable illness. If Christ could conquer fear in these areas, he could be victorious in any endeavor. And conquer fear he did!

I. The fear of the demoniac (Mark 5:2–20).

A. *Fear involved.* Fear soared in four directions in the experience with the Gadarene demoniac. First, other people feared the one possessed by demons. They sought to chain him for their own protection (Mark 5:3–4). He was beyond human help. No men could "tame him." Second, the man feared himself. He was continually hurting himself (v. 5). This is a perfect analogy of what sin causes. Third, the demons feared Jesus Christ (v. 7). They were afraid Jesus was going to torment them. Fourth, after Jesus sent the demons into the pigs, the people in the surrounding area were afraid of his power (v. 17). Perhaps they feared that the loss of their herd was God's judgment and that he would do more.

B. *Forces involved.* Two powers were involved—the force of evil in Legion (Mark 5:12) and the might of righteousness found in Jesus Christ.

C. *Fierceness involved.* Jesus caused the demons to leave the victim and go into a herd of swine. They were destroyed when they ran down the steep hillside and into the water and drowned. When the news of this reached the local town, a group (probably owners of the swine) begged Jesus to leave the area (Mark 5:17).

D. *Faith involved.* The cured man was so overwhelmed with thanksgiving that he wanted to forsake all to follow Jesus. Jesus felt the man would be more effective as a witness in his own hometown.

II. The fear of the ruler (Mark 5:21–24, 35–43).

A. *Fear involved.* Jesus encountered one of the rulers of the synagogue who had a very sick child. This father pleaded with Jesus, saying his daughter was dying. His fear became a reality when he received news of the child's death.

B. *Force involved.* All the power of physical death stalked this scene. This same ominous force haunts humankind today. But the might of Jesus Christ was also present.

C. *Faith involved.* When the heartbroken father received the news of his daughter's death, there was the temptation to give up hope. Jesus sought to banish his fear and instill faith in his soul. Only a word from the Christ could comfort a broken heart in this situation.

D. *Freedom involved.* Jesus immediately rebuked the professional mourners at the home of Jairus. He then freed the child from the clutches of death and commanded that she be fed.

III. The fear of the woman (Mark 5:25–34).

A. *Fears involved.* A woman who was hopelessly ill, not helped by doctors, reached out to just touch Jesus's cloak in the press of the crowd. Trembling with fear, she fell at his feet when he asked who had touched his clothes.

B. *Faith involved.* The text declares that when the woman "heard of Jesus, [she] came in the press behind, and touched his garments." Her faith rested totally in what she had heard other people say about him. Her faith led her to touch his cloak.

C. *Forces involved.* When the woman touched Jesus's clothes, he felt the force of his power leave him (Mark 5:30), and she was healed. Jesus's holiness contained a power within itself. The overwhelming mercy (v. 34) of the Lord sent the woman away in peace, healed of her plague.

Conclusion

Faith in the person of Jesus Christ relieves one of fear and extends peace to take its place.

SUNDAY MORNING, OCTOBER 14

Title: Nicodemus

Text: "Jesus answered him, 'Truly, truly, I say to you, unless one is born anew, he cannot see the kingdom of God'" **(John 3:3 RSV)**.

Scripture Reading: John 3:1–15; 7:50; 19:39

Hymns: "Come, Thou Almighty King," Anonymous
"Jesus Saves," Owens
"Ye Must Be Born Again," Sleeper

Offertory Prayer: Father, we thank you for listening to our prayer and praise. We thank you for receiving our gifts, which we need to bring more than you need them to use. Help us to give generously because our gifts are expressions of love. In Jesus's name we pray. Amen.

Introduction

Many years ago I was the evangelist in a church in Memphis, Tennessee. The pastor and I went to talk to a family about the Lord. No one answered the door. A woman in the adjoining apartment came to explain that they were away. The pastor introduced us as being from a nearby church. The lady smiled graciously and said she knew about the church. The pastor invited her to services.

Again the nice woman smiled, thanked us, and explained that she would like to attend services sometime but that she was Jewish. The pastor assured her that she was welcome. She said her deceased father, a rabbi, would turn over in his grave.

The following day the pastor and I went back to see the family we had missed. Again they were away. And again the Jewish woman came to the door. "I'm sorry you missed my neighbors again. It is so nice of you to be trying to see them. If I were not Jewish, I think I would go to your church." She went on to explain that her widowed mother was teaching Hebrew in a local synagogue and would probably lose her job if she, the daughter, attended a Christian church.

By now the pastor and I detected her interest in becoming a Christian. We witnessed to her faithfully and respectfully. The next day when we rang the doorbell next door, we hoped that they would not be at home. Sure enough, they didn't answer the door, but the Jewish woman did. She demonstrated real conviction and concern as we explained how any person, regardless of religious and racial background, could and should become a Christian. With tears she thanked us as she explained that she "just could never become a Christian."

On Sunday morning I recognized her in the evangelistic service. I preached on the death of Jesus and emphasized the question of Pilate, "Then what shall I do with Jesus who is called Christ?"

The young Jewish lady responded to the invitation, came down the aisle, shook hands with the pastor, and didn't stop until she was on the platform shaking hands with me. Her laughter was mixed with tears as she asked, "Is everybody this happy when he or she becomes a Christian?" She had apparently forgotten the difficulties.

It is difficult for any of us to leave the religion of our parents and become a Christian. Judaism is closer to Christianity than any other religion, and yet it is still not easy for a person born and reared a Jew to become a Christian. Three questions come to mind.

I. Is It Necessary?

We constantly hear people say or imply, "It doesn't make any difference what your religion is just so you believe." Well, the Bible never says that. And you don't use that logic about anything else. What about, "It doesn't matter what medicine you take just as long as you are sincere"? They also say, "We are all headed for the same place. We are just taking different roads." It is not only false today that all roads lead to Rome, but you can even go in the wrong direction on the right road.

If any person in the world could be in God's kingdom without being a Christian, Nicodemus could.

A. *He was a good man.* No one ever raised the question about his altruistic spirit, his morality, or his honesty. In fact, he was criticized by some as being super-pious and displaying an attitude of being too good to associate with common people.

B. *He was a religious man.* He never missed a synagogue service, and he participated actively in all worship activities. If they had had a Sunday school, he would have been the director or the teacher of the largest adult class. He memorized large portions of Scripture and spent long hours in the study of them. The truth is that probably no one in Jerusalem knew more about the Bible than Nicodemus. He believed in the immortality of the soul, the resurrection of the body, and the existence of angels and spirits.

C. *He was a judge in the civil court and even sat on some criminal cases.* Without any doubt, Nicodemus was one of the most respected men in Jerusalem. He was respected by the Roman government as well as his own people, the Jews.

If a man in this community met all of the aforementioned qualifications, would he be on the prospect list for Tuesday night visitation? There might be a little rivalry between churches about who would "reach him" if he moved into the community, or there might even be some efforts at "sheep stealing." Not a soul would be trying to "win him to the Lord," however.

How do we know all these things about Nicodemus? The three passages of Scripture we read at the outset tell us this about him. He was a member of the Pharisees and a ruler of the Jews, and he sat on the court of the Sanhedrin. All of these characteristics are required to fill these roles.

Yet when the record says that Jesus told someone of the necessity of a spiritual rebirth to become a member of God's kingdom, it was to this good man Nicodemus. He needed a complete conversion, a new birth. But how?

II. Is it possible?

If the new birth is necessary, it is possible. With humans it is impossible, but with God all things are possible. "But to all who received him, who believed in his name, he gave power to become children of God; who were born, not of blood nor of the will of the flesh nor of the will of man, but of God" (John 1:12–13 RSV).

An Indian who had faithfully followed the Hindu religion for fifty years said at the close of an evangelistic service, "Just think! I am an old man, yet I have just been born." It has been my privilege to see Hindus, Buddhists, Roman Catholics, and Baptists be born again. Every person present in this service who is a Christian has been born again. And any rational, accountable person here who desires the new life in Christ can be born again before you leave this service.

III. Is it understandable?

Nicodemus said, "I don't understand this. How can a man be born when he is old?"

Jesus virtually said to him, "You don't really have to understand, Nicodemus. You are a brilliant man. You are well trained and there are many things you do know, but there are some things you do not understand. You feel the gentle breeze of the evening and hear the rustling of the leaves as the wind passes through them, but you do not understand the wind."

What Jesus said to Nicodemus about the wind is even more interesting when we know that the same word in the Greek language is used for wind, breath, and spirit. Jesus was saying that you do not have to understand the wind that blows or the breath that is necessary for life. You can benefit by them without understanding them. He was saying that just as you receive these as wonderful and necessary gifts from God, you accept the spiritual birth on the basis of faith.

I have seen people come to experience the new birth the first time they heard about it. It is like the medication you take when you are sick or the surgery the physician performs; you do not have to understand it to benefit by it. You do have to put your life in the hands of the doctor. In this case, when you put your life in the hands of the Lord, he performs the new birth within you.

Conclusion

The Hebrew people did not understand how the fiery serpent could cure a snake bite, but Jesus said, "As Moses lifted up the serpent in the wilderness, so must the Son of man be lifted up, that whoever believes in him may have eternal life" (John 3:14–15 RSV).

SUNDAY EVENING, OCTOBER 14

Title: Look unto the Hills

Text: "I will lift up mine eyes unto the hills, from whence cometh my help. My help cometh from the LORD, which made heaven and earth" **(Ps. 121:1–2)**.

Scripture Reading: Psalm 121:1–8

Introduction

God is a God of the mountains. His footprints can be traced from mountain peak to mountain peak through the Bible. In fact, there are 467 references to mountains in the Scriptures. Early Israel thought of the mountains as the dwelling place of God.

A beautiful legend tells about the creation of the mountains. Once, long ago, the earth was flat or gently rolling plains. There were beautiful flowers; rich, luxuriant grasses; groves of tall, leafy trees; and peaceful lakes mirroring the fleecy clouds and blue sky. God looked down, and everything was so beautiful and his heart was filled with so much love that he wanted to embrace the whole world. He must have thought, "Oh, world, I cannot hold you close enough!" With infinite tenderness, forgetting his great power, he stroked the earth, caressing it with his mighty fingers. The force of his touch dredged out the valleys and piled the mountains high, stretching them out for miles along the earth. He looked again, saw what he had done, and it was good.

The mountains do declare the glory of God, and every rock, tree, and spring shows his handiwork. No wonder the psalmist wrote, "I will lift up mine eyes unto the hills, from whence cometh my help. My help cometh from the LORD, which made heaven and earth."

I. As we look to the hills, they seem to say, "Life is ascent."

A. *The road to life is upward.* There is no downhill road to living. My grandfather was eighty-six years old when he died. I loved to visit him and listen to him quote Bible verses. He was aged, wrinkled, and gray, and he became very feeble, but he always had a sparkle of humor about him. He would say with eyes twinkling, "I'm on the downhill road and can't reach the brake." I knew that he was speaking figuratively about his physical being when he said that, but I have since seen the tragedy of that statement in people's spiritual lives. Many people seem to be on that downhill road and cannot reach the brake. They are not able to resist the downward pull of life and its temptations.

B. *God says to us, "If ye then be risen with Christ, seek those things which are above, where Christ sitteth on the right hand of God. Set your affections on things above, not on things of the earth"* (Col. 3:1–2). Paul gave us his personal testimony, saying, "I count not myself to have apprehended: but this one thing I do . . . I press toward the mark for the prize of the high calling of God in Christ Jesus" (Phil 3:13–14). The life and character of Christ challenge us: "Be ye therefore perfect, even as your Father in heaven is perfect" (Matt. 5:48).

Though we may never be able to attain perfection, humanly speaking, we are challenged to keep climbing. The heights appeal to the daring, heroic, adventurous nature of people. Christian living captivates the courageous.

C. *When Captain George Mallory, who later lost his life trying to scale Mount Everest, spoke at Harvard, he said, "Someone is bound to ask me why I wish to climb to the top of Everest. My answer is, 'Because it is there.'"* Doesn't the life of Christ beckon you? Doesn't it challenge you to keep reaching heavenward? It is said that the higher mountain climbers climb, the higher they want to climb. The higher you climb in Christ, the higher you want to climb.

In the Valley of Arve in Switzerland stands the statue of Horace Savesure, who pioneered the trail up Mount Blanc. His body is thrust forward, his hand extended toward the mountain. The inscription reads, "This is the way." Christ, the pioneer in living, stands in the valley beckoning all humankind, pointing upward, saying, "I am the way, and the truth, and the life" (John 14:6).

II. Look unto the hills, for the atmosphere is so invigorating.

A. *Who has not stood on Mount Mitchell, Clingman's Dome, Pike's Peak, Roan Mountain, or some other tall peak and felt the refreshing breeze, smelled the clean air, eyed the enchanting scenery, and felt like saying with Simon Peter, "Lord, it is good for us to be here" (Matt. 17:4)?* Life on the heights is uplifting and strengthening to the soul. It brings a lift to the spirit. It heightens the vision. It empowers the will.

B. *Paul wrote to the Ephesians, "[God] hath raised us up together, and made us sit together in heavenly places in Christ Jesus" (Eph. 2:6).* I have been on some mountain peaks with Jesus. I have stood on some high places spiritually—places of joy, service, and worship.

At Ridgecrest, North Carolina, I went one morning on a hike up Mount Kitazuma to greet the sunrise. As I neared the summit, I heard the singing voices of those who had arrived first: "There's a land that is fairer than day, and by faith we can see it afar." I stood there and looked across the broad expanse of the heavens, high enough that morning that I felt I could almost take the Lord's hand. Tears welled up in my eyes and an inspiration that will live forever came to my heart. I was not only on a mountain peak physically, but emotionally and spiritually as well. Life is so invigorating on the heights with Christ! Life is flat and stale on the low levels of sensual living. Live on the heights.

C. *One man advised another, "Live above the snake line."* There is a level on every mountain that marks the place above which snakes cannot live. Live above the snake line, above the cheap pettiness of the world, above the bitter jealousies and seething resentments, and above the burning prejudices and brooding hatreds. If you live on the heights with Christ, you can face the temptations and evils of the world about you and be victorious.

III. Look unto the hills to get the proper perspective.

A. *On the heights we get God's viewpoint.* Study the life of Jesus and you will see that time after time he withdrew to the mountains to pray, then returned with power to serve in the valleys. This same rhythm characterized the life of Elijah. A voice told him to "hide thyself" (1 Kings 17:3). Later the voice told him to "shew thyself" (18:1). We must hide ourselves away, taking time for prayer and meditation, and then come forth to show ourselves strong on behalf of the cause of Christ.

B. *A psychologist advised a woman who had trouble with stress and emotional difficulties to go away and see something big.* Distance lends enchantment to the view. Our fears, problems, and troubles seem so small from the distance. A missionary in the Balkans once took a small boy who lived at the base of the mountain on a journey up its side. When they gained the summit, the little climber looked this way and that and said with astonishment, "My, what a wonderful world. I never dreamed it was so big!" On the heights our horizons are broadened, our imaginations are kindled, and our vision of God is greatened.

IV. Look unto the many different hills of God.

A. *Mount Calvary.* It is the place where Jesus died for our sins. Look in faith to Calvary's cross and experience God's forgiving grace and saving power.

B. *Mount Sinai.* This is the mountain of a well-disciplined life. It is the place where God calls us to keep his commandments. The Bible says, "Blessed are they that keep my ways" (Prov. 8:32). Will you climb the mountain of obedience? It leads to happiness.

C. *Mount Hermon.* This is the Mount of Transfiguration where Jesus was transfigured before his disciples and they saw him as the divine Son of God. They heard Moses and Elijah talking with him and knew that he had direct communion with heaven. They heard the voice of God saying, "This is my beloved Son . . . hear ye him" (Matt. 17:5).

D. *Mount Olivet, the mount of the ascending life.* It is the place where Jesus ascended to heaven and his disciples looked up desiring to follow him. As we lift our eyes heavenward and strive to be with him and to be like him, we can live that ascending life.

Conclusion

A father bought his son some parallel bars for Christmas. Out in his backyard every day, the little fellow would reach up and try to take hold of the bars. One day a neighbor asked him what he was doing. He replied, "I am reaching up, trying to take hold of the bars. My father says if I keep reaching, one day I will be able to take hold of them."

Keep your eyes on the hills of God and keep reaching upward.

WEDNESDAY EVENING, OCTOBER 17

Title: One Provoking Recognition

Text: "And when the sabbath day was come, he began to teach in the synagogue: and many hearing him were astonished, saying, From whence hath this man these things? and what wisdom is this which is given unto him, that even such mighty works are wrought by his hands?" **(Mark 6:2)**.

Scripture Reading: Mark 6

Introduction

Jesus had a reputation among the people as being a humble carpenter. This profession placed him in the serving class of society. Yet his ministry was so revealing of his inner character that the populace was provoked into asking, "From whence hath this man these things? and what wisdom is this which is given unto him, that even such mighty works are wrought by his hands? Is not this the carpenter?" In this sixth chapter, Mark gives a narration that takes Jesus from the position of the unknown (v. 3) to that of the known (v. 54). He is recognized from five sources.

I. Recognition from his kin (Mark 6:1–6).

A. *He taught truth.* When Jesus arrived in his "own country," he taught the same basic truth he had shared in other locations.

B. *They remembered when.* The local people could only remember Jesus when he was the local carpenter. They could not make an immediate mental transition.

C. *He could do no great work.* Because of the limited ability of his own kin and friends to accept him, he was limited in his work in their midst.

D. *He was saddened.* Though the villagers recognized his works and heard his teaching, they refused to give him the honor due his prophetic role. He left this locale saddened because of their unbelief.

II. Recognition from the Twelve (Mark 6:7–13).

A. *He called them.* It was an act built on inner confidence that caused Jesus to call the Twelve. It was an act built on inner faith that caused the Twelve to respond.

B. *He gave power.* Jesus backed his challenge to the disciples by sharing his inner power with them. They found that his instructions and guidance outfitted them for the task.

C. *They were successful.* This small band of men discovered a new way of victory and power. They were victorious because of their association with Jesus Christ.

III. Recognition from Herod (Mark 6:14–29).

A. *Political authority rested with Herod.* Any threat to his rule would come to his attention. He took note of Jesus.

B. *Herod was confused.* Being plagued by a guilty conscience on one side and a jealous concern on the other, Herod confused the ministry of Jesus with that of John the Baptist.

C. *Herod was haunted.* Something Herod recognized in the life and ministry of Jesus reminded him of John and made him afraid.

IV. Recognition from the sheep (Mark 6:30–44).

A. *People meandering about.* The scene moves from the bustle of Herod's halls to the lazy wandering of people in the meadows. Jesus was concerned with those who were as "sheep not having a shepherd."

B. *He met immediate needs.* Jesus took the role of the Servant and fed the multitudes where they were.

C. *He met future needs.* The miracle of Christ did not only meet the present needs, but it took care of the future. Twelve baskets were filled with the leftovers. This was enough for everyone to have lunch on the return trip home.

V. Recognition from the troubled (Mark 6:45–54).

A. *Disciples in trouble.* The disciples were caught in a storm as they tried to row across a large lake.

B. *Jesus walked on water.* The Lord went to the aid of his followers. The sight of their leader walking on water caused grave concern among the disciples.

C. *Jesus identified himself.* In an attempt to calm their fears, Jesus immediately identified himself. He then came into the boat and caused the winds to cease.

Conclusion

When Jesus and the disciples got off the boat, the people recognized Jesus. "They knew him" (Mark 6:54). This was more than a simple awareness of Jesus's name. They had come to recognize Jesus as the true protector of humankind.

SUNDAY MORNING, OCTOBER 21

Title: A Conversion in a Ghetto

Text: "Every one who drinks of this water will thirst again, but whoever drinks of the water that I shall give him will never thirst; the water that I shall give him will become in him a spring of water welling up to eternal life" **(John 4:13 RSV)**.

Scripture Reading: John 4:7–26

Hymns: "Glorious Is Thy Name," McKinney
"The Great Physician," Hunter
"I Am Praying for You," Clough

Offertory Prayer: Lord, help us to allow your compassion to fill our lives that we may see people in need as you see them. We thank you now for an opportunity to express our concern as we bring our tithes and offerings. In Jesus's name. Amen.

Introduction

Do you know of population pockets where little or no evangelism is done? These pockets exist in all kinds of communities. A man who lives in a town of about one thousand told me about members of his church spending a Saturday visiting house to house in a community less than five miles from their church building. They found people who had never been to church and many who had never been witnessed to.

We are familiar with ghettos in large cities. People there are isolated economically, socially, educationally, culturally, racially, and often even religiously. But ghettos are not the only place where there are individuals who have never had an evangelistic witness. Every community has economic, social, educational, cultural, racial, and even religious barriers that intimidate Christians and keep them from sharing the gospel. This should not be. Superficial barriers never hindered Jesus.

In Jesus's day there was a region in the hill country of Palestine between

Judea and Galilee known as Samaria. It was completely isolated religiously. In 722 BC the conquest of the northern kingdom of Syria resulted in inter-marriage between some Israelites and foreigners. Pagan religious infiltration added to an already intolerable racial mixture, resulting in a social and religious island.

As the curtain rises on the fourth chapter of John, Jesus is in Jerusalem. He wanted to go to Galilee. The usual Jewish road map would have led him and his party across the Jordan River and up on the east side to avoid Samaria. However, the priorities of Jesus were not determined by prejudice. Therefore, John says, "He had to pass through Samaria."

Passing through Samaria, Jesus and his disciples came to the city of Sychar. Sitting by historic Jacob's well to rest while his friends went into the city to get food, Jesus had a visitor, a Samaritan woman who came to the well for water. Jesus offered the woman more than well water; he gave her the "spring of water welling up to eternal life."

The dialogue that followed presents two messages for our consideration.

I. A message to Christians.

A. *Every Christian to whom I speak is represented by the woman.* Had the door not been opened to foreigners, I, an Anglo-white, could never have been a child of God. The gospel did not begin with my kind of people. The same is true for most of you.

   A Jewish convert said, "If a Gentile Christian woman had not been to me the witness the Jewish Jesus was to the Samaritan woman, I could never have been a Christian."

B. *We are witnesses to all kinds of people.* I didn't say we *ought* to be. Jesus said, 'You are witnesses" (Luke 24:48).

   Have you ever seen a court trial? Have you ever heard a witness testify? Can one be a bad witness as well as a good witness? We are witnesses every day of our lives, at work, school, play, or in our social contacts.

   One Tuesday night my wife and I went to church visitation. Being an itinerant evangelist, we are not home for much of this. On this night I asked for the names of people who were not known to be professing Christians. We received a name on a street in our neighborhood. I was a little puzzled because I thought I knew who lived at this familiar address and this name was unfamiliar. We went anyway. The lady we thought lived there came to the door. She explained that the name we had was an African American yardman who lived in a house in the backyard. She called him on the intercom, and we met in the backyard between the two houses.

   I have no idea what he thought as he came out to meet me. It was easy to see his surprise when he learned that I had come to talk with him about becoming a Christian. After his conversion, we learned that his employer and several of her friends had been praying for him for weeks.

C. *We are witnesses to all the world.* Billions of people in the world need the Lord. If they are ever to receive him, we must share him. "And there is salvation in no one else, for there is no other name under heaven given among men by which we must be saved" (Acts 4:12).

On the day of his resurrection, Jesus said, "As the Father has sent me, even so I send you" (John 20:21). How do we obey this command? What are the logistics? You say, "I want to do what Jesus commands. I want to help the people of the world hear about Jesus, but I can't go to some foreign country, much less the entire world."

Don't rule that out. Many people who never thought they would—have. I am one of them. Recently, when I was on a mission tour, a farmer in our group said, "I can't believe I am here in a foreign country, much less on a Christian mission." Also, most denominations have some cooperative plan of missionary support for those who feel called of God to serve in distant places. They would be disobedient to their heavenly vision if they did not go. The churches will be derelict unless they support them.

I have no doubt that when you get to heaven someone from some faraway land will approach you on a golden street and thank you for sending the gospel to him or her through some missionary. That will be an added joy to one you felt when you gave your tithe last Sunday.

II. A message inviting you to become a Christian.

A. *The Samaritan woman knew she needed help.* She was an extremely unhappy woman. She had already had five unsuccessful marriages, and no marriage has ever been broken without unhappiness. She was now living with a man outside of marriage. Much unhappiness is read between the lines in this story. Jesus loved this woman though he had never previously seen her and, to her surprise, was able to help her.

B. *The Samaritan woman did not expect help.* She had some religious background. She knew about Jacob and considered him her religious father. She knew about the temple that had been built by Herod on Mount Gerizim for the Samaritans, and she referred to "this mountain" as a place of worship. She knew the Jews worshiped in Jerusalem (v. 21), and she knew about the promised Messiah (v. 25).

Her attitude clearly revealed her resignation to her plight. She never expected help, and certainly never from a Jewish religious leader. It was a part of their religious practice to stone people like her. Unfortunately, many hurting people feel that churches only throw stones at those like themselves. I would like to convince you that Jesus loves you and can help you.

C. *The Samaritan woman received the highest spiritual blessings available to anyone in the world.* She became a true worshiper when by faith she received Jesus.

Whatever your situation in life, Jesus desires to give you assurance of eternal life, forgiveness of sin, and, yes, a complete new life. If he can't do that, he is not the Son of God and cannot keep his promises. How far away he seems has nothing to do with it. Whatever the nature of your sins has nothing to do with it. "Though your sins are like scarlet, they shall be as white as snow; though they are red like crimson, they shall be like wool" (Isa. 1:18 RSV).

Your life may be entirely different from that of the Samaritan woman. Your sins may be entirely different. Society may condone your sins of selfishness, pride, arrogance, impatience, unkindness, and unforgiveness, but these sins are as much in need of forgiveness as her sin of adultery. Jesus is as willing to forgive you, and you need it as much.

Your thirst will never be satisfied any other way. You may drink from the wells of the world and you may receive superficial quenching, but remember God's Word through Jeremiah: "For my people have committed two evils; they have forsaken me, the fountain of living waters, and hewed out cisterns for themselves, broken cisterns, that can hold no water" (Jer. 2:13).

Conclusion

Jesus's arms of welcome are extended to you. Will you right now turn your eyes upon Jesus? His eyes are right now turned on you. If you will receive him, he will become yours and you his. "But to all who received him, who believed in his name, he gave power to become children of God" (John 1:12).

SUNDAY EVENING, OCTOBER 21

Title: Consider the Lilies

Text: "Consider the lilies of the field, how they grow; they toil not, neither do they spin: And yet I say unto you, That even Solomon in all his glory was not arrayed like one of these" **(Matt. 6:28–29).**

Scripture Reading: Matthew 6:25–34

Introduction

There was a grand simplicity about the life of Christ. He lived close to nature and loved it. I grew up on a Texas dairy farm where I fed chickens, milked cows, and baled hay. When spring or fall comes, I am thankful that Jesus Christ lived in the country. He found his parables in the clustering of the vine, the springing of the corn, the rocking of boats on the lake, and the rising and setting of the sun. He found them in the birds that flew overhead, the sheep in the pastures, the fig trees in the grove, and the fowl in the farmyard.

So much of his teaching was in the imagery of pastoral life. I fear that those who live in cities may miss that sense of the presence of God that people who live close to nature know.

I. Consider the God of the lily.

A. *Nature does reveal God.* The psalmist said, "The heavens declare the glory of God; and the firmament sheweth his handiwork" (Ps. 19:1). Who has not gazed at the starry heavens or looked upon a golden sunset and felt near to God? The order, beauty, perfection, and intelligence we see in nature remind us of God. God speaks in the regularity of the seasons; the movements of the sun, moon, and stars; the cycles of night and day; and in the balance between humankind's consumption of life-giving oxygen and its production by plant life.

No wonder the apostle Paul said, "For since the creation of the world God's invisible qualities—his eternal power and divine nature—have been clearly seen, being understood from what has been made, so that people are without excuse" (Rom. 1:20 NIV).

B. *Our generation is fast becoming an urban society.* Seventy percent of people now live in cities. The symbolism of the lilies, sparrows, grasses, and vines may not be as relevant to urban people.

C. *Whether we live in the country or in the city, we must live by faith.* Contrast Paul and Christ. Paul was not at home in the country. It was the city that appealed to Paul. He thrived on its problems, its pageantry, its bustle, and its crowds. But God was no less real to him. The kingdom of heaven was not like a seed to Paul. The kingdom of heaven was like some noble building. When he illustrated things of grace, he did not turn to the vine or the lily. He turned to the soldier polishing his armor, to the gladiator fighting before ten thousand eyes, to the freeborn citizen whose civic charter had been won in the senate of imperial Rome. Our God is the Lord of all. He is the God not only of the lily but also of the city; not only of the shepherd but also of the astronaut; not only of the Stone Age but also of the Space Age. Through faith God is real wherever we live.

II. Consider the growth of the lily.

Jesus said, "Consider the lilies of the field, how they grow; they toil not, neither do they spin" (Matt. 6:28).

A. *What is he saying?* He is not saying that the way to grow beautiful, stately, and strong is to be free from all toil and work and tension in life. He is not patting us on the back and saying, "Don't worry. Everything will come out all right." He is not saying that God will step in to correct all our follies and omissions. He is not promising a trouble-free road. He is not saying to those who trust God that they will never be injured or persecuted. He is not saying that the lilies and the grasses will live happily ever after.

B. *Look at the words: "Consider the lilies of the field."* The lilies grow in the valley. Here is a parable of life. We too must grow in the valleys of life. Whether we live in the country or in the city, we have problems, sorrows, troubles, pains, and frustrations.

C. *What is God trying to say to us here?* He is saying, "Do not be anxious about life." The word *anxious* means "to choke." If you choke, the food won't go up or down. How many of us live all choked up by the problems of our daily existence? Five different times in this passage Jesus tells us not to be anxious. Since God provides for the birds and the flowers and the grass, he will take care of his children, for they are made in his image. Through a life of faith, we can link our feebleness with his strength, our temporariness with his eternity, our emptiness with his fullness, our lack of direction with his purpose.

We must learn how to grow in the midst of tension. The secret of this growth is found in Christ. The great apostle Paul knew it:

In labours more abundant, in stripes above measure, in prisons more frequent, in deaths oft. . . . Thrice was I beaten with rods, once was I stoned, thrice I suffered shipwreck, a night and a day I have been in the deep; in journeyings often, in perils of waters, in perils of robbers, in perils of mine own countrymen, in perils by the heathen, in perils in the city, in perils in the wilderness, in perils in the sea, in perils among false brethren; in weariness and painfulness, in watchings often, in hunger and thirst, in fastings often, in cold and nakedness. (2 Cor. 11:23, 25–27)

Yet he knew the strength of God's grace. People grow in the valleys facing hardships and trials.

III. Consider the glory of the lily.

A. *The lily is beautiful.* Few flowers can compare with it in beauty. But the glory of the lily is not in its beauty alone. The glory of the lily is in its immortality. Solomon in all his glory passed away, but the lily blooms again each spring. Such is the glory of the Christian life, for God's people will live forever.

B. *Whether we live in the city or the country, death is still a reality.* You may say that our generation does not care about golden streets and pearly gates. We are not so much afraid of the fires of an eternal judgment. But I say Christ not only offers abundant life here and now, not only is the Christ life the best life and the happiest life, not only does Christ give us a worthy purpose while we are on the earth, but there is more. Paul declares that "Christ . . . hath abolished death, and hath brought life and immortality to light through the gospel" (2 Tim. 1:10).

My mother and I recently visited the little cemetery where my father and brother are buried in Cresson, Texas. We stood by the grave of my brother, who died at the age of eighteen just as he was entering manhood, and by the grave of my father, who died at the peak of his manhood. I had mixed emotions as I stood there. It is difficult to understand the mysteries of life and death. I was reminded of the beautiful scene from Ivan Turgenev's great book *Fathers and Sons,* which describes a village graveyard in one of the remote comers of Russia. Among the many neglected graves was one untouched by man, untrampled by beasts. Only the birds rested on it and sang at daybreak. Often from the nearby village two feeble old people, husband and wife, moving with heavy steps and supporting one another, came and visited this grave. Kneeling down at the railing and gazing intently at the stone under which their son was lying, they yearned and wept. After a brief word they wiped the dust away from the stone, set straight a branch of the fir tree, and then began to pray. In this spot they seemed to be nearer their son and their memories of him. Then Turgenev asks, "Can it be that their prayers, their tears, are fruitless? Can it be that love, sacred, devoted love is not all powerful?" The flowers growing over the grave peep serenely with their innocent eyes. They tell not only of eternal peace, of that great peace of indifferent nature, but also of eternal reconciliation. But upon what is that hope based? It is based on the resurrection of Jesus Christ.

Conclusion

The glory of the Christian life is the glory of immortality. We will live forever, and one day all the injustice and inequality and the mystery of life shall fade away and we shall understand the meaning of it all through Jesus Christ.

WEDNESDAY EVENING, OCTOBER 24

Title: One Defining Defilement

Text: "He answered and said unto them, Well hath Esaias prophesied of you hypocrites, as it is written, This people honoureth me with their lips, but their heart is far from me" (**Mark 7:6**).

Scripture Reading: Mark 7

Introduction

As beauty is in the eye of the beholder, so Satan attempts to make sin a relative matter. "Evil is a matter of interpretation by the persons involved," he says. In the passage under consideration, the critics of Jesus accused him and his followers of being guilty of sin (Mark 7:2). The major issue of right and wrong is faced. Sin (and/or defilement) is not left up to any individual interpretation. Our Lord proceeded to define defilement, thus settling the issue for his followers.

I. Defilement is from the heart (Mark 7:3–6).

A. *Concerned about unwashed hands.* The Pharisees and scribes exposed a shallow concern about defilement. They observed only the particulars of hand washing. They obviously were nit-picking about the behavior of the Lord's disciples.

B. *Concerned about tradition of elders.* There was an undue concern about certain traditions established within the Pharisees' ranks. They were attempting to force human rituals on God's righteousness.

C. *Jesus charged hypocrisy.* Jesus was very direct in charging the critics with hypocrisy. A hypocrite is someone who pretends to be something he or she is not. These men were not really interested in preserving righteousness.

D. *Heart is not "near him."* Jesus struck at the heart of the issue by declaring that "their hearts were far from him." No moral standard may be substituted for a "heart experience" with Christ. When we love Jesus Christ and his teachings, we will develop the proper Christian ethic.

II. Defilement perverts doctrines (Mark 7:7–13).

A. *Worship in vain.* It does matter what one believes. By substituting biblical truths with the tradition of men, these hypocrites were unable to have a valid worship experience. Their outward acts of devotion were vanity.

B. *Reject commandments of God.* Jesus pointed out an additional danger involved when one substitutes error for truth. The Pharisees were in reality rejecting the way God had taught. It was not a "both/and" situation. It is an "either/or" circumstance. If we choose man's traditions, we reject God's commandments.

C. *Make Word of God ineffective.* The thoughts of Christ followed the rebellious actions of the critics to another step. If the commandments of God are rejected, God's Word is made ineffective in the lives of the rejectors. This is tragic. The source of help is God and his Word. People condemn themselves when they deny the Word of God free access to their souls.

D. *Foundation corroded.* Jesus used an illustration from the life of the family to show what would happen if a man let his foundation corrode. But the application of the Word of God could reestablish the family.

III. Defilement comes from within (Mark 7:14–23).

A. *Defilement is not from without.* Our Lord made a simple statement regarding spiritual defilement. We may never blame our environment for our personal failures. God always makes a way of escape (1 Cor. 10:13).

B. *Defilement is from within.* We may or may not allow evil in our heart.

C. *Defilement listed.* In case his hearers might misunderstand, Jesus proceeded to list the varied sins that "come from within man."

IV. Defilement is not ethnic (Mark 7:24–30).

A. *Home of a Greek.* Jesus exploded the myth that sin and/or salvation is the sole property of any ethnic group. He gave an illustration of an "unclean spirit" being in a Grecian woman's child.

B. *Need for exorcism.* The Lord recognized the need that existed. He cast out the "unclean spirit."

C. *Identified ethnic problem.* Jesus did recognize the ethnic problem involved. Yet his emphasis was that the kingdom of heaven superseded any earthly kingdom.

V. Defilement is not physical handicap (Mark 7:31–35).

A. *Physically handicapped.* Jesus was approached by one who was deaf and could not speak clearly. Society castigated these and often declared them unclean.

B. *Healed with spittle.* Christ touched the one in need with clay he had made with his own spittle.

C. *Normalcy restored.* The health of the individual was restored by the touch of God's Servant.

Conclusion

The chapter concludes with this assessment of Jesus: "He hath done all things well!" (Mark 7:37). One who was defiled could not do these things and get this kind of reputation.

SUNDAY MORNING, OCTOBER 28

Title: The Conversion of the Jewish Scholar

Text: "What shall I do, Lord?" **(Acts 22:10 RSV).**

Scripture Reading: Acts 22:6–16

Hymns: "Blessed Be the Name of the Lord," Wesley
"Light of the World," Monsell
"Open My Eyes," Scott

Offertory Prayer: Father, we praise your name and thank you for the privilege of worship. We thank you for the gift of abundant life. We thank you for the gift of earning that we may share. Bless, we pray, the tithes and offerings we now bring, through Jesus Christ our Lord. Amen.

Introduction

Can a person become a Christian if he or she doesn't want to? When you become a Christian, who takes the initiative, you or the Lord? Can a scholarly cynic suddenly become a humble, obedient Christian? You might not remember to look for all of these answers during this message, but you can look for the answers you are most interested in.

We will look at the remarkable conversion of Saul in terms of (1) his life before he became a Christian, (2) the forces used of the Holy Spirit to lead him to Jesus, (3) how he became a Christian, and (4) how the new life began to express itself.

I. Saul's life before he became a Christian.

A. *He was well born.* Paul was proud to be a descendant of Abraham (2 Cor. 11:22) of the tribe of Benjamin (Phil. 3:5) and of the line of another Saul, the first king of the Hebrew people. His father was a strict Jew and a Pharisee. He said proudly, "My brothers, I am a Pharisee, the son of a Pharisee" (Acts 23:6 NIV). Not only that, his father was a Roman citizen. Paul was pleased to say, "I was born a citizen" (22:28 NIV).

It is not necessary to be well born to be born again, but this is another reminder that one is never so well born that he or she does not need to be born again.

B. *He was well educated.* He grew up in the university city of Tarsus and, whether or not he attended the university there, the whole environment was one of education and culture. We do know that he studied at the feet of Gamaliel, the outstanding theological teacher of his day among Jews. He gave evidence of some acquaintance with Greek literature. This bilingual student learned the art of debate and became a good writer if not a good speaker (2 Cor. 10:10).

336

C. *He was a born leader.* There is no question that he who classified himself as the chief of sinners has long since been recognized as the chief of saints. His ambitions and talents combined to make him a leader among his fellow students (Gal. 1:14).

Paul combined scholarship and activism in an unusual way. He who always wanted his books nearby (2 Tim. 4:13) had a keenness of intellect that challenges the respect of the greatest minds of the world. He also gave himself, both before and after he became a Christian, to being perhaps the most energetic personality we read about in the New Testament.

D. *This well-born, well-educated leader was a sinner.* To put it bluntly, Paul was a bloodthirsty murderer. True, his position as a leader among persecutors of Christians prevented his actually throwing the stones that took the lives of Stephen and others, but he said, "And when they were put to death, I gave my vote against them" (Acts 22:4). In speaking later of his blasphemy and persecution, he said he had "acted ignorantly in unbelief" (1 Tim. 1:13). "But Saul began to destroy the church. Going from house to house, he dragged off both men and women and put them in prison" (Acts 8:3 NIV).

There is never any meaner sinner than a religious sinner. Some of the bloodiest wars have been religious wars. How did Saul, with his gentle, cultured, educated background, come to be such a passionate murderer? He had become so fanatically dedicated to the defense of his own religious traditions that he persuaded himself he was committing these sins in the name of God. Some of us have seen some pretty dirty tricks performed by people even in the name of the Christian religion.

II. How Saul came to know he needed to be a Christian.

A. *As always the Lord took the initiative in the actual conversion experience.* While Paul was on his way to Damascus, the Lord spoke to him. Where I went to church as a child, nearly everyone became a Christian at "the mourner's bench." The way to "get saved" was to go and sit or kneel on the front pew and have the people come and plead with God to save you from sin. Not only did I see people go forward in every service for an entire week of revival before they became Christians, but I knew some who went year after year before they became Christians. When later, however, they experienced conversion, they were able to see that the Lord had been more willing than they all along. Jesus always meets people more than halfway. His Holy Spirit convicts of sin, of righteousness, and of judgment. Without his convicting power, there is no such thing as becoming a Christian.

B. *From a psychological standpoint, it is easy to see that Paul was aware of the weaknesses and failures of his own legalistic religion, and this explains much of his defensive bitterness toward those who had surrendered to Jesus.* Subconsciously he was beating himself black and blue in his persecution of others.

A friend and I were ordered out of the house of a man to whom we were trying to witness. In less than a year I saw him come forward in an evangelistic service with tears streaming down his face, confessing his sins, and asking for membership in the church.

C. *Saul was familiar with the Old Testament Scriptures, and though he was using them outwardly to defend his selfish ambition, there is no doubt that these same passages spoke conviction to his heart.* The Lord said to him, "It hurts you to kick against the goads" (Acts 26:14). Like the sharp spikes used by animal drivers in training them to pull a load, the Holy Spirit was using the Scriptures to let Saul know that he needed something he did not have.

Recently a new convert said to me, "I could never get away from the things I learned in Vacation Bible School as a child."

D. *Saul could not escape the positive influence of the Christians he had been persecuting.* He especially could not forget the testimony of Stephen as he was martyred.

Thirteen years after I witnessed to a young Jewish man, he said to me, "You were right and I was wrong. You cannot be neutral about Jesus. I have thought about what you said many times, and I am glad I will not be neutral about him anymore because I have just trusted him as my Savior." I have not seen him since that night, but if I were to talk to him now, I am sure he would recall how many other Christians influenced him over those same years.

A preacher asked a new convert, "What did I say in my sermon that led you to accept Jesus?"

The man answered, "It was nothing you said. It was the life of the man with whom I work every day."

III. The actual conversion of Saul.

As Saul and his party came near the city of Damascus at noon, he saw a light from heaven brighter than the sun shining around him. When they had all fallen to the ground, he heard a voice saying to him, "Saul, Saul, why do you persecute me?" When Saul asked who was speaking to him, the voice answered, "I am Jesus, whom you are persecuting; but rise and enter the city, and you will be told what you are to do." When he arose from the ground, he could not see because of the brightness of the light and remained in blindness for three days. It was all so completely incomprehensible that even Paul himself could never fully articulate the experiences of those moments. You who tell your own experience perhaps have some of this same difficulty. About the only people who always relate their Christian testimony in the same way are those who have memorized a certain manner of telling it. One time we are likely to recall one portion of it and another time another portion. Sometimes we remember the details in one manner and sometimes in another. This does not weaken, but strengthens the testimony.

Since one's conversion always comes at the moment of his or her surrender, Saul's likely took place at the moment he said, "What shall I do, Lord?" When I was willing to admit to the Lord that I did not know how to become a Christian but that he knew how, and I said to him, "From now on it's in your hands. I am not going to worry about it anymore," I felt safe in his eternal hands.

IV. How the new life began to express itself.

When Saul asked the Lord what he must do, the Lord told him to go into Damascus and he would be told what to do. He promised him help from a man named Ananias. The Lord also appeared to Ananias and prepared him to go to Saul and give him the assurance he needed.

Following the testimony of Ananias, Saul took food for the first time in three days and obeyed the Lord in baptism. He immediately entered as ardently and fervently into the new life as he had followed the old life.

Conclusion

Not only did the Lord take initiative in Paul's salvation, but he also immediately called him into his service to be a witness. Paul had no more doubt about his call to witness than he did about his conversion. For Paul it was impossible to be a secret disciple, and it will be just as impossible for you. When Jesus lives in you, you will live like Jesus.

SUNDAY EVENING, OCTOBER 28

Title: Palm Tree Christians

Text: "The righteous shall flourish like the palm tree: he shall grow like a cedar in Lebanon" **(Ps. 92:12)**.

Scripture Reading: Psalm 92:7–14

Introduction

As a boy I loved to play under the shade of the trees on our farm. I loved to climb those trees and to gaze upon their strength and watch them grow and weather storms. Joyce Kilmer saw a message in the trees:

> I think I shall never see
> A poem lovely as a tree.
>
> A tree whose hungry mouth impressed
> Against the earth's sweet flowing breast.

Upon whose bosom snow has lain,
Which intimately lives with rain.

A tree that looks at God all day,
And lifts its leafy arms to pray.

Poems are made by fools like me,
But only God can make a tree.

Our text says, "The righteous shall flourish like the palm tree." How is a child of God like a palm tree?

I. The roots of the palm tree go down deep into the earth.

A. *The palm tree has great roots that make the tree strong and substantial.* The psalmist said that a godly man "shall be like a tree planted by the rivers of water" (Ps. 1:3). The palm tree bends and strains in the wind and the storm, but it stands because of its deep roots. A Christian rooted in Christ can stand the winds of temptation and the storms of trial.

B. *Can we stand up against the enemies of our souls?* The palm tree has many enemies that threaten its life—the dryness of the desert, the burning heat of the sun, the fierceness of the winds, and animals that rub away its trunk; but it lives on because it is rooted deep in the earth. Paul mentioned some of the enemies of the Christian life in Romans 8: "tribulation, or distress, or persecution, or famine, or nakedness, or peril, or sword" (v. 35), and cried, "Nay, in all these things we are more than conquerors through him that loved us" (v. 37).

II. The palm tree is upright.

A. *Jeremiah spoke of people being as "upright as the palm tree."* The palm tree rears itself straight up in the air, erect, stately, and strong. It is a fitting image of a good person who is not crooked, but is upright in character and in conversation.

B. *Dr. T. L. Holcomb used to speak to the boys at the Ridgecrest Boys' Camp at Ridgecrest, North Carolina.* All around there are tall, straight, stately trees. In one of his messages he told the boys, "Go out into the mountains and back up next to one of these giant trees and pray this prayer: 'Lord, make me like one of these trees—tall, straight, and strong.'"

C. *When Charles Elliott became engaged to Ellen Peabody, Miss Peabody's family received a congratulatory letter saying of him, "He is a regular cedar post—firm, sound, and always in the same place."* How much it would mean in the home, in the church, and in the nation if we could be like that in our manner of life—strong, firm, and upright. This is the palm tree Christian.

340

III. The palm tree is graceful.

A. *It is the emblem of grace and beauty.* In the Old Testament, palm trees adorned the temple. Jericho was called the "city of palm trees" and was one of the most beautiful cities of the ancient world. In heaven the saints are portrayed as those clothed in white robes with palms in their hands, the emblem of beauty, grace, and victory.

B. *John spoke of Christ as being "full of grace and truth."* The New Testament says of the early Christians, "Great grace was upon them all." There are many facts of meaning of the word "grace," but here it means charm and attractiveness. There is something attractive about those who live near to Christ.

IV. The palm tree is an evergreen.

A. *Other trees turn dark and gray during the winter, but the palm tree holds its rich, deep color.* It shows its colors in all seasons. It is the symbol of faithfulness. Paul said, "Preach the word; be prepared in season and out of season" (2 Tim. 4:2 NIV). The psalmist said, "I will bless the LORD at all times; his praise shall continually be in my mouth" (Ps. 34:1). Can you say, "I will be an evergreen. I will be like that palm tree, showing my colors at all times"? Can you say, "Anytime, Lord, day or night, in summer or winter, in darkness or light, I will follow you; in sickness, in health, in joy, in sorrow, in adversity, or in prosperity, I will be true"?

B. *While I was in seminary, I was a pastor of the Evergreen Baptist Church.* I was there several months before I learned why it was named the Evergreen Church. It was a country church with a handsome building and a wonderful congregation, and it had a heritage of fine preachers. The building had many large, stately trees around it. You never noticed the evergreens, which almost completely surrounded the church, until the wintry winds and rains had stripped the leaves from all the other trees. Then you could see the evergreens showing their colors. There are church members like that; they show their colors in all seasons. They are palm tree Christians.

V. The palm tree is a fruitful tree.

A. *This illustration refers to the date palm.* It produces up to six hundred pounds of fruit each year. There are many uses for its fruit, including medicinal use. The camel feeds on the date stones. The leaves are used in making a variety of household articles. Thread and rope are made from the fiber of the bough. A drink is made from the sap. No wonder it was said that an Arab's very existence depended on the palm tree. Likewise, the Christian is useful and fruitful.

B. *The influence, example, spirit, words, deeds, and life of a Christian are a blessing.* Being in touch with the source of fruitfulness, he or she lives a fruitful life. "But the fruit of the Spirit is love, joy, peace, longsuffering, gentleness, goodness, faith, meekness, temperance" (Gal. 5:22–23). The fruitfulness of the palm tree continues for hundreds of years, for this tree is noted for its long life. The ministry of a Christian may bear fruit even for years after he or she has reached the heavenly home.

VI. The palm tree grows in the desert.

A. *The palm tree thrives in burning sand under the hot sun in the dry desert climate.* The Christian flourishes in difficult places. It was said of God's people when they were enslaved under Pharaoh, "The more they were afflicted, the more they . . . grew" (Ex. 1:12). God's people grow under tribulation. Moses spent forty years on the back side of the desert of Midian. God was getting him ready to lead his people through the wilderness. It was said that John the Baptist was trained in the desert. No wonder he was such a great man—he was trained in the discipline and difficulty of desert life.

B. *Christ was led into the desert to be tempted, to be tested, and to be prepared for his life's work.* The Christian grows and thrives in difficult places and becomes Christlike.

VII. The palm tree is an oasis of refreshment.

A. *The traveler looks across the burning sands, parched with thirst, and sees a palm tree.* His heart leaps for joy because he knows there is water, shade, food, and refreshment for his tired body and spirit.

B. *The Christian is like that, for God in Christ makes his people the means of refreshment to a weary world.* Paul spoke of Onesiphorus coming to him while he was in prison in Rome and said, "He oft refreshed me." Here was one of those refreshing personalities who comes to bless us in our sorrow, discouragement, sickness, doubt, and need.

C. *Palm tree Christians are a means of refreshment to those who live about them.* Christ refreshes our minds and hearts and we, in turn, refresh others. True Christians can be an oasis of refreshment to friends, family, and all who know them. Would you be a refreshing personality? Then get close to Christ, the source of refreshment.

Conclusion

Live in the light of God's love, and he will make your life flourish like the palm tree.

WEDNESDAY EVENING, OCTOBER 31

Title: One Offering a Second Chance

Text: "For what shall it profit a man, if he shall gain the whole world, and lose his own soul?" **(Mark 8:36)**.

Scripture Reading: Mark 8

Introduction

The compassion of the Servant-Messiah was exposed as he observed the multitude growing weak and hungry. This scene is almost identical to the situation in Mark 6. This chapter pictures our Lord dealing with people beyond an initial experience. In his love he encourages people "more than once." He has the heart of a persistent Servant who continually tries to help others.

Jesus exercised "second effort" on behalf of the multitudes, the Pharisees, the disciples, the blind man, the apostle Peter, and the people.

I. To the multitude (Mark 8:1–9).

A. *Failed to bring food.* We are not able to determine an exact time span between the settings of chapters 6 and 8, but there is such a similarity of fact that we may easily make note of one lesson. Jesus did not reject this group of people because they made the same mistake as the other group. He had the same compassion on this hungry multitude as he did on the crowd in chapter 6.

B. *Questions of the disciples.* These followers of Jesus asked almost the identical question, yet Jesus did not respond to them in anger or with impatience.

C. *The miracle feeding.* Jesus took the available food and multiplied it as he had done on a previous occasion. In spite of the absent-mindedness of human nature and the spiritual forgetfulness of his followers, he fed the people again.

II. To the Pharisees (Mark 8:10–13).

A. *Seeking a sign.* This is not the first encounter Jesus had with the Pharisees. They were anxious to require Jesus to prove that he was from heaven.

B. *Reason behind question.* These hypocrites were not as concerned about signs as they appeared to be. They were trying to trap Jesus in his ministry.

C. *Opportunity for faith.* Jesus made no attempt to exhibit his authority. He only furnished these men with another opportunity to have faith in him. This was not the first, nor would it be the last, time Christ encouraged belief in the activities of the unseen God.

III. To the disciples (Mark 8:14–21).

A. *Teaching of the Lord.* Jesus sought to make his followers aware of the "leaven of the Pharisees and of Herod." He tried to lead them into a discernment of truth and/or error.

B. *Ignorance of disciples.* They misunderstood Jesus's message. Their thoughts were so centered on the immediate facts that they could not readily discern eternal truths.

C. *Spiritual interpretation given.* Jesus restated the lesson he was trying to get across to the men. He again attempted to get his thoughts into their thoughts.

IV. To the blind (Mark 8:22–26).

A. *Condition of the blind.* Jesus met a man in Bethsaida who could not see. It was God's will for the man to be healed. There was a special lesson he wanted to teach through this man's experience.

B. *Partial healing.* Jesus did not complete the healing of the man with his first efforts. The man could only partially see.

C. *Total healing.* Jesus made a second effort on behalf of the man. He was then completely healed. We all desire Jesus to present an instantaneous cure for our problems. Most of the time we are made to realize that the answer to our problems came in a progressive manner. Salvation is instantaneous. Christian growth and experience are progressive in nature.

V. To Peter (Mark 8:27–33).

A. *Leader.* When Jesus asked Peter to tell him who people thought he was, Peter gave him a summary answer.

B. *Exacting theology.* Jesus gave Peter another chance to answer the question. He required Peter to be specific in his reply. Peter identified him as the Christ.

C. *Corrected deeds.* Peter dared to challenge Jesus when he declared that the "Son of man" must die. The Lord corrected this chief apostle with a sharp rebuke.

VI. To the people (Mark 8:34–37).

A. *People sought profit.* The flesh has always encouraged people to seek the way of profit (v. 36). Jesus knew of the gluttony of the people to whom he spoke.

B. *The life of the "second chance."* Jesus encouraged the people to "deny self, take up the cross," and follow him.

C. *The value.* Eternal souls of people would be saved if they followed the way proposed by Christ.

Conclusion

In the last verse the Lord encourages his followers to bear witness of the way of righteousness (Mark 8:38).

NOVEMBER

■ Sunday Mornings

The theme for Sunday mornings this month is "The Christian's Response to Material Values." Modern disciples of our Lord live in a world in which materialistic values can become a rival for the place that belongs to God in their life. Stewardship is more than being a faithful tither and a generous contributor. It is a way of life.

■ Sunday Evenings

"Christ Is Our Contemporary" is the theme for messages based on texts from the book of Revelation. The Christ is more than a historical figure of the past. We must recognize and respond to him as our contemporary.

■ Wednesday Evenings

Continue the series from the gospel of Mark using the theme "Jesus As Mark Saw Him."

SUNDAY MORNING, NOVEMBER 4

Title: The Faithful Steward Is Faithful in Living

Text: "Let a man so account of us, as of the ministers of Christ, and stewards of the mysteries of God. Moreover it is required in stewards, that a man be found faithful" **(1 Cor. 4:1–2).**

Scripture Reading: Matthew 25:14–30

Hymns: "Guide Me, O Thou Great Jehovah," Williams
"I Love Thy Kingdom, Lord," Dwight
"Take My Life, and Let It Be," Havergal

Offertory Prayer: Heavenly Father, we rejoice in this day you have made. We worship you and praise you with all our hearts. Out of the abundance of your fullness, you have ministered to us generously. Add your blessings to these gifts to the end that others might come to know the Lord Jesus Christ. In his name we pray. Amen.

Introduction

Can you imagine anything more wonderful than hearing the God of all creation pronounce the final benediction on your life in these words: "You have been faithful . . . enter into the joy of your master"? Can you imagine any statement more totally devastating than that other verdict, "You wicked and slothful servant"?

I. The faithful steward has faith in God the Creator.

A. *Faith says that God is the owner of all.*

1. "The earth is the LORD's and the fulness thereof, the world and those who dwell therein" (Ps. 24:1 RSV). God is the ultimate owner of all that is. He created and sustains the world; the world answers to God. Both Old and New Testament statements constantly remind us that God holds the title of ownership to all the world.

2. We belong to God. The story of creation in Genesis tells us that God created man in his own image. The parable in our Scripture lesson reminds us that our lives are a sacred trust from God. Paul reminded the Corinthians that we belong to God because of Christ's redemption. Listen to those beautiful words: "You are not your own; you were bought with a price. So glorify God in your body" (1 Cor. 6:19–20 RSV). This marvelous statement is the classic expression of Christian stewardship. We belong to God even more than we belong to our own families.

3. "God gave us this land." Deuteronomy 26:9 illustrates how people of faith acknowledge that God gives to them the small portions of land that they in turn till for their needs and for his glory. The Old Testament further stresses the tentativeness of this trust by reminding us that God gives the power to get wealth. Furthermore, the Hebrews were forbidden to sell the land in perpetuity, since it always reverts to God.

B. *Things, then, are understood in terms of faith.*

1. Work has a religious purpose. Human toil, when seen in this light, becomes creative. It has a religious meaning because people work with God in creation.

2. So, responsibility to God includes both the sacred and the secular. People who have faith blend the sacred and the secular because their God is Lord of all. Earning a living is endowed with the same sacred meaning as is the worship service on Sunday morning.

II. The faithful steward has faith in man, God's creature.

A. *Man's origin is in God.*

1. Life is focused on God. Since God is my creator, my life must be lived in terms of God's purpose for me. This requires that I constantly look up to him to get my bearings.

2. I am not my own to do as I will with my life. Freedom is never the license to "do as I please," but is rather liberation from my bondage so that I can fulfill the task for which God created me.

B. *Man's purpose in life is to serve God.*
   1. To care for the earth—dominion. At creation God placed man in dominion over the rest of his creation. The proper care of it related to man's purpose in living. The waste and exploitation of nature in modem times would be inconceivable if people were really living by faith.
   2. To care for other people—love. Biblical faith constantly reminds us that we can express our love for God only as we care for God's creation and especially for the other people God has created. We are told that we cannot claim to be honoring God if we are oppressing our neighbor. We show our love to God through our love for fellow humans.
   3. To glorify God—serve and worship. Glorifying God is living in such a relationship to God within creation that we reflect his own holiness back to him. We do this through serving and worshiping.

III. The faithful steward translates all of life into personal terms.

A. *Faith in God and humanity endows creation with a personal character.*
   1. People are the masters of things. Not only does the Bible teach us that people are to have dominion over created things and use them for the good of humanity and the glory of God, but it also tells us that people commit idolatry when they allow things to master them. People are forbidden to bow down to idols of wood or stone or precious metal. They also are forbidden to worship the money and the affluence it will buy in our day, for this too is idolatry.
   2. So people are always more important than things. The faithful steward keeps personal values in clear focus and never allows the things of the world to be used for injustice toward people. It is precisely for this reason that faithful stewards will give of their means to care for the needs of others and to see that others hear the good news of God.

B. *So, people are trustees under God over nature.*
   1. We are servants of God and masters of nature. We always live in this "in-between" role, and therein we learn what it is to be made in the "image of God." We have a measure of sovereignty over nature as he has total sovereignty over all. We express this sovereignty by serving him.

2. We are coworkers with God. As we subdue nature and serve our fellow humans, we enter into God's creative work. Human life could have no greater meaning nor depth than this conviction of faith.

IV. The faithful steward lives "by faith."

A. *Living by faith is different than living by sight.* Paul reminded the Corinthians, "We walk by faith, not by sight" (2 Cor. 5:7). This reminder has several applications.

1. Life faces uncertainty. The parable of the stewards laid stress on that uncertainty. Two of the stewards faced their uncertainty by faith; the other rejected faith. Faithful Christian stewards are able to face the uncertainty of tomorrow because of the strength of their religious convictions today.

2. Living involves taking risks. The unfaithful steward was condemned precisely because he would not take the risk that faith is willing to take. Furthermore, when he faced his master, he denied the responsibility of his stewardship and actually blamed the master for being a hard man. His last excuse was "I was afraid, and went and hid thy talent in the ground" (Matt. 25:25). Fear is the opposite of faith. Fear cringes and withdraws and hides; faith stands up and takes the risk of tomorrow with confidence.

3. But life has promise. Faithful stewards accept the promises of God and walk by faith where they cannot see.

B. *The condemnation of the wicked steward is for his refusal to take the risk of faith.*

1. The risk was investment. The unfaithful steward refused to invest the talent entrusted to him that it may grow. By hiding it, it was actually diminished.

2. Stewardship is synonymous with management. God has entrusted us with certain abilities, talents, possessions, and time. Life consists of the management of those for God's glory and humankind's usefulness. This man rejected the essence of life.

3. He was condemned for unbelief. All of judgment comes to bear on this theme of stewardship. John tells us, "He who believes in him is not condemned; he who does not believe is condemned already, because he has not believed in the name of the only Son of God" (John 3:18 RSV).

C. *The faithful steward is commended for "being faithful."*

1. Faithful stewards live by faith. This means that their life is determined by their convictions about God and humanity and the world. This means that they are willing to face the uncertain future and take the risks of life by living in a world

under God with people and over things. The rejection of faith is the rejection of God. The apostle Paul argues persuasively that our justification before God is purely a matter of our faith in Jesus Christ.

2. The commendation also emphasizes the quality of faithfulness as one lives by faith. There are degrees of faithfulness; some people are more faithful than others. Some are more capable than others; God knows the difference. You and I are challenged by this parable to understand the basic truth that human life is a sacred trust from God. We are stewards of God. The question is whether or not we are faithful stewards.

One of the clearest insights into our faithfulness is the way we manage the material resources entrusted to us. You are asked to consider your own stewardship of material things. Next Sunday we will deal precisely with this theme.

Conclusion

A baseball player once indicated that his ambition in life was to hear his coach say at the time of the player's retirement, "You are the best baseball player I have ever coached." How much more should we Christians live our lives with the joyful expectation and determination that at the end of the journey God will say to us, "You have been faithful." Bankers must be honest; soldiers must be brave; watchmen must be vigilant; runners must be swift; weightlifters must be strong; stewards must be faithful.

SUNDAY EVENING, NOVEMBER 4

Title: A Throne Was Set in Heaven

Text: "And immediately I was in the Spirit; and, behold, a throne was set in heaven, and one sat on the throne" **(Rev. 4:2)**.

Scripture Reading: Revelation 4:2–11

Introduction

The book of Revelation must be interpreted as every other book must be interpreted—against the historical background out of which it came. Revelation was written during the last decade of the first Christian century when the emperor of the Roman Empire was trying to eradicate Christianity from the face of the earth. By imperial decree it was declared throughout the empire that every individual must bow down before an image of Caesar and say, "Caesar is lord." Christians refused to do this, and thus were threatened with death or exile. The book of Revelation was written to meet the needs of the church during that specific age and every age.

These early Christians were faced with the question of what was going

349

to happen to the church. Every time there is a crisis, God raises up someone to deliver a message that meets the needs of his people. John, the beloved apostle, had been assigned to share the unveiling of Jesus Christ. Revelation reveals Christ. The book was meant to meet the needs of those living on the very precipice of death. Much of the contents will happen in the future, but much also applies to today.

John was called to heaven that he might view the activity there as well as look down and see earth. The first thing he saw was a guarantee of the ultimate victory of God. We, as did John, need a revelation of God's holiness and magnitude as he is seated on the throne.

I. God is a Spirit.

John does not exactly describe the one seated on the throne. He would affirm that God is a Spirit not limited to time and space. They that worship him must worship him in spirit and in truth. He does not have a physical body like ours. If he did, he would be limited to one place at a time. Following Jesus's crucifixion, he went back to heaven so that he might come back in spirit to be everywhere present at all times. A personality is not a body with a spirit, but a person with a spirit who has a body. God is a spirit, and we too are spirits dwelling in the flesh. It is in a spiritual nature that we are made like God.

II. God is eternal (Rev. 4:3).

In the Old Testament God established the rainbow as a promise that he would never destroy the race again. People were to look at the rainbow and remember the promise of God and in reverent fear open their hearts to the eternal God who preserved Noah. The God John and Noah worshiped is the same God you and I worship, a sovereign and supreme God.

III. God is sovereign (Rev. 4:4).

"And round about the throne were four and twenty seats: and upon the seats I saw four and twenty elders sitting, clothed in white raiment; and they had on their heads crowns of gold" (Rev. 4:4).

The twenty-four seats may be symbolic of the twelve patriarchs and twelve kings. Kings and patriarchs worshiped God and wore golden crowns. They cast their crowns before the throne saying, "Thou art worthy, O Lord, to receive glory and honour and power: for thou hast created all things, and for thy pleasure they are and were created" (Rev. 4:11). Caesar wanted the people to bow before him and say that he was lord.

IV. God is power.

"And out of the throne proceeded lightnings and thunderings and voices" (Rev. 4:5). The lightning belongs to God. Thunder is said to be the voice of God. Caesar claimed to have all power.

V. God is immanent in his creation.

"And there were seven lamps of fire burning before the throne, which are the seven Spirits of God" (Rev. 4:5). This verse refers to the Holy Spirit who has come to dwell in the heart of each of us. The eternal God, who in incarnation came and dwelled in the person of Jesus Christ, comes to dwell in our hearts to lead, guide, and help us to become what God wants us to be.

VI. God is holy (Rev. 4:6).

Like a blinding light, the throne of God was symbolizing that God is unapproachable by those who are defiled by sin. When Isaiah saw God in a vision, he said, "Woe is me! for I am undone; because I am a man of unclean lips, and I dwell in the midst of a people of unclean lips: for mine eyes have seen the King, the LORD of hosts" (Isa. 6:5). To see God is always an overwhelming experience.

VII. God is the source of all life.

He is God of all that was, is, and is to come.

In Ezekiel's vision (Ezek. 1), which is similar to Revelation 4:6–8, the lion was the king of the wild beasts, the ox was the king of domestic animals, man was the crown of creation, and the eagle was the ruler of the birds of the air. These represent every area of life. They are there before the throne to worship him who is sovereign, supreme, majestic, and holy.

Conclusion

With this picture of God, Jesus Christ through John sought to encourage and strengthen the faith of those who were threatened with death. Knowing that your God is that big and that great will take away your fear of death and the grave. John's God gave strength, courage, and victory to people who were threatened with defeat, and he does so today. May God help us to bow to him and worship him.

WEDNESDAY EVENING, NOVEMBER 7

Title: One Possessing Power

Text: "And he said unto them, Verily I say unto you, That there be some of them that stand here, which shall not taste of death, till they have seen the kingdom of God come with power" (**Mark 9:1**).

Scripture Reading: Mark 9

Introduction

The Servant-Messiah, Jesus, had a responsibility to reveal that the kingdom of God had come with power. With this in mind, this chapter reveals that he had inner power, an intellectual power, a consoling power, a resurrection power, a social power, and a power in his very name.

I. Inner power (Mark 9:2–10).

A. *Transforming power.* A strange incident occurred in Jesus's life. His body was transfigured, transformed into a wonderful radiance that mystified those about him. In reality, his inner glow of godliness burst forth to be seen by the immediate witnesses.

B. *Backward projection.* Moses, representing the law, and Elijah, representing the prophets, stood with Jesus. These two talked with the Servant-Messiah. In all probability, the conversation centered around the fact that Christ was the fulfillment of the law and the prophets.

C. *Forward projection.* As Jesus and the disciples descended from this mountain of glory, Jesus commanded them that this incident should remain secret until the time of his glory in the Resurrection (Mark 9:9).

II. Intellectual power (Mark 9:11–13).

A. *Perplexing question.* The scribes pondered much over the question of Elijah's return. This teaching is found in Malachi 4:5–6.

B. *Explanation.* Jesus maintained that the truth of the scriptural question found its explanation in the story of the Son of Man. Elijah would prepare the way for the Son of Man.

C. *Application.* The Lord proceeded to apply this prophecy of Elijah to John the Baptist.

III. Consoling power (Mark 9:14–29).

A. *Agony involved.* A father was suffering over the illness of his son. He had sought the help of the disciples to no avail.

B. *Failure of disciples.* The disciples' failure multiplied the father's frustration. They tried to accomplish a job they did not believe they could do. This was their sin.

C. *Situation settled.* Jesus performed two major operations of consolation. He cast the evil spirit out of the son, and he shared with his disciples the way of spiritual power. He consoled the physically and spiritually downcast.

IV. Resurrection power (Mark 9:30–32).

A. *Prophecy of death.* Jesus attempted to prepare his followers for his impending death. He felt it necessary to reveal to them the stark reality of the horrible days ahead.

B. *Misunderstanding disciples.* They were so overwhelmed with Jesus's presence that they could not conceive of his death. They could not understand that his death would be temporary. This teaching made them afraid.

C. *Resurrection foretold.* Along with the fact of his death, Jesus shared with the disciples the fact of his resurrection. The idea of his resurrection did not seem to register with them.

V. Social power (Mark 9:33–37).

A. *Disagreements.* The despicable sin of vainglory worked its way into the fellowship of disciples. They argued among themselves as to who "should be the greatest."

B. *Disposition of service.* Jesus shared with the disciples the true attitude of a servant. If a man desired to be first, he should be last, servant to all.

C. *Living illustration.* Jesus clinched his discussion by settling this social and spiritual problem with a common illustration. He placed a small child among the disciples and said, "Whosoever shall receive one of such children in my name, receiveth me."

VI. Power in his name (Mark 9:38–49).

A. *Miracles in his name.* Jesus rebuked the disciples for their tendency to exclude others from the ministry of Christ. He maintained that "no man which shall do a miracle in my name . . . can lightly speak evil of me." He was aware that his name contained a miraculous power. This is still true today.

B. *Service in his name.* The Servant-Messiah encouraged his followers to perform the role of servant in relation to others. He maintained that those who served in his name would be rewarded.

C. *Searching in his name.* Jesus then said that his disciples should have a period of heart-searching (Mark 9:42–43).

Conclusion

In the final verse of this chapter, the Lord issued a challenge for his fellow servants to "have peace one with another." This could come to pass only if the salt retained its seasoning—that is, if Christians retained their power and testimony.

SUNDAY MORNING, NOVEMBER 11

Title: The Faithful Steward Is Faithful in Giving

Text: "On the first day of every week, each of you is to put something aside and store it up, as he may prosper, so that contributions need not be made when I come. And when I arrive, I will send those whom you accredit by letter to carry your gift to Jerusalem" **(1 Cor. 16:2–3 RSV)**.

Scripture Reading: Matthew 5:23–24

Hymns: "Glory to His Name," Hoffman
"A Child of the King," Buell
"Our Best," Kirk

Offertory Prayer: Loving Father, we come to you as the giver of every good and perfect gift. We thank you for your gift of your Son, Jesus Christ. We thank you for the gift of the indwelling Holy Spirit. We thank you for the privilege you have granted us of being coworkers with you in bringing the saving message to a needy world. Add your divine blessings to these gifts to the end that men and women, boys and girls will be brought into your kingdom. In Jesus's name we pray. Amen.

Introduction

Last Sunday we talked about faithful stewards. We dealt primarily with the religious beliefs of stewards and what might be called the underlying foundations of stewardship. Today we talk specifically about faithful stewards and the matter of giving their money.

Probably everyone here has some connection with this church or another church and some interest in the causes for which our church stands. Furthermore, we know that our church will be able to accomplish its task only in proportion to our financial support of its efforts. We also are well aware that our support of our church is a much broader concept than the financial support alone; but this in no way minimizes the need for our financial support.

I. Faithful stewards must give themselves first.

    A. *Worship is personal.*

        1. Jesus taught that we cannot make a gift to God unless we are first right with God and with our neighbors. He said, "If you are offering your gift at the altar, and there remember that your brother has something against you, leave your gift there before the altar and go; first be reconciled to your brother, and then come and offer your gift" (Matt. 5:23–24 RSV).

        2. Giving is a part of worship. In both the Old and the New Testaments there is a high premium on giving. People are expected to share their possessions with others in need. In the New Testament an additional cause arose that called for Christian support: As the church saw its mission to the entire world and began sending missionaries to proclaim the gospel, it faced the need for the financial support of those who were already believers. This kind of giving has been a far more meaningful offering to God than the kinds of offering we see in the Old Testament. In Christian giving we must never forget the personal aspects; giving is never a legal or external affair.

B. *Paul cited the Macedonians as good examples of giving.*
   1. They gave themselves first. Paul wrote of the Macedonians, "First they gave themselves to the Lord" (2 Cor. 8:5 RSV). At the time, Paul was encouraging the Corinthians to give of their money for the support of the poor in Jerusalem. He cited the Macedonians as an outstanding example of Christians who had given liberally of their money for the same cause, precisely because they had first given of themselves.
   2. The Macedonians had given their money cheerfully. In the verses preceding this statement, Paul pointed out how the Macedonians, though poor themselves, had overflowed "in a wealth of liberality" and had begged for the favor of taking part in this noble cause. Cheerful giving is possible only for people who have first given themselves to God.

C. *Paul urged the Corinthians to see the relationship between giving themselves and giving their money to God.*
   1. Paul sought the Corinthians, not their possessions. He wrote, "I seek not what is yours but you" (2 Cor. 12:14 RSV). Paul thought the Corinthians had given themselves to God, but some of them either had not or had made very little progress in their Christian lives. Their dedication of themselves to God was of primary importance.
   2. Giving their money for the Christian cause was evidence of their having given themselves. Paul repeatedly urged them to grow in the grace of Christian giving for the support of the needy in Jerusalem.

II. Faithful stewards give voluntarily.

A. *Christian stewardship replaced legalism.*
   1. Tithing is an inadequate expression of Christian stewardship. Tithing in the Old Testament involved the giving of 10 percent of one's earnings to God. Today many Christians would never think of giving less than 10 percent of their money to God through their churches. They give not because the law requires it, but because they have given themselves to God through Jesus Christ and because they attach importance to the cause of Jesus Christ. Christians should not be satisfied with giving as little as 10 percent of their money to their churches. Some are so prosperous that they should give 50 percent or more to the cause of Jesus Christ. Christian stewardship does, in fact, insist on giving oneself totally to God and managing all of one's possessions for the glory of God.
   2. Christian stewardship is not the result of external coercion, but of internal conviction. This is why Paul commended

the Macedonians: "They gave . . . of their own free will"
(2 Cor. 8:3 RSV).

B. *Voluntary giving is cheerful giving.* Nowhere is the voluntary element summed up in a better way than in Paul's statement, "Each one must do as he has made up his mind, not reluctantly or under compulsion, for God loves a cheerful giver" (2 Cor. 9:7 RSV). We can grow into cheerful stewards only as we understand more thoroughly our own commitment to God and our dedication to the cause of God in loving and caring for other people.

III. Faithful stewards give proportionately.

A. *In proportion to one's ability.*

1. Paul indicated that Christians should give in accordance with their ability to give, "as [they] may prosper" (1 Cor. 16:2 RSV). It is always a wise guideline to give to the church in proportion to one's ability to give. It is also a practical way that is fair and equitable. Paul further emphasized this principle by his comment, "It is acceptable according to what a man has, not according to what he has not" (2 Cor. 8:12 RSV). Christians should never feel uncomfortable if others are able to give more than they are. Christian stewardship of money is in proportion to one's ability to give.

2. Proportionate giving is characteristic of Christian giving. Early in the history of the church, Christians gave of their material means for the support of Christians in other areas who were in need. Paul and Barnabas took such a collection of funds to Jerusalem on one occasion. The narrative states, "And the disciples determined, everyone according to his ability, to send relief to the brethren who lived in Judea; and they did so" (Acts 11:29–30 RSV). The principle of proportionate giving is well established and well recommended. However, there is one other proportion often overlooked.

B. *In proportion to one's dedication and vision.* Some Christians gauge their giving not only in proportion to their ability to give, but in proportion to their dedication to Christ and their vision of the accomplishment to be made through their giving. In the passage cited previously (2 Cor. 8:3), Paul testified that the Macedonians had given "beyond their means." In the same letter (9:6ff.), Paul compared giving to sowing seed. "The point is this: he who sows sparingly will also reap sparingly, and he who sows bountifully will also reap bountifully." Then Paul goes on to talk about giving. This giving is in proportion to the expectation of a bountiful harvest and is not limited only by one's reasonable ability to give.

IV. Faithful stewards give systematically.

A. *They give regularly.* Paul recommended to the Christians of Corinth that they give "on the first day of every week" (1 Cor. 16:2). The emphasis here is on systematic giving to meet the ongoing needs of the congregation. Many people receive their money on a monthly basis or even on an annual basis; regular systematic giving to them would be regulated by the time in which they receive their income.

B. *Systematic giving may involve more than regular giving.* Many Christians become excited about one or two causes and neglect all the others. Giving through churches provides some protection against such incomplete giving.

V. Faithful stewards give generously.

A. *Generous giving is measured again in terms of ability to give and in terms of enthusiasm for the cause.* The Macedonians had suffered severe affliction, but still "their abundance of joy and their extreme poverty have overflowed in a wealth of liberality on their part" (2 Cor. 8:2). Generosity is a Christian virtue that should never be restricted by legalistic requirements, either minimums or maximums. The Christian spirit should always be free to respond to the needs of people and the challenges of the Christian cause.

   The Bible says a great deal about the dangers of wealth in that it often is the occasion through which rich people become calloused and indifferent to the needs of those about them.

B. *There is a promise to those who give generously.* Paul wrote, "You will be enriched in every way for great generosity, which through us will produce thanksgiving to God" (2 Cor. 9:11). This is not a promise that generous givers will become rich immediately. Neither is it a promise that they will become rich in the future. The promise has to do with the quality of life and the rewards we receive by responding generously to the people and causes about us.

VI. Faithful stewards give accountably.

A. *Accountable in safeguarding the funds.* Paul told the Corinthians to collect their financial resources for the relief of the poor in Jerusalem and then promised, "When I arrive, I will send those whom you accredit by letter to carry your gift to Jerusalem. If it seems advisable that I should go also, they will accompany me" (1 Cor. 16:3–4). In other words, Paul taught and practiced the principle that money given by stewards to their churches should be carefully handled and, in this case, he promised both letters and messengers to guarantee the delivery of the money for the purposes intended.

B. *Accountable in its proper use.* Christian stewardship always requires stewards to be responsible, or accountable, for the proper use of the money they give and that is entrusted to them. It is surprising that some Christians will give their money to their churches but will not bother to attend business meetings or participate in budget planning to assure that their gifts accomplish the purposes for which they are given.

It is even more incredible that many Christians will send gifts to television and radio ministries about whose handling of funds they know nothing. Great caution must be used and much research done before giving to such ministries. Giving money to irresponsible people is not Christian stewardship; it is misappropriation of funds.

Conclusion

You and I are stewards of every aspect of our lives, including the wealth God entrusts to us. How shall we respond to the teachings of the New Testament? Let us resolve to be faithful stewards in every area so that others might be helped and God glorified.

Would you be willing to determine that you will move beyond the minimum in giving and give in proportion to a dream or a hope for the full accomplishment of the cause of Christ in our time? Remember the requirement of stewards: They must be faithful. Are you and I faithful? When we stand before God at the end of the journey, will he speak that welcome benediction, 'You have been faithful over a little. Enter into the joy of your Lord"?

SUNDAY EVENING, NOVEMBER 11

Title: Ephesus: Remember, Repent, and Repeat

Text: "Remember therefore from whence thou art fallen, and repent, and do the first works" **(Rev. 2:5)**.

Scripture Reading: Ephesians 2:1–7

Introduction

The Christ introduces himself as the one who holds the seven churches in his right hand. They are precious to him, dear to his heart, and he has noble and redemptive purposes for each of them. He loved them to the extent that he gave himself in death on the cross for them (Eph. 5:25–27).

Jesus describes himself as the one "who walketh in the midst of the seven churches." It is interesting to note that during his earthly ministry the Savior had promised that "where two or three are gathered together in my name, there am I in the midst of them" (Matt. 18:20). He has promised never to leave us nor forsake us. He is always near if we but have faith to believe in the precious promise of his abiding presence.

I. The Savior's commendation.

The Savior found many things in the church at Ephesus worthy of commendation and praise.

A. *"I know thy works."* This was a working congregation.

B. *"I know thy labor."* The Lord himself needs laborers who are willing to labor in the fields, which are white unto harvest (Matt. 9:37–38).

C. *"I know thy patience."* The congregation at Ephesus had stayed under the load. They were a people with a persistent attitude that produced a gallant endurance.

D. *This congregation was intolerant of evil.* They practiced church discipline so as to ensure the purity of their church membership. In many respects Ephesus was a remarkable church. It was famous for many things.

II. The Savior's complaint.

In spite of all that our Savior found worthy of commendation, he had one great complaint. Have you ever known someone who had the appearance of being in perfect health and yet deep within had a fatal malady that would soon produce death? This was the case with the remarkable church at Ephesus. There was something dreadfully wrong with the heart of this church that had not yet manifested itself to the eyes of the casual observer.

The eyes of him who so loved that he endured the cross was about to see beneath the surface and issue his complaint. "Nevertheless I have somewhat against thee, because thou hast left thy first love" (Rev. 2:4). The Savior discovered that the congregation at Ephesus had forsaken their first love, the love they had for the Lord when they first knew him. He discovered that while the activities continued, the emotion, the enthusiasm, and the energy of first love was lacking. The ardent fervency of that love had disappeared.

III. The Savior's counsel.

Because love is the master motive behind obedience and service, the loss of that love will eventually be disastrous to any church. Knowing this, our Savior gave counsel, voiced a challenge, and provided a prescription to cure the church of this fatal malady of the loss of first love.

A. *"Remember therefore from whence thou art fallen" (Rev. 2:5).*

1. The first step back to God is by the pathway of memory.

2. Memory can bring depression and despair (Luke 15:17).

3. Memory can bring delight and joy (Luke 15:18–24).

Have you forgotten what it is like to be lost? Do you remember what it felt like to be under the condemnation of God? Can you remember the burden of the guilt of your sin? Do you remember the joy, the sense of relief, the blessed peace that entered your heart when you let Jesus become your Lord and Savior?

Have you forgotten what it cost God to save you? Have you forgotten that Jesus Christ died for you? Have you forgotten that heaven is going to be your eternal home?

If we are to return to the love we had at first, we need to exercise our memory.

B. *Remember . . . and repent.* "Remember therefore from whence thou art fallen, and repent" (Rev. 2:5).
   1. Repentance is more than remorse for past sins.
   2. Repentance is more than an initial experience in which there is a change of mind about God and his will for our lives.
   3. Real repentance is a continuing experience in which we journey from the natural mind of the flesh to the mind of Jesus Christ. It is a continuing experience in which we accept his viewpoint, his perspective, his scale of values, and his design for life.
   4. We need to reverse our thoughts of selfish satisfaction and indifference, confess our sins, forsake all evil, and commit ourselves to Christ.

Conclusion

Remember and repent. "Remember therefore from whence thou art fallen, and repent, and do the first works" (Rev. 2:5).

1. Set yourself again on the right path.
2. By inspired imagination, visit Calvary to discover the indescribable love of God for unworthy sinners like you and me.
3. Renounce and make a clean break with personal sins, whether they be sins of omission, sins of commission, or sins of disposition.
4. Renounce and begin again your life of adoring love, your affectionate gratitude that issues in a life of praise and obedience.

WEDNESDAY EVENING, NOVEMBER 14

Title: One Teaching Reality

Text: "And he arose from thence, and cometh into the coasts of Judaea by the farther side of Jordan: and the people resort unto him again; and, as he was wont, he taught them again" **(Mark 10:1)**.

Scripture Reading: Mark 10

Introduction

A grave temptation in life is to yield to the lure of the world of fantasy or make-believe. Christians often are given over to too much dreaming. Due to the harsh life he faced, the servant was more often in touch with the realism of life than was his master. In this portion of Scripture, Jesus, the Servant, led his followers into an understanding of some of the basic facts (realisms) of life.

I. Realism of marriage (Mark 10:2–12).

A. *Question of divorce.* The divorce question has always been very difficult. The Pharisees attempted to place Jesus in an untenable position with the question.

B. *Heart of marriage.* Jesus delved into the very heart of marriage. He defined marriage as being when "the two will become one flesh" (v. 8 NIV). He challenged the Pharisees with the command, "What therefore God hath joined together, let not man put asunder" (v. 9).

C. *Result of fantasy.* The Lord warned against the dangers of neglecting the reality of marriage. To desecrate it is to commit adultery (vv. 11–12).

II. Realism of childhood (Mark 10:13–16).

A. *Sincere rebuke.* Some well-meaning people were rebuked by the disciples when they brought children to Jesus. These men did not feel children were a real issue with Christ. Thus, they should not absorb his time.

B. *Heart of the kingdom.* When Jesus became aware of this incident, he rebuked his disciples. He taught that children and their simplicity of faith were the very heart of the kingdom of God.

C. *Result of fantasy.* If a person rejects the value of the "little people" of this world, he or she will be rejected by the Master.

III. Realism of salvation (Mark 10:17–22).

A. *Question of concern.* An inquirer came and asked Jesus a most important question: "Good Master, what shall I do that I may inherit eternal life?" He longed for eternal security.

B. *Heart of salvation.* Jesus outlined a procedure for the man to follow. This was designed to show the man he was neither capable nor willing "to earn" eternal life. The heart of salvation is found in the command "Follow me."

C. *Result of fantasy.* The man had hoped for a formula that did not involve sacrifice. Jesus emphasized the great cost involved in salvation.

IV. Realism of riches (Mark 10:23–27).

A. *Difficult circumstances.* In light of the rich man's rejection of God's way, Jesus pointed out the difficulty people have with wealth (vv. 23–25).

B. *Heart of riches.* Because of the very nature of wealth, it is impossible for rich people to enter the kingdom of heaven on their own volition. Jesus hastily adds that only with the aid of God can rich people be saved (vv. 26–27). Of course, this is true also of people without wealth.

C. *Results of fantasy.* Jesus taught that unless we see the reality of worldly wealth and its lack of spiritual power, we will be tempted to place our trust in possessions (v. 24).

V. Realism of sacrifice (Mark 10:28–31).

A. *Self-centeredness.* Peter served as a spokesman for the group when he said, "We have left all, and have followed thee." He longed for some kind of statement of praise from Christ.

B. *Heart of sacrifice.* Jesus shared the real meaning of sacrifice in the statement: "There is no man that hath left house, or brethren, or sisters, or father, or mother, or wife, or children, or lands, for my sake, and the gospel's, but he shall receive an hundredfold now in this time, houses, and brethren, and sisters, and mothers, and children, and lands, with persecutions; and in the world to come eternal life" (vv. 29–30). Peter seemed to feel he was due certain merit for his sacrifice. Jesus maintained it should be done for "his sake."

C. *Result of sacrifice.* Genuine sacrifice will bring about a blessing in the present life, plus eternal life in the world to come.

VI. Realism of death (Mark 10:32–34).

A. *Frightened disciples.* The disciples sensed an impending danger. There was something different about this trip with the Master.

B. *Heart of death.* Jesus shared with his followers the events that were to transpire in Jerusalem. His death was to be determined by the Jews and carried out by the Gentiles.

C. *Way of resurrection.* As in many other instances, Jesus sought to overshadow the ominous scene of death with the joy of the Resurrection. The realism of death would be overwhelmed by the realism of new life.

VII. Realism of honor (Mark 10:35–45).

A. *Pride of service.* Even during this crucial hour, some of the disciples were ambitious for worldly honor and glory.

B. *Heart of honor.* Jesus maintained that honor was something that must be obtained through service. It was not something to be indiscriminately passed around (v. 40).

C. *Results of honor.* Genuine honor will cause people to be servants to others. We should follow the example of the Servant-Messiah (v. 45).

VIII. Realism of faith (Mark 10:46–52).

A. *Blind man.* A blind man came into contact with Jesus outside the city of Jericho. He desired his sight.

B. *Heart of faith.* The man got to the heart of realistic faith when he addressed Jesus as "Lord." Then he directed his appeal to the Master.

C. *Results of faith.* Jesus maintained that the faith of the blind man had made him whole. Immediately after Jesus recognized the man's faith, the man received his sight. Faith is the "eye-opener" for believers today!

Conclusion

We must accept the truths of God if we are ever to know real life!

SUNDAY MORNING, NOVEMBER 18

Title: An Imperative for Christian Stewards: Living Within Our Means

Text: "Let the thief no longer steal, but rather let him labor, doing honest work with his hands, so that he may be able to give to those in need" **(Eph. 4:28)**.

Scripture Reading: 2 Thessalonians 3:6–13

Hymns: "Love Divine, All Loves Excelling," Wesley
         "Something for Thee," Phelps
         "All Things Are Thine," Whittier

Offertory Prayer: Holy heavenly Father, we pray that your Holy Spirit will open our eyes and help us to see how richly you have poured out your blessings on us. We thank you for both spiritual and material blessings. We come today bringing our gifts and asking that you will bless them so that others might come to know the saving grace and redeeming power of our Lord and Savior, Jesus Christ. Help us to worship you not only with our gifts but also with our hearts. Through Jesus Christ we pray. Amen.

Introduction

Most Christians give too little money to our churches because we spend too much elsewhere. And, despite all our complaints to the contrary, we spend a great deal for things we do not need. To put it another way, the Christian cause is suffering because we are wasting our resources on ourselves. Our greed for things exceeds our dedication to God.

I. The Christian attitude about earning a living.

A. *The attitude we should have about earning a living is found in Jesus's attitude about his life and mission.* Jesus identified his task: "For the son of man also came not to be served but to serve, and to give his life as a ransom for many" (Mark 10:45 RSV).
   1. Life comes to focus not in being served but in serving others.
   2. Jesus stressed giving rather than getting. Jesus's entire life was an example of giving himself to others. It was in keeping with the spirit of the heavenly Father: "For God so loved . . . that he gave." Our Lord Jesus Christ was always giving life away with both hands.

3. Jesus indicated that the secret of living is giving. When he invited people to be his disciples, he said, "For whoever would save his life will lose it, and whoever loses his life for my sake will find it" (Matt. 16:25 RSV). He went on to say that we might gain the entire world and yet lose the meaning of our own life in the process unless we learn the secret of giving. This same sentiment is expressed well by the apostle Paul in the great ethical admonition of Philippians 2. He encouraged the Philippians, 'Your attitude should be the same as that of Christ Jesus: Who, being in very nature God, did not consider equality with God something to be grasped, but made himself nothing, taking the very nature of a servant . . . and became obedient to death—even death on a cross!" (Phil. 2:5–8).

B. *Jesus frequently warned his followers against greed and covetousness.*

1. "Do not lay up for yourselves treasures on earth, where moth and rust consume and where thieves break in and steal, but lay up for yourselves treasures in heaven, where neither moth nor rust consumes and where thieves do not break in and steal. For where your treasure is, there will your heart be also" (Matt. 6:19–21 RSV).

2. In Jesus's story of the rich young ruler (Matt. 19:16–22), he indicated that the young man walked away sorrowful because he was unable to break loose from his possessions. He had acquired great wealth, a high standard of morality, and a beginning appreciation for eternal life. But the young man failed the test when Jesus told him he lacked only one thing, and that was to give away his possessions. Jesus did not usually require his converts to give away all their possessions, but this individual did not own his possessions; his possessions owned him. The test of whether we own our money is if we have the freedom and the power to give it away. If not, our money owns us. The young man could not give his allegiance to God; he had given it all to his wealth.

3. In the story of the successful farmer (Luke 12:13–21), the farmer's sin was not his successful farming nor his building plans. Rather, Jesus called him a fool because the decision of what to do with his surplus showed that he had made the wrong decision about the meaning of life. He thought that all of life centered in himself; he had forgotten God.

4. In Jesus's story about the rich man and Lazarus (Luke 16:19–31), the rich man stood condemned before God not because he was rich but because he tried to keep all his riches for himself and allowed his wealth to blind him to the presence of a poor man who lay begging at his gate. Modem Christians

had better pay attention to that story when they decide what to do with the surplus of wealth that comes through their hands.

C. *Paul's comments about earning a living.*

1. In our text of the morning (Eph. 4:28), a thief who has become a Christian is admonished to do honest work with his hands. Such honest toil will contribute toward his continuing salvation and also make it possible for him to contribute to others who are in need.

2. The Scripture lesson of the morning limits food and services to those who work. Obviously, the text assumes that one is healthy, able, and has opportunity to work. Provisions are made for those who cannot work.

II. The Christian attitude toward management of resources.

A. *The word* stewardship *means "management."* The word designates the role of a trustee who serves as the manager of a house for its original owner.

1. The Christian sees life as a matter of total stewardship. All of life, with its resources, is a gift from God to be managed. The Christian finds it meaningful to be a trustee under God over life as a trust.

2. Faithfulness in such management is the basis for final judgment. Jesus told several parables that clearly indicate that we will stand before God and give an account to him of all that we did with all that was entrusted to us. It is not merely a matter of money, although that may be a very important part of it.

B. *Christians must pay their obligations.* Of course, there should never be any doubt about this matter and an explanation is unnecessary. However, it might prove profitable to read an ethical section from Paul's letter to the Romans. In 13:1–7 he admonishes Christians to pay all of their taxes, revenue, and respect to whom such things are due. There can be no doubt but that Christians must bear their full share of the costs of society.

C. *Christians must avoid unnecessary indebtedness.* While the modem world is quite different from the ancient world with reference to credit practices and indebtedness, there is a principle that must be heeded today. The apostle said, "Owe no one anything, except to love one another" (Rom. 13:8 RSV). There are also parables that teach of the dangers of indebtedness. Indebtedness limits our freedom of choice and increases the pressure against being free to do what we know we ought to do. Worst of all, many Christians are poor stewards of their money to God because of their heavy indebtedness for material things. If our indebtedness prevents us from serving God with our resources, a serious wrong has been done.

III. Modern spending habits that threaten Christian stewardship.

A. *The habit of buying things we don't need.* Modem Americans, even when they term themselves poor, live in great luxury. We buy too many things we do not need, many of which are detrimental to us and to others.

    1. We do not distinguish between greed and need. We might define need as a reasonable standard of living including food, clothing, shelter, transportation, various insurances, medical care, and so on. Somewhere in the list we go from "needs" to "wants."

    2. We do not distinguish between enough and surplus. We express our greed in our earning power as well as in our spending. Somewhere along the line of necessities we reach a point that should be marked "enough." Beyond that point, we should apply the label "surplus." One small responsibility increases when we move from the area called "necessities" into the area called "surplus."

B. *The habit of spending beyond our means—buying on credit.* One of the two or three greatest sins of modern Christians, in terms of stewardship, is living beyond our means.

    1. There are the "need suppliers." These individuals and/or corporations manufacture or import for us numerous luxuries we not only do not need, but we cannot afford.

    2. Then there are the "need creators." These are the advertisers who convince us that we need things we really don't need. Their advertising is so persuasive that we buy the items to satisfy our greed.

    3. The third conspirator is credit buying. Easy credit makes it possible for us to buy things we cannot afford and do not need. This tragic mismanagement of resources has not only robbed many people of some of the necessities of life later but has all but crippled stewardship practices within the churches. However, lest we lay the blame on the wrong party, let us Christians recognize that need suppliers, need creators, and easy credit could not succeed without our greed.

C. *Disastrous results for our Christian stewardship.*

    1. Individual Christian stewards. Many Christians are so enslaved to their mortgages that they actually find it hard to practice Christian stewardship. The tragedy of this situation is compounded by the fact that frequently their indebtedness is for things they really don't need. With easy credit they have bought cottages, travel trailers, boats, and recreational vehicles whose depreciation alone will eat up all of the financial surplus that could have gone into education, contributions,

and savings. But the greater tragedy is the loss of personal freedom that people should have but cannot have when their "souls belong to the company store."

2. For churches and denominational institutions. The disastrous results here have been twofold: Churches have received less financial support because of the greed and wasteful spending of their members, and churches have themselves fallen into the same greedy and wasteful habits.

In the first instance, churches spend most of their money on the operation of their own building and ministry and have little left for world missions. Even major denominations sometimes do little more than maintain their weakened outposts. One of the largest denominations in the United States records statistics that its churches spend over 90 percent of all their money on their own local operation and give less than 10 percent of it to missions beyond the church.

In the second instance, many churches have followed the disastrous course of falling to the temptations of the same conspiracy. They think that churches ought to be air-conditioned throughout, and have such things as wall-to-wall carpeting, assembly grounds and camps for weekend retreats, and fleets of buses to take them back and forth. When churches are so preoccupied with the same kind of things, how can they expect their members to be spiritually minded? A church can raise $500,000 to renovate its sanctuary more easily than it can raise $50,000 for hunger relief on the other side of the world. No wonder people don't believe in the church!

Conclusion

Christians must determine a "Christian lifestyle" and then live it.

1. This means that we must allow our lifestyle to be determined by Christian values and teachings rather than by the world around us. We are the ones who believe that God is the Creator and the world belongs to him. We are the ones who believe that we have a responsibility to God for the world and for others. We cannot meet those obligations apart from a Christian lifestyle.

   We will have to decide when enough is enough, and we will have to be content with it. If we live within our means, we then will be able to contribute adequately to support these genuine needs.

2. We must recognize that our greed has led to the rape of nature and to the robbery of civilization and society. We have participated in crime, and we must repent first. Then we must lead in establishing a way of life that is more compatible with the faith we profess.

3. We must designate and give a reasonable portion of our earnings for genuinely Christian causes. There is no way for Christian institutions to accomplish their tasks of teaching, witnessing, nurturing, and winning the world apart from this support.
4. We must give a higher percentage of our surplus to worthy causes than we have ever done before.

SUNDAY EVENING, NOVEMBER 18

Title: Be Sure to Let Him In

Text: "Behold, I stand at the door and knock; if any one hears my voice and opens the door, I will come in to him and eat with him, and he with me" **(Rev. 3:20 RSV)**.

Scripture Reading: John 1:11–13

Introduction

The resurrection declared Christ to be the Son of God with power. By his Spirit, he has walked down through the corridors of time ministering to the spiritual needs of those who are willing to look to him in faith and to follow him in faithfulness. The beautiful words of our text present a picture of the living Christ full of pathos. He is standing at the door of the churches eager to come in and to bring the blessings of God.

This text has been used effectively as the basis for many evangelistic sermons. The Christ stands at the heart's door of the lost person wanting to come in to bring forgiveness and eternal life. However, to interpret this verse in its context, we must recognize that it refers primarily to the seven churches in Revelation 2 and 3.

Is it possible that you have been neglecting to let Jesus Christ come fully into the services of your church?

We can shut him out in a number of different ways. Some shut him out because of their lack of faith. They do not come to the house of God with an attitude of expectancy that Jesus will keep his promise to meet with those who gather in his name. Many shut him out through irreverence because they do not recognize that the worship service is a time and place where Jesus comes to meet with his disciples. Some shut him out because of a self-righteous and critical attitude toward those about them. One cannot be self-righteous and critical toward others and enjoy the full blessings of Jesus's presence at the same time.

Let's allow Jesus Christ to come fully into our church life.

I. Let Jesus Christ come into worship services of the church.

Do not shut him out. Let him come into worship services when you meet together with other believers.

A. *Let him come in as the Savior who is eager to save everyone who has not yet come to know him in the forgiveness of sin.*

B. *Let him come in to be your leader.* He told the fisherman, "Follow me." Expect him to give you guidance for the road of life.

C. *Let him come in to be your healer.* He can heal the emotional hurts of your heart and life. He can bring health to your soul if you will let him have his way in your life.

D. *Let him come into the worship service as your Friend who loves you, accepts you, and is eager to assist you.*

E. *Let him come into the worship service as the Lord of Lords with the authority to give you orders for your life.*

II. Let Jesus Christ come into your Bible class.

Jesus Christ, the living Lord, will use your Bible teacher to help you better understand the Word of God. Jesus Christ has given the gift of the Holy Spirit to open up the Scriptures to your understanding and your understanding to the Scriptures.

You expect your Bible study teacher and the students to be present. Would it not be wise to expect Jesus Christ to come into your classroom to enlighten your minds as you open up his Word?

III. Let Jesus Christ come into the song service of your church.

We should not be singing for applause. Neither should we be singing for our own spiritual enrichment alone. We should be singing out of our hearts to the Lord and for the Lord. This will bring spiritual warmth into our hearts and make it possible for the Lord to bring his blessings into our lives through the ministry of music.

IV. Let Jesus Christ come into the service of the church.

Often we think of church services in terms of the stated meeting times. We have morning worship and evening worship and midweek prayer services. These are actually but the times when the congregation comes together for prayer and worship and praise. In reality the church service is that which is rendered seven days a week out in the community in the name of Jesus Christ and on behalf of others.

As we go out into the world where we live and work and play, we should go as the servants of the living Lord. His promise is, "Lo, I am with you always, to the close of the age" (Matt. 28:20 RSV).

Conclusion

Jesus Christ wants to come into the worship services where you meet with others, into the classroom where you study God's Word, and into the service that you render in his name during the week. Be sure and let him come in. Beware lest you shut him out. To do so is to impoverish your life and to deprive him of the honor and glory of working in you and through you to bring others into the family of God.

WEDNESDAY EVENING, NOVEMBER 21

Title: One Exercising Authority

Text: "And Jesus answering saith unto them, Neither do I tell you by what authority I do these things" (**Mark 11:33**).

Scripture Reading: Mark 11

Introduction

The chief priests, scribes, and elders were overwhelmed by Jesus's teachings and deeds. He had performed in such a responsible manner that they asked him pointedly, "By what authority doest thou these things? and who gave thee this authority to do these things?" (v. 28). These people had witnessed an authoritative display of deeds and wisdom; they had to know his source. Jesus displayed his power in four areas: over the people, over prayer, over the temple, and over religion.

I. Over the people (Mark 11:1–11).

A. *Actions of the people.* When Jesus and his disciples approached Jerusalem, he commanded two of his followers to go and get a colt that had never been ridden. They immediately obeyed without question.

B. *Property of people.* Some people were gathered near the colt. They questioned the actions of the disciples as they untied the animal. Their reply was, "The Lord hath need of him" (v. 3) The owners of the beast apparently gave permission for the disciples to take the colt. Whether Jesus had prior contact with the owner or not, the Lord had authority over the possession of this animal.

C. *Worship of people.* As Jesus entered the city of Jerusalem on the back of the colt, people spontaneously worshiped him as he passed by. The crowd made some strong claims for Christ, and he did not reject their compliments or rebuke them. Rather, he approved of their actions.

II. Over prayer (Mark 11:12–14, 20–26).

A. *Fig tree incident.* The withering of the fig tree seemed beyond reasoning. But this is exactly what Jesus wanted to teach his followers. His power to make and answer requests superseded all reasonable and natural sequences.

B. *Faith taught.* When the disciples returned to the fig tree, they noticed that it was dried up from the roots. Jesus used this as an object lesson to express the need for faith.

C. *Lesson in prayer.* Jesus then challenged his followers to attempt things that appeared to be impossible. Through faith in Christ, "nothing shall be impossible" (Matt. 17:20).

III. Over the temple (Mark 11:15–19).

A. *Abuses in the temple.* The populace had made the temple a den of thieves. They were selling inferior animals for sacrifice and charging too much to exchange money. The very purpose of the temple had been perverted.

B. *Cleansing the temple.* To the common observer, Jesus was an ordinary Jew with no authority. Yet, using physical force, he took it upon himself to cast the thieves, blasphemers, and animals out of the temple area. He exerted an authority that could have come only from God through him.

C. *Teaching concerning the temple.* Jesus quoted Isaiah 56:7 to reveal the teaching of God regarding the temple. The scribes and chief priests actually responded in fear rather than with righteous indignation. Though they did not like Jesus or approve of him, they had to respect his doctrines of truth and righteousness.

IV. Over the religious (Mark 11:27–33).

A. *Religious leaders.* When Jesus returned to Jerusalem, he was met by the full force of religious leadership. The chief priests, the scribes, and the elders all joined forces for the sole purpose of bringing Jesus into account before their vigilante committee. They obviously felt threatened by his recent activities in the temple.

B. *Questioning of Jesus.* These leaders asked Jesus two questions: "By what authority doest thou these things? and who gave thee this authority to do these things?" (v. 28). They wanted to challenge him and also anyone who might be supporting him. They were admitting by the very nature of these questions that Jesus had been acting with spiritual authority, for they questioned the source of this authority.

C. *Authority and truth equated.* Jesus placed the men in a quandary by bringing up the issue of the authority of John the Baptist. They were unable to answer Jesus's question, and he refused to answer theirs. But by raising the issue of John the Baptist, Jesus taught the maxim that authority finds its source in truth. Anytime truth is present, it carries a built-in authority to accomplish its purpose.

Conclusion

This chapter on authority is concluded with the concept that Jesus exercised authority, even over those who challenged his authority.

SUNDAY MORNING, NOVEMBER 25

Title: Big Deal, Big Barn, Big Fool

Text: "But God said to him, 'Fool! This night your soul is required of you; and the things you have prepared, whose will they be?'" **(Luke 12:20 RSV)**.

Scripture Reading: Luke 12:13–21

Hymns: "We Gather Together," Anonymous
"Count Your Blessings," Oatman
"Make Me a Channel of Blessings," Smyth

Offertory Prayer: Holy heavenly Father, we thank you for revealing your love to us through the Scriptures. We thank you for the manner in which you have worked in and through the lives of believers in ages gone by. We thank you for the blessings you have sent into our lives through pastors, teachers, parents, and others. We thank you for every uplifting influence that has crossed the pathway of our life. Today, Lord, we come bringing tithes and offerings as symbols of our desire to be totally involved in your service. Bless these gifts and use them for your glory and for the good of all humankind. We pray in Jesus's name. Amen.

Introduction

Jesus's parables are marvelous little stories taken from everyday life that reveal profound truths. The one before us today is a very disturbing drama. It was prompted by what appeared to be an innocent request that Jesus settle a dispute about a family inheritance. Jesus warned his hearers against covetousness. He reminded them that life "does not consist in the abundance" of material wealth. Then he told a story about a successful farmer with a bountiful harvest, a grand building plan, and a retirement plan that would gain 99 percent approval in modern America. Finally, he called the man a fool.

I. This successful farmer really did have a "big deal."

A. *Such success is the justifiable reward for many stewards.* We can safely assume that this farmer had planned well, had labored long, and now was bountifully rewarded for his investment. This is what life is about, and God has never condemned anyone for being a good steward.

B. *There are many "big deals" among contemporary Christian stewards.*
   1. I knew of some rice farmers in the Mississippi delta who planted a crop in 1942 expecting to receive fifty cents a bushel for their rice. Instead, they received more than two dollars per bushel for a bountiful harvest. That was a big deal.
   2. A schoolteacher moved to Las Vegas, Nevada, in its early days and invested her small earnings in plots of real estate that later magnified in value until she was a rich woman. That was a big deal.

3. I know a Christian layman, an attorney, who purchased some newspaper establishments for $250, 000, which just a few years later were worth more than $3 million. That was a big deal.

C. *There is nothing necessarily wrong with big deals.* The farmer in Jesus's story and the three people in my illustrations did nothing wrong. A combination of factors had caused their initial investment to grow considerably.

D. *But something went wrong with this big deal that Jesus told about.* Jesus called the man a fool. What was the problem? The man was covetous and seemed to think that life consisted in the abundance of possessions.

II. Building the big barn was not his sin.

He was not called a fool because he chose to change vocations from farming to building. He was not a fool because he chose to build a bigger barn, unless, of course, his bigger barn would cover the whole farm and leave no land for farming.

A. *Proper management of surplus is responsible stewardship.* Jesus would not condemn the man for building adequate storehouses in which to preserve the grain he had grown. Rather, Jesus would approve of such responsible management of the rewards of the man's labor.

B. *Furthermore, waste is sinful.* There is a rich tradition in Scripture and in Christian understanding that discourages waste and encourages the careful management of physical resources.

C. *What was wrong with the decision to build a bigger barn?* This man was a fool for reasons that lie deeper in the story. They involve covetousness, selfishness, the wrong understanding of life, and perhaps something even more deadly to the human spirit.

III. Why did God call this diligent farmer a fool?

A. *The farmer considered only one option—keeping it all.* According to the narrative before us, the farmer asked the important question: "What shall I do, for I have nowhere to store my crops?" (Luke 12:17 RSV). And then he announced his plan: He would find some way to keep it all.

One wonders about the employees on the farm and about the neighbors whose crops did not yield so bountifully. And what about the poor who had no farms at all? There is no mention of sharing or of making an offering. There is no hint of an obligation to God who sent the rain and the sun and gave the increase. There is consideration of only one option—keeping it all.

B. *He failed to recall his religious instruction.*

373

1. "The earth is the LORD's, and the fulness thereof, the world and those who dwell therein" (Ps. 24:1). The setting in Palestine requires that we think of this man in terms of his Jewish religious training. In biblical faith, one always looks to God as the source of all that is.
2. People are stewards under God. While the earth belongs to God, it has been entrusted to people. People live "in-between"—under God and above nature. The details of our story indicate that this rich farmer did not recall these religious lessons.
3. The man's life was focused in the wrong place. Since people are creatures of God, our lives are supposed to be focused on God. However, the successful farmer was concerned only about himself. Did you notice how often he used the first person pronoun I? Did you notice that his plans for the future included references to no one but himself?

C. *Apparently, he lived and labored for the wrong reasons.* A wise man lives and works for reasons beyond himself. A fool thinks of no one but himself. Who could know joy without the love and respect of a family? Who could live a meaningful life without reference to neighbors and friends? Who could work and live without recognizing his obligation for the stranger within and without his gates? Who could call it living if he had no other reason in life but that expressed in his enthusiastic statement, "Soul, you have ample goods laid out for many years; take your ease, eat, drink, be merry" (v. 19 RSV). Surely this man was a fool.

D. *He was a fool because of his attitude and action regarding the surplus.*
1. There is a distinction between needs and surplus. We face a tremendously important question after we have achieved the necessities of life for ourselves and our families. The additional resources entrusted to our care present both an opportunity and a peril. The farmer in our story did not recognize the tremendous challenge and responsibility that come along with the surplus entrusted to us. Its potential for good or ill is enormous, and it is potentially good or ill for us as well as for others. Now it begins to be clear why God called him a fool. He did not recognize the basic distinction that would solve so many of the inequities of human existence.

   If the men and women of faith in Christ would consider this distinction, they could solve many of the injuries and hurts that afflict the human family in our time. Is it not obvious that we, like the rich fool, have failed to recognize when we passed from the realm of needs and necessities into that area in which we too enjoyed a large surplus? God called this man a fool for missing that distinction and for failing to act in the light of his added opportunity.

2. Are the barns too big on your farm and mine? On your journey in life, have you progressively moved to larger and more expensive houses? Have you progressively bought automobiles beyond the normal need for transportation but expensive in cost and operation in the realm of luxury? Have you and I been satisfied when our earnings provided a reasonable retirement plan, or have we fallen into the pit of hoarding up for the future beyond normal expected needs?

   It seems reasonable to believe that God would expect us to make normal provision for the uncertainties of life and for tomorrow if we can do so without hurting ourselves or depriving others. But, at the same time, it seems that this story may be saying to us that on our farms the barns are too big and they will stand as awful evidence against us when we come before God and answer for our greed and luxury while we lived in a world that was beset with hunger and lack. Yes, God might also call you and me "fools."

E. *Perhaps this man had forgotten his dreams or, worse than that, had never had any.*

1. How many times have we wanted to give to our church or to some other worthy cause but were unable to do so? How many times have we said, "I would like to do this certain thing, but I cannot afford it"? How many times have we seen people really suffering and wished we were able to relieve that suffering? How often do young people look to their mature years with strong resolves that they will not exhibit the same grasping greed as their predecessors?

   Was this man an exception to the rule? Had he never dreamed about the good things he could do with such a bountiful harvest? Had he never had any hopes or goals worthy of such a harvest? Had he never felt the need of human beings around him and wished that he had the means to do something about it?

2. But what about those dreams? Had he forgotten them or had he never had them? In either case, he would still be called a fool. Life does not consist in the abundance of possessions, but it may consist of using those possessions for some worthy person or cause.

   Jesus had warned about laying up treasure on earth where it would be attacked by moth and rust. He suggested that while we could not take it with us, we could send it on ahead by laying up treasure in heaven as in escrow. But this man sought to lay it all up for himself and was shocked with the awareness with which we may be shocked someday. The only difference is that this man knew the precise day of judgment. The judgment is the same if we have lived selfishly and thought of life only in terms of ourselves. God will say to us "Fool! This night your soul is required of you" (v. 20 RSV).

IV. Would God call us fools for our use of surplus?

A. *It boils down to a basic question:* How are we handling the surplus that comes to us? Do we, like the rich fool in the Bible, deal only with the option of keeping it all for ourselves? Do we recall our stewardship role under God? Do we labor and live for ourselves instead of for God? Do we deal responsibly with surplus?

B. *What is the evidence against us?* The answer to our first question will point us to the answer to this question. What have we done with our surplus? What percentage of it has gone to the church? What percentage of it has gone to help others and to relieve human suffering? What percentage of it are we zealously guarding for ourselves?

C. *What about our dreams, our hopes, and our visions?* This also will tell us whether or not we consider life to consist in the abundance of possessions or whether we are laying up treasures in heaven and are rich toward God.

Do you recall the youthful hopes and aspirations you had about what you would do when you were financially independent or when you had more money than you really needed? Do you recall the enthusiasm you had for the mission effort, and is that enthusiasm still alive? Do you remember how you wanted to help someone who was poor but were unable to do so? Are you able to do so now? There are still poor people.

Conclusion

Earlier I mentioned a schoolteacher who had bought land in Las Vegas, Nevada, which escalated in value. This woman died before she was fifty years of age, but she gave far more of her life and her means to the cause of Christ than most wealthy people give. At the time of her death, she was giving about 30 percent of her current earnings to her local church. In addition, she kept money available for mission pastors in remote and poor areas. She gave additional money to missionary causes outside this country. Many people knew that they could secure money from her to help people in their times of need. She lived modestly, happy with the things she really needed. She never did know the lust for luxury that afflicted so many of her contemporaries. But surely she stored up great treasure in heaven by her giving. Perhaps in this parable of Jesus there is a message that will turn you and me from the course of life that leads to the final verdict "Fool" into that other direction that hears the benediction, "You have been faithful."

SUNDAY EVENING, NOVEMBER 25

Title: How Well Do You Hear?

Text: "He that hath an ear, let him hear what the Spirit saith unto the churches" **(Rev. 3:22)**.

Scripture Reading: Revelation 3

Introduction

Jesus said imperatively, if you have ears to hear, use them. Hear what the Spirit of God is saying to the church. Jesus declared that humans are spiritual receiving stations. We have the capacity to receive communication from God if we will pay attention, listen, and concentrate on what God is trying to communicate. Jesus gave his disciples the same command: "He that hath ears to hear, let him hear" (Mark 4:9).

Our capacity to receive is determined by our listening. If a student enrolls in a class and for some reason quits paying attention as the teacher speaks, the time will come when the pupil will not be able to comprehend what the teacher is saying. We develop our capacity to hear and to receive what we hear.

I. A person is a spiritual receiving station.

Are you aware that you are a spiritual receiving station? That God is trying to get through to you? God is trying to communicate with you. Sometimes he puts forth great effort before we finally realize that he is speaking and decide to listen.

I remember one night while in Japan, I decided to call home. I placed the call at 10:00 p.m., which was 7:00 a.m. in Tulsa, Oklahoma. I called the international operator and told her whom I wanted to call, and at 12:00 my phone rang. We had established communication with Tulsa at 9:00 Sunday morning. I was able to give my wife the results of our Sunday night services in Japan so she could report them to the Sunday morning service in Oklahoma. There are times when God spends a great deal more time than that trying to get through to us.

How well do you hear? Some people hear better than others. Some creatures can hear much better than a human being while others hear less. An alligator can hear only one-fifth as well as man. A minnow can hear only one-fourth as well as man. A frog can hear one-half as well as man. A dog can hear more than twice as well as man. Some of us have noticed that when sirens go off, our dogs seem to be in agony. This is due to sound waves vibrating the eardrums and causing pain. A cat can hear two and a half times as well as humans, and bats can hear five times as well as humans. When it comes to listening to God, instead of listening like the alligator or the frog, listen like the cat or bat to hear everything that God is trying to say to you.

II. The ability to hear.

A. *Only one in approximately six thousand babies is born without the ability to hear.* This is a tragic loss, but we can be grateful that only one out of six thousand comes into the world without the ability to hear.

B. *It is true not only in the physical life but also in the spiritual life that the ability to hear often declines as one grows older.*

C. *The ability to hear can be lost by disease or accident in both the spiritual and the physical realm.* Have you ever thought about the fact that you could lose your ability to hear God? You can destroy your own spiritual hearing, your ability to hear God's voice. One of the strange teachings of the Bible is that when people hear the call of God, unless they hear and heed and respond properly, they do something to their capacity to hear the second time. One of the most dangerous things a person can do is to say no to the clearly known will of God, for to do so is to deaden one's spiritual eardrum.

III. The invitation to hear.

A. *God spoke through Moses to encourage the people to hear (Deut. 31:11–15).*

B. *God spoke through Isaiah to encourage the people to hear (Isa. 55:3).* To hear and refuse to heed is to deaden your own eardrum and bring about insensitivity to the voice of God. Most of us at sometime in life will reach over and turn off our alarm clock and go back to sleep. If we did this morning after morning, the time would come when we in complete slumber could reach over and turn off the alarm and not be aware that we turned it off. This also happens in the spiritual realm. A lost person comes to church and hears the call of God over and over and reaches out and turns the alarm off. The time will come when this person can hear God speaking but will turn off his voice without realizing that he or she has done so. This person has lost the ability to hear.

IV. The importance of hearing.

The ability to hear enables one to both give and receive communications. Since warnings, invitations, commissions, comfort, and counsel from God come to us through the avenue of hearing, we need to recognize how important it is. God spoke through Moses to the people of Israel. Through Moses, God invited the people of Israel to open up their ears and to hear the truth that would lead them to the abundant life.

Have you been listening? Have you been hearing what God is saying to you?

Jesus repeatedly encouraged his disciples to hear what God would have them to hear, and to not close their ears by tolerating and encouraging sin in their lives.

V. Are you listening? God speaks.

A. *Are you deaf because of sin?* It is dangerous to make a practice of sin, for it will deceive you. To know that there is something in our life that is contrary to God's will and do nothing about it will dull our hearing.

B. *Some of us are deaf because of preoccupation.* We never take time out to be alone with God and let him speak to us. How long has it been since you have gotten away from everything to the extent that you could hear nothing? I hope that during our worship services we can hear what God is saying to us. The best time spent in prayer is when we are trying to listen to what God is saying.

Conclusion

How well do you hear? As well as the frog or the alligator or the cat or the bat? Some people can hear better than others. This is a capacity that can be developed if we will just be still and listen to what God is saying to us. God is speaking to some of us right now, and he will be trying to break through and communicate with all of us tomorrow and every day. Let those who have ears hear.

WEDNESDAY EVENING, NOVEMBER 28

Title: One Probing Man's Heart

Text: "And thou shalt love the Lord thy God with all thy heart, and with all thy soul, and with all thy mind, and with all thy strength: this is the first commandment. And the second is like, namely this, Thou shalt love thy neighbour as thyself" **(Mark 12:30–31)**.

Scripture Reading: Mark 12

Introduction

A servant's responsibility is to carry out tasks for his or her master. The task of the Servant-Messiah in this portion of Scripture was to probe human hearts about several major questions of importance to their own well-being. Consequently, this chapter is a painful, introspective search of the heart.

I. Question of ownership (Mark 12:1–12).

A. *Parable of the heir.* Jesus gave a parable about a vineyard that was leased out to husbandmen. The husbandmen rebelled against the servants of the owner as they came to collect the rent. Finally, the owner sent his son. They killed the son with the intent of stealing the vineyard. The eventual end was the destruction of the husbandmen. This is the story in capsule form of Jesus's ministry.

B. *Probe of the heart.* The people present felt that he had spoken this parable against them. And so he had! The piercing message had reached its target.

C. *"They . . . went their way" (v. 12).* The response was tragic. Instead of repenting and turning to Jesus, "they . . . went their way." "Their way" was one of self-condemnation.

II. Question of rulership (Mark 12:13–17).

A. *Issue of Caesar's rule.* The Pharisees' stated purpose for asking Jesus the question regarding Caesar was "to catch him in his words." The Pharisees and the Herodians quizzed him, "Is it lawful to give tribute to Caesar, or not?" (vv. 13–14). They felt they had Jesus in a dilemma. Either way he answered would be wrong according to the interpretation of the questioners.

B. *Probe of the heart.* Jesus looked beyond the surface of the question. In the depths of their hearts, he detected hypocrisy. He chastised their hearts with the sincere reply, "Why tempt ye me?" (v. 15).

C. *"Render unto Caesar."* After an inspection of their hearts and of the coin of Caesar, he perplexed their minds with the reply, "Render to Caesar the things that are Caesar's, and to God the things that are God's" (v. 17). The image of Caesar was stamped on the coin. The image of God was stamped on man.

III. Question of resurrection (Mark 12:18–27).

A. *Distorted belief.* Jesus exposed an error in the theology of the Sadducees regarding the Resurrection. They sought to mock the fact of the Resurrection by an absurd illustration using a teaching of Moses.

B. *Probe of the heart.* Jesus immediately discerned their ignorance of the Scriptures and of the power of God. The mockers of God's truths are always ignorant of the scope of Scripture. They have not tasted of God's power.

C. *"God of the living."* After giving an authoritative answer to their question, Jesus emphasized the heart of it. He replied, "He is not the God of the dead, but the God of the living" (v. 27). Consequently, the Resurrection is absolutely essential.

IV. Questions of commandment (Mark 12:28–34).

A. *Genuine concern.* With a sincere heart, a scribe asked Jesus which of the commandments he considered to be the greatest. The Servant responded to this inquiry with tenderness and a straightforward answer. He maintained that love of God was primary. But this would lead to a consequential love of one's neighbor.

B. *Probe of the heart.* The heart of the scribe was probed in light of the truth proposed by Christ. He adapted his ways to the way of Truth.

C. *"Not far from the kingdom."* Jesus shared with this scribe a very intimate response. He declared that he was "not far from the kingdom of God" (v. 34). The scribe's yieldedness had allowed him access to the kingdom of God.

V. Question of David (Mark 12:35–37).

A. *Jesus raised a question.* Jesus took the offense in perplexing his critics. He knew of the reverence the religious leaders had for King David. They tenaciously held that David's words were divine truth. Jesus quoted a messianic passage from David where the great king had avowed allegiance to the Christ. Jesus asked them, "How could David call the Christ his Lord if the Christ was supposed to be the Son of David?" (see v. 37).

B. *Probe of the heart.* Though both facts of David's relationship to the Christ are true, the purpose of the question was to reveal to the critics their extreme limitations in understanding the things of God.

C. *"Son revealed as Lord."* Jesus's emphasis to the "common people" was to reveal the Son of God as the Lord, even of David.

VI. Question of sincerity (Mark 12:38–44).

A. *Outward religion.* As one would expect him to do, Jesus questioned the validity of the outward show of religion of these people.

B. *Probe of the heart.* The heart was exposed when the prayers of the so-called righteous ones were placed alongside their deeds. They prayed and then took advantage of the widows.

C. *"Widow's mite."* An illustration of total sincerity is given in the story of the widow casting her mite into the temple treasury.

Conclusion

The Lord has probed deeply into the hearts of his followers and critics in this portion of Scripture.

DECEMBER

■ **Sunday Mornings**

The theme for Sunday mornings is "Preparing the Heart for Christmas."

■ **Sunday Evenings**

The theme for Sunday evenings is "The Living Christ and the Marks of His Church."

■ **Wednesday Evenings**

Close out the year by completing the series "Jesus As Mark Saw Him."

SUNDAY MORNING, DECEMBER 2

Title: Christmas: Star and Scepter

Text: "There shall come a Star out of Jacob, and a Sceptre shall rise out of Israel" (**Num. 24:17**).

Scripture Reading: Numbers 24:12–17; Matthew 2:1–12

Hymns: "Brightest and Best," Heber
"We Three Kings of Orient Are," Hopkins
"As with Gladness Men of Old," Dix

Offertory Prayer: O Lord, our God, we thank you for the dawning of another season when we remember that the great God of this universe entered the stream of history and came down to earth to dwell among us. All things are yours, and we are yours; and as we lay our gifts on your altar today, we remember that "we give you but your own." Bless this service this morning. May its every part be an offering on your altar. Bless our gifts, but may we first give ourselves. In Jesus's name we pray. Amen.

Introduction

What blessings did Christ's coming bring to the world? What blessings does he offer to our hearts now? The answer from this text is a star and scepter, guidance and security, revelation and sovereignty. What blessings do we need more today than light amid our darkness and power amid our weakness? What light can compare with the light of Bethlehem's star, and what power can compare with the power of the King of Kings and Lord of Lords? The message of our text is carried in two figures—the star and the scepter.

I. The blessing of Christ's coming is set forth by a star.

Put two widely separated Scriptures together, our text and Matthew 2:1–2, and you have prophecy and fulfillment, both symbol and fact. "There shall come a Star out of Jacob." That is prophecy. "Now when Jesus was born in Bethlehem of Judaea in the days of Herod the king, behold, there came wise men from the east to Jerusalem, saying, Where is he that is born King of the Jews? for we have seen his star in the east, and are come to worship him" (Matt. 2:1–2). That is fulfillment of prophecy. What did that star symbolize?

A. *That star was and is a harbinger of hope, an announcement of hope's fulfillment.* Jeremiah spoke of "the hope of Israel" (Jer. 14:8; 17:13). That was a stock phrase in Jesus's day used to refer to the coming Messiah. Paul, imprisoned in Rome, used it in the past tense, "that for the hope of Israel I am bound with this chain" (Acts 28:20). That star over Bethlehem said, "Look! Hope is fulfilled! The Christ has been born! He is here! See his star!"

B. *That star was and is a symbol of revelation and light.* The prophet Isaiah said, "The people that walked in darkness have seen a great light: they that dwell in the land of the shadow of death, upon them hath the light shined" (Isa. 9:2). After the birth of John the Baptist, his father, Zacharias, steeped in the messianic prophecies and led by the Holy Spirit, spoke of the visitation of "the dayspring from on high . . . to give light to them that sit in darkness" (Luke 1:78–79). In the first verses of his gospel, John says, "In him was life; and the life was the light of men. And the light shineth in darkness; and the darkness comprehended it not" (John 1:4–5). The tragedy of the darkness that has settled down in our day is that it is so unnecessary. The light has come. The light shines.

C. *That star was and is a fixed point by which to steer, a faithful standard to guide us on our way.* Before instruments, charts, and radar, it was the stars that guided ships into the harbor. The stars were fixed, stable, unvarying. This is the message of Bethlehem's star: God is faithful.

D. *That star was and is the only anchor for our faith.* If we are living in a stormy time when darkness often settles upon us, we know that above the darkness the stars of God's love are shining still, holding the world together. Christmas brings hope, light, guidance, and faith.

II. The blessing of Christ's coming is also set forth by a scepter.

An Oriental monarch was always provided with a scepter that he carried as a symbol of his authority. If, as the king sat upon his throne, one of his subjects came and bowed down before him, the touch of the king's scepter was a signal to arise. A scepter in the hand of a king meant authority and rule, majesty and power.

383

When Jeremiah said, "And a Scepter shall rise out of Israel," he was saying a king shall come out of Israel. And so say all the prophets. Christmas is "good tidings of great joy" (Luke 2:10). What are the "good tidings"?

A. *First, they say the king has been born.* When the strange visitors appeared in Jerusalem to ask, "Where is he that is born King of the Jews?" Herod was troubled for fear of a possible rival. Being unable to answer, he called together the chief priest and scribes of the people. They cited an ancient prophecy, chapter and verse, "But thou, Bethlehem Ephratah, though thou be little among the thousands of Judah, yet out of thee shall he come forth unto me that is to be ruler in Israel; whose goings forth have been from of old, from everlasting" (Mic. 5:2). The king has been born. A scepter has indeed risen out of Israel.

B. *But again, the news of Christmas is that a government has been established, not will be, but has been.* The first truth of life is this: God rules! His sovereignty remains. All authority, in heaven and on earth has been committed unto our Lord and King who was born that day (Matt. 28:18). A government has been established. "Of the increase of his government . . . there shall be no end" (Isa. 9:7). Thank God the rule of this world is in his hands and not in the hands of mere humans.

C. *And last, the news of Christmas is that the consummation of his kingdom is coming.* The king has been born? Yes, long since. His government has been established. All authority and rule is his, even now. But there are still those who rebel against his rule, and it will not always be so. A time will come when every knee will bow and every tongue will confess that he is King (Phil. 2:10–11). That time has not yet come, but it is coming.

Conclusion

In this dark hour, who knows what to do? Who knows what decisions to make? Who knows which way to turn? It is too much for humans, but not for our Lord. Revelation and sovereignty? Thank God both truths are in our world this morning if we have eyes to see and ears to hear.

SUNDAY EVENING, DECEMBER 2

Title: Hey, That's Our Church!

Text: "Is there any among you afflicted: let him pray. Is any merry? let him sing psalms. Is any sick among you? let him call for the elders of the church; and let them pray over him, anointing him with oil in the name of the Lord: And the prayer of faith shall save the sick, and the Lord shall raise him up; and if he have committed sins, they shall be forgiven him. Confess your faults one to another, and pray one for another, that ye may be healed. The effectual fervent prayer of a righteous man availeth much" **(James 5:13–16)**.

Scripture Reading: James 5:13–20

Introduction

Lyle E. Schaller, a distinguished church planner and analyst, wrote a book titled *Hey, That's Our Church!* (Nashville: Abingdon, 1975). The main thought expressed in the book is that churches can be classified by types. Just as human beings can be classified by basic body types, so churches can be classified by types. And, like people, churches often turn out to be combinations of two or more types rather than a clear-cut expression of one type.

The benefits of looking at churches in this way are at least twofold: you can understand the type of congregation that you are; and understanding the type of church that you are, you can better plan, analyze, and set goals for the performance of your church. This can help a church avoid the errors of what Schaller calls "scapegoating" or "hero worship."

The living Lord does his work through the church. What, then, are the marks of the Lord's church? By looking at the characteristics of a New Testament church, we can see some of the marks of the church of the living Lord. And we can also see what we are and where we are in ministry and mission.

For a basis of this examination, look at the concluding verses of the book of James, the most practical of the New Testament books. James deals with Christianity on the level of faith and works. He argues that faith without works is dead. What you believe will show up in what you do. It is not enough simply to affirm that you have faith, that you love God, and that you are concerned about your brother without doing something tangible about it. This shows up in church life. From these last verses in James, we see some of the marks of the early church. These must also be the marks of any church that stays true to its ministry.

I. Our church must be a worshiping church.

James expressed the idea of worship in the church with one aspect of worship—singing. The early Christian church was a singing church. More than once the apostle Paul told the church to which he wrote that as the Word of God dwelled in them they would teach one another in psalms and spiritual songs.

Singing is not incidental to what we do; it is integral to what we do. It is not just to warm us up for the sermon; it is to express something of the praise and the joy we all feel. By singing we can express something we cannot say. A famous dancer was once asked what she meant by a certain interpretive dance. She replied that if she could have said it, she would not have danced it. We sing what we cannot say. God has worked a great work in our hearts, and we have joy because of that. We must express praise to God because of that.

Worship is the primary business of the church. All else that we do grows out of it. For that reason the worship service is planned. Order in worship has been called "God's table manners." We try to come into the presence of the almighty God with good manners. The main motive of Jesus's ministry was to bring people into the presence of God. This we try to do through the worship of God.

II. Our church must be a caring church.

James first focused on caring for one another by praying for one another and especially for the healing of the sick. Then he wrote of the importance of confession of sin. If we care for one another, we will be concerned with one another's needs. The prayer meeting service of one church is given almost totally to prayer for persons in need. Those for whom prayer has been offered are sent a little card telling them that the church has prayed for them. The responses to those cards indicate that people are pleased that other Christians care enough for their needs to pray for them.

If we care for one another, people will be important. We should never be so intent on growing larger and counting people that we lose sight of individuals. Jesus centered on individuals in his ministry, and so must we. And if we care for one another, we cannot become complacent. A church must always be open to God and responsive to him.

III. Our church must be a praying church.

It is instructive that so much of this passage has to do with prayer. For the Christian and for the church, prayer can never be optional. Tennyson said, "More things are wrought by prayer than this world dreams of." We believe this; we do not always practice it.

What will prayer do? It will show us our needs. The need mentioned in this passage is illness. Prayer will lead to the confession of sin. We cannot pray without honestly facing our needs and confessing our sins to God. This sounds rather like a share group. John Wesley borrowed the practice of sharing requests from the Moravians and made it a part of the early Methodist movement, in which a weekly meeting was important.

Prayer will bring the power of God to bear on our problems. The experience of Elijah is the one the writer of James mentions (5:17–18).

IV. Our church must be a witnessing church.

The importance of witnessing can be seen in the last two verses of James. Through the church, witness is given in many ways: personal visitation, ministry, the corporate witness of the church with other churches, witnessing to friends and neighbors, lifestyle evangelism, and public preaching and worship services.

How important is Christian witness? Leonard Griffith expressed it when he said, "Outreach, evangelism, and mission are not optional activities like bowling, billiards, and Ping-Pong for the members of a religious club. They are mandates from Christ himself, a part of the original givenness of the gospel" (*We Have This Ministry* [Waco, Tex.: Word, 1975], 87). Foremost in any church's purpose must be the winning of the unsaved for Christ. And the witness must be the witness of the whole gospel. So each of us must ask ourselves that significant question put by an American tourist to a guide in Westminster Abbey: 'Young man, stop your chattering and tell me: Has anyone been saved here lately?"

Conclusion

These are the marks of the living Lord's church. Can you say, "Hey, that's our church"?

WEDNESDAY EVENING, DECEMBER 5

Title: One Issuing Warnings

Text: "And what I say unto you I say unto all, Watch" **(Mark 13:37)**.

Scripture Reading: Mark 13

Introduction

The greatest aid a servant can render to his or her master is to warn of impending events. In this portion of Scripture the Servant-Messiah issued several warnings to his followers. Each effort on his part was designated to encourage righteousness on earth. He issued warnings:

I. Concerning establishments (Mark 13:1–8).

A. *Temple to be destroyed.* The Jewish religion was centered around the temple of Jerusalem. Jesus startled his disciples with a warning that the temple would be destroyed. They were keenly interested in the details of this matter, for it was close to Jewish hearts and minds.

B. *Christ to be imitated.* Jesus issued a warning to his followers that evil ones would even try to imitate the Christ, God's greatest "establishment." The purpose of this would be to draw people away from truth into error.

C. *International conflict.* In the last days, even the solidarity of nations would be challenged. There would be problems within national groups, natural circumstances, and social needs.

II. Concerning individuals (Mark 13:9–13).

A. *Christians persecuted.* A warning was issued to the Christians that they would face persecution. Jesus gave the divine assurance that all of this would be done "for my sake." Thus, this suffering would be on behalf of Christ.

B. *Gospel to be preached.* Through the persecutions and trials, the gospel of Christ will be sent to the nations of the world.

C. *Faithful to be saved.* The warning of trial and tribulation was intensi-fied in this passage. But Jesus closed with these comforting words: "He that shall endure unto the end, the same shall be saved."

III. Concerning tribulation (Mark 13:14–23).

A. *Fulfillment of prophecy.* Obviously, this portion is not made to be enjoyed, but to be heeded. The tribulation that the world is to experience will be a fulfillment of the prophecy of Daniel (12:1).
B. *Horrible affliction.* This period will be characterized by a horrible affliction. It will be the greatest time of difficulty since creation.
C. *Elect to be saved.* As with the previous warning, the Lord concluded this ominous prophecy of events to come with a statement of comfort. The elect of God will be favored during this tragic period of history. Jesus said, "Except that the Lord had shortened those days, no flesh should be saved: but for the elect's sake, whom he had chosen, he hath shortened the days."

IV. Concerning the Second Advent (Mark 13:24–31).

A. *Son of Man returns.* To the righteous ones on earth at this time, the second coming of Christ is to be a blessing. But it is a warning to those rejecting God's way of life, for they will be chastised.
B. *Gather up his elect.* When Christ returns from heaven at the conclusion of this horrible tribulation period, he will gather his elect to himself. These are the ones who repented and turned to him for conversion during this trial.
C. *Certainty of prophecy.* Jesus proclaimed the certainty of his message. Though all tangible matters passed away, one could rely on his Word.

V. Concerning indifference (Mark 13:32–36).

A. *"Son" on journey.* Jesus presented a parable to warn his hearers of the futility of indifference. The story is about a master of a household who assigned duties to his servants before leaving on a trip.
B. *Commanded to watch.* The major task of the household was to watch for the return of the master. The task of "watching" is mentioned four times in the passage.
C. *Coming is sudden.* The purpose of the continual surveillance on the part of the workers is to take note of the return of the master. His return will be sudden and without warning.

Conclusion

The major lesson to be derived from this chapter is that God's people must "be alert." Believers are responsible to always be ready for Jesus's coming.

SUNDAY MORNING, DECEMBER 9

Title: Our Ultimate Ruler

Text: "Pilate therefore said unto him, Art thou a king then? Jesus answered, Thou sayest that I am a king. To this end was I born, and for this cause came I into the world, that I should bear witness unto the truth" **(John 18:37)**.

Scripture Reading: John 18:28–38

Hymns: "Joy to the World! The Lord Is Come," Watts
"Angels from the Realms of Glory," Montgomery
"Crown Him with Many Crowns," Bridges-Thring

Offertory Prayer: Heavenly Father, we praise your name this day for your majesty and might, your wisdom and power. We give thanks that all authority and power in heaven and on earth is yours and is not in the hands of humans. We give thanks that the whole world is in your hands. But above all, we thank you that you loved us so much that you sent your Son into this world to share all we are, except our sins, and to die on a cross for our sakes. Bless us as, like the Magi of old, we bring our gifts to lay at the feet of our King. In his name we pray. Amen.

Introduction

Jesus was bound over to Pilate by the Jewish rulers on the trumped-up charge of sedition. They said he was a threat to Caesar, that he made himself a king. Jesus set the record straight by explaining, "My kingdom is not of this world" (John 18:36). Then when Pilate asked, perhaps in jest, "Art thou a king then?" (v. 37), Jesus replied, "Thou sayest that I am a king. To this end was I born, and for this cause came I into the world" (v. 37).

This is the scriptural basis of our Advent message today. Jesus is our ultimate ruler, King of Kings and Lord of Lords, before whom, one day, every knee shall bow and every tongue confess. Three simple, biblically based affirmations will develop the thought.

I. Jesus was born to rule. He came into the world to be a king.

A. *He establishes his rule by witnessing.* "To this end was I born . . . that I should bear witness unto the truth."
1. He bore witness in his own person. No other New Testament book is more concerned with the person of Christ than John's gospel. "In the beginning was the Word, and the Word was with God, and the Word was God" (John 1:1). He refers to Christ as "king of the Jews," "the son of David," "the son of God."
2. Jesus bore witness by his works. He said, "The same works that I do bear witness of me" (John 5:36). When the Jews were at the point of stoning him he said, "Many good works have

389

I showed you from my Father; for which of those works do ye stone me?" (John 10:32).

3. He bore witness by his words. Clement Atlee once said of Winston Churchill's oratory, "Words at great moments of history are deeds." There was kindling power in Jesus's speech. When officers sent to arrest him at the Feast of Tabernacles returned empty-handed, their explanation was, "Never man spake like this man" (John 7:46). He told a multitude in a Capernaum synagogue at the conclusion of his discourse on the Bread of Life, "The words that I speak unto you, they are spirit, and they are life" (John 6:63).

B. *He establishes his rule by serving.* One way of establishing rule is by force, but inevitably this recruits the opposition that ultimately overthrows the rule. The other way is by serving others until they crave your cooperation. This is Christ's way: "I am among you as he that serveth" (Luke 22:27).

C. *He establishes his rule by redeeming.* He is the King-Redeemer. Jesus never left the world in doubt as to the purpose of his coming, "to seek and to save that which was lost" (Luke 19:10). Again he said, "I am come that they might have life, and that they might have it more abundantly" (John 10:10). He is King by the choice of his subjects, those who have believed on him unto eternal life.

II. Jesus is ruling now.

Not only was Jesus born to rule, but he is ruling now.

A. *He was born a king when an infant's wail broke the stillness of the night in a rude cattle shed in Bethlehem, and shepherds saw a great light and heard the angels sing.*

B. *He was proclaimed King when, in exact fulfillment of the prophecy of Zechariah (9:9), he entered Jerusalem to the plaudits of the multitude who cried, "Blessed be the King that cometh in the name of the Lord" (Luke 19:38).*

C. *He was crowned King when he came forth from the tomb and the angel then rolled the stone away that his disciples might enter and see and believe.* The Son of God came forth in majesty and power from the dark realm of death "because," as Peter told his audience at Pentecost, "it was not possible that he should be holden of it" (Acts 2:24). He is the King of life and death and time and eternity.

Jesus is reigning now. Paul wrote in one of his great doxologies, "Now unto the King eternal, immortal, invisible, the only wise God, be honour and glory for ever and ever. Amen" (1 Tim. 1:17). He reigns in the realm of spiritual reality. The kingdom of God is not a state or condition of this world. It is not an ideal order of nations and life. It centers around a person—the King. He is reigning now.

How wonderfully that encourages us in our discouragement. How that lifts us up out of our depression and defeat. How that strengthens us and nerves us for the battle when the odds against morality and decency and integrity are so overwhelming.

III. Ultimately, Jesus will rule over all people and over all things.

"The kingdoms of this world are become the kingdoms of our Lord, and of his Christ; and he shall reign for ever and ever" (Rev. 11:15).

A. *This was the prophet's vision.* Isaiah said, "He shall not fail nor be discouraged, till he have set judgment in the earth" (42:4). Again he said, "Thine eyes shall see the King in his beauty" (33:17). The prophets dared to dream of a time when nations would beat their swords into plowshares, their spears into pruning hooks, when nation would not lift up sword against nation, nor learn war anymore (see Isa. 2:4; Mic. 4:3).

B. *This was the psalmist's dream: "The LORD is king for ever and ever; the nations shall perish from his land" (Ps. 10:16 RSV).* Another psalmist sang, "The LORD reigns; he is robed in majesty" (93:1).

C. *This was the great apostle's faith.* To Paul, crowning Christ as King was the long-range or ultimate significance of the Resurrection (see 1 Cor. 15:24–25).

D. *This was the substance of John's apocalyptic vision.* He speaks of Christ reigning for ever and ever (Rev. 11:15). On a higher note he says, "For he is Lord of lords, and King of kings" (17:14). The highest note of all, the climax of the Bible, is Revelation 19:6: "And I heard as it were the voice of a great multitude, and as the voice of many waters, and as the voice of mighty thunderings saying, Alleluia: for the Lord God omnipotent reigneth."

E. *This is the dynamic of Christian missions, the prophet's dream that "the earth shall be full of the knowledge of the LORD, as the waters cover the sea" (Isa. 11:9).*

F. *This is the ground of Christian hope.* There is no hope except in Jesus. Every other kind of life is bounded by the limits of this shrinking world, but Christianity has all the windows open toward the limitless expanse of eternity.

Conclusion

"Thou sayest that I am a king. To this end was I born, and for this cause came I into the world" (John 18:37). "Alleluia: for the Lord God omnipotent reigneth" (Rev. 19:6). Do we believe this? This is the Christ who would meet with us this blessed season.

SUNDAY EVENING, DECEMBER 9

Title: When a Church Worships

Text: "Then the same day at evening, being the first day of the week, when the doors were shut where the disciples were assembled for fear of the Jews, came Jesus and stood in the midst, and saith unto them, Peace be unto you" **(John 20:19)**.

Scripture Reading: John 20:19–24

Introduction

Peter Marshall told this story. It was quiet on the battlefield. In the bright early summer sunshine, the air was balmy and had a breath of a garden in it. By some grotesque miracle, a bird was singing somewhere near at hand. On the firing step with his rifle laying in a groove in the parapet stood a young soldier in field gray, his uniform stained with mud and blood. On his face, so young yet strangely marked with the lines of war that made him look old, was a wistful, faraway expression. He was enjoying the sunshine and the quiet of this strange lull in the firing. The heavy guns had been silent. There was no sound to break the eerie stillness.

Suddenly a butterfly fluttered into view and alighted on the ground almost at the end of his rifle. It was a strange visitor to a battleground. But it was there, a gorgeous creature, the wings like gold leaf splashed with carmine swaying in the warm breath of spring.

As the war-weary youngster watched the butterfly, he was no longer a private in field gray. He was a boy once more, fresh and clean, swinging through a field in sunny Saxony, knee deep in clover, buttercups, and daisies. That strange visitor to the front trench recalled to him the joys of his boyhood when he had collected butterflies. It spoke to him of days of peace. It was a symbol of the lovelier things of life. It was the emblem of the eternal, a reminder that there still was beauty and peace in the world.

He forgot the enemy a few hundred yards across no man's land. He forgot the danger and privation and suffering. He forgot everything as he watched that butterfly. With all the hunger in his heart, with the resurrection of dreams and vision that he thought were gone, he reached out his hand toward that butterfly. His fingers moved slowly, cautiously, lest he frighten away this visitor to the battlefield. In showing one kind of caution, he forgot another. The butterfly was just beyond his reach, so he stretched, forgetting that watchful eyes were waiting for a target.

He brought himself out slowly until he had just a little distance to go. He could almost touch the wings that were so lovely. Then—*ping, ping.* A sniper's bullet found its mark. The stretching fingers relaxed. For the private soldier in field gray, the war was over (in Clyde E. Fant Jr. and William M. Pinson Jr., *Twenty Centuries of Great Preaching* [Waco: Word, 1971], 12:43–44).

There is always a risk when you reach for the beautiful. And worship is a reach for the beautiful. It is our attempt to reach from the squalor of the earth to the very beauty of God himself.

Notice the marks of the church that belong to the living Lord. Worship is one of those marks. Perhaps the group of believers that met together on the first day of the week following the resurrection of Jesus was a prototype of the church. They met at an accustomed time for worship. From their experience we can see what happens when a church worships.

I. When a church worships, notice the time of worship.

Notice that these people met on the first day of the week for worship. It was not the seventh day, the Sabbath, but the first day, the Lord's Day. Christians worship on Sunday, the first day of the week. The seventh day was a memorial to creation. The first day is a memorial to the Resurrection, to the new creation.

While every day has meaning to God, and for Christians every day is sacred and all time is to be used wisely, this one day each week that we dedicate to God is special. It is a token of the fact that all of time is in God's hand and that we therefore owe God a portion of our time in worship.

II. When a church worships, observe the purpose for worship.

Hebrews 10:25 admonishes us not to forsake the assembling of ourselves together. There is an instinctive call to worship in all of us. We worship to see God. We move aside all of the other things of life that crowd out and obscure God so that we can seek his face.

Why? We are literally pushed into the arms of God. Notice that the disciples were gathered together that day because they were afraid. Pushed by our sins, the weight of the world, and the problems of life, we move into God's presence. During the blitz of London in World War II, the ladder into a dugout had broken. The father stood in darkness at the foot of a well and his child stood uncertain on the upper edge. He could see her dimly against the night sky; she could not see him at all in the depth. But she could hear his voice: "Jump!" he said, "Daddy can see you. Now, right into my arms!" And so we jump into the arms of God through worship.

III. When a church worships, recognize the person of worship.

The central element in the worship service is Christ. It was when Jesus was in their midst that the disciples knew something unique had happened.

There are many reasons for corporate worship, such as gathering the family of faith, witnessing to the world, sharing joys and sorrows, and deriving strength from meeting with others of like hearts and minds. But the primary reason for worship is to meet with the resurrected Christ. It is then that we can claim his promise of Matthew 18:20, "Where two or three come together in my name, there am I with them" (NIV).

IV. When a church worships, see the product of worship.

This is what happens when we worship God.

    A. *We receive the Word of comfort from Christ.*
    B. *We receive the gift of God's peace (John 20:19–20).*

C. *We receive a commission for service, a responsibility for life (John 20:21).*
D. *We receive the Spirit of power (John 20:22), who empowers us to share the gospel with others.*

Conclusion

Someone has observed that in the church in which William Shakespeare worshiped in Stratford-on-Avon, the woodcarver had the privilege of carving his own inspiration under the choir seats after he had carved the ornate reredos of the altar. Clearly visible to visitors are the pious, serene, and holy carvings. But underneath the choir seats are carvings that are dark and unseemly: monsters, dogs biting people, unholy and impious acts. But that is what worship does: It delivers us from the dark and unredeemed impulses that would destroy us. It is a reach for the beautiful, for God.

WEDNESDAY EVENING, DECEMBER 12

Title: One Pondering Death

Text: "After two days was the feast of the passover, and of unleavened bread: and the chief priests and the scribes sought how they might take him by craft, and put him to death" **(Mark 14:1).**

Scripture Reading: Mark 14

Introduction

The major role of God's Servant-Messiah is to suffer for humankind. This portion of Scripture is overwhelming in its content of Jesus's death.

I. Threat of death (Mark 14:1–2).

A. *Time of sacred feast.* The feast the Jews were celebrating was a memorial of the time God's death angel passed over the homes of the Israelites in Egypt. The death angel passed over every home that had the sacrificial blood on the doorposts. The remembrance of death was in the air.
B. *Death by "craft."* At this crucial moment in the Jewish religious year, cruel men sought to take Jesus by deceit and put him to death. He was aware of this.
C. *Fear of people.* It is ironic and hypocritical that these deceivers feared the people while they had no fear of God. They respected the feast day but not the Lord's Son.

II. Anointed for death (Mark 14:3–9).

A. *House of Simon.* Jesus and his disciples went into the home of a friend. While there, a woman came and anointed Jesus's head with expensive spikenard ointment.

B. *Misunderstanding disciples.* The disciples thought that this act was an extravagant waste. They considered the cost of the ointment and began to murmur against the woman who anointed Jesus.

C. *Purpose given.* Jesus immediately came to the defense of the woman and her deed. He then explained, "She hath done what she could: she is come aforehand to anoint my body to the burying." The disciples could not fully appreciate this fact at the time, but the Lord saw it as part of God's preparation of the sacrifice.

III. Traitor unto death (Mark 14:10–11).

A. *Judas sought enemies.* Mark's account of Judas's betrayal was very direct. He had a personal hatred for Jesus that forced him into the company of the chief priests, the ones who sought to take him by craft.

B. *Betrayal of Jesus.* Judas's purpose was to use the trust the Master had in him for a weapon to be used against Jesus. He found these men glad to share with him.

C. *Purpose of Judas.* The motivating power in the life of Judas was revealed to be money. When money was promised him, he proceeded to plot how he could most conveniently betray Jesus.

IV. Picture of death (Mark 14:12–25).

A. *Passover killed.* The death of the paschal lamb permeated the minds of the Lord and his disciples as they planned a meal in the large upper room. During this meal, Jesus revealed that one of the men would betray him. This betrayal would lead to his death.

B. *Broken body.* At one particular point in the meal, Jesus took bread, blessed it, and broke it. He encouraged them to eat it with these words of memorial: "This is my body" (v. 22). As the bread was broken, so would his body be broken.

C. *Blood of new covenant.* He took a cup of the "fruit of the vine," gave thanks, and gave it to them. He declared, "This is my blood of the new testament, which is shed for many" (v. 25). He pictured his death in the broken bread and the blood of the covenant.

V. Prayer before death (Mark 14:26–42).

A. *"Sorrowful unto death."* Jesus led three of his disciples out to the garden of Gethsemane for a time of prayer. Jesus's mind was full of the fact of his death. All the pathos of human nature was revealed in his statement to his followers: "My soul is exceeding sorrowful unto death." He felt the heaviness of love in Gethsemane.

B. *"Not my will."* Jesus had to struggle with the reality of death. He first asked that if it was possible, the hour would pass from him. Finally, he conceded, "nevertheless not what I will, but what thou wilt."

C. *"Could not watch."* To multiply his burdens for the hour, his faithful followers went to sleep. He chastised them for not watching with him during this crucial time.

VI. Condemned to death (Mark 14:43–65).

A. *Judas revealed him.* The events of Jesus's final hours began when Judas led the arresting band to Gethsemane. He proceeded to kiss the Master to complete his betrayal.
B. *Others forsook him.* The disciples fled one by one after Jesus's arrest. Details of Peter's denial show the extent of the confusion and fear of Jesus's followers.
C. *High priest condemned him.* The high priest was supposed to direct his people to righteousness. Instead, he condemned righteousness in the person of Jesus Christ. He cried out, "What need we any further witnesses? Ye have heard the blasphemy: what think ye?" The response was, "And they all condemned him to be guilty of death!"

Conclusion

In almost every verse of this chapter, the death of Jesus is emphasized. Praise God this is not the final chapter in the Bible!

SUNDAY MORNING, DECEMBER 16

Title: The Hinge of History

Text: "Fear not: for, behold, I bring you good tidings of great joy, which shall be to all people. For unto you is born this day in the city of David a Saviour, which is Christ the Lord" (**Luke 2:10–11**).

Scripture Reading: Luke 2:1–10

Hymns: "Hark! The Herald Angels Sing," Wesley
"Silent Night, Holy Night," Mohr
"While Shepherds Watched Their Flocks," Tate

Offertory Prayer: Our Father who art in heaven, we praise your name for the joys of this season. We thank you for your unspeakable gift, your Son, our Savior and Lord. Accept the tithes and offerings we bring to you. Grant us your blessings through every part of this service. In Jesus's name we pray. Amen.

Introduction

How remarkable is heaven's announcement of the birth of Christ. Not to Caesar Augustus in the city of Rome did the news come. Not to Herod the Great, nor to the Sanhedrin in Jerusalem was the announcement made, but "to certain poor shepherds in fields as they lay." The angel's announcement is the heart of the Christmas story.

Christ's birth is the hinge of history, the dividing line. Every date affixed to a check or legal document is witness that the central event in history was the birth of Christ. Our thinking is in terms of either BC, "before Christ," or AD, *anno domini*, meaning "in the year of the Lord."

In his annunciation the angel tells us that Jesus's coming may be regarded from five points of view.

I. Jesus's coming had a universal dimension.

"I bring you good tidings of great joy, which shall be to all the people" (Luke 2:10). Christianity is for all people of all time. Jesus was born a world Savior. He so understood his mission. Thus Paul interpreted it. And thus his early followers preached.

Most of the world's religions—Confucianism, Buddhism, Islam, Hinduism—have a limited appeal, but Christianity has followers in all countries. People everywhere need a Savior from sin and a hope for eternal life. Christ came to meet these needs.

As we come together today, we are conscious of being part of a great company, a worldwide fellowship. Though in many lands Christ's followers differ in language, in customs, in manner of celebrating his birth, the joy in the hearts of all Christians is the same.

II. Jesus's coming had a historical dimension.

"Unto you is born this day," the angel said. "This day." Jesus was born at a point in time. Something happened, and that event is dated. This is not an abstract proposition; it is a historical fact. This is not an ancient legend or a bit of Jewish folklore; this is the record of a historical event, an event by which all others are dated. The faith of Christendom is that at one point in history, God broke directly into this world. Our faith centers in what God has done. Seeing or failing to see this will shape our whole philosophy of history.

The Greeks defined history as a series of nonunique, ever-recurring events. They were saying that history repeats itself. Their cynical attitude was, "That which shall be has already been." But the birth of God's Son assures us that they were wrong. History does repeat itself, it does recur in cycles, but nonetheless it is moving toward a goal, a consummation; and along the way there are great towering mountain peaks. The highest of them is this: "Unto you is born this day."

III. Jesus's coming had a geographic dimension.

"Unto you is born this day in the city of David," was the angel's tidings. "In the city of David." Jesus was born at a place on the earth, at a spot on the map you can pinpoint. Humanity has always wanted to believe that the universe has meaning, that something more than human power makes for righteousness, and that the world operates within the framework of moral law. In the historical appearance of Jesus, born at a certain time in a certain place, God assures us that this is true. Jesus was not born in some hypothetical place, in some dim and distant never-never land, but at a definite place—"the city of David." Not only was Jesus born at a definite point in time, he was born at a definite place on the world's surface. The third fact confirms and supports the second.

IV. Jesus's coming had a redemptive dimension.

"Unto you is born this day in the city of David a Saviour." How joyous was the good tidings of the angel messenger! "There is born . . . a Saviour." Not only was he born at a specific time and place, but for a specific purpose, announced by God's angelic messenger before his birth: "And thou shalt call his name JESUS; for he shall save his people from their sins" (Matt. 1:21). Always God is the initiator in the redemptive drama. In a way people did not suspect, God was invading human life.

The consciousness of Jesus's redemptive mission bore heavily on his mind and heart and drove him on with an imperious sense of urgency never before known to mortal man (see John 9:4).

V. Jesus's coming had a prophetic dimension.

"Unto you is born this day in the city of David a Saviour, which is Christ the Lord." This was "good tidings of great joy" indeed. None of the shepherds could have misunderstood. No devout Jew of that day, steeped in the religion of his fathers, could have misunderstood the phrase "which is Christ the Lord." This was the glad announcement that the promised Messiah and "King of David's line" had been born.

This was the hope that enabled the Jews to survive the shock of national destruction and to preserve their national identity during seventy years of exile and return to their own land. This was the hope that enabled them to survive the persecution of the interbiblical period and to throw off the yoke of the Greek oppressor. This was the hope that strengthened them in Jesus's day and enabled them to endure the iron heel of Rome upon their necks. The angel said, "This day that hope is fulfilled. The one born is 'Christ the Lord.'" God's prophets had promised, and God kept the promise made through his prophets.

Conclusion

Beloved, that promise is to all, even to us. This event at Bethlehem is no private matter. Let me emphasize in closing a phrase of the text that is near its beginning. "Unto you is born this day in the city of David a Saviour, which is Christ the Lord." Hear him. That herald angel is speaking "unto you."

SUNDAY EVENING, DECEMBER 16

Title: When a Church Prays

Text: "And when they had prayed, the place was shaken where they were assembled together; and they were all filled with the Holy Ghost, and they spake the word of God with boldness" **(Acts 4:31)**.

Scripture Reading: Acts 4:23–31

Introduction

On New Year's Eve 1975, Pope Paul VI in Rome took a silver trowel in his hand and ceremonially and symbolically began closing with brick and mortar a certain door in the vestibule of St. Peter's Church in Rome. It was the door known as the Porta Sancta, the sacred door. That door is marked by a cross and normally is walled up. It is opened but four times a century for a holy year. For Roman Catholics 1975 was a holy year, and thousands of people made a pilgrimage to Rome. In holy years the pope begins the ceremony on Christmas Eve prior to the first day of the holy year when he begins the demolition of the door by tapping it three times with a silver hammer. Then when the holy year ends, he seals the door and the entrance into the cathedral by which most of those who made up his party will never enter again.

Now suppose that we could pray only once every twenty-five years. Suppose that it had been ten years since you had prayed and fifteen years before you could pray again. Wouldn't you look forward to that day!

But now we have neglected the opportunity we have to pray every day. Probably one of our greatest weaknesses as churches is our weakness in prayer.

It was not so in the early church. Prayer was much a part of the life of the early church. When Peter and John were arrested after the healing of the lame man in the temple, the church prayed. And when they prayed, God demonstrated that their prayer had been heard.

One of the marks of the church of the living Christ must be prayer. Christ's church must be a praying church.

I. When a church prays, there is a response.

When Peter and John were released from jail, they joined other Christian friends in Jerusalem. While Acts does not say it, those friends may have been praying for Peter and John's release at that moment.

And what did Peter and John do upon their release? They did not hold a conference or plan retaliation or try to find a way to keep from being arrested again. They prayed.

Prayer is the natural response of the Christian to God's grace. It often is difficult to teach children to write thank-you notes after receiving gifts. They are quick to receive but slow to respond. Christians are much the same—quick to receive the gifts of God but slow to respond to him. Prayer is our most immediate response.

The God to whom we respond is described in these verses:

A. *He is the sovereign Lord (Acts 4:24, 28).*
B. *He is the self-revealing Lord (Acts 4:25–27).*
C. *He is the seeing Lord (Acts 4:29).*

II. When a church prays, there is a request.

Request or petition is only a part of prayer, but it is the part we practice most often. Prayer should involve praise, thanksgiving, confession, and intercession as well as petition.

399

Notice the request in this prayer as expressed in Acts 4:29. It was a request that centered on their obedience to God and on their task of witnessing. The believers did not pray, "Grant that we may be kept safe," or "Grant that Peter and John may be protected," or "Lord, don't let it happen again," but "Lord, help us to get on with the job of proclaiming the gospel."

That may be our most needed request. We pray for all sorts of personal and physical matters, and that is right. But we also should pray for boldness in proclaiming the gospel of Christ.

The late Harry Emerson Fosdick once observed that we seek for a *thing*, and God gives us a *chance*. Then he illustrated his observation with a statement from Henry Ward Beecher who said, "A woman prays for patience and God sends her a green cook."

The request is for adequacy for the task. Daniel Poling was editor of the *Christian Herald* for many years. He had a preacher son who was one of the four chaplains who went down on the *Dorchester* not far from the British coast early in World War II. The four chaplains gave their life belts to their fellow men and went down with the ship praying at the rail. Clark Poling had written a letter to his family shortly before he left on that voyage. It said, "I know I shall have your prayers; but please don't pray simply that God will keep me safe. War is a dangerous business. Pray that God will make me adequate" (Paul S. Rees, *The Adequate Man* (Westwood, NJ: Revell, 1959], 6).

III. When a church prays, there is a resource.

They prayed with expectancy. They expected God to do something for them. They knew that there was an adequate and powerful resource in the hand of God, and they claimed it.

Do you really expect God to do something when you pray? Even this same group of Christians fell short later. In Acts 12 they again prayed for Peter and John to be released from prison. They were. But when they came to the prayer meeting, they were not recognized.

Sometimes we feel that it is an admission of weakness to admit that we need outside help. That is what it is, and that is what we need: God's help.

How ridiculous it is for the greatest resource of all—the power of God—to be present and available and for us not to use it.

IV. When a church prays, there are results.

The presence and the power of the Holy Spirit were with them. What a result of prayer!

One result of prayer is that something will happen. It may not always be like you expected it to happen, but something will happen. God may deny the form of your request and grant to you the substance of your prayer. Monica, the mother of St. Augustine, prayed that he would not go to Italy, but he did. And it was there that he became converted. Her prayer was ultimately answered but not in the way she expected.

Another result is that we can know the power of God. The place was shaken with the power of God.

Yet another result is that there will be boldness for witness and mission. Jerry Golden was a tough guy incarcerated in the Louisiana State Penitentiary at Angola. While there he was visited by an eighty-year-old Christian businessman and was converted. After his release he founded Christian Prison Ministries.

Conclusion

When a church prays, something happens. It is for God and it is good.

WEDNESDAY EVENING, DECEMBER 19

Title: One Accepting Kingship

Text: "And Pilate asked him, Art thou the King of the Jews? And he answering said unto him, Thou sayest it" **(Mark 15:2)**.

Scripture Reading: Mark 15

Introduction

It would be sheer foolishness to make a humble servant into a king. In the world's sight that is exactly what this scene was—a cruel, deadly jest. It was not so with Christ. He accepted his kingship with all of its responsibilities and sorrows. Notice the plight of the King in this chapter.

I. Pilate questioned the King (Mark 15:1–8).

A. *"Art thou the King?"* The religious rulers did not have sufficient power to actually put Christ to death. They had to ask the civil authority to accomplish this. Thus, they brought him to Pilate. The charges against him constituted a threat to the civil order of the Roman rulership. Pilate asked him concerning the charge, "Art thou the King of the Jews?" No doubt this ruler was trying to discern if Jesus was planning some kind of civil insurrection.

B. *"Thou sayest it."* Jesus knew the futility of giving a defense against Pilate at this time. His curt reply to Pilate indicated that Pilate had spoken the truth in the question asked. Christ was the King of the Jews.

II. People rejected the King (Mark 15:9–14).

A. *"What will . . . I do?"* Pilate was convinced that Jesus was innocent of the charges. Yet the populace was capable of bringing pressure on his rulership before higher authorities within the Roman government. He appealed to the people as to what to do with "the King of the Jews." The immediate shout was, "Crucify him!"

B. *"What evil . . . ?"* Pilate became a pawn in the hands of the mob. Seeking some justification for the way the riot scene was going, Pilate cried out, "Why, what evil hath he done?" They needed no justification. The satanic chant of "Crucify him, crucify him!" intensified.

III. Soldiers mocked the King (Mark 15:15–20).

A. *"They clothed him."* Pilate tried to appease the crowd by having Jesus scourged. The soldiers assigned the task dressed him in purple clothes and made mock worship of him. This was an hour of great shame to these foolish men.

B. *"His own clothes."* As if to desecrate him, they took off the purple clothes and placed his clothes back on him. Little did they realize that their purple clothing was sheer hypocrisy, while his rags were garments of the King of Kings and Lord of Lords.

IV. Cross announced the King (Mark 15:21–31).

A. *"The King of the Jews."* The most important monarch to ever reign over the greatest kingdom of the world was heralded by a simple sign at the top of a shameful instrument of death. How ironic was this entire scene.

B. *Numbered with transgressors.* To further intensify the shame of humankind, two convicted criminals were put to death with Jesus. He was literally placed among the transgressors to die.

V. Crowds reviled the King (Mark 15:32).

A. *"Let Christ . . . descend."* Misguided mockers played games with his kingship. They cried, "Let Christ the King of Israel descend now from the cross." They taunted him in shame and disgrace—their shame and disgrace!

B. *"May see and believe."* As sinful people did throughout Jesus's sacred life, they now called for him to reveal signs at his death. They had to wait for the greatest sign of all times—the Resurrection!

VI. Christ bore the kingship (Mark 15:33–41).

A. *Alone.* Christ Jesus took the full burden of the kingship upon himself. This was especially emphasized when he prayed, "My God, my God, why hast thou forsaken me?" He dared not shun one iota of responsibility that went with the kingship of Israel.

B. *Wall of partition.* Jesus died. When he had completed the suffering for sin, the veil of the temple was torn down the middle. People now had access to God through the person of Jesus Christ, the King of Israel.

VII. Joseph buried the King (Mark 15:42–47).

    A. *Begged for his body.* Joseph of Arimathea was deeply involved in his love for Jesus. A practical task was now at hand. Someone had to care for the earthly tabernacle of Jesus. Joseph took that responsibility upon himself.

    B. *Fine linen.* Joseph wrapped Jesus's holy body in fine linen. This was the type of cloth used in making kings' garments. Joseph felt Christ was the King of the Jews, and as best he could, he tried to bury him accordingly.

Conclusion

How dismal is the scene of the rock being rolled across the ground to seal the tomb of the King of Israel. But wait . . .

SUNDAY MORNING, DECEMBER 23

Title: Where Is He?

Text: "Where is he that is born King of the Jews? for we have seen his star in the east, and are come to worship him" **(Matt. 2:2)**.

Scripture Reading: Matthew 2:1–12

Hymns: "There's a Song in the Air," Holland
           "O Come, All Ye Faithful," Anonymous
           "O Little Town of Bethlehem," Brooks

Offertory Prayer: Our heavenly Father, we praise your name as we meet to worship in your house. We thank you for the joy of these days with our families and with our church family. Grant that we may be faithful to teach our children about the Savior who was born long ago. Take our thoughts beyond his nativity to remember that he grew to manhood, walked among people, taught them, healed them, died for them, and then arose from the dead. Bless us now as we recognize our stewardship in the giving of money. Consecrate our gifts to your cause. In Jesus's name. Amen.

Introduction

Perhaps no part of the Christmas story has a greater appeal to popular fancy than that of the wise men mentioned in Matthew's gospel. Who were they? Where did they get the information they had to have about the promised Messiah of the Jews? What was their country, their nationality? How many of them were there?

But far more important than any of these is the question they asked when they came to Jerusalem: "Where is he that is born King of the Jews? for we have seen his star in the east, and are come to worship him" (Matt. 2:2). "Where is he?" Our attitude toward and our answer to that question make all the difference in the world in our lives this Christmas season.

I. This question may be asked in the spirit of the implacable, the relentless enemy who seeks to destroy.

"Where is he?" Herod asked. He wanted to know, and he was exact, diligent, and thorough in his efforts to find an answer, for his motive was murder. He inquired privately of the Magi, not because he cared anything about prophecies of where or when or how the Christ was to be born, but because he saw the possibility of a rival for his throne and wanted to eliminate him. Jesus's kingdom was not of this world, and he was really no rival at all. But in the truest, highest sense, Christ is against Herod and all his kind and all he stands for.

"Where is he?" Modern Herods are still asking that question. And as long as Herod continues to be Herod, he will seek to destroy Christ and all he stands for; and therefore, peace can never be declared. There are vast areas of the earth where Christ is cast out and where people would banish him by decree.

II. This question may be asked in the spirit of the unbeliever who scoffs.

This is the person who ridicules the idea of a Christ born in Bethlehem. The scoffers were no doubt present when the shepherds reported what they had seen and heard. From time to time during Jesus's earthly ministry, they circled him to taunt him. Some despised him, fulfilling Isaiah's prophecy that he would be "despised and rejected of men" (53:3). When he was on the cross, some scoffed, saying, "If thou be the Son of God, come down from the cross" (Matt. 27:40).

Scoffers are still with us today. Some ask in scorn, "This Jesus who was born some two thousand years ago—where is he? He was to be the Prince of Peace (Isa. 9:6). There is no peace." Or they ask, "With the breakdown of integrity and character in high places and with the morals of the pigsty paraded on the front pages as news, has his coming made any difference at all? Where is he?"

III. This question may be asked in the spirit of the cynic who sneers at and ridicules the things of Christ.

"In the midst of all this pagan holiday you call Christmas," they ask, "where is he? Where is the Christ in your Christmas celebration? The holly and the mistletoe, the colored lights on your streets, the gaily decorated windows and counters of your department stores, your secular songs about reindeer and Santa Claus, your commercial shot in the arm—all of these we see, but where is he? Where is Jesus in all this?"

Some have the cynical spirit that would say, "Maybe he is the Son of God, maybe he isn't. As far as I am concerned it doesn't matter, but believe me, I am going to cash in on this thing while I can." Christmas! A great gala time, but where is Jesus in it all? And how long, we wonder, will it be before merchants put up Christmas lights and display Christmas merchandise on the fifth day of July?

IV. This question may be asked in the spirit of the believer.

This is the person who seeks, who follows on until he or she finds. The Magi had a spirit that believed yet inquired. So strong was their faith that the Christ had been born that they followed the only clue they had—the gleam of a star. They showed their faith not only by starting on a difficult journey but also by their diligent inquiry in Jerusalem and by hastening on to Bethlehem when they learned the way. Their faith was abundantly rewarded. "Where is he?" they asked. They sought, they found, they fell down and worshiped him; and for them life was never the same again.

Let any person ask in sincere faith, "Where is he?" And then let that person seek wholeheartedly with all the light available, and that person will find the Christ.

Conclusion

A learned professor, a decent and respected man, professed not to believe in God, and he was attempting to teach his children not to believe in God. He did permit his eight-year-old daughter to attend Sunday school, however, and she believed in God as most children do.

One night the professor was very busy in his study, and his little girl insisted on talking to him. He took a long strip of paper and with a black crayon printed the words, "God is nowhere." He showed the sentence to her and quickly cut it apart, letter by letter. He mixed the letters up in a box and said, "Now, honey, put those words back together like I had them." Quickly she put the letters back together, but it didn't come out like he had it. Her sentence read, "God is now here." And so he is!

SUNDAY EVENING, DECEMBER 23

Title: The Night before Christmas

Text: "For unto you is born this day in the city of David a Saviour, which is Christ the Lord" **(Luke 2:11)**.

Scripture Reading: Luke 2:1–20

Introduction

"'Twas the night before Christmas" begins Clement Clark Moore's poem written in 1823. Perhaps nothing ever written has so influenced our secular view of Christmas. But we want to think of this "holy night" in spiritual terms. As we muse on that first Christmas Eve, and on the one we will celebrate this week, we want to think in terms of heaven and earth and our own hearts. In three circles of application, beginning at the outer rim and moving toward the center, let us ask, "What was and what is taking place?"

I. What was taking place in heaven on that first Christmas Eve?

Here we must rely on our Spirit-led imaginations.

A. *Can we not imagine the angel Gabriel reporting on the events preceding Christ's birth that had been committed to his care?* He could have told the assembled angels of his visit in a vision to Zacharias (Luke 1:8–20) and of the events leading up to the birth of John the Baptist. He could have reported on the annunciation to Mary, a virgin in Nazareth, and of her obedient response (vv. 26–38). He could have told of the visit of Mary to her relative Elizabeth and of their mutual joy (vv. 39–56). He could have told how he reassured Joseph in a dream so that both the child to be born and his mother would be protected (Matt. 1:20–23). He could even have told how God used the decree of Caesar Augustus to bring it about that the Christ should be born in Bethlehem of Judea as the prophet had foretold (Mic. 5:2).

B. *Again, can we not imagine a great congregation of angels around the throne awaiting the moment Paul calls "the fulness of the time" (Gal. 4:4) to sweep down to earth to herald his birth?* Perhaps as they waited they interrupted Gabriel's report with songs of praise to their Lord and ours. They were ready for instant obedience. Earth was oblivious to the great event about to happen in lowly Bethlehem, but heaven was trembling with expectancy.

C. *Again, can we not imagine a farewell conversation in heaven that night between the Father and the Son?* One writer has seen in Hebrews 10:5–7, where the writer quotes from Psalm 40, a record of this conversation. This is fanciful exegesis, but we can still imagine that such a conversation did take place that night. The nature of Christ's incarnation, for his human body was the result of a divinely creative act; the purpose of the Incarnation, to do the Father's will; and the glory it would bring—all these could well have entered into that conversation that night.

II. What was taking place on earth on that first Christmas Eve?

Here we have the clear Scripture record of four events.

A. *First, there was the arrival of Joseph and Mary in Bethlehem, their frantic search for quarters, and their settling down in a shelter for cattle.* The "fulness of the time" had come for Mary. For months she had been pondering in her heart the annunciation of the angel, the words of her relative Elizabeth (Luke 1:39–45), the angel's assurance to Joseph, and the Old Testament prophecies she incorporated in what we call the Magnificat (vv. 45–55). All these things probably came to a climax in Mary's heart as she and Joseph arrived in Bethlehem.

B. *Second, there was the virgin birth of Jesus.* Isn't it remarkable that the event on which all history turns was unheralded, unattended, and unknown except for the animals and the angels? This was the advent of that ancient prophetic sign that a virgin should conceive and bear a son and call his name Immanuel, "which being interpreted is, God with us" (Isa. 7:14; Matt. 1:23). Hosts of angels fell down to worship, then rose up to sing.

C. *Third, there was the appearance of the angels to the shepherds.* Unto these simple and faithful men who believed the prophecies and had prepared their hearts, the veil that separates earth from heaven was drawn back; and they saw and heard the heavenly hosts. How wonderful was the announcement, how glorious their praise.

D. *Fourth, in some far-off land the Magi, as they studied the skies, saw the appearance of a new star that night.* They were men chosen of God because of their search for truth. When they saw the star, they knew somehow that the King had been born. In them we have the forerunners of many Gentiles who were, and are yet, to come to worship the King. In them also we have God's provision, through their gifts, of safety and financial security for the long journey to Egypt.

III. What will be taking place on this Christmas Eve in our hearts?

Across two thousand years, what is the factor that will make this "night before Christmas" meaningful for us? It is the fundamental Bible truth that Christ is reborn in the regeneration of every child of God. When a person is born again, there is, in a very real sense, another incarnation of God, so that that person can say, "Christ lives in me" (Gal. 2:20 NIV). We are living in a world that seems to have no room for Christ, but you can make room for him in your heart.

Conclusion

Have you worshiped and adored Jesus as did the angels? Have you sought to see him for yourself as did the shepherds? Have you crowned Christ King in your heart by the gifts you bring, as did the Magi? He is the Lord's Christ, the Savior of the world. He wants to be your Savior too.

WEDNESDAY EVENING, DECEMBER 26

Title: One Erasing Doubts

Text: "And afterward he appeared unto the eleven as they sat at meat, and upbraided them with their unbelief and hardness of heart, because they believed not them which had seen him after he was risen" **(Mark 16:14)**.

Scripture Reading: Mark 16

Introduction

The scene of Calvary would be final unless some great phenomenon occurred. The suffering Servant's ministry could be validated only by a resurrection from the grave. This final chapter of Mark pictures Jesus Christ erasing all doubts that were brought on within his ranks by his crucifixion.

I. Doubts concerning Jesus's death (Mark 16:1–4).

A. *The archenemy.* Death has always been considered the chief enemy of humankind. It had carried with it a pall of finality as far as the human scene was concerned. This was known as "the way of flesh."

B. *Conquering stone.* When the stone was rolled before the tomb, it became a symbol of eternal resistance. It had "sealed" Jesus into the tomb. Who could roll away the stone from the sepulcher?

C. *Open tomb.* On the first day of the week, a small group went to the tomb. There they found that the stone was rolled away and the tomb was empty. The seal of death was conquered!

II. Doubts concerning Jesus's resurrection (Mark 16:5–8).

A. *Body not stolen.* The first impressions would have made these startled followers wonder if the body had been stolen. A young man of angelic appearance announced, "He is risen, he is not here!" No, Jesus's body was not stolen. He was resurrected from the dead.

B. *Proof given.* To give proof of this amazing event, the gaping women were shown the place where the body had been placed after it was prepared for burial.

C. *He announced plans.* The angelic creature proceeded to instruct the followers in the plans the risen Christ had for them. The disciples (and Peter) were instructed to meet him in Galilee.

III. Doubts within Jesus's followers (Mark 16:9–14).

A. *Mary Magdalene.* Jesus appeared first to Mary Magdalene. She immediately shared this joy with his disciples.

B. *Unbelieving ones.* Some of the disciples simply would not accept the fact of Jesus's resurrection, even after talking with Mary Magdalene. They would not believe the testimony of two others. Then it happened! He appeared before the Eleven and chastised them because of their hardness of heart.

C. *They believed.* All doubts about Jesus's resurrection were removed after a fellowship meal with him.

IV. Doubts concerning Jesus's mission (Mark 16:15–20).

A. *Reach of his kingdom.* When Jesus was crucified, the momentum of his kingdom was stopped. All the disciples felt there was no hope. When he was resurrected from the dead, hope was not only revitalized, but it was also greatly intensified. All doubts were removed. Jesus announced to his followers that he expected them to go "into all the world." His vibrant message was intended for every person on the face of the earth.

B. *Activity of his kingdom.* Jesus specifically requested his adherents to "preach the gospel" as they went. The activity of preaching is one of the most sacred in God's program. To "preach the gospel" means to "announce the good news." There is so much excitement in the fact of the resurrected Lord. He has conquered death! He has conquered sin! He has conquered the hearts of people!

C. *Results of the kingdom.* When the gospel of the kingdom is preached, people may either accept or reject it. Those who accept it have eternal life. Those who reject the gospel will be damned.

Conclusion

When the resurrected Christ confronted his disciples, he instilled a confidence in them that caused them to go far and wide victoriously proclaiming the gospel.

Thus Mark presents the Servant-Messiah in his story of redemption. May God continue to use this accounting of our Lord in our ministry for him.

SUNDAY MORNING, DECEMBER 30

Title: Is There Any Word from the Lord?

Text: "Then Zedekiah the king sent, and . . . asked him secretly . . . Is there any word from the LORD? And Jeremiah said, There is" **(Jer. 37:17)**.

Scripture Reading: Jeremiah 37:16–21

Hymns: "A Mighty Fortress Is Our God," Luther
"O God, Our Help in Ages Past," Watts
"He Is Able to Deliver Thee," Ogden

Offertory Prayer: Our Father, we come into your presence today, thankful for all your blessings in the year past and confident of your love and care as the new year dawns. Accept these tithes and offerings as a part of our very selves laid on your altar, consecrate them to your kingdom's purposes, and multiply their ministry throughout the earth to the end that all people may know your Son as Savior and Lord. In his name we pray. Amen.

Introduction

"Is there any word from the LORD?" This question was asked by Judah's last king, Zedekiah, a weak and vacillating unbeliever, who did not mean to be as bad as he was. It was answered by the prophet Jeremiah, who had now become the iron pillar and brazen wall God had predicted. Upon Josiah's untimely death his three sons, Jehoahaz, Jehoiakim, and Jehoiakin followed him in that order upon the throne; and last, his uncle, Zedekiah. Things had gone from bad to worse for Judah. Now the Chaldeans had surrounded the walls of Jerusalem as the trembling king asked God's prophet, "Is there any word from the LORD?" "There is," Jeremiah replied; and then as if drumming a lesson into the head of a dull child, he repeated his message: "Thou shalt be delivered into the hand of the king of Babylon."

Viewed broadly, Jeremiah's message as he gave God's word to Zedekiah was a word of judgment, of faith, and of salvation. There was a word from the Lord, but the weak and fearful king would not heed it.

This text is relevant. Our own age is asking, "Is there any word from the Lord?" If those who try to be preachers of God's Word are true, they must echo Jeremiah's reply of long ago, "There is." What is God's word for us in our day? Let me mention three things as we apply this ancient text.

"Is there any word from the Lord?" First of all there is:

I. A word of affirmation.

That word is this: God lives. He is alive. He rules. The God whom Isaiah saw almost three millennia ago "sitting upon a throne, high and lifted up" (Isa 6:1), still reigns in this world, and "He must reign, till he hath put all enemies under his feet" (1 Cor. 15:25). Of all the Christian hymns I know, this is my favorite stanza:

> *He rules the world with truth and grace,*
> *And makes the nations prove*
> *The glories of his righteousness,*
> *And wonders of his love.*
> *And wonders of his love.*
> *And wonders and wonders of his love.*

That is the gospel's word, the gospel's affirmation: "He rules the world." He may not be ruling the world in the way some people want him to, but he is on the throne.

Our world is afraid and confused. It is perishing for some sure word out of which hope may arise. We have it: God lives and rules. Since we have it, we had better give it. "Alleluia: for the Lord God omnipotent reigneth" (Rev. 19:6).

"Is there any word from the Lord?" Second, there is:

II. A word of warning.

God created man innocent, sinless, free: innocent in that he had not been tempted and therefore had not fallen into sin; sinless in that he had not, as yet, exercised his power to choose between good and evil; and free in that he could choose to do whatever he liked within prescribed boundaries. By its very nature, freedom must have boundaries. Our first parents crossed those boundaries in willful disobedience. They fell, and this is the history of our race.

This was the history of Judah in Jeremiah's day. They had transgressed God's laws and thrown down his covenant. Jeremiah's message was simple:

410

Because of sin, Judah and Jerusalem would be punished. Jerusalem would be destroyed and her people would be carried into captivity. After seventy years of purging in a foreign land from her sins of idolatry and unfaithfulness, the nation would be restored. A remnant would return. This was God's prophet's word of warning.

"Is there any word from the Lord?" There is a word of warning. The Bible is full of this word. "The soul that sinneth, it shall die" (Ezek. 18:4). "The wages of sin is death" (Rom. 6:23). "Be not deceived; God is not mocked; for whatsoever a man soweth, that shall he also reap" (Gal. 6:7).

"Is there any word from the Lord?" Last of all, there is:

III. A word of salvation.

As King Zedekiah sent for Jeremiah a third time, his request was, "I will ask thee a thing; hide nothing from me" (Jer. 38:14). He was saying, "Tell it like it is, preacher. Tell me, what is the score? What will come of all this?" After receiving the king's assurances of fair dealing, Jeremiah said: "Thus saith the LORD . . . ; If thou wilt assuredly go forth unto the king of Babylon's princes, then thy soul shall live, and this city shall not be burned with fire; and thou shalt live, and thine house. But if thou wilt not go forth to the king of Babylon's princes, then shall this city be given into the hand of the Chaldeans, and they shall burn it with fire, and thou shalt not escape out of their hand" (vv. 17–18). This was a word of salvation for his own life, the life of his family; and it would save the city from destruction. But we read the sad word, "And Zedekiah the king said unto Jeremiah, I am afraid" (v. 19).

We have a word. We can tell the world, "We see Jesus." The writer of Hebrews had seen it all—the terror, the wretchedness, the hatred on the earth, the mess humans make of things. Yet he said, "Now we see not yet all things put under him. But we see Jesus" (Heb. 2:8–9).

Again, we know our marching orders. The word, through Christ, is to go into all the world with the gospel. Our loved ones, our city, our world must be reminded that God lives and rules, that God warns people of impending judgment, and that he saves all who will believe.

Conclusion

There is a word from the Lord, but will we heed it, will we hear? Let us leave this place, let us bid farewell to this year with that word ringing in our ears.

SUNDAY EVENING, DECEMBER 30

Title: Closing the Door on 2018

Text: "And the angel of the God, which went before the camp of Israel, removed and went behind them; and the pillar of the cloud went from before their face and stood behind them: and it came between the camp of the Egyptians and the camp of Israel; and it was a cloud and darkness to them, but it gave light by night to these: so that the one came not near the other all the night" **(Ex. 14:19–20)**.

Scripture Reading: Exodus 14:10–20

Introduction

As we meet to worship in this final service of the year 2018, I am not as concerned with an appraisal of the year past or with predictions about the year to come as I am with our attitudes as we look both ways. So much depends on the way we view things. How shall we come by truths that will fashion right attitudes within us?

This Exodus record will help us. The Israelites had reached the Red Sea, which blocked their path, when suddenly, as if to make a bad situation worse, they saw the Egyptians in hot pursuit. They were literally between the devil and the deep.

The year's last day reminds us that we too are on a journey "hastening stormfully across the astonished earth," as Carlyle once put it. Like the Israelites, we too often are caught between the Red Sea before us, blocking our advance, and the army of the Egyptians behind. What happened in this emergency reveals three great truths shining through this vivid record.

First, in our text, we see that:

I. Some of our greatest enemies are not those that confront us, but those that pursue.

It was not so much the Red Sea in front of the Israelites as the Egyptian army behind them that created panic in the camp. This is a parable of our situation tonight. We think we have escaped these ghosts of yesteryear, when suddenly we hear the clatter of their horses' hooves and see the dust of their chariot wheels. Think of the realms in which this truth applies.

A. *Some of us are pursued by fears, complexes, inhibitions, frustrations, and phobias that psychologists solemnly tell us are the fruition of the seeds sown in childhood experiences.* We leave our childhood days behind, but these ghosts out of our past pursue us.

B. *Some of us are pursued by grief.* It may be that during the past year sorrow has laid a heavy hand on us and our families. It is not some possible future grief we fear, but a past one that pursues us.

C. *Still others are pursued by some old sin, some old temptation to which we once gave in.* Like the Israelites, we have thrown off the yoke and started toward the Promised Land, but now that old temptation follows us on and on.

This is our first truth here. The Israelites left Egypt but not the Egyptians. The hindrance to our progress toward maturity of

Christian character in 2019 may spring not from something out in the future, but from some carryover from 2018.

Second, in our text we see that:

II. God not only goes before us, he is also our rear guard.

God's angel, who had been out in front as their guide, now came behind them as their defense and stood between them and their pursuers.

As we begin a new year, we think of God out there behind the veil of the future. In faith and praise we sing, "He Leadeth Me! O Blessed Tho't!" "Guide Me, O Thou Great Jehovah," and "Lead On, O King Eternal." This thought is wonderfully true.

But it also is true that we need a God who is not only before us but behind us as well. How profound was the insight of the psalmist as he said, "Thou hast beset me behind and before, and laid thine hand upon me" (Ps. 139:5). It is almost certain that the prophet had the Exodus in mind as he wrote, "For the LORD will go before you, and the God of Israel will be your rear guard" (Isa. 52:12 RSV). These words would also apply to the return from exile.

F. W. Boreham tells of a man in his congregation who was always poised and serene, wasting no time on the fruitless exercise of worry. When asked how he could do this, he replied, "I've always made it a rule of my life that when I've shut the door, I've shut the door." He had set the Lord not only before him but also behind. Since he is our rear guard, let us close the door on 2018. Let us trust in God, who can shut the door on the hosts who pursue.

Finally, there is a third truth in our text:

III. Every experience of life has a double meaning depending on to whom the experience comes.

The pillar of cloud that stood between the Israelites and the Egyptians caused darkness upon the Egyptians and gave light by night to the Hebrews. With faith our experiences mean one thing, without faith another. The same fire that melts wax hardens clay. The Egyptians saw only a dark cloud, but to the Israelites it gave light.

A. *Consider this truth as it applies to the world situation.* Surely it is dark enough. To take it at face value, Egyptian-like, is to see nothing but darkness, confusion, danger, and chaos—a black cloud. But to people of faith, the cloud is not all darkness, because we see the reason for the darkness, and that releases a flood of light. The presence of God in history means darkness to some but light to others. People of faith know that God is at work in history. The revolutionary periods have always been the most creative. God often does more when the waters are stirred.

B. *Again consider the afflictions, disappointments, and tragedies that come to us.* They mean darkness to the Egyptians who cry out, as did Job's wife, "Curse God, and die" (Job 2:9). But to people of faith, there is light shining in these dark experiences.

C. *Or consider the fact of death.* To the Egyptians it is darkness unrelieved, as said the wisdom writer, "For that which befalleth the sons of men befalleth beasts . . . as one dieth, so dieth the other" (Eccl. 3:19). But people of faith say, "Though our outward man perish yet the inward man is renewed day by day" (2 Cor. 4:16). "We know that if our earthly house . . . were dissolved, we have a building of God" (5:1).

D. *Or consider the cross.* Unbelievers cannot understand it: "Unto the Jews [the cross is] a stumblingblock, and unto the Greeks foolishness" (1 Cor. 1:23). "But," Paul said, "unto us which are saved it is the power of God" (v. 18). The light of the Resurrection streams across the darkness of the cross.

Conclusion

In this last Sunday evening service of 2018, let us do two things:

1. As God gives us the grace and the faith, let us close the door on 2018, on all the Egyptians of temptation and evil habits and old grudges and sins. God can shut that door if we trust him.

2. Let us take courage and go on. The past is God's, the future is God's, and his power is greater than all.

MISCELLANEOUS HELPS

Title: Breaking Bread Together

Text: "When ye come together therefore into one place, . . . when ye come together to eat . . . ye come not together unto condemnation" **(1 Cor. 11:20, 33–34).**

Scripture Reading: 1 Corinthians 11:17–34

Introduction

Vance Havner once said, "A church needs to take time out to tune up." This is what Paul is talking about in 1 Corinthians 11. The Lord's Supper will enable a church to be in tune with Jesus Christ.

When a church has the mind of Christ, the observance of the Lord's Supper is meaningful. When a church is demonstrating love for Christ and for one another, the Lord's Table is a blessing beyond expression. What makes breaking bread together so significant?

I. Breaking bread together is a distinctive experience.

A. *The Lord's Supper was distinctive in the heart of Christ.* It was uniquely given against the background of the Passover. The Lord's Supper was given during the Passion Week, Jesus's last week before the cross. It was his last official act before being arrested in the garden of Gethsemane. It also was the seal of the new covenant that God gave to humanity in that the covenant was sealed by the blood of Jesus. Thus, Jesus commanded that his followers perpetuate the Lord's Supper throughout the ages.

B. *It is distinctive in the life of the church.* The church practiced breaking bread together often. The book of Acts indicates that it was a vital part of the church's life (Acts 2:42–46; 20:7).

C. *It is distinctive in the lives of believers because the Lord's Supper is for members of Jesus's body.* In that personal relationship, it is a part of a believer's life and worship and faithful continuance in Christ (see Acts 2:41–47).

However, the Lord's Supper needed to be more distinctive in the church at Corinth because they were surrounding "breaking bread together" with selfish attitudes and divided relationships. First Corinthians 11:17–22 describes these circumstances. What the church needs today is a new distinctiveness regarding the Lord's Supper in our lives.

II. Breaking bread together is an act of discernment.

Verse 28 of our text says, "Let a man examine himself." This means that each of us is responsible for the manner in which we approach the Lord's Supper. There are three areas in which we need to examine ourselves.

A. *We need to examine ourselves in our relationship to Jesus Christ.* In the light of Luke 22:21–24, is our attitude toward Christ one that is genuine and transparent, or are we secretly betraying him? In light of 2 Corinthians 13:5, are we truly in Christ, and are we growing in Christ? In light of 1 Corinthians 11:27, is there any area of guilt toward the Lord in breaking his bread and drinking his cup?

B. *We need to examine ourselves in relationship to ourselves.* Verse 29 of our text refers to "damnation to himself." Let us accept our personal responsibility so that we are not guilty before God and within ourselves. All unworthy attitudes and unconfessed sins, any spiritual insensitivity toward others and carelessness toward needs in our lives, all must be spiritually confronted and corrected.

C. *We need to examine ourselves in relationship to the church.* We are members of the body of Christ, but it is possible that we lack discernment in this area (v. 29). What results in Christians when this is overlooked? Verse 30 says that many become weak and sickly and may die. According to Luke 22:25–27, we are to have a servant's attitude toward other members of the church. Strength and love and unity will characterize the church that does.

III. Breaking bread together is an act of devotion.

Verse 24 of our text clearly states the purpose of the Lord's Supper: "This do in remembrance of me." Observing the Lord's Supper is remembering that Jesus gave his life for us in his sacrificial sufferings. When we have that focus, our lives will be centered on all that he desires for us.

Conclusion

If we acknowledge that the Lord's Supper is a distinctive experience, an act of discernment, and an act of devotion, it will indeed be a dynamic experience for both individual believers and the church as a whole. It will result in a spirit of renewal in our lives.

Title: Sitting at the Lord's Table

Text: "Ye cannot drink the cup of the Lord, and the cup of devils: ye cannot be partakers of the Lord's table, and of the table of devils" (**1 Cor. 10:21**).

Scripture Reading: 1 Corinthians 10:16–21

Introduction

I remember what our table was like when I was growing up at home. I remember where I first sat, where I was later promoted, and finally the time when I sat at my dad's right hand. That was a special table to me, as it should be. But there is a table even more meaningful spiritually, and that is the "Lord's Table." To sit at the Lord's Table is a unique experience in that we identify ourselves with Christ and we share in fellowship with other believers. Two things may occur as we sit at his table.

I. We share in the blood of Christ.

It means that as we take the cup of the Lord, we are identifying ourselves with the meaning of Christ's blood. We share in the sacrificial spirit of his death, but we also share in the victory of Christ's blood. "There is power in the blood" as we have so often sung.

A. *Victory over our sins.* Romans 3:23 says that we stand before God as sinners, and Romans 3:24–26 teaches that we need forgiveness of our sins. It also says that God forgives our sins, not because he overlooks them, but because he sees the blood of Jesus. On the Day of Atonement, blood was shed for sins, and this pleased God. At the Passover, God said, "When I see the blood, I will pass over you" (Ex. 12:13). Thus, there is forgiveness, as Colossians 1:14 says: "We have redemption through his blood, even the forgiveness of sins."

B. *Victory over guilt.* Hebrews 10:22 tells us that the blood of Christ cleanses our conscience. A guilty conscience reveals that there is a barrier between us and God, and when we confess our sins to him, Christ's blood cleanses. We ought to keep short accounts with God when we sin.

The blood of Christ brings us near to God initially (Eph. 2:13) and continually (Heb. 10:22). Therefore, I do not enter into nor abide in God's presence by who I am or what I have done, but by the precious blood of Christ. The Lord's Table revives our memory of this truth.

C. *Victory over the devil.* Satan's activity is to accuse us (Rev. 12:10), but God forgives us of every sin (1 John 1:7). So, on what ground can Satan accuse us? None whatsoever. How does he do this then?

1. Satan accuses us to God. The answer to that accusation is in Romans 8:31: "If God be for us, who can be against us?" God points Satan to the blood of his Son by which Satan was utterly defeated. No one can accuse us (Rom. 8:33–34), because the blood of Christ is sufficient (Heb. 9:11–12, 14; 1 John 2:1–2).

2. Satan accuses our conscience. He reminds us that we have sinned. He tempts us to look within, to our self-defense, or to look to our feelings instead of to faith. We are not to listen to Satan but to rely on Christ's victory, in which we eternally stand. Drinking of "the Lord's cup" provides that touch of faith that blesses the Christian's life.

II. We share in the body of Christ.

Sitting at the Lord's Table means there is to be a oneness in the body of Christ. Verse 17 of our text speaks of "one bread" and "one body" and says that "we are all partakers of that one bread." This means that we share in a unity with others who also sit at the Lord's Table.

It is God's will that his people be one in the Spirit. This was the burden of Jesus's high-priestly prayer in John 17, not only for his immediate disciples but also for all who would come to know him.

The church at Corinth illustrates that the body of Christ may be marked with envy, strife, and divisions (1 Cor. 3:1–3). It was Paul's purpose, however, that they recognize their essential oneness, as 1 Corinthians 3:8 teaches: "Now he that planteth and he that watereth are one." Disunity is promoted by Christians who are carnal (1 Cor. 3:1–3); that is, they are not filled with the Spirit and under his control.

The observance of the Lord's Supper is a pointed reminder that it grieves the heart of Christ for Christians to sit together at his table when there is a lack of oneness in spirit. Only a renouncing of pride and a confession of the sin of self-centeredness will open the way for the unity of the Spirit to be experienced. But what meaning when it is!

Conclusion

Each one of us holds the key to true fellowship with Christ and our fellow believers. As we submit ourselves to Christ and his purpose in the Lord's Supper, and as we come to his table spiritually prepared, his cup does become "the cup of blessing."

Title: Honoring Jesus Christ

Text: "This do ye, as oft as ye drink it, in remembrance of me" (**1 Cor. 11:25**).

Scripture Reading: 1 Corinthians 11:23–26

Introduction

"In remembrance of me" calls for the highest sense of honor to Jesus Christ our Lord. Were the president of the United States here in this service, we would honor him magnificently. Now we honor one who is supremely greater, Jesus Christ, the Lord of heaven and earth.

Let us be on guard lest we pervert the meaning of the Lord's Supper for our lives. This is what the Corinthian church was doing as they observed a love feast. It was intended to be a time of sharing and fellowship, but it had degenerated into a time of ill will, divisions, arguing, and selfishness. So when they began to observe the Lord's Supper, it was not a time when Jesus Christ could be honored.

We may not be members of a "Corinthian church" to the extent described in our text, but to attempt to observe the Lord's Supper in an attitude of selfishness hinders the church from giving true honor to Christ. Two questions need to be answered if we are to honor him.

I. Why do we observe the Lord's Supper?

A. *It is a specific command of Jesus.* He said, "This do ye . . ." (v. 25). The verb is a present imperative, indicating that it is a divine command that is to be obeyed by continual observance or frequent remembrance.

B. *It awakens us to Jesus Christ.* He said, "in remembrance of me." This is not just memory but an active calling to mind. Remember his person, his life, his death, and his coming again. All these are vitally related to the Lord's Supper.

C. *It reminds us of the one way of salvation.* All believers eat of the same bread and drink of the same cup. We have only one Savior. All of us come to the Father the same way.

D. *It witnesses to the world of our devotion to Jesus Christ.* Observing the Lord's Supper demonstrates that we believe him and we yield ourselves to him and his way.

II. How do we prepare for the Lord's Supper?

We are not to observe it unworthily (v. 27), and this refers to the manner of participation and not the person. All of us are unworthy to observe the Supper. How are we to observe it then?

A. *Examine ourselves spiritually (v. 28).*

B. *Confess our sins and be cleansed of any attitude, words, or actions that are displeasing to the Lord.*

C. *Observe the Lord's Supper according to Jesus's instructions.*

D. *Observe it in the spirit of love and unity.* First Corinthians 13 is God's will for love in the church.

E. *Approach the Lord's Table in the spirit of yieldedness to Jesus Christ.*

Conclusion

What is your attitude toward Jesus Christ? Is he Lord of your life? Nothing short of his being Lord will bring honor to his name.

MESSAGES FOR CHILDREN AND YOUNG PEOPLE

Title: God Has a Plan for Your Life

Text: "He went away again the second time, and prayed, saying, O my Father, if this cup may not pass away from me, except I drink it, thy will be done" (**Matt. 26:42**).

Scripture Reading: Matthew 26:36–46

Introduction

Jesus in Gethsemane is one of the most stirring scenes in the Bible. He was alone and in deep agony making a choice. He was tempted not to do the will of his heavenly Father, but as he battled in his warfare, he said finally, "Thy will be done."

Just as God had a plan for Jesus's life, so he has a plan for yours and mine. He is a great and good God, loving, providing, caring, and purposing in your life. Your life is important to him. He has a plan for you.

I. God has a plan for your life—believe it.

A. *Just as God has a plan for the universe, so he has a plan for your life.* Life cannot be attributed to chance. There is every evidence of supreme intelligence behind it. A. C. Morrison says that humans do not stand alone; God stands behind them. He cites numerous examples of how astronomy, biology, zoology, and anthropology affirm this truth. For example, the earth rotates on its axis at a rate of a thousand miles per hour. If it were one hundred miles per hour, our days and nights would be ten times as long. In the summer all vegetation would be burned up during the long days or freeze in the long nights. According to science, we are just the right distance from both the sun and moon or else life would be destroyed. God has a plan for the universe and he has a plan for people—for you (Ps. 8).

B. *Just as God has a plan for the ages for humanity, so he has a plan for your life.* The Bible tells us God's plan of redemption by which sinful humans are forgiven through Jesus Christ. His plan is that we become like Jesus Christ and glorify him in our lives. God's eternal purpose is that all things are summed up in Christ. In light of these truths, we may know that he has a plan for us.

C. *Just as God had a plan for Jesus's life, so he has a plan for you.* Jesus said, "I have finished the work which thou gavest me to do" (John 17:4). God had a definite plan that Jesus knew and could accomplish. Jesus didn't live by accident or chance or fate, and neither do we. We live by his plan for our lives.

II. God has a plan for your life—discover it!

We need not be afraid of God's will, for he is "our Father." Rather, we can be like the psalmist who said, "I delight to do thy will, O my God" (Ps. 40:8). We need not fight God's plan. Yet how often we do. In our pride we contend with God, preventing his plan from being revealed to us.

To discover God's plan for our lives, we must:

A. *Desire it.* We must choose God's will. He will not force us. This involves a seeking spirit on our part, and this is the attitude he rewards (Heb. 11:6).

B. *Ask the counsel of those whom God puts in authority over us.* God works through parents to help us to find his will. Ephesians 6:1–3 teaches the importance of this relationship. There may be others whose counsel we will seek also, such as a pastor, teacher, or Christian friend, but God especially works through parents.

C. *Recognize circumstances that help to identify the "open door" that God is providing.* We need in this regard to consider our abilities, experiences, opportunities, and needs.

D. *Pray about his plan.* God reveals his plan through prayer. This involves companionship with God.

E. *Let God speak to you through the Bible, his Word.* This is where his ageless plan is recorded, and as we consult it, his principles are revealed to us.

F. *Surrender yourself to God.* Be willing to be and to do whatever he leads you to be and do. Yield your life upon his altar, purposing to do his will. Be assured that he will let you know.

III. God has a plan for your life—enjoy it.

God is not asking you to consider something dull, detrimental, or destructive. Rather, his plan is truly delightful. Once again the psalmist says, "I delight to do thy will, O God." Jesus said, "My meat is to do the will of him that sent me." This means deepest satisfaction, inner peace, true joy.

Conclusion

As we yield ourselves to the Lord, his plan becomes personal, fulfilling, and spiritually exciting. He has a plan for your life. Believe it, discover it, and enjoy it!

Title: A Disciplined Life

Text: "Forasmuch then as Christ hath suffered for us in the flesh, arm yourselves likewise with the same mind" **(1 Peter 4:1)**. "And he said to them all, If any man will come after me, let him deny himself, and take up his cross daily, and follow me" **(Luke 9:23)**.

Scripture Reading: 1 Peter 4:1–7; Luke 9:23

Introduction

Disciplined people are those who express a control in their lives that is gained by enforcing obedience. Athletes discipline themselves to be in top condition physically. Athletes who participate in marathons must discipline themselves to run twenty-six miles in any kind of weather. They discipline themselves not to be distracted by crowds and to run their own style of race and not that of another. Disciplined people live by a pattern of behavior that expresses the control they have gained.

Who is a disciplined Christian? One who expresses self-control gained by becoming obedient to Christ, who lives by a pattern of behavior empowered and guided by the Holy Spirit. How much of your life has been brought under the control of Christ? How obedient are you as a Christian? Is your pattern of behavior any different from that of people who do not know Christ? If so, how different is your life? How disciplined are you?

I. Description of a disciplined life.

First Peter 4:7 says, "Be ye therefore sober." Here "sober" may be translated "disciplined." First Peter 4:1–7 describes a disciplined life.

A. *It has a particular mind (v. 1).* It is the mind of Christ.
B. *It has the mark of militancy (v. 1).* We are to "arm ourselves." This is a term for spiritual warfare. We are truly soldiers of the cross.
C. *It has a sharp meaning (v. 2).* We are to live according to God's will. The past life is described as an undisciplined life, and the new life calls for a change—God's way of living.
D. *It is a life that is misunderstood (v. 4).* A disciplined life is considered a "strange" life. Former friends are surprised and speak evil of us. Jesus taught that we can expect this (Matt. 5:10–12). At times we must stand alone, even as Jesus did.

Verse 7 says, "The end of all things is at hand." We must bring life under Christ's control and live by his pattern of behavior if we are to be prepared for his return.

II. Directions for a disciplined life.

These directions come from Jesus as they are recorded in Luke 9:23.

A. *Denial.* This is to renounce our selfish ways for a disciplined life. To deny self is to refuse to acknowledge our self-life and its control.
B. *Death.* The "cross" means death—Christ's death and ours. To "take up the cross" is an act of acknowledging death to our old sinful self-nature. Galatians 2:20 says it clearly: "I am crucified with Christ."
C. *Daily.* To take up the cross daily is the extent of a disciplined life. How disciplined are we to be? Sunday morning? Sunday all day? Special occasions? Or daily? We are to be so disciplined that "every thought" is brought into captivity to the obedience of Christ (2 Cor. 10:4–5).
D. *Devotion.* We are to "follow" Jesus, making him Lord of our lives every day.

III. Dimensions of a disciplined life.

What does a disciplined life include?

A. *Disciplined mind and thought life.* "As he thinketh in his heart, so is he" (Prov. 23:7). Paul admonishes, "Let this mind be in you, which was also in Christ Jesus" (Phil. 2:5).

B. *Disciplined attitudes.* In Matthew 5:3–12 Jesus teaches the eight qualities that will make life meaningful and full of divine blessing.

C. *Disciplined time.* Psalm 90:12 says, "So teach us to number our days, that we may apply our hearts unto wisdom."

D. *Disciplined worship.* "Not forsaking the assembling of yourselves together, as the manner of some is" (Heb. 10:25).

E. *Disciplined Bible study.* This means that we are to not only possess a Bible, but we are to read it, study it, memorize it, and meditate upon it (Prov. 2:1–6; 2 Tim. 3:14–15).

F. *Disciplined prayer life.* Jesus is our example. Paul says, "Pray without ceasing" (1 Thess. 5:17). Spiritual warfare calls for continual praying (Eph. 6:10–18).

G. *Disciplined family life.* Joshua 24:15 describes one man who disciplined himself to lead his family.

H. *Disciplined finances.* This will involve Christ's control of our giving, receiving, and spending. In this way we honor the Lord (Prov. 3:9–10; Matt. 6:19–34).

I. *Disciplined friendship.* We need to commit ourselves to companions who build up our lives rather than tear them down.

J. *Disciplined tongue.* "Set a watch, O LORD, before my mouth; keep the door of my lips" (Ps. 141:3).

K. *Disciplined conscience,* whereby we discern both good and evil (Heb. 5:13–14).

L. *Disciplined purity.* "Keep thyself pure" (1 Tim. 5:22; see 2 Tim. 2:19–22).

M. *Disciplined social life.* This is doing what glorifies God.

N. *Disciplined body in all categories, including eating and exercise.* First Corinthians 9:27 says we are to keep our bodies under control.

O. *Disciplined eyes.* We are to make a covenant with our eyes, lest we use them for lust (Job 31:1).

Conclusion

Not all Christians are disciplined, but those who are bear the fruits of a disciplined life. Gideon's army was reduced from 32,000 men to 300 disciplined ones, and how victorious they were! God is waiting for his people to discipline themselves today for his glory.

FUNERAL MEDITATIONS

Title: Three Things to Remember

Text: "Bless the LORD, O my soul: and all that is within me, bless his holy name. Bless the LORD, O my soul, and forget not all his benefits" **(Ps. 103:1–2)**.

Scripture Reading: Psalm 103

Introduction

The Scripture lists some benefits the Lord shares with us: he forgives all our sins, he heals all our diseases, he redeems our life from destruction, he crowns us with loving-kindness and tender mercies, and he satisfies our mouth with good things.

If something then happens in life that seems, from a human point of view, to be a contradiction of these benefits, what may be said? Verse 7 helps us. It refers to God's ways and God's acts. We do not know his ways with us, like Moses did, because his ways are so much greater than ours. His purpose is larger. We do not understand, but we can draw comfort and strength from remembering three truths for a time like this.

I. Let us remember God's mercy.

Notice the Scripture verses that describe God's mercy. He is merciful: "The LORD is merciful and gracious, slow to anger, and plenteous in mercy" (v. 8). His mercy is great: "For as heaven is high above the earth, so great is his mercy toward them that fear him" (v. 11). In his mercy he forgives our sins: "As far as the east is from the west, so far hath he removed our transgressions from us" (v. 12). In his mercy he treats us tenderly: "Like as a father pitieth his children, so the LORD pitieth them that fear him" (v. 13). His mercy is everlasting: "But the mercy of the LORD is from everlasting to everlasting upon them that fear him, and his righteousness unto children's children" (v. 17). His mercy is never failing: "It is of the LORD's mercies that we are not consumed, because his compassions fail not. They are new every morning; great is thy faithfulness" (Lam. 3:22–23).

II. Let us remember our makeup.

Verses 14–16 of our text tell us how we are made. "For he knoweth our frame; he remembereth that we are dust. As for man, his days are as grass: as a flower of the field, so he flourisheth. For the wind passeth over it, and it is gone; and the place thereof shall know it no more."

Even at our best and strongest times, we are but dust. Our days are as grass, and like a flower they flourish. Then the wind passes over the field and life is gone. This is such a reality for us as we share today in this service.

It is in an experience like this that we truly need to remember the Lord's mercy and that he still loves us and cares for us and desires to bless us.

III. Let us remember the manner of our response to the Lord.

A. *For one thing, we are to bless him.* Psalm 103:1–2 tells us: "Bless the LORD, O my soul: and all that is within me, bless his holy name. Bless the LORD, O my soul, and forget not all his benefits."

We bless God by thanking him in all circumstances. I do not understand this event of sorrow, but I do know that unless we give thanks to the Lord, we will miss the wonderful victory that he gives. We can thank him on the basis of our believing that he is Lord, that his way is best, and that we belong to him.

B. *Another response is that we are to fear him.* Verse 11 of our psalm says, "For as the heaven is high above the earth, so great is his mercy toward them that fear him." Fearing the Lord is a reverential awareness of his presence. We are in his presence today as we live through this event. Therefore, we tread softly.

C. *Third, we are to obey him.* "The mercy of the LORD is from everlasting to everlasting upon them that fear him, and his righteousness unto children's children; to such as keep his covenant, and to those that remember his commandments to do them" (vv. 17–18). This involves an obedient spirit to his will and his plans for us. The greatest example of obedience in all of life is Jesus Christ who, at an early age, faced the cruel agony of the cross. Yet he said to his Father, "Thy will be done." Just as he passed through the darkness of the cross into the brightness of the Resurrection, so now is the time to wait quietly upon the Lord.

Conclusion

Ella Wheeler Wilcox wrote about faith in these words:

I will not doubt, though all my ships at sea
Come drifting home with broken masts and sails;
I shall believe the Hand which never fails,
From seeming evil worketh good to me;
And, though I weep because those sails are battered,
Still will I cry, while my best hopes lie shattered, "I trust in Thee."

Title: God Cares!

Text: "Casting all your care upon him; for he careth for you" (**1 Peter 5:7**).

Scripture Reading: Psalm 23; 1 Peter 5:5–7

Introduction

The Phillips translation of 1 Peter 5:7 says, 'You can throw the whole weight of your anxieties upon him, for you are his personal concern." The Living Bible paraphrases the verse with these words: "Let him have all your worries and cares, for he is always thinking about you and watching everything that concerns you." According to the King James Version, there are four words in the verse that constitute the distinctive truth of the Bible, "He careth for you." This is the sweep of the message of the entire Bible. In countless ways we discover that God cares.

One great Scripture passage that reflects God's care is Psalm 23. It begins by saying, "The LORD is my shepherd; I shall not want." This means that he cares for us in all our circumstances.

The highest evidence that God cares for us is in the giving of his Son, Jesus Christ, and the meaning of his coming. God felt a concern for people's needs and expressed his love in Jesus Christ. "Jesus Christ" is God saying to the world that he cares for us. Every time he healed the blind, every time he touched diseased bodies to make them whole, and every time he came into the presence of death and sorrow with his calm assurance, he was saying that God cares for us.

Just how does he care for us today?

I. God cares for all the needs of life.

Matthew 6:30–32 says: "Wherefore, if God so clothes the grass of the field, which today is, and to morrow is cast into the oven, shall he not much more clothe you, O ye of little faith? Therefore take no thought, saying, What shall we eat? or, What shall we drink? or, Wherewithal shall we be clothed? For after all these things do the Gentiles seek: for your heavenly Father knoweth that ye have need of all these things." God knows all our needs, and implied in that knowledge is his care for us so that we have every need met. We are made aware through these words that God is the source of our supply. This means that he will provide our personal and emotional needs in the loss of a loved one—even for us today.

II. God's care is indescribably deep.

Romans 5:8 beautifully says, "But God commendeth his love toward us, in that, while we were yet sinners, Christ died for us." This tells us how deep and unconditional his love and care is. When we did not care for him—in fact, our backs were turned against him in willful rejection—he loved us. This is what the cross is all about!

III. God cares at the time of death.

This is the simple but meaningful truth of Jesus's visit to the home of Mary and Martha at the time of Lazarus's death. John 11 describes not only the words and actions of Jesus related to Lazarus's resurrection, but also the presence of Jesus that illuminated the darkness of the experience. Jesus's very presence was God the Father saying through him, "I know your loss, your hurt, and your need, and I do care for you!" God is still saying this through the ministry of the indwelling Christ in the Holy Spirit. Why not let him make his care real to you now?

IV. God's care is eternal.

Romans 8:35–39: "Who shall separate us from the love of Christ? shall tribulation, or distress, or persecution, or famine, or nakedness, or peril, or sword? . . . Nay, in all these things we are more than conquerors, through him that loved us. For I am persuaded that neither death, nor life, nor angels, nor principalities, nor powers, nor things present, nor things to come, nor height, nor depth, nor any other creature, shall be able to separate us from the love of God, which is in Christ Jesus our Lord." Nothing can separate us from his love and care. We know it now, and we are assured that it will be fully and finally experienced in heaven.

Conclusion

A poet expresses it this way:

> When his eye is on the sparrow
> And each budding leaf that grows;
> When he sends the dew each morning,
> And the sunshine to the rose;
> You may know beyond all doubting,
> In this trial you're passing through,
> God cares . . . and every moment
> He is watching over you!

Title: In Times Like These

Text: "God is our refuge and strength, a very present help in trouble. . . . Be still, and know that I am God" **(Ps. 46:1, 10)**.

Scripture Reading: Psalm 46

Introduction

In a time like this, the sudden death of a young person, it is a time to examine the basics of life, because they are eternal and unfading and inescapable.

I. It is a time to turn to God's Word.

Other literature may be beautiful and helpful, but today we need something that is eternal yet relevant for this moment. And God's Word is just that. Isaiah 40:8 says, "The grass withereth, the flower fadeth: but the word of our God shall stand for ever." Romans 15:4 says, "For whatsoever things were written aforetime were written for our learning, that we through patience and comfort of the scriptures might have hope." As you read the Bible, the Holy Spirit will comfort your heart with its words.

II. It is a time to test ourselves.

Second Corinthians 13:5 says, "Examine yourselves to see whether you are in the faith; test yourselves. Do you not realize that Christ Jesus is in you . . . ?" (NIV). This is a challenge to examine our relationship to Jesus Christ. This is essential, for life's basics include a personal hope in him. We need to examine ourselves to see if we really are in Christ.

The time is always short for us and death is sure to come, sometimes unexpectedly. Let us let this experience be a warning from God to be ready for life and death.

Jesus Christ is our answer, as John 14:6 says, "Jesus saith unto him, I am the way, and the truth, and the life: no man cometh unto the Father, but by me."

III. It is a time to trust God's will.

It is so easy for us not to trust the Lord in a time like this. Mary and Martha had difficulty trusting God at the death of their brother, Lazarus. According to the story in John 11, these two sisters sent word to Jesus about the illness of their brother. Jesus delayed his going to their home because he could see the "bigger picture." When he did arrive, Lazarus had already died and had been buried. In fact, Jesus arrived there four days after Lazarus's death. Martha's first words to Jesus indicate a feeling of resentment: "Lord, if thou hadst been here, my brother had not died" (John 11:21). Her words breathe an element of distrust. She is really saying, "Why, Lord?"

We too have probably asked the same question or in some way expressed our inward feeling of hurt toward the Lord. But it must not continue. Jesus said on the cross, "My God, my God, why hast thou forsaken me?" But later he said, "Father, into thy hands I commend my spirit." He was saying, "Father, I trust you."

What kind of will is God's will? Romans 12:2 says that his will is "good, and acceptable, and perfect." He never makes a mistake. Romans 8:28 says that it always leads to good "to them that love God, to them who are the called according to his purpose." What we see may be a jumble of marks and lines, but what the Father sees is a special design that only he can create.

A mine disaster occurred in England in which forty miners lost their lives. The families of the men gathered, grief stricken and bewildered. Someone asked Bishop Ed Stanley to say something that would help these people. He said, "We stand here today in the face of mystery, but I want to tell you about something I have at home, a bookmark embroidered in silk. On one side the threads are crossed and recrossed in wild confusion, and looking at it you would think it had been done by someone with no idea of what he was doing. But when I turn it over, I see the words beautifully worked in silken threads, 'God is love.' Now we are looking at this tragedy from one side, and it does not make sense. Someday we shall be permitted to read its meaning from the other side. Meanwhile, let us wait and trust."

Conclusion

This trust will lead us to say that "God is my refuge and strength, a very present help in trouble"; and it will lead us to be still and know that he is God. It will lead us to the time when we can even say, "Thank you, Father," for your will. First Thessalonians 5:18 says, "In every thing give thanks: for this is the will of God in Christ Jesus concerning you."

WEDDINGS

Title: A Wedding Ceremony

Marriage is God's solemn and sacred institution, and we stand in the presence of that reality this evening. On the first page of Scripture, it is written: "And God said, Let us make man in our image, after our likeness. . . . So God created man in his own image, in the image of God created he him; male and female created he them" (Gen. 1:26–27). He also said, "It is not good that the man should be alone; I will make him an help meet for him. . . . Therefore shall a man leave his father and his mother, and shall cleave unto his wife: and they shall be one flesh" (2:18, 24). What God did then, he still does today. He brings together two persons to become one flesh, thus creating from two families, one new family.

Marriage is not only a divine relationship, it is the deepest human relationship there is. God is the Creator of this human relationship, about which an Old Testament writer wrote: "To every thing there is a season, and a time to every purpose under the heaven: a time to be born, and a time to die; a time to plant, and a time to pluck up that which is planted . . . a time to weep, and a time to laugh; a time to mourn, and a time to dance . . . a time to embrace, and a time to refrain from embracing . . . a time to keep silence, and a time to speak; a time to love, and a time to hate; a time of war, and a time of peace. . . . He hath made every thing beautiful in his time: also he hath set the world in their heart, so that man can find out the work that God maketh from the beginning to the end. . . . And also that every man should eat and drink, and enjoy the good of all his labour, it is the gift of God" (Eccl. 3:1–13).

This, then, is a joyful time for us. As guests, you are here because of your involvement in the lives of the bride and groom. By your presence you encourage, support, and share their joy. You experience with them the awesomeness of two persons being united into one. Therefore, let us rejoice with them and their families.

Minister to Father of the Bride: Who gives this woman to be wed to this man?

Father: Her mother and I.

Minister to Groom: Will you have this woman to be your wife? And will you pledge yourself to her, in all love and honor, in all duty and responsibility, in all faith, to live with her and to cherish her, according to God's will, in the holy bond of marriage?

Groom Answers: I will.

(Minister joins the right hands of the bride and groom)

Exchange of Vows: _____ and _____, as you pledge your vows to each other, you are publicly pledging your love to one another, as described in

1 Corinthians 13: "This love of which I speak is slow to lose patience—it looks for a way of being constructive. It is not possessive: it is neither anxious to impress nor does it cherish inflated ideas of its own importance. Love has good manners and does not pursue selfish advantage. It is not touchy. It does not keep account of evil or gloat over the wickedness of other people. On the contrary, it shares the joy of those who live by the truth. Love knows no limit to its endurance, no end to its trust, no fading of its hope; it can outlast anything" (1 Cor. 13:4–7 Phillips).

You may repeat after me the following vows:

Groom: I, _____, take you, _____, to be my wedded wife. I promise before God and these witnesses to be your loving and faithful husband, in plenty and in want; in joy and in sorrow; in sickness and in health, for the rest of our lives.

Bride: I, _____, take you, _____, to be my wedded husband. I promise before God and these witnesses to be your loving and faithful wife, in plenty and in want; in joy and in sorrow; in sickness and in health, for the rest of our lives.

Ring Ceremony: These rings you are about to exchange will be ceaseless reminders of the vows you have just taken. As a circle, the ring is a symbol of the completeness of the marriage relationship.

Groom to Bride: This ring I give you as a symbol of my love for you.

Bride to Groom: This ring I give you as a symbol of my love for you.

Pronouncement of Marriage: Since you have pledged your faith in and love to each other, and have sealed your solemn marital vows by giving and receiving the rings, I, acting in the authority vested in me by the laws of this state, and looking to heaven for divine sanction, do now pronounce you husband and wife in the presence of God and these assembled guests.

Prayer by the Minister

Benediction: The grace of our Lord Jesus Christ, and the love of God, and the communion of the Holy Spirit, be with you all. Amen.

Title: A Marriage Ceremony

Jesus spoke these words concerning marriage: "From the beginning of creation, 'God made them male and female.' 'For this reason a man shall leave his father and mother and be joined to his wife, and the two shall become one flesh.' So they are no longer two but one flesh. What therefore God has joined together, let not man put asunder" (Mark 10:6–9 RSV).

Love is the secret to a beautiful relationship in marriage. The apostle Paul wrote, "Love is patient and kind; love is not jealous or boastful; it is not arrogant or rude. Love does not insist on its own way; it is not irritable or resentful; it does not rejoice at wrong, but rejoices in the right. Love bears all things, believes all things, hopes all things, endures all things. Love never ends" (1 Cor. 13:4–8 RSV).

This is a beautiful and hallowed moment, the time of your commitment to one another in marriage. It is a time, in the words of Ruth, when you are saying to one another: "Intreat me not to leave thee, or to return from following after thee: for whither thou goest, I will go; and where thou lodgest, I will lodge: thy people shall be my people, and thy God my God: Where thou diest, will I die, and there will I be buried: the LORD do so to me, and more also, if ought but death part thee and me" (Ruth 1:16–17).

From this moment of the beginning of your home, may your lives radiate with a new depth of joy. May they be lived in the Spirit of Christ who alone can enable your home to be a lasting one. This is my challenge to you.

Minister: Who gives this woman to be wed in holy matrimony? (The father or person giving away the bride may respond with an appropriate reply.)

The Vows: (The minister may ask the couple to join right hands or may assist them in doing so, and then proceed with the vows.)

_____, in taking the woman whom you hold by the right hand, to be your lawful and wedded wife, you may repeat after me the following vow:

"I promise to love and cherish her, to honor and sustain her, in sickness as in health, in poverty as in wealth, in the bad that may darken our days, in the good that may light our ways, and to be true to her in all things until death alone shall part us."

_____, in taking the man who holds you by the right hand, to be your lawful and wedded husband, you may repeat after me the following vow:

"I promise to love and cherish him, to honor and sustain him, in sickness as in health, in poverty as in wealth, in the bad that may darken our days, in the good that may light our ways, and to be true to him in all things until death alone shall part us."

Then are you devoted to each other until death parts you.

Ring Ceremony:

And now for the rings.

From time immemorial the ring has been significant to seal important covenants. These rings symbolize the completeness of marriage and love. They will abide as ceaseless reminders of the vows you have just exchanged.

To the Groom: Do you, _____, give this ring to _____ as a token of your love for her?

He replies, "I do."

To the Bride: Will you, _____, receive this ring as a token of love for you, and will you wear it as a token of your love for him?

She replies, "I will."

To the Bride: Do you, _____, give this ring to _____ as a token of your love for him?

She replies, "I do."

To the Groom: Will you, _____, receive this ring as a token of love for you, and will you wear it as a token of your love for her?

He replies, "I will."

Proclamation:

(Prior to the climax of the ceremony, the bride and groom may rejoin their right hands.)

Since you have pledged your faith in and love to each other, and have sealed your solemn marital vows by giving and receiving the rings, I, acting in the authority vested in me by the laws of this state, and looking to heaven for divine sanction, do now pronounce you husband and wife in the presence of God and these assembled guests. Let us pray.

Sentence Sermonettes

Hope is brightest when it dawns from fears.

Life is fragile. Handle with prayer.

An act of kindness is the shortest distance between two hearts.

The sun never rises in hell.

If God sends us on stony paths, he provides strong shoes.

Some tears are liquid prayers.

There could be no mountaintops without the valleys.

The only ability God asks for is availability.

The flowers of tomorrow are the seeds of today.

A child is someone who passes through your life and then disappears into an adult.

Love is the medicine for the sickness of the world.

Your attitude determines your altitude.

Life is too short to be little.

It takes clouds to make a beautiful sunset.

When the night is the darkest, the stars shine the brightest.

Suffering and success go together.

The prayer of faith shall save.

Our God is limitless. He can change the situation.

Tired bodies and tired minds make a good breeding ground for despondency.

Obstacles can be stepping-stones.

Worry is pulling tomorrow's cloud over today's sunshine.

It is never too late and never too early to pray to God.

Worry is like a rocking chair. It gives you something to do but doesn't get you anywhere.

Faith plus patience equals hope.

Worry is a circle of inefficient thoughts whirling about a pivot of fear.

God in our heart can mean the difference between despair and victory.

Worry does not empty the day of its trouble, only of its strength.

Flying into a rage ensures a bad landing.

Some give and forgive: others get and forget.

If you find life empty, try putting something into it.

You cannot put things across by getting cross.

Parents are God's best commentaries, and home is heaven's best interpreter.

Salvation is free, but being Christian is costly.

Making excuses does not change the truth.

All people smile in the same language.

The grass is greener on the other side, but it is just as hard to mow.

A smooth sea never made a skillful mariner.

The man who walks humbly with his God is not likely to run over his fellow men.

The secret of success is constancy of purpose.

If it is to be, it is up to God—and *me*.

Hate is suicide by slow degrees.

A cheerful friend is like a sunny day.

Subject Index

Index of Scripture Texts